THE WELFARE STATE

THE WELFARE STATE

Edited by

**Ellen Frankel Paul, Fred D. Miller, Jr.,
and Jeffrey Paul**

CAMBRIDGE
UNIVERSITY PRESS

Published by the Press Syndicate of the University of Cambridge
The Pitt Building, Trumpington Street, Cambridge CB2 1RP, England
40 West 20th Street, New York, NY 10011, USA
10 Stamford Road, Oakleigh, Melbourne, Victoria 3166, Australia

First published 1997

Printed in the United States of America

Library of Congress Cataloging-in-Publication Data

The Welfare State / edited by Ellen Frankel Paul,
Fred D. Miller, Jr., and Jeffrey Paul.   p.   cm.
Includes bibliographical references and index.
ISBN 0-521-62731-1
1. Welfare state.   2. Public welfare—United States—History.
3. United States—Social policy.   I. Paul, Ellen Frankel.   II. Miller,
Fred Dycus, 1944-   .   III. Paul, Jeffrey.
HB846.W465   1997
361.6′5′0973–dc21   97-14489
CIP
ISBN 0-521-62731-1 paperback

The essays in this book have also been published,
without introduction and index, in the semiannual journal
Social Philosophy & Policy, Volume 14, Number 2,
which is available by subscription.

CONTENTS

INTRODUCTION

The legitimacy of the welfare state has been challenged in recent years by critics who contend that, rather than fulfilling its original promise of providing a safety net against the vicissitudes of economic life, it has instead undermined individual responsibility and fostered a debilitating dependence among the poor. Has the welfare state lived up to its promises, or would people be better served by a system that relied less on government intervention and more on self-help, voluntarism, and private charity and insurance? How sound is the justification for the welfare state, and what viable alternatives exist to the public provision of aid?

The twelve essays in this volume—written from a range of viewpoints by philosophers, historians, economists, and political and legal theorists—seek to address these questions and confront related issues. Some essays explore the history of voluntarist arrangements, such as mutual aid societies and fraternal organizations, that provided life insurance, medical care, and other benefits to their members before the establishment of the welfare state. Some focus on social insurance programs designed to provide for the elderly after their retirement, asking whether these programs are consistent with principles of fairness, or whether they should be replaced by a system of individual retirement savings accounts which would give workers a greater measure of control over their funds. Other essays discuss the nature of personal responsibility, the role of government, the impact of identity politics on the welfare state, or the various strategies that have been proposed to deal with the problem of poverty. Still others assess the success or failure of public housing, government assistance to veterans, or other specific programs, suggesting ways of reforming, expanding, or replacing them.

In the opening essay, "Guarantees," David Schmidtz notes that the history of market society is a history of people flourishing under conditions of uncertainty, without the assurance that their needs for food, clothing, shelter, and medical care will be met. A common response to such uncertainty is the desire to guarantee, through government programs, that people's basic needs will be met. Schmidtz argues, however, that the attempt to provide such governmental guarantees can actually leave people worse off, by discouraging them from taking responsibility for their own lives and well-being. In the absence of guarantees, Schmidtz observes, people have historically taken it upon themselves to produce what they need and to devise voluntary collective arrangements—such as mutual aid societies—that can help individuals and families to flourish in spite of uncertainty. The key to the success of these societies, Schmidtz contends, was that they internalized responsibility for welfare provision rather than externalizing it: they allowed people to cooperate in providing for their own welfare rather than forcing productive people to provide for those who were not productive. Schmidtz sketches the history of mutual aid societies prior to the emergence of the welfare state, and suggests that similar arrangements might be developed today to provide old-age pensions, unemployment insurance, life insurance, medical care, and other services. In the course of the essay, he attempts to explain the emotional reactions of people who debate about the welfare state, arguing that those who favor governmental solutions to the problem of poverty tend to take a static (or "snapshot") view of the conditions of the poor; a more fruitful approach, he argues, is to take a dynamic view which recognizes the processes that lead to poverty and those that lead to prosperity. He concludes that the extent to which a society is peaceful and prosperous depends on the extent to which responsibility is internalized through voluntary arrangements.

The next two essays elaborate on the history and operation of mutual aid societies. In " 'This Enormous Army': The Mutual Aid Tradition of American Fraternal Societies before the Twentieth Century," David T. Beito explores the development of mutual aid or "fraternal" societies, which were leading sources of social welfare provision in the United States at the beginning of the twentieth century. Beito shows how American fraternal orders grew out of British orders, which in turn had their roots in much older European mutual aid traditions, such as the confraternities and craft guilds of the Middle Ages. He describes two main types of fraternal orders—insurance orders and secret societies—which became increasingly popular in Great Britian and the United States in the eighteenth century. Secret societies favored approaches of informal assistance, while insurance orders promised regular cash benefits for members who became sick and burial benefits for those who died. National life-insurance orders, which specialized in providing substantial benefits for the survivors of members who died (rather than mere burial benefits), arose in the U.S. after the Civil War and gained widespread membership. Unfortunately, Beito observes, the popularity of such orders, as measured by the number of local organizations or "lodges," peaked in 1925 and declined rapidly during the Depression; and while some lodges remain, many exist primarily as social organizations. The decline of such orders, Beito concludes, can be attributed to the rise of the welfare state and to a number of other factors: competition from employers and commercial insurers in the provision of benefits; changing social customs; restrictive government regulations; and the opposition of medical societies which fought the efforts of fraternal orders to offer health care to their members.

Stephen Davies discusses mutual aid as part of a wider voluntarist approach to improving the welfare of the poor, an approach which also includes self-help and the cultivation of individual responsibility. In "Two Conceptions of Welfare: Voluntarism and Incorporationism," Davies examines the shift from voluntarism, which was dominant until the late nineteenth century, to incorporationism—the theory that state action, in the form of welfare programs, was needed to incorporate the poor into the mainstream of society. Davies offers a detailed discussion of the voluntarist ideals of self-help and mutual aid, showing that the concrete results of both were substantial improvements in the economic and social conditions of the poor. In the course of his discussion, he dispels some common misconceptions about the self-help movement and describes the operation of a number of mutual aid institutions, including day schools, savings clubs and working-class savings banks, and fraternal orders (or "friendly societies") which provided a range of benefits to their members. Davies explores several factors that may have contributed to the shift from voluntarism to incorporationism and the growth of the welfare state: the need of nation-states to secure the loyalty of their citizens; opposition to self-help on the part of some professionals with a vested interest in state measures; and the belief on the part of reformers that some of the poor were simply unable to practice self-help or to participate in mutual aid. He argues that the contemporary crisis of the welfare state is leading to a reexamination of the role of government in welfare provision and to the growth of new self-help practices which may yet bring about a revival of voluntarist ways of thinking.

Like Davies, Howard Husock addresses the tension between self-help and individual responsibility, on the one hand, and welfare-state programs, on the other. Husock's essay, "Standards versus Struggle: The Failure of Public Housing and the Welfare-State Impulse," focuses on the desire of reformers to reduce or eliminate the need for economic struggle on the part of the poor, by using the apparatus of the state to provide some minimum level of goods, services, or income. Husock discusses the motives of such reformers and the impact of their proposals. Using publicly subsidized housing projects as a central example, he shows how the attempt to establish minimum levels of economic security for the poor leads to unintended (and often disastrous) results. He argues that these projects, as well as other policies such as minimum-wage laws, serve to undermine self-sufficiency and encourage dependence. The alternative to these sorts of welfarist policies—insisting that government refrain from interfering while individuals struggle to gradually and incrementally improve their condition—seems cruel. Yet, Husock contends, it may be the only way to achieve sustained economic improvement. This does not preclude the possibility of voluntary efforts to assist individuals in their struggles, however, and Husock examines a pair of voluntarist programs which have offered such assistance: settlement houses, which provided social, recreational, and educational programs for the poor during the late nineteenth and early twentieth centuries; and Habitat for Humanity, which, since the late 1970s, has built homes for people of low income. Such programs have achieved success, Husock argues, by requiring and fostering responsibility on the part of the poor—something which welfare-state programs generally fail to do. Nevertheless, Husock acknowledges that the government may have a narrowly restricted role in assisting the poor in their struggles: by ensuring that children receive an adequate education, and by supporting the severely disabled.

The next five essays examine specific welfare-state policies and suggest ways to reform them or replace them with alternative programs. Taking a more sympathetic stance toward the welfare state, Theda Skocpol explores the possibility of reviving the kind of government assistance embodied in the United States' G.I. Bill of 1944, which authorized educational loans, family assistance, employment assistance, and home, business, and farm loans open to about sixteen million American veterans of World War II. In "The G.I. Bill and U.S. Social Policy, Past and Future," Skocpol sketches the history and impact of the G.I. Bill, noting that it stands out as the major example of extensive federal government involvement in helping young men and their families—as opposed to earlier and later social programs which have focused on the elderly or on impoverished mothers and children. The success of the G.I. Bill, Skocpol argues, could provide a model for future programs, especially given current anxieties about education and training, stagnating wage-rates, and family security. Indeed, conservative Democrats have proposed offering educational loans in exchange for national service (an idea which has been implemented on a modest scale in President Clinton's AmeriCorps program), while liberal Democrats have suggested more extensive educational loans, perhaps subsidized through the Social Security trust fund. Skocpol discusses both proposals and argues that the latter might hold more promise of recreating major federal investments in the education and training of working-age Americans. She recognizes, however, that such a program would need to be tied to a moral rationale and a contemporary national challenge, in order to recapture a sense of solidarity and purpose of the sort which provided a foundation for the G.I. Bill in the aftermath of World War II.

A central component of modern welfare states is social insurance for the elderly, and this is the focus of Daniel Shapiro's contribution to this volume, "Can Old-Age Social Insurance Be Justified?" Shapiro sets out the central features of social insurance systems of the sort that are common to Western democracies and asks whether such systems should be replaced by compulsory private pension systems. Under a compulsory private system, each employee would be required to contribute a certain percentage of his or her income to an individualized retirement investment account. In contrast, social insurance systems such as Social Security in the U.S. operate on a pay-as-you-go basis, with contributions of current workers going into a collective fund used to pay for the benefits of current retirees. Shapiro argues that a compulsory private system would be superior to a social insurance system according to a number of criteria: a compulsory private system would be more just; it would provide greater security and would ensure a wider sphere of freedom for individuals; and it would do better at meeting the requirement that basic political institutions should be publicly justified. In making his case, Shapiro contends that our current old-age social insurance programs produce significant transfers from later (younger) generations to earlier generations, and thus harm the members of the later generations, particularly those who are worst off. He argues that such social insurance systems provide less security, since the relationship between one's contributions and one's benefits is less direct than it would be under a compulsory private system; and he maintains that a compulsory private system would provide greater freedom for citizens to decide how to invest their contributions. He notes, finally, that information about a compulsory private system would be far more accessible, when compared to complex social insurance systems, which are often misunderstood by the public. Given the many problems of current old-age social insurance systems, problems which are likely to be exacerbated as populations age, Shapiro concludes that such systems should be phased out and replaced with compulsory private pension systems.

Peter J. Ferrara describes how such a compulsory private system could function in his contribution to this collection, "Privatization of Social Security: The Transition Issue." Ferrara notes that the key issue in the current debate over privatization of Social Security in the U.S. is whether the transition from the public, pay-as-you-go system to a private, fully funded system is feasible. Since Social Security benefits of current retirees are paid out of revenues from payroll taxes on current workers, the primary concern is the so-called double payment problem: in a transition, members of the current generation of workers would have to finance their own retirement while at the same time meeting Social Security's obligations to current retirees. A major fear of privatization opponents is that this double payment problem would lead to large and unmanageable transition deficits. To respond to this worry, Ferrara sets out a specific proposal for reform, projects the transition deficits that would occur, and argues that they are manageable. Under Ferrara's proposal, individual employees could opt out of the Social Security system and begin directing a significant portion of their Social Security payroll taxes into private retirement accounts. Individuals would use part of the money from these accounts to purchase life and disability insurance, and the remainder would be invested for long-term growth. The Social Security system's obligations to current retirees could be met from a number of sources: from a small portion of the payroll tax which would continue to be paid into the Social Security trust fund, even after a worker opts into the private system; from the sale of long-term government bonds; from taxes on the investment returns in the private retirement accounts; and from reductions in government spending. Ferrara projects that after about fourteen years, the transition deficits would be eliminated, and that after about twenty-three years, the reform would start producing net surpluses. He concludes that the transition is feasible because the privatization reform would lead to significant gains in production, efficiency, and economic growth: the transition costs could be financed out of these gains, while still leaving present workers with much better benefits than they could hope to receive under Social Security.

While the essays by Shapiro and Ferrara focus on programs which transfer income to the elderly, such as Social Security, James M. Buchanan's essay explores welfare-state transfer programs more generally. In "Can Democracy Promote the General Welfare?" Buchanan questions whether transfer programs are consistent with a principle of nondiscrimination. He begins by noting that the basic logic of majority-rule democracy embodies discriminatory or nongeneral treatment of members of the polity: the minority must accept the decisions of the majority, even if those decisions impose unequal burdens on different groups. Of course, it is possible to impose constitutional constraints on majoritarian processes in order to secure generality of treatment, as we do when we prohibit discrimination on the basis of gender, race, or religion. Buchanan suggests that we should institute a similar generality requirement in welfare-state transfer programs. We could do so, he argues, by financing such programs through a flat-rate tax on incomes, without exemptions or special treatment for certain kinds of income—and by distributing benefits in the form of "demogrants": equal-per-head transfer payments without regard to the need or income of the recipients. The net result of such a system would be a transfer of income from those with higher pre-tax income to those with lower pre-tax income; yet such a system, Buchanan contends, would not be subject to partisan political manipulation. If it could be effectively constitutionalized, the flat-tax/demogrant system could ensure that specific groups are not targeted for differentially favorable or unfavorable treatment. Moreover, by eliminating means-testing and reducing opportunities for political exploitation, such a system could reduce the potential for conflicts of interest between various groups, and thus could lend stability and legitimacy to the welfare state. Buchanan concludes by examining a number of current welfare-state programs—including social insurance programs for the elderly and the disabled, disaster-relief programs, and in-kind transfer programs such as food stamps—to determine the extent to which they are consistent with the kind of generality norm embodied in the flat-tax/demogrant system.

Central to Buchanan's discussion is the idea that there are limits to what states may legitimately do in formulating and imposing welfare programs on their citizens. H. Tristram Engelhardt, Jr. also explores the notion of limits—specifically, limits on the provision of health care by the state. In "Freedom and Moral Diversity: The Moral Failures of Health Care in the Welfare State," Engelhardt argues that there are moral grounds for severely limiting the establishment of a government-enforced universal welfare right to health care. He contends that fundamental disagreements about equality, fairness, and justice—disagreements that he takes to be irresolvable in secular moral terms—make any attempt to establish a right to health care highly problematic. Even if one assumes that states may legitimately acquire resources to aid the poor in obtaining medical care, the distribution of such resources raises difficult issues. Is it legitimate for states to deny patients treatments that might offer them some relief from suffering, if the costs of such treatments are judged to outweigh the possible benefits? To what extent would risky behaviors and lifestyle choices become politicized under a government-run health-care system? May states impose egalitarian restrictions forbidding individuals from purchasing a better basic health-care package than the one available under the state's health plan? Engelhardt maintains that these issues— together with disagreements over contraception, abortion, third-party-assisted reproduction, physician-assisted suicide, and other practices— should lead states to establish health-care policies that respect the diverse moral views of their citizens. The best way to proceed, he suggests, may be to provide health-care vouchers or health-care purchase accounts for the poor—a policy which would allow individuals to tailor their coverage to their own needs and beliefs, and one which would allow them to distance themselves from practices of which they do not approve.

The next two essays address the origins and justification of welfare programs, drawing on the work of British sociologist T. H. Marshall and other early theorists of the welfare state. In "Citizenship and Social Policy: T. H. Marshall and Poverty," Lawrence M. Mead argues that the legitimacy of welfare policies is being challenged today not merely because of their cost but, more fundamentally, because of the growth of dysfunctional poverty in Western cities. Mead notes that Marshall viewed the welfare state as an expression of citizenship—a collection of claims and duties people have as members of a social order. Since employment is taken to be one of the central duties of citizenship, Mead contends that poor adults must work more regularly if Marshall's civic case for social provision is to remain persuasive. Mead discusses the contrast between the "deserving" and the "undeserving" poor, and surveys evidence of large and growing disparities in levels of employment between the poor and the nonpoor. He sketches various approaches to dealing with the problem of poverty—the institution of new entitlement programs; investments in education, training, child care, and health care; the privatization of welfare programs; and the enforcement of work requirements in exchange for benefits—and he argues that work enforcement is the option which is most consistent with Marshall's vision and also the one most likely to be effective. Mead believes that the political disputes surrounding poverty today are bound up in issues of competence and responsibility among the poor, and that a policy of enforcing work requirements for the poor would reaffirm their competence and reestablish their claims to inclusion in society and enjoyment of its benefits.

The relationship between welfare policies and the ideal of inclusion is the focus of Alan Wolfe and Jytte Klausen's contribution to this volume, "Identity Politics and the Welfare State." Wolfe and Klausen note that the attempt to ensure an inclusive social order—one which encourages the participation of members of minorities and disadvantaged groups—may lead social reformers to embrace two conflicting objectives: the establishment of a strong welfare state designed to enhance the life choices of individuals; and the promotion of policies which guarantee respect for the autonomy and integrity of groups based on race, ethnicity, nationality, and gender. To show how these objectives can come into conflict, Wolfe and Klausen examine the ideas associated with the founding of the welfare state. They draw on the work of T. H. Marshall, R. H. Tawney, William Beveridge, and other theorists, who held that in order to build a welfare state, one first had to build a state, which required an expansive conception of national citizenship and the suppression of challenges to state authority—challenges which could arise both from outside the country and from subgroups within the country. These theorists also held that welfare-state policies should be designed to break up the power of artificial constellations of interest such as class. Thus, there seems to be a tension between the principles of national citizenship required to sustain a welfare state and the demands for recognition of particular identity groups. After describing the nature and impact of this tension, Wolfe and Klausen go on to explore the view of inequality that underlies the institutions of the welfare state, distinguishing between natural differences among individuals (first-order inequalities) and inequalities in social status or access to education and employment (second-order inequalities). The original aim of the welfare state, they note, was to reduce or eliminate second-order differences, while sustaining, and even celebrating, first-order ones. Wolfe and Klausen conclude with a discussion of current calls for privatization and a general weakening of welfare policies, suggesting that a preoccupation with identity politics has prevented some social reformers on the left from properly responding to the welfare state's critics.

The final essay in this collection deals with the concept of personal responsibility as it has evolved under the welfare state, and with the concept of forfeiture—the idea that individuals may in certain cases forfeit some of their rights due to their own irresponsible conduct or wrongdoing. In "The Problem of Forfeiture in the Welfare State," Richard A. Epstein analyzes changes in the legal system that have arisen in the twentieth century as a result of the view that special legal protections must be accorded to employees, consumers, recipients of charity, and others who are taken to be vulnerable to exploitation. Epstein compares the nineteenth-century view of responsibility with the twentieth-century view with respect to contract law, tort law, and laws governing charitable organizations. He argues that the nineteenth-century view was better able to recognize the potential for misconduct on the part of both parties to a contract or transaction, and that the twentieth-century view has had some costly negative effects, reducing access to jobs and medical treatment. In the area of tort law, Epstein maintains that twentieth-century product-liability laws embody an unreasonable view of personal responsibility, holding a manufacturer liable even when a given injury or loss is the result of a consumer's misuse of its product. In the case of charitable organizations, Epstein contends that the nineteenth-century legal system encouraged charitable activity by, for example, limiting liability for medical malpractice in charity clinics and hospitals, and allowing organizations to make better use of limited resources by denying aid to some potential recipients based on alcoholism, misconduct, or refusal to work. In contrast, modern laws requiring hospitals to provide emergency medical care to all comers, regardless of their ability to pay, have had the perverse effect of reducing the number of institutions dispensing emergency care. With respect to the law of contract, Epstein shows how the modern view, in assuming that employees must be accorded special protection, tends increasingly to make hiring and firing decisions the subjects of litigation, in a way that is detrimental to job-creation in the long run. He concludes that in all these areas—contract, tort, and charitable provision—it may be time to consider a return to the earlier legal view of individual responsibility.

These twelve essays offer valuable insights into the history of the welfare state, the proper role of government in ameliorating distress, and the nature of individual and collective responsibility. They explore important controversies regarding the legitimacy and effectiveness of public welfare programs, and the viability of private, voluntaristic alternatives.

ACKNOWLEDGMENTS

The editors wish to acknowledge several individuals at the Social Philosophy and Policy Center, Bowling Green State University, who provided invaluable assistance in the preparation of this volume. They include Mary Dilsaver, Terrie Weaver, and Pamela Phillips.

We wish to thank Executive Manager Kory Swanson, for his tireless administrative support; Publication Specialist Tamara Sharp, for her patient attention to detail; and Managing Editor Harry Dolan, for editorial assistance above and beyond the call of duty.

CONTRIBUTORS

David Schmidtz is Associate Professor of Philosophy and, by courtesy, Associate Professor of Economics at the University of Arizona. He is the author of *Rational Choice and Moral Agency* (1995) and *The Limits of Government: An Essay on the Public Goods Argument* (1991). He and Robert Goodin are currently preparing a book for Cambridge University Press on responsibility and welfare.

David T. Beito is Assistant Professor of History at the University of Alabama. His current research interests are focused on the history of the nongovernmental provision of public services. He is the author of *Taxpayers in Revolt: Tax Resistance during the Great Depression* (1989) and of articles in the *Journal of Urban History*, *Critical Review*, and the *Journal of Policy History*. He is currently working on a book entitled *From Mutual Aid to the Welfare State*, which discusses the role of fraternal societies as sources of social welfare during the twentieth century.

Stephen Davies is Senior Lecturer in the Department of English and History at Manchester Metropolitan University in Manchester, England. He received a degree in Medieval and Modern History at the University of St. Andrews in 1976, and earned his Ph.D. from the same university in 1984. He is the author of *Beveridge Revisited: New Foundations for Tomorrow's Welfare* (1986) and is currently at work on a book which examines the successful provision of charitable services by private organizations in England during the nineteenth century.

Howard Husock is Director of Case Studies in Public Policy and Management at the Kennedy School of Government, Harvard University, where he is also affiliated with the Taubman Center for State and Local Government. He has published widely on housing and social policy, and his work has appeared in such periodicals as the *Wall Street Journal*, the *New York Times*, *City Journal*, *The Responsive Community*, *Critical Review*, and *The Public Interest*. He is a 1972 graduate of the Boston University School of Public Communication and was a 1981–92 Mid-Career Fellow at the Woodrow Wilson School of Public and International Affairs, Princeton University.

Theda Skocpol is Professor of Government and Sociology at Harvard University. She received her B.A. in 1969 from Michigan State University, and her Ph.D. in 1975 from Harvard University. She was the 1996 President of the Social Science History Association, and is a member of the Council of the American Political Science Association and a fellow of the

American Academy of Arts and Sciences. She is the author of *States and Social Revolutions: A Comparative Analysis of France, Russia, and China* (1979), *Protecting Soldiers and Mothers: The Political Origins of Social Policy in the United States* (1992), and *Boomerang: Clinton's Health Security Effort and the Turn against Government in U.S. Politics* (1996).

Daniel Shapiro is Associate Professor of Philosophy at West Virginia University. He received his B.A. from Vassar College in 1976 and his Ph.D. from the University of Minnesota in 1984, and has held visiting appointments at Rice University, the University of North Carolina at Chapel Hill, and Bowling Green State University. He has published a variety of articles in social and political philosophy in such journals as *Philosophical Studies, Social Theory and Practice, Public Affairs Quarterly, Journal of Political Philosophy*, and *Law and Philosophy*. He is currently at work on a book which compares welfare-state institutions to more free-market alternatives, as judged by central values or principles in contemporary political philosophy.

Peter J. Ferrara is General Counsel and Chief Economist at Americans for Tax Reform and an Associate Scholar at the Cato Institute. He has served as Associate Deputy Attorney General of the United States (1992–1993), as Associate Professor of Law at George Mason University School of Law (1987–1991), and as a senior staff member at the White House Office of Policy Development (1981–1983). He has written numerous books, studies, and articles on Social Security, including *Society Security: The Inherent Contradiction* (1981). He is a graduate of Harvard College and Harvard Law School.

James M. Buchanan is Harris University Professor at George Mason University and Advisory General Director of the Center for Study of Public Choice. He received his B.A. from Middle Tennessee State College in 1940, his M.S. from the University of Tennessee in 1941, and his Ph.D. from the University of Chicago in 1948. He is the recipient of the 1986 Nobel Prize in Economic Sciences, the editor of *The Return to Increasing Returns* (with Yong J. Yoon, 1994), and the author of *Ethics and Economic Progress* (1994), *The Economics and the Ethics of Constitutional Order* (1991), *Constitutional Economics* (1991), *Economics: Between Predictive Science and Moral Philosophy* (1987), *The Limits of Liberty* (1975), and *The Calculus of Consent* (with Gordon Tullock, 1962).

H. Tristram Engelhardt, Jr. is Professor of Medicine at Baylor College of Medicine, Professor of Philosophy at Rice University, and Member of the Center for Medical Ethics and Health Policy at Baylor College of Medicine. He is the editor of the *Journal of Medicine and Philosophy* and the coeditor of *Christian Bioethics*. He is also the coeditor of the book series *Philosophy and Medicine* and *Clinical Medical Ethics*, and the editor of the book series *Philosophical Studies in Contemporary Culture*. A revised second edition of his book *The Foundations of Bioethics* was published by Oxford University Press in 1996.

Lawrence M. Mead is Professor of Politics at New York University, where he teaches public policy and American government. He has also been a visiting professor at Harvard University, Princeton University, and the University of Wisconsin. A specialist on social policy and poverty, he has been a leading advocate and scholar of work requirements as an approach to welfare reform. He has published *Beyond Entitlement* (1986), *The New Politics of Poverty* (1992), and many journal articles on social policy, welfare, and welfare reform.

Alan Wolfe is University Professor of Sociology and Political Science at Boston University. He is the author of a number of books including *Whose Keeper? Social Science and Moral Obligation* (1989) and, most recently, *Marginalized in the Middle* (1996). A contributing editor of *The New Republic* and *The Wilson Quarterly*, he is currently writing a book on middle-class morality.

Jytte Klausen is Assistant Professor of Comparative Politics at Brandeis University and a Fellow at the Center for European Studies, Harvard University. She is currently completing a book on the social dimension of postwar economic policy, *Parity Politics in European Capitalism, 1945–1995*. She is also the author of articles on citizenship and the European welfare state, and on the position of women in trade unions, and is the coeditor (with Louise A. Tilly) of *European Integration as a Social Process: Historical Perspectives, 1850–1995*.

Richard A. Epstein is James Parker Hall Distinguished Service Professor of Law at the University of Chicago. He is the author of *Takings: Private Property and the Power of Eminent Domain* (1985), *Forbidden Grounds: The Case against Employment Discrimination Laws* (1992), *Bargaining with the State* (1993), and *Simple Rules for a Complex World* (1995). He is an editor of the *Journal of Law and Economics* and a member of the American Academy of Arts and Sciences.

GUARANTEES*

By David Schmidtz

I. Individual versus Collective Responsibility: Not the Real Issue

People have accidents. They get old. They eat too much. They have bad luck. And sooner or later, something will be fatal. It would be a better world if such things did not happen, but they do. There is no use arguing about it. What is worth arguing about is whether it makes for a better world when people have to pay for other people's misfortunes and mistakes rather than (or as well as) their own.

Misfortune and mistakes aside, it is sometimes said that even in the ordinary course of events, people should not have to pay for basic human needs. There is no use arguing about that, either. Someone, after all, has to pay. The question is who. Edwin Baker claims that "[i]f the practices of the society indicate that certain things are necessary in order to be a full member, then the community must assure the provision of these things to all who are expected to be part of the community."[1] Is that true? Baker leaps straight from the premise that certain things are necessary to the conclusion that guaranteed provision of those things is also necessary. That is a dangerous leap. Our need for food, clothing, and shelter is beyond question; our need for guaranteed provision is not. That we are better off having food, clothing, and shelter is beyond question; that we are better off having guaranteed provision of such things is not. After all, the guarantee does not mean the goods are free. What it means is that someone else has to pay.

This essay is about guarantees. It is about trying to ensure that no one ever loses. It is about trying too hard, and making people worse off in the process. This essay is also about what actually happens in the absence of guarantees. How do people respond when left to fend for themselves, with no guarantee that their needs will be satisfied at someone else's expense? Do they roll over and die? Do they thrive in the manner of Robinson Crusoe? Do they pour out of the country in order to avoid such

*This essay uses material from a forthcoming book, David Schmidtz and Robert E. Goodin, *Social Welfare as an Individual Responsibility: For and Against* (New York: Cambridge University Press, 1997). For helpful discussion, I am grateful to the members of my seminar at the University of Arizona in the spring of 1996 and to the other contributors to this volume. For written comments, I am especially grateful to Lawrence Mead, Ellen Paul, and Elizabeth Willott.

[1] Edwin Baker, "Utility and Rights: Two Justifications for State Action Increasing Equality," *Yale Law Journal*, vol. 84 (1974), p. 52.

responsibility and the prosperity that comes with it, or do they pour into the country in search of it?

Do they cooperate, voluntarily coming together to pool resources, share risks, and help each other in times of trouble? If they do, then to that extent they are accepting responsibility for their welfare as a group rather than as individuals. Are they making a big mistake? It depends. Collective responsibility is not a problem in and of itself, and individual versus collective responsibility is not the crucial distinction. More crucial is the distinction between *internalized* and *externalized* responsibility. Economists say a decision has a negative external effect when someone other than the decision maker ends up bearing some of the decision's costs. A pulp mill dumping wastes into a river, leaving them to be dealt with by those who live downstream, is a classic example of a negative externality. The cost of cleaning up the mess is foisted upon people who played no part in causing it.

When I speak of responsibility being externalized, I have something similar in mind. Responsibility is externalized when people do not take responsibility: for messes they cause, for messes in which they find themselves. Responsibility is externalized when people regard the cleanup as someone else's problem. We can speak of responsibility being externalized whether the messes result from mistake, misfortune, or (in the case of the pulp mill) from business as usual. In contrast, responsibility is internalized when agents take responsibility: for their welfare, for their futures, for the consequences of their actions.

The contrast between internalized and externalized responsibility does not neatly track the contrast between individual and collective responsibility. Collective responsibility can be a form of internalized responsibility. It can, in other words, be an example of people taking responsibility for themselves. A group collectively internalizes responsibility when, but only when, the group is composed of members who willingly take responsibility for themselves as a group.[2] So, when family members willingly accept responsibility for each other, we can see them as internalizing responsibility even though the responsibility takes a collective form. To some extent, this is a semantic issue, but it points to a real difference: some people see their welfare as someone else's problem; other people willingly take responsibility for each other's welfare as well as their own. Whatever terms we use, there is a real difference here, and it is something other than a difference between individual and collective responsibility.

Some forms of collective responsibility help to internalize responsibility. They have a history of enabling people to take responsibility for

---

[2] Someone could say that redistributive taxation is a government's way of internalizing responsibility—it sees people from whom it takes as part of the same group as people to whom it gives. That is not how I use the term, but I do not want to quibble about definitions. Our task is to explore what makes people better off, not to explore what counts as internalization.

themselves as a group, and consequently have been important contributors to human welfare. My thesis is that a society is trying too hard when, to avoid the prospect of leaving individuals to "sink or swim," it issues guarantees that not only collectivize responsibility but externalize it at the same time. Such guarantees do not merely help decision makers spread costs among themselves but also help them pass costs on to third parties without consent.

II. A COOPERATIVE VENTURE

When people take responsibility for their own welfare, this tends to put both them and the people around them in a better position to lead peaceful and productive lives and thereby turn their society into a "cooperative venture for mutual advantage."[3] In contrast, when people are taught that someone else owes them a living—when they consider it only fitting that they should have guaranteed free access to the fruits of other people's labor—both their lives and the lives of the people around them almost inevitably are rendered less productive and also less peaceful.[4] To let people tap the fruits of other people's labor without consent is to convert society into something less than a cooperative venture for mutual advantage.

We want to know which economic, political, and cultural institutions enable people to make meaningful, satisfying, and rewarding contributions to society as a cooperative venture for mutual advantage. We also want to know what such institutions can do to minimize the suffering that can result when some people are unable to contribute. To the first question, I would say that social structures enable people to contribute to society as a cooperative venture by encouraging them to take responsibility for their own welfare. To the second question, I would say that if we truly want to minimize suffering, we have to tackle that problem within the context of the overarching goal of encouraging people to take responsibility. We have to do it that way because if we fail to pay enough attention to the overarching goal, we will not minimize suffering either.

We think of famine as a shocking aberration, yet being on the edge of famine is and always has been more or less normal in nonmarket societies. We should pause to reflect on how amazing it is that anyone could *ever* afford what the average person in a market society today can afford. None of us wants to let people starve, but if we genuinely want to help our fellow citizens, then we should stop to remind ourselves that most of them do not need our help, and we should above all make sure we do not

---

[3] I borrow the phrase from John Rawls, *A Theory of Justice* (Cambridge: Harvard University Press, 1971), p. 4, but I do not claim to be interpreting the phrase in a Rawlsian way.
[4] My reference to the welfare of "the people around them" is not a throwaway line. Whether a person learns to be self-supporting or learns to expect free access to the fruits of other people's labor will affect the whole community.

change that. Above all, we should avoid disrupting the processes in virtue of which most people do not need our help.[5]

III. Leaving the Poor Behind

Welfare programs, though, often seem highly disruptive. No one thinks they encourage people to take responsibility for their own lives. Some people say welfare programs encourage (or even require) people to drop out of the work force.[6] Is it true? No one doubts that it is true to a degree. How large a degree? Economists Sheldon Danzinger, Robert Haveman, and Robert Plotnick estimate that every dollar in U.S. welfare-program transfers leads recipients to reduce the labor they contribute to the economy by an amount worth twenty-three cents.[7] Citing this same study by Danzinger et al., and describing it as a masterly synthesis, philosopher Robert Goodin writes that "the major U.S. income transfer programs, all taken together, are probably responsible for a total reduction of work hours by recipients amounting to 4.8 percent of total work hours for all workers in the U.S."[8]

Some authors have inferred from this that welfare recipients are 4.8 percent less likely to work. As Danzinger et al. note, though, "the percentage of reduction in work per transfer recipient implied by this estimate is substantially larger than 4.8 percent" (p. 998). How large? Danzinger et al. estimate that "AFDC reduces work effort of the average recipient by roughly 600 hours per year" (p. 997). Since the average recipient would work substantially less than 2,000 hours (i.e., fifty weeks) per year, AFDC—Aid to Families with Dependent Children—therefore is reducing work effort by substantially more than 30 percent on average. If the figure of 600 hours is anywhere near the truth, then AFDC is indeed inducing people to drop out.[9]

When adults drop out, they are less able, and perhaps less willing, to send their children a signal that taking responsibility for their own welfare is part of growing up. If their parents do not send that signal—if children grow up without firsthand experience of what it would be like to be productive—what will become of them? The answer, for better or

[5] Part of this thought is that even people who do need help (children, for example) get the help they need from their families, friends, and neighbors. That is part of the social structure and social process that we should try not to disrupt.

[6] See Lawrence M. Mead, *Beyond Entitlement: The Social Obligations of Citizenship* (New York: Free Press, 1986).

[7] Sheldon Danzinger, Robert Haveman, and Robert Plotnick, "How Income Transfer Programs Affect Work, Savings, and the Income Distribution: A Critical Review," *Journal of Economic Literature*, vol. 19 (1981), p. 1020.

[8] Robert E. Goodin, *Reasons for Welfare* (Princeton: Princeton University Press, 1988), p. 233.

[9] Why do they drop out? There is no simple explanation, but part of the explanation is that AFDC payments, together with food stamps and other benefits that go to AFDC recipients, add up to a pre-tax hourly wage equivalent of $14.76 in New York, $12.45 in Philadelphia, $11.35 in Baltimore, and $10.91 in Detroit. See Michael Tanner, Stephen Moore, and David Hartman, "The Work vs. Welfare Trade-Off," *Policy Analysis*, vol. 240 (1995), p. 27.

worse, is that the financial gap between people who accept responsibility for themselves and people who do not cannot help but grow over time. The only way to share fully in society's growing wealth is to participate fully in the process that makes wealth grow. If we wanted to guarantee that the poor would be left behind, here would be the way to do it: teach them that their welfare is someone else's responsibility.

IV. STATIC AND DYNAMIC PERSPECTIVES

When evaluating the welfare state's performance, what should we be hoping for? Robert Goodin proposes that "[p]reventing the exploitation of dependencies by making assistance to needy, dependent people largely nondiscretionary is the hallmark of the welfare state."[10] In the hands of public officials, the power of discretion is the power to exploit. *Exploitation* is objectionable when it consists of "laying down conditions in circumstances wherein the other party has no reasonable choice but to comply. The same thing that makes the other person have no other choice—his vulnerability to and dependence upon us for the needed resource—gives rise to a strong obligation on our part to provide him with that needed resource."[11] Goodin concludes that his arguments "dictate aiding the needy through rule-bound systems of welfare entitlements, wherein those dispensing the benefits have minimal discretion to withhold or lay down conditions for receipt of benefits by those entitled to them."[12]

What about people who are vulnerable through their own improvidence? If officials lack discretion, how will such people be excluded from the receipt of aid? Goodin proposes not to exclude them. He writes: "[C]ausal histories—how they ended up in their weak position or you in your strong position—are irrelevant to the strength of this moral duty. The fact that they got into this position through their own improvidence does not relieve you of your duty."[13]

When I first read this, I was puzzled. Why would anyone say that who caused a mess (through their own improvidence!) is not even *relevant* to the question of who should clean it up? I now see that there are two fundamentally different ways to look at it, each legitimate in its own way. From a static perspective, we see society as a snapshot, and what is wrong with the picture is that some people have unmet needs for food, clothing, and shelter, while others have plenty. From that perspective, causal histories do seem irrelevant. The only issue is how to get needed resources to needy people. We might worry that if resources keep getting diverted to purposes other than the purposes for which producers are producing them, production will decline or go offshore. If we do worry about that,

[10] Goodin, *Reasons for Welfare*, p. 177.

[11] *Ibid.*, p. 196. This characterization will suffice for my purposes, but Goodin himself offers several others (pp. 124, 147). See also his discussion of when dependents are exploitable (pp. 175–76).

[12] *Ibid.*, p. 19.

[13] *Ibid.*, p. 165n.

we will appear, from a static perspective, to be willfully out of touch. We will be talking about history or economics, perhaps, but not about the real world. The real world is the snapshot.

From a more historical or dynamic perspective, though, society is a *process* by which one snapshot evolves into another. People who take a dynamic perspective worry that when we focus on the snapshots, we can lose sight of the process that links the frames together; they believe that if we look at the process rather than the frames, we will come to radically different conclusions about what ought to be done. From a static perspective, the issue is how to rearrange the resources visible in the snapshot, on a frame-by-frame basis. In contrast, from a dynamic perspective, the issue is how to nurture processes that produce those resources, and thereby produce better snapshots in the future.

What should be our first priority: to clean up messes, or prevent them? I do not deny the first task's importance, but I do want to say that if we focus on the first task and ignore the second, we miss most of the point of encouraging people to take responsibility for their own welfare. Encouraging people to take responsibility can help many of the people who need help right now, but that is not the main reason for such encouragement. The main reason is that when people take responsibility, they are less likely to need help in the first place. Therein lies the significance of the distinction between static and dynamic perspectives.

Lest this be misunderstood, when I refer to the static perspective as static, I do not mean the adjective to be taken as pejorative. What we see from a static perspective is, after all, really there. Unfortunately, there are things we do not see from a static perspective. The things we do not see are more abstract. They lack the visceral urgency of the crises of the day. But they are no less real.

From a static perspective, it may seem that people would care about causal histories—how a needy person came to need—only insofar as they want to know whom to blame. (Some people want to blame the individual; others want to blame the "system.") From a dynamic perspective, though, causal histories are crucial in the analysis of exploitation. If Jane comes to be in need by virtue of knowingly building (and then not insuring) a house on a floodplain, for example, that bit of history is highly relevant to the question of whether those who are given no choice in the matter of paying to rebuild Jane's house are being exploited. If we guarantee Jane that, when in need, she will have access to other people's income no matter how she comes to be in need, then we are giving Jane a guaranteed right to exploit in an attempt to prevent Jane from being vulnerable to exploitation. I would agree with Goodin that, even if Jane is to blame, that does not entail that she ought to be left to fend for herself. By the same token, if the "system" is to blame, that does not entail that other individuals have a duty to help. Who is to blame for her plight and who ought to take responsibility for her welfare are distinct questions. They are not unrelated questions, though. Even if the only thing we care about is how to help Jane escape her current predicament, the fact remains that before we can know what it will take to get her out of her predicament, we have to know what it took to get her into it. If she is in need because an insurance agent pocketed her premium while fraudulently leading her to believe that she was paying for flood insurance, that is not the same problem as need that results from Jane's half-conscious assumption that the government would lack the stomach to deny her aid in the event of a flood. An approach that ameliorates one problem might exacerbate the other.

From a static perspective, what would solve the discretion/exploitation problem? Goodin writes: "[I]t is necessary both (a) that adequate resources be transferred to guarantee that people's basic needs will be met and (b) that that transfer occur in ways that are substantially independent of any discretionary power on the part of those responsible for effecting the transfer."[14] Is it possible to meet both of these conditions at once? There certainly is a financial obstacle. Meeting the first condition would be expensive, but the second condition, minimal discretion, ultimately translates into minimal ability to contain costs by limiting access. Goodin's solution, in any case, is to *over*fund the system, "systematically erring on the side of generosity."[15]

Goodin calls this the rule of generosity, and concludes: "The only real objection to my rule of generosity is the economic one."[16] This seems unlikely. For example, we might wonder what gives anyone the right to be so generous with other people's money, knowingly giving recipients more than most of them need.

Moreover, the economic problem is by no means trivial. Arthur Okun says we can fund a more generous welfare state by "twisting some other dials" so as to produce budget surpluses.[17] Goodin quotes this approvingly.[18] Okun published his remark in 1975; Goodin quoted it in 1988. I do not know whether Goodin feels the same way today. Oddly, Goodin allows that under conditions of scarcity, different rules apply, rules other than the rule of generosity.[19] It is hard to know what to make of this

---

[14] *Ibid.*, p. 177.

[15] *Ibid.*, p. 221ff.

[16] *Ibid.*, p. 223.

[17] Arthur Okun, *Equality and Efficiency: The Big Tradeoff* (Washington, DC: Brookings Institution, 1975), p. 99. Presumably, one of the dials Okun had in mind was the tax rate. When contemplating tax hikes, even people who know better routinely make budget projections on the assumption that raising tax rates by 20 percent will raise tax revenues by 20 percent as well. But twisting the revenue dial is not so easy. While some people deny that tax rates affect investment decisions, others question whether raising tax rates has much effect on government revenues. W. Kurt Hauser, "The Tax and Revenue Equation," *Wall Street Journal*, March 25, 1993, says that between 1949 and 1993, top marginal personal income tax rates were as high as 92 percent and as low as 28 percent, but federal tax receipts never went higher than 21.5 percent of gross domestic product (in 1981, when the top tax rate was 50 percent) and never went lower than 17.9 percent of GDP (in 1964 and 1965, when the top tax rate was 77 percent).

[18] Goodin, *Reasons for Welfare*, p. 234.

[19] *Ibid.*, p. 223n.

concession. Goodin does not say what the other rules are. On its face, the concession amounts to an admission that different rules *always* apply, since scarcity, as the term is normally used, is ubiquitous. On its face, then, we should conclude that the rule of generosity is of no consequence. Surely this is not what Goodin intends. Since he makes the concession in passing, as if it had no great significance, he may be supposing that so long as rich people are out there, there is no genuine scarcity. We could tap them at will, if only we had the courage. It is not true, though, that we can force the stream of wealth produced by other people's labor to flow wherever we choose without affecting the volume of wealth flowing down the stream. We have experience with large-scale systems that ask people to take according to need and give according to ability. The experience is all bad. It is time to ask, what are our real options?

V. NEED-BASED DISTRIBUTION

The first thing to consider is that, upon reflection, asking the welfare state to guarantee that rich people will never be able to exploit poor people is asking both too much and too little. It is asking too little, because if people starve when minimum-wage laws cut them off from jobs that would have paid them $4 an hour, it is no comfort that the laws also prevent them from being exploited. It is asking too much, because to eliminate exploitation, we would have to do something other than give people who do not work a license to exploit people who do; the only guaranteed way to eliminate opportunities to exploit poor people is to eliminate contact with poor people, thereby eliminating opportunities to help them too.[20] A more plausible general goal would be to enable poor people to prosper, or more concretely, to enable them to support themselves.[21] Ending exploitation sometimes would help, but it is neither necessary nor sufficient as a means to that end.

If we suppose that the point of the welfare state is to help poor people prosper, what role does that suggest for need-based distribution? From a static perspective, the answer is obvious. Need-based distribution meets needs. Or is that not as obvious as it sounds? Need-based distribution is meant to meet needs, but how well does intent match reality? Can we safely assume that distributing according to need is the most reliable way of meeting needs? The record of the

[20] For those concerned about rich people exploiting poor people, though, one obvious remedy would be to eliminate a program like Social Security. Retired people in the United States today are, as a group, far wealthier than young workers, yet the pay-as-you-go system employed in the United States transferred $334 billion from the latter to the former in 1995 alone, amounting to 22 percent of the entire federal budget. The cost of the system as currently constituted is projected to increase to $566 billion (in constant dollars) by the year 2005, according to the Congressional Budget Office, *Baseline Projections for Mandatory Spending* (Washington, DC: Congressional Budget Office, April 1995).

[21] Supporting oneself is not to be equated with living like Robinson Crusoe. What people mean when they speak of supporting oneself is living on one's earnings, however cooperative and interdependent the enterprises may be from which those earnings derive.

twentieth century's attempts to distribute according to need is not encouraging. Although there surely is a place in social life for need-based distribution, we should neither exaggerate this place nor jump to any conclusions about how centralized or how bureaucratic the administration of such distribution ought to be. It would be a fallacy to assume that those who object to need-based distribution by a central bureaucracy do not care about need. Many of them think that need-based distribution (especially by a central bureaucracy) is not what people need.

Goodin knows that need-based distribution is not the only way to meet needs, but he thinks that state-administered, tax-financed redistribution is superior to the market when it comes to meeting the needs of the poor. He observes: "What a straightforward redistribution would accomplish in an instant, supply-side policies would accomplish only in due course."[22] Goodin has a point. To put it in terms of a proverbial metaphor, giving someone a fish accomplishes in an instant what teaching the person to fish accomplishes only in due course. The problem is that, in general, giving someone a fish *helps* for only an instant too. The nice thing about supply-side policies is that what they accomplish tends to stay accomplished. We certainly want to know what constitutes "due course." However, it misconceives the nature of a free society to think that, within it, poor people have no choice but to patiently wait for wealth to "trickle down."[23] There was a time in the nineteenth century when poor people found it hard to afford the price of health care. They did not passively wait for the "long term." They got together and solved the problem.

VI. FRIENDLY SOCIETIES IN A SOMETIMES HOSTILE WORLD

If we honestly sought to identify social arrangements with a history of helping people to become self-supporting, would we find that collective responsibility has a history of failure, while individual responsibility has a history of success? Not exactly. Certainly, the prosperity of any society depends substantially on the ability of its culture and institutions to inculcate expectations of individual responsibility. Just as certainly, though, some ways of collectivizing responsibility can be and have been important contributors to economic and cultural development. Certain kinds of collective responsibility, it turns out, are compatible with a culture of personal initiative and accountability.

Francis Fukuyama writes: "[T]he United States has never been the individualistic society that most Americans believe it to be; rather, it has always possessed a rich network of voluntary associations and community structures to which individuals have subordinated their narrow in-

---

[22] Goodin, *Reasons for Welfare*, p. 271.
[23] I thank Dan Russell for discussions of this point.

terests."[24] Fukuyama is right. Institutions of collective responsibility per se are nothing new.

They seem to have taken a new shape, though. Collective responsibility once manifested itself primarily in family-based and community-based norms that sustained neighborhoods and a rich network of mutual aid, and thus made crucial contributions to social welfare. Today, collective responsibility is a concept we associate with a distant bureaucracy. It has been externalized. People we never meet decide what to deduct from our paychecks and how to spend it. It has become commonplace to accuse the welfare state of eroding norms of individual responsibility by encouraging dependence, but that may not be the worst of it; in some ways the welfare state seems also to undermine people's sense of collective responsibility. Historian David Green writes that, in recent times, "socialists have not seen the good person as someone who gave his own time and energy in the service of others, but as the individual who demanded action by the state at the expense of other taxpayers."[25]

In his 1996 "state of the union" address, President Clinton said we cannot go back to the time when people were left to fend for themselves. But what time was that? Mr. Clinton did not say, but we can suppose he had in mind the time before Franklin Roosevelt's New Deal. Were people in fact left to fend for themselves before the New Deal? If so, what actually happened? Did people roll over and die? Did they thrive as hermits, in the manner of Robinson Crusoe? Or did they get together with neighbors and figure out how to solve their problems? Perhaps Mr. Clinton is right: it may be impossible to go back to such a time. I suppose no one knows for sure. What I do know is that it is a false dichotomy to suppose that the only alternative to the welfare state is everyone having to fend for him- or herself.

As in many other countries, the United States included, there once flourished in England organizations known as friendly societies that, according to Green, historically share with trade unions an older kind of collectivist philosophical underpinning, one based on the idea of self-help.[26]

> Through the trade unions workers would win the wages necessary to sustain a decent existence, and through the friendly societies they would organize their own welfare services—social insurance, medical care, even housing loans. The profit motive, too, was to be supplanted: in the factory by the mutuality of the workers' co-op; and in

[24] Francis Fukuyama, *Trust: The Social Virtues and the Creation of Prosperity* (New York: Free Press, 1995), p. 29.

[25] David G. Green, *Reinventing Civil Society: The Rediscovery of Welfare without Politics* (London: IEA Health and Welfare Unit, 1993), p. 3.

[26] David G. Green, *Working-Class Patients and the Medical Establishment: Self-Help in Britain from the Mid-Nineteenth Century to 1948* (Aldershot: Gower Publishing Co., 1985) pp. 1, 4–5.

retailing by the co-op store. Not all of these working-class hopes were realized, but the friendly societies, the trade unions, and the co-op stores were successful and offered a fraternal alternative to the sometimes cold world of commercial calculation. Particularly striking is the success of the friendly societies, whose social insurance and primary medical care schemes had attracted at least three-quarters of manual workers well before the end of the nineteenth century. Until the 1911 National Insurance Act every neighborhood of every town was dotted with friendly society branches, each with their own doctor, who had usually been elected by a vote of all the members assembled in the branch meeting.[27]

How *expensive* was participation in such societies? Access to club medical care was inexpensive to the point of being an outrage to the organized medical profession. Historian David Beito writes that, in America in 1900, a lodge member "could acquire a physician's care for about two dollars a year; approximately a day's wage for a laborer at the time."[28] David Green and Lawrence Cromwell report that, in Australia in the 1830s and 1840s, fees charged by private doctors were sometimes over ten shillings per visit—well beyond the means of most people. By 1869, friendly societies had emerged in Australia, providing medical service at a rate of ten shillings per *year* for each member, plus an additional ten shillings per year for a member's wife and children. To win election to a post as club doctor, candidates offered competitive rates, submitted to questioning by the assembled members regarding their training and experience, and offered perks such as free house visits within three or four miles of the lodge.[29]

How *widespread* was participation in such societies? Green estimates that "at least 9 million of the 12 million originally included in the National Insurance scheme were already members of friendly societies offering medical care."[30] Moreover, between friendly societies, voluntary hospitals, provident dispensaries,[31] private charity, regular insurance, fees for service (which competition from friendly societies eventually forced down to levels that average workers could afford), and, as a last resort, the Poor

---

[27] *Ibid.*, p. 1.

[28] David T. Beito, "The 'Lodge Practice Evil' Reconsidered: Medical Care through Fraternal Societies, 1900–1930," *Journal of Urban History*, vol. 23 (July 1997).

[29] David G. Green and Lawrence G. Cromwell, *Mutual Aid or Welfare State? Australia's Friendly Societies* (Sydney: George Allen and Unwin, 1984), pp. 76–80.

[30] Green, *Working-Class Patients*, p. 95.

[31] Voluntary hospitals provided free care. Provident dispensaries charged nominal fees. "[T]he provident dispensaries aimed to enable the poor to make as much of a contribution as they could afford to the cost of their health care. It was felt that the beneficiaries would feel greater self-respect if they were able to pay at least something towards their own health care. They therefore paid a low annual contribution, felt to be within the means of the very poor, and the balance was supplied by the honourary members." See Green, *Reinventing Civil Society*, p. 73.

Law,[32] universal coverage had, for all practical purposes, been achieved. "No one, therefore, went without some sort of primary medical care."[33]

How *adequate* was the care provided by such societies? Green reports disputes between the societies and the organized medical profession over the societies' refusal to exclude wealthy members; means-testing would have been contrary to the societies' principle that all joined on equal terms.[34] The fact that there was an issue over wealthy members using the service suggests that the quality of service must have been reasonably good—good enough that rich people in significant numbers wanted access to it.

For what it is worth, the friendly societies were a remedy for exploitation as well. When there are multiple providers of relevantly similar services, people who dislike terms offered by one provider can look elsewhere, which minimizes their dependence on, and consequent vulnerability to, any particular provider. No particular provider, nor any coalition of providers, was in a position to dictate terms to clients. The friendly societies, together with provident dispensaries, voluntary hospitals, and so on, decentralized collective responsibility for medical care without turning it into a strictly individual responsibility. Individually and collectively, they gave people a range of choices at prices that almost anyone, even then, could afford.[35]

So, what happened to them? Several factors contributed to their decline. First, employer-provided benefit packages became common as tax-free benefits packages became an increasingly attractive form of compensation compared to taxable wages. Those packages made friendly societies' services somewhat redundant. There was less reason for workers to pay dues for services that they were already receiving through their employers.

Meanwhile, professional medical associations hated the friendly societies, correctly believing that friendly societies gave medical consumers the bargaining power they needed to undermine price collusion by doctors. By the early 1900s, medical associations had become a powerful political force, especially when they joined forces with for-profit insurance companies (which also viewed friendly societies as an obstacle to higher profits). Together, they played an active and highly visible role in the friendly societies' decline. In England, they were a major influence on

---

[32] England's Poor Law Amendment Act of 1834 sought to limit access to (and desirability of) government poor relief, so as to ensure that it would indeed be treated as a last resort. The general idea was that the standard of living made possible by public assistance ought to be less desirable than that available to the humblest of self-supporting laborers. See Gertrude Himmelfarb, *The De-Moralization of Society* (New York: Alfred A. Knopf, 1994), ch. 4.

[33] Green, *Working-Class Patients*, p. 179.

[34] *Ibid.*, pp. 19–21.

[35] A Royal Commission assigned to investigate whether the poor were systematically deterred from joining friendly societies found that, in 1901–1902, "registered friendly society membership was highest in rural areas where wages were lowest" (Green, *Reinventing Civil Society*, p. 68).

the process of amending early drafts of the 1911 National Insurance Act so as to make the final legislation as prejudicial as possible to the friendly societies.

Two features of the National Insurance Act are crucial. First, the act established price floors that made it illegal for friendly societies to offer health care at lower prices. Second, the act made it compulsory for male workers earning less than a certain income to purchase government medical insurance, thereby making it more difficult if not pointless for workers to pay friendly society dues (which the price floors had made more expensive) on top of what they paid for government services. (Interestingly, in some respects, the act hardly even pretended to be providing national insurance. For example, the act made no provision for the care of widows and orphans, because insurance companies felt that such provision would make it harder to sell life insurance.[36])

Similar forces were at work in the United States. David Beito reports that medical associations warned their members that if they accepted work as club doctors, they faced "forfeiture of membership or, just as seriously, a boycott" by other medical providers.

> In 1913, for example, members of the medical society in Port Jervis, New York vowed that if any physician took a lodge contract they would "refuse to consult with him or assist him in any way or in any emergency whatever." In this instance, and many others, boycotts extended to patients as well. One method of enforcement was to pressure hospitals to close their doors to members of the guilty lodge.[37]

Their demise notwithstanding, friendly societies seem to have had many of the features that we wish our health-care system had today: cost-containment, state-of-the-art service, personal attention, and the ability effectively to reach all segments of society. Such societies also provided services like old-age pensions, unemployment insurance, life insurance, workmen's compensation, day care, and so on, while at the same time serving as a form of community association.

Is it realistic to suppose that friendly societies in the twenty-first century could emulate their earlier success?[38] Realistically, they could never be like they were, simply because they would be responding to needs that are not the same as the needs of nineteenth-century lodge members. Times change. Conditions essential to an institution's history of success may no longer be operative, and we may not realize that until after we try

---

[36] Green, *Reinventing Civil Society*, p. 99.

[37] Beito, "The 'Lodge Practice Evil' Reconsidered," p. 30.

[38] Given the lack of modern actuarial and accounting techniques, it is easy to imagine how nineteenth-century friendly societies could have run into financial difficulties. Yet none of them, to my knowledge, ever appealed to financial hardship as a reason for refusing to provide promised benefits.

and fail to replicate its success in another time and place.[39] Thus, policy-makers have to live without guarantees. This is no reason not to explore alternatives, especially when those alternatives have been tried with success.

I do not know exactly how such a system would work, any more than I know exactly how a toaster works. But that is no reason to forbid people to make toasters, or to invent better ones. Nor is it a reason to ignore alternatives to government-provided health care, social security, and even unemployment insurance.[40] It may be hard to imagine how such things could work, but potted *a priori* arguments that they are impossible will not do. Theorists cannot match the creativity of people on the ground needing to solve real-world problems.

In any case, friendly societies comprise a class of tested examples of how institutions can collectivize responsibility and still succeed. They are not a thought experiment; they are not a utopian dream. Medical savings accounts and privatized pension plans can help people to internalize and at the same time individualize responsibility for their health care and their retirement. Friendly societies comprise a distinct alternative. They have a history of allowing people to internalize responsibility in a collective form.[41]

VII. THE POSSIBILITY OF POLITICAL DISARMAMENT

There are reasons why people voluntarily seek to join groups that collectivize responsibility. Certain forms of collective responsibility help to spread risk, for example.[42] For some people, sharing is intrinsically desirable, and understandably so. It is intrinsically a form of community.

---

[39] As recently as the 1960s, though, the Taborian Hospital of Mound Bayou, Mississippi, provided basic medical coverage for as little as $30 per year, according to David T. Beito, "Our Temple of Health: Black Fraternal Hospitals in the Mississippi Delta, 1942–1967," paper presented to the American Historical Association, January 1996.

[40] Private unemployment insurance was once available in Michigan, and insurance companies spent decades fighting against laws prohibiting wider selling of unemployment policies. See Michael B. Rappaport, "The Private Provision of Unemployment Insurance," *Wisconsin Law Review*, vol. 61 (1992), pp. 61–129.

[41] Lawrence Mead, in conversation, acknowledges that friendly societies were once effective providers of health care to the poor, but questions whether welfare recipients today have the competence to do for themselves what poor people did a century ago. If Mead is right, then we are left with a question of how to instill competence. One might begin by observing that we acquire competence in any particular activity through practice. We are not born with it. One of the ways in which our social environment contributes to our developing competence is by making it clear that we are expected to become competent. An environment that does not present us with such expectations is likely to hold us back.

[42] There is some evidence, though, that the advantages of communal management as a form of collective responsibility tend to decrease as an economy matures. See Robert C. Ellickson, "Property in Land," *Yale Law Journal*, vol. 102 (1993), pp. 1315–1400, esp. p. 1342ff. See also my chapter on property rights in Schmidtz and Goodin, *Social Welfare as an Individual Responsibility: For and Against*.

Theda Skocpol[43] defends the welfare state and is skeptical about mutual aid societies on the grounds that the welfare state has woven into it a pattern of sharing (to use Skocpol's apt phrase) while mutual aid societies do not. I think the exact opposite is true. What is woven into the welfare state is literally a pattern of transfer, not a pattern of sharing. It is mutual aid societies, not welfare-state programs, that are knit together by a pattern of sharing. It is not true that where the welfare state goes, community spirit flourishes. Nor is it true that authentic community spirit was dead before fifty years of expanding federal programs gradually brought it back to life.

Fraternal feeling is possible in a small group, but when we institutionalize altruism on a national scale, the possibility of genuine community is precisely what we give up.[44] At present, the welfare state's actual operation plainly provides more occasion for mutual resentment than for fraternal feeling.

If we want a system that nurtures fraternal feeling, we have to start by acknowledging that compulsory deductions from paychecks do nothing of the kind. Rightly or wrongly, taxpayers often feel victimized by the welfare state. Rightly or wrongly, beneficiaries often feel the same way. Both sides find it unfathomable that people on the other side would feel like victims. The bottom line is that the welfare state externalizes responsibility, and in the process does the opposite of engendering a sense of community. If communitarians are right to say that Western society has been atomized, then surely one of the causes has been the state's relentless drive to turn public life into a matter of standing in line, filling out forms, and arguing with bureaucrats.

What we need are ways of bringing people together that are (in their own eyes) in their common interest, in order that they may come together willingly.[45] We have to look for ways that enable people to live peaceful and productive lives, pursuing their own projects in such a way as to make themselves better off by making the people around them better off. The idea that government should strive to be an impartial referee, enforcing rules that enable people to pursue their own plans in peace, is no longer widely shared. But when government becomes a player rather than a referee, getting government to play for your side becomes a key objective. When the power of government is up for grabs in a game with no referee, those who love that kind of power (and also those who fear it) inevitably fight over it, creating nothing of value in the process.

---

[43] In conversation.

[44] I thank James Buchanan for this point.

[45] The proposal is not to appeal exclusively to self-interest so much as to appeal to interests that people actually have. There is also sometimes a place for appealing to latent interests (in their community, say) that people could have reason to develop and pursue under the right conditions.

In contrast, voluntarily assumed responsibility, whether individual or collective, reduces the extent to which people represent threats to each other. By enabling people to help themselves and each other without first needing to fight for political power, voluntarily accepted responsibility becomes a form of political disarmament. As with literal disarmament, it is a recipe for peace and prosperity.

VIII. Making Progress

We all want guarantees, but the cost of trying to purchase them is high. Systematically *rewarding* productive effort helps people internalize responsibility and thus helps make for a peaceful and productive society.[46] Trying to guarantee that productive effort will be *unnecessary* helps make for the opposite. It is in response to a lack of guarantees that people take responsibility for their own welfare and for the welfare of those they care about. Like it or not, a lack of guarantees has been one of the great engines of human progress.[47]

Within a nation's population, Goodin observes, there is "much productive potential; but to bring out that productive potential, people must be healthy, educated, well fed, etc. The welfare state guarantees that such basic needs are met. . . . That the welfare state contributes in this way to economic efficiency is pretty well indisputable."[48] I only wish it were actually true that children of welfare recipients tend to be healthy, educated, and well fed.

Nevertheless, in Western market societies more generally, children today are healthier, better educated, and even better fed (to the point of being significantly taller on average) than children were a century ago. Someone must be doing something right. Looking at the long run, it is obvious that the poor have not been getting poorer.[49]

---

[46] Alan Wolfe suggests (in conversation) that we could distinguish between positive and negative guarantees. An adequately enforced system of property rights, for example, provides a negative guarantee to the extent that it secures people against interference with their productive efforts. Positive guarantees secure access to the fruits of other people's productive efforts. Negative guarantees help make for a peaceful and productive society; positive guarantees help make for the opposite.

[47] A similar theme is suggested by Howard Husock in "Standards versus Struggle: The Failure of Public Housing and the Welfare-State Impulse," elsewhere in this volume.

[48] Goodin, *Reasons for Welfare*, p. 237.

[49] Short-run trends are harder to discern, of course. It is often claimed that wages for the poor and middle classes have stagnated since 1980, but data for the United States do not support this claim:

> The Census Bureau keeps statistics separately for "families" and "unrelated individuals." Census Bureau figures show that between 1980 and 1989, real income for the middle quintile of families increased by 8.3 per cent, while real income for the middle quintile of unrelated individuals increased by 16.3 per cent. The CBO [Congressional Budget Office] manipulated this Census Bureau data by combining "families" and "unrelated individuals" into the single category of "families." Since demographic

For the sake of argument, though, suppose we look at the short run, and suppose we find that the average income of people in the bottom income quintile has not risen in thirty years. What would that mean? Would it mean that a fifth of the population have incomes that were low to begin with and that have not risen in thirty years? Or would it mean that a fifth of the population are barely out of high school; they pump gas and work in fast-food restaurants, and their wages are about the same as what people their age were earning in the same jobs thirty years ago?

If the latter interpretation (corrected for overstatements of inflation and so on) is closer to the truth, then what became of all those people who were young and poor thirty years ago? They are now about fifty years old. Are they still pumping gas? If their place in the bottom quintile was inherited by people who are barely out of high school now, then where did they go as they grew older? Which quintile do they occupy today?

Philosopher Thomas Nagel finds it "appalling that the most effective social systems we have been able to devise permit so many people to be born into conditions of harsh deprivation which crush their prospects for leading a decent life,"[50] but the Census Bureau found that 25.7 percent of those who were below the poverty line in 1987 were no longer below it *one year later*.[51] In absolute terms, "[i]ndividuals in the lowest income quintile in 1975 saw, on average, a $25,322 rise in their real income over the 16 years from 1975 to 1991. Those in the highest income quintile had a $3,974 increase in real income, on average."[52] The U.S. Treasury Department's Office of Tax Analysis found that of people in the bottom income quintile in 1979, 65 percent moved up two or more quintiles by 1988.[53] That finding has been corroborated. Tracking a separate group of

---

trends produced more rapid growth in the number of unrelated individuals in the 1980s, and since families headed by two adults on average have far higher incomes than unrelated individuals, combining these groups into a single category of "families" greatly depressed average "family" incomes.

Thus, even though the incomes of middle-quintile families increased at a rate of 8.3 per cent and the incomes of middle-quintile individuals increased by 16.3 per cent, middle-quintile "families" in the CBO's new sense saw their total incomes decline by 0.8 per cent over the same period. (John H. Hinderaker and Scott W. Johnson, "Wage Wars," *National Review*, April 22, 1996, p. 35)

Robert Samuelson suggests a further explanation for the misperception of statistical stagnation. "The notion that most people's incomes and living standards are stagnating is simply false. Not only is it contradicted by the outpouring of new consumer products and services. It is also contradicted by official statistics, which, once corrected for slight overstatement of inflation, show sizable gains. No one knows precisely the extent of the overstatement of inflation. A good guess is ten to twenty percent over the past two decades." Robert J. Samuelson, "Great Expectations," *Newsweek*, January 8, 1996, p. 32.

[50] Thomas Nagel, *Equality and Partiality* (New York: Oxford University Press, 1991), p. 64.

[51] Reported by D. Eric Schansberg, *Poor Policy* (Boulder: Westview Press, 1996), p. 8.

[52] My source for these figures is Census Bureau data reported in W. Michael Cox and Richard Alm, "By Your Own Bootstraps," *Annual Report of the Federal Reserve Bank of Dallas* (1995), p. 8.

[53] See Schansberg, *Poor Policy*, p. 8.

people occupying the lowest quintile in 1975, the Census Bureau saw 80.3 percent move up two or more quintiles by 1991.[54]

The idea of being in the bottom quintile conjures up images from the novels of Charles Dickens. What is it really like? Consider that people with an income of $11,000 (roughly that of a typical American graduate student) are squarely in the middle of America's bottom quintile.[55] Yet many of them own a telephone, a microwave oven, a radio, a toothbrush, a closet-full of factory-made clothing, even an automobile. All have access to flush toilets, electric light, and hot running water. As recently as a century ago, these amenities and thousands of others would have been rare if not inconceivable for people in the bottom quintile. In 1900, the average life expectancy was 47.3 years in the United States. By 1990, it had risen to 75.4 years.[56] I suspect the increase in life expectancy would be even more dramatic if we compared only people in the bottom quintile for income. I am not suggesting that everyone in the bottom quintile has a lifestyle as comfortable as that of graduate students, of course. The point, rather, is that people in the middle of the bottom quintile are spectacularly wealthy compared to people in the same relative position a hundred years ago. We could show that by comparing today's graduate students to nineteenth-century graduate students, or by comparing representative manual laborers, and so on.

There are people, though, who find it offensive to compare the snapshots of today to the snapshots of a century ago. The comparison will seem complacent to those who think that the only things that really matter are the problems they see in the snapshots of today. The fact that things are a lot better than they were a century ago is beside the point. I tried to explain the vitriolic nature of debates concerning the welfare state by positing two kinds of perspectives, static and dynamic. One of this essay's themes is that the world and what we should do about it look very different from the two perspectives. People who take the static perspective sometimes think that those who see things differently are indifferent to suffering, and in some cases they are probably right. People who take a dynamic perspective sometimes think that those who see things differently must simply hate it when a society's institutions enable people to prosper, and in some cases they too are probably right.

---

[54] See Cox and Alm, "By Your Own Bootstraps," p. 8.

[55] About 9 percent of U. S. families earn under $11,000 in 1996 dollars. (These are Congressional Budget Office numbers, so a graduate student counts as a family, as per Hinderaker and Johnson; see note 49.) A household bringing in two graduate student salaries is still (just barely) in the bottom quintile. See Don L. Boroughs, "Workers Take It on the Chin," *U.S. News and World Report*, January 22, 1996, p. 50.

[56] Ann Hardie, "Why We're Living Longer," *Atlanta Journal/Constitution*, August 28, 1995, p. A3. Hardie does not list original sources, but Samuelson, "Great Expectations," p. 27, says that, according to the U.S. Census Bureau, average life expectancy increased from 65.9 years in 1945 to 75.7 years in 1994.

A second theme is that the extent to which a society is peaceful and prosperous depends on the extent to which responsibility is internalized, that is, on the extent to which people bear the cost of their own mistakes and misfortunes, and are not made to bear the cost of other people's mistakes and misfortunes without consent. At the same time, certain social arrangements for collectivizing responsibility have a history of making people better off—specifically, those that avoid externalizing responsibility in the process of collectivizing it. Internalizing responsibility is a form of political disarmament. As with literal disarmament, it is a recipe for peace and prosperity.

A third theme is that although the direct approach to meeting needs is the most obvious, it is not always the best. Could a welfare safety-net be packaged in such a way that people would willingly pay for it? It would have to avoid treating those who work for a living as mere means to the ends of those who do not. It would have to serve the ends of both those who support it and those supported by it. It would have to institutionalize reciprocity rather than free-riding. Is that possible?

The answer is that such schemes are not only possible; they have a long history. The history of friendly societies is a history of people producing and paying for their own guarantees. Friendly societies never were perfect, and never would be, but in many countries they have a history of doing what a welfare safety-net is supposed to do, and doing it increasingly well over time as they evolved in response to consumer demand.

I conclude that there are reasons for endorsing certain forms of group responsibility, but that the best arguments for group responsibility are bad arguments for the welfare state as a set of institutions for administering that responsibility. The welfare state undertakes to offer people the wrong kind of guarantee, namely a guarantee that externalizes responsibility. It is a better world when people come together of their own free will to share each other's burdens. It is a worse world when people can foist the cost of their misfortunes and misadventures on others without consent.

Philosophy, University of Arizona

"THIS ENORMOUS ARMY": THE MUTUAL AID TRADITION OF AMERICAN FRATERNAL SOCIETIES BEFORE THE TWENTIETH CENTURY*

By David T. Beito

I. Introduction

The tendency to join fraternal organizations for the purpose of obtaining care and relief in the event of sickness and insurance for the family in case of death is well-nigh universal. To the laboring classes and those of moderate means they offer many advantages not to be had elsewhere.

—New Hampshire Bureau of Labor, *Report* (1894)

The social-welfare world of the poor has changed considerably since the turn of the century. It is not difficult to find dramatic evidence of progress. Most obviously, there has been a substantial reduction in the percentage of Americans who are poor. Even in 1929, about 40 percent of the population still lived in poverty. The corresponding figure for 1993 was 15.1 percent. The poor have also enjoyed notable material and physical gains in terms of income, diet, health, and housing conditions.[1]

There are other, much less reassuring statistical measures, however. The decline in poverty has coincided with increased rates of dependence on governmental aid. In 1905, only one out of every 150 Americans (excluding prisoners) resided in a public or private institution of any kind, including almshouses, asylums, orphanages, and hospitals. The number of Americans who depended on outdoor relief (aid delivered outside of any institutional setting) was also small. As late as 1931, only 93,000 families received mothers' pensions, the state-funded antecedents to Aid to Families with Dependent Children (AFDC). In 1993, by contrast, the caseload for AFDC was just over five million families.[2]

* I would like to thank David Schmidtz, Theda Skocpol, Danny Shapiro, Ellen Frankel Paul, Bradley J. Young, Stephen Davies, Richard Epstein, Howard Husock, Alan Wolfe, Lawrence Mead, James Buchanan, H. Tristram Engelhardt, Jr., and Peter Ferrara for their valuable help.

[1] Sar A. Levitan, *Programs in Aid of the Poor* (Baltimore: Johns Hopkins University Press, 1990), pp. 5–6; U.S. Department of Commerce, Bureau of the Census, *Statistical Abstract of the United States* (Washington, DC: U.S. Department of Commerce, 1995), p. 480.

[2] *Charities and Commons*, vol. 16 (1906), pp. 488–91; U.S. Department of Labor, *Mother's Aid, 1931* (Washington, DC: U.S. Government Printing Office, 1933), p. 8; *Statistical Abstract*, p. 387.

Paradoxically, this rise in the welfare rolls has occurred despite a substantial decline in poverty rates. This raises an obvious question: How were poor people once able to avoid dependence? Part of the answer is that they could fall back on a wide diversity of self-help and mutual aid arrangements, most of which no longer exist. Some of the most important of these were fraternal societies such as the Knights of Pythias, Sons of Italy, the Polish National Alliance, and the Independent Order of Odd Fellows.

The defining characteristics of a fraternal society were (more or less) the following: an autonomous system of lodges, a democratic form of internal government, a ritual, and the provision of mutual aid for members and their families. Members of female organizations which met these criteria generally embraced the term "fraternal" rather than "sororal." In contrast to the hierarchical methods of modern welfare, fraternal aid rested on a principle of reciprocity. Donors and recipients often came from the same, or nearly the same, walks of life; today's recipient could be tomorrow's donor, and vice versa.

By the early nineteenth century, two types of fraternal organization were predominant: secret orders and insurance orders. The former emphasized ritualism and eschewed uniform payment schedules. The second type devoted somewhat less attention to ritualism and openly solicited recruits with the lure of health and life insurance protection. This dichotomy should not be exaggerated. The line between the secret order and the insurance order was often a blurred one. Moreover, both types of fraternal organization shared a common emphasis on mutual aid. As a spokesman for the Modern Woodmen of America (which called its members "neighbors" and its lodges "camps") wrote in 1927:

> [A] few dollars given here, a small sum there to help a stricken member back on his feet or keep his protection in force during a crisis in his financial affairs; a sick Neighbor's wheat harvested, his grain hauled to market, his winter's fuel cut or a home built to replace one destroyed by a midnight fire—thus has fraternity been at work among a million members in 14,000 camps.[3]

II. Confraternities and Guilds

It is not my purpose here to provide a comprehensive history of fraternal societies in the United States. Instead, I will try to sketch some highlights of their development prior to the twentieth century. Any thorough attempt to study this subject must take into account the work of

---

[3] Este Erwood Buffum, *Modern Woodmen of America: A History*, vol. 2 (Rock Island, IL: Modern Woodmen of America, 1935), p. 5.

Alexis de Tocqueville. His famous discussion of voluntary associations
from the 1830s has become a staple of the literature:

> Americans of all ages, all conditions, and all dispositions constantly
> form associations. . . . The Americans make associations to give en-
> tertainment, to found seminaries, to build inns, to construct churches,
> to diffuse books. . . . Wherever at the end of some new undertaking
> you see the government in France, or a man of rank in England, in
> the United States, you will be sure to find an association.[4]

Contrary to the impression that might be left by this quotation, the American love affair with voluntarism had deep roots in the Old World. Tocqueville's words, with only slight modification, could have been applied to
the role of associations in England and Spain during the Middle Ages.
The two European associational forms which most closely resembled
American fraternal orders were confraternities and craft guilds. For this
reason, I will discuss their development in some detail.

Like fraternal societies, confraternities were oath-bound, lay-controlled
voluntary organizations which were open to members of all classes and
occupations. They grew rapidly in Western Europe after the twelfth century. A confraternity usually derived its name from a religious figure,
such as a patron saint or the Virgin Mary. Women could, and often did,
join, but both custom and formal rules generally barred them from leadership positions. In theory, and to a great extent in reality, confraternities
were democratic and egalitarian. The members, garbed in hooded "liv-
eries," marching in procession, with candles in hand, regularly appeared
at funerals of brethren to pray for their safe journey through purgatory to
paradise.[5]

Much like the fraternal societies of a later age, confraternities were
leading outlets for sociability and prestige in many communities. They
also served as sources for social welfare. Confraternities dispensed cash
to relieve sickness and other emergencies, endowed hospitals, paid for
funerals, underwrote dowries for poor women, advanced low-interest
loans, arbitrated legal disputes, established schools, and built bridges for
religious pilgrims. Historian Maureen Flynn characterizes the confraternities of medieval Spain as "collective insurance agencies" as well as
pioneering " 'institutions' of social welfare." She concludes that they an-

---

[4] Alexis de Tocqueville, *Democracy in America* (New York: Random House, 1981), pp.
403–4.

[5] Maureen Flynn, *Sacred Charity: Confraternities and Social Welfare in Spain, 1400–1700* (New
York: Cornell University Press, 1989), pp. 5, 13, 23, 33, 40, 43; Ronald F. E. Weissman, *Ritual
Brotherhood in Renaissance Florence* (New York: Academic Press, 1982), pp. 66–81; Christopher
Black, *Italian Confraternities in the Sixteenth Century* (Cambridge: Cambridge University Press,
1989), pp. 35, 150; Susan Brigden, "Religion and Social Obligation in Early Sixteenth-
Century London," *Past and Present*, no. 103 (March 1984), p. 98; J. J. Scarisbrick, *The Refor-
mation and the English People* (Oxford: Basil Blackwell, 1984), p. 19; George Unwin, *The Gilds
and Companies of London* (London: Methuen and Company, 1908), pp. 122, 123.

ticipated modern actuarial practices (at least in a crude way) by assessing members on the basis of risk and age. According to historian Ronald F. E. Weissman, Italian confraternities were purveyors of "vital forms of social insurance in life and death."[6]

Attempts to draw analogies between the functions of confraternities and those of modern welfare and insurance institutions, while valid to some degree, should not be overdone. As many historians of the subject have cautioned, the spiritual agenda always took precedence over any monetary benefits. Many confraternal budgets in Italy and England, for example, allocated far more to the purchase of candles than to social welfare. The candle was an essential investment because it lighted "the path through the vale of tears" to the bliss of "eternal life." These religious priorities probably made sense to most recipients, who did not join primarily for economic rewards.[7]

Confraternities also anticipated fraternal societies in their ability to win a mass following. There were over 160 confraternities in London alone during the fifteenth century. Zamora, Spain, a city of about eight thousand people, had one for every fourteen households during the same period. In Italy, confraternities established footholds in almost every sizable village. Historian Christopher Black has estimated that about one out of four Italian adults in the sixteenth century were members at one time in their lives.[8]

Many features of the craft guilds of the Middle Ages can also be detected in modern fraternal societies. Like confraternities, craft guilds relied on rituals, an elective form of internal government, and the provision of sickness and burial benefits. Taking the analogy still further, they built hospitals, operated joint stock companies, and subsidized the arts. Some founded towns and cities. In contrast to confraternities, which were open to all believers, craft guilds restricted membership to members of a single occupation.[9]

[6] Flynn, *Sacred Charity*, pp. 37–39, 44, 49, 51–58; Scarisbrick, *The Reformation and the English People*, p. 22; Black, *Italian Confraternities*, pp. 14, 163, 184, 223–33; Michel Mollat, *The Poor in the Middle Ages: An Essay in Social History* (New Haven: Yale University Press, 1986), p. 283; and Weissman, *Ritual Brotherhood*, p. ix.

[7] Richard Mackenney, *Tradesmen and Traders: The World of Guilds in Venice and Europe* (Totowa, NJ: Barnes and Noble Books, 1987), pp. 71–73; Black, *Italian Confraternities*, p. 127; Flynn, *Sacred Charity*, p. 41; and Ben R. McRee, "Charity and Gild Solidarity in Late Medieval England," *Journal of British Studies*, vol. 32 (July 1993), p. 207.

"Unlike the modern welfare state," writes Christopher Black, "involvement with confraternities satisfied more than basic physical needs. For donors and recipients, for those praying and those being prayed for, for comforters and patients, the confraternities could satisfy the needs for fraternity, social solidarity and spiritual comfort in this world as they contemplated the possibilities of joining the ultimate fraternity of Christ and his saints" (*Italian Confraternities*, p. 281).

[8] Brigden, "Religion and Social Obligation," p. 94; Flynn, *Sacred Charity*, p. 16; Black, *Italian Confraternities*, p. 270.

[9] One of the founders of Londonderry, for example, was a craft guild. Antony Black, *Guilds and Civil Society in European Political Thought from the Twelfth Century to the Present* (Ithaca, NY: Cornell University Press, 1984), pp. 55–65, 151; Mackenney, *Tradesmen and Traders*, p. 7; Steven A. Epstein, *Wage Labor and Guilds in Medieval Europe* (Chapel Hill: University of North Carolina Press, 1991), pp. 157–58.

In other respects, craft guilds more closely resembled arms of governments than they did voluntary associations. An individual joined primarily to gain an entrée to political and regulatory privilege. "Freedom of the
gild," writes sociologist Jack C. Ross, "was never an unlimited right for all
people, and it was this selectivity that gave the gilds their place in the
stratification system and the ability to provide rewards, financial, social,
and religious, to members."[10]

While craft guilds and confraternities eventually declined throughout Europe, the timing and details varied greatly. In Spain and Italy, confraternities were still forces to be reckoned with during the late eighteenth century,
and even later. They also established footholds in Latin America. German
craft guilds in many cases maintained their preeminent status until the middle of the nineteenth century. In Great Britain, on the other hand, craft guilds
and confraternities had suffered serious reversals by the sixteenth century.
Both types of institution reeled under accusations of harboring sedition and
creating unfair economic privilege. Confraternities were especially suspect
because of their Catholic trappings, such as the worship of saints, belief in
purgatory, and prayers for dead. The Chanceries Act of 1547 dealt a fatal
blow. Under its provisions, confraternities became branded as subversive
organizations and lost their property holdings.[11]

III. THE RISE OF FREEMASONRY

The demise of confraternities and craft guilds confined mutual aid, as
manifested by formal voluntary associations, to the margins of British
social life for well over a century. Other sources of welfare assistance,
such as the poor law, Protestant churches, and elite-endowed philanthropic organizations, struggled to fill the gap. This era was also one of
transition. New institutions of mutual aid slowly emerged. Many of them
built upon medieval precedents such as confraternities and craft guilds.[12]

---

[10] Jack C. Ross, *An Assembly of Good Fellows: Voluntary Associations in History* (Westport,
CT: Greenwood Press, 1976), pp. 175, 194.

Ben R. McRee writes that confraternities even at their apex constituted "but one link in the
chain of medieval poor relief," which included "hospitals, help-ales [cooperative feasts],
monastic alms, family aid, individual acts of charity, handouts to mourners at funeral and
obit services, and parish assistance" ("Charity and Gild Solidarity," p. 224).

[11] Flynn, *Sacred Charity*, pp. 138–39; Christopher Black, *Italian Confraternities*, p. 22; Antony
Black, *Guilds and Civil Society*, pp. 123, 128, 167; Ross, *An Assembly of Good Fellows*, pp.
138–39; Brigden, "Religion and Social Obligation," pp. 101–2; Scarisbrick, *The Reformation
and the English People*, pp. 36–37.

A good measure of the waning health of English confraternities and guilds was a fall-off
in bequests from wills, a major source of funds. From 1522 to 1539, 23.6 percent of wills in
London included such bequests, but between 1539 and 1547 this figure declined to just 8.5
percent; see Brigden, "Religion and Social Obligation," p. 101. While the grand totals of will
bequests to charity of all types continued to increase after the Chanceries Act, such bequests
did not recover in per-capita terms until the 1650s; see Paul Stack, *Poverty and Policy in Tudor
and Stuart England* (London: Longman, 1988), pp. 164–65.

[12] Brigden, "Religion and Social Obligation," pp. 104–7. A leading form of organized
mutual aid during this period was the "help ale" (or cooperative feast); see Judith M.

Freemasonry stands out as the most famous example of mutual aid which arose during the seventeenth and eighteenth centuries. Historians have yet to reach a consensus on the origins of this paradigmatic secret society. Much of this confusion can be traced to the early Masonic fascination with secrecy and habit of inventing fantastic tales of antiquity. The overriding goal of the Masonic ritual was not historical verity but to "instruct" the society's members. It was a means to teach them about Freemasonry's supposed illustrious role in the construction of Solomon's temple, the design of the pyramids of Egypt, and the founding of the Knights Templars of the Middle Ages. The earning of each new "degree" filled in another piece of the puzzle. By moving up the degree ladder, the member gradually gained more access to the secrets of the organization and the moral lessons which it imparted. The highest possible honor for any member was to earn thirty-three degrees.[13]

Nowadays, even official historians of Freemasonry dismiss these fanciful accounts, and most scholarly studies trace Masonic origins to either England or Scotland in the seventeenth century. Beyond that, there is still a lack of consensus. A common theory holds that Freemasonry emerged in some way out of stone (or operative) masonry. The groundwork may have been laid by the gradual admission of nonoperatives to the lodges, or other organizations, which had been founded by stonemasons. If this was the case, it is still unclear why these new members joined. Perhaps they had been lured by the mystique of the rituals or the prospect of gaining hidden knowledge about fields such as geometry. For some, membership may have been a means to recall the values, either real or imagined, of the moribund craft-guild tradition. In any case, by the first decade of the eighteenth century, a network of lodges controlled by nonoperatives existed in both England and Scotland. The nonoperative members of these lodges came to be officially known as "accepted" masons because they were not workers in stone. Despite the probable origins of Freemasonry as a craft guild, the new members were primarily from the wealthier and best-educated segments of the community, including professionals and businessmen.[14]

Fraternal societies of all types borrowed much from the structure and practices of Freemasonry. Most obviously, they imitated its system of decentralized, but affiliated, lodges. They also embraced key elements of

---

Bennett, "Conviviality and Charity in Medieval and Early Modern England," *Past and Present*, no. 134 (February 1992), pp. 19–41.

[13] John Hamill, *The Craft: A History of English Freemasonry* (Leighton Buzzard, Bedfordshire: Crucible, 1986), pp. 15–16, 21; Dorothy Ann Lipson, *Freemasonry in Federalist Connecticut* (Princeton: Princeton University Press, 1977), pp. 35–37. For another recent study, see Margaret C. Jacob, *Living the Enlightenment: Freemasonry and Politics in Eighteenth-Century Europe* (New York: Oxford University Press, 1991).

[14] Hamill, *The Craft*, pp. 27–40; David Stevenson, *The Origins of Freemasonry: Scotland's Century, 1590–1710* (Cambridge: Cambridge University Press, 1988), pp. 7, 22, 123–24, 156, 197–98, 216–33.

Originally, "Free Mason" was a contraction of "freestone mason." The term referred to a specialist "who worked in freestone—usually limestone—capable of being immediately carved for decorative purposes" (Hamill, *The Craft*, p. 27).

the ritual, especially the stress on artisanship and graded degrees. Free-masonry repopularized ritualism for an increasingly secular age by break-ing free from the old constraints of craft interests or Roman Catholic doctrine.[15]

IV. BRITISH FRIENDLY SOCIETIES

The rise of the sickness and burial insurance order, known in Great Britain as the "friendly society" or "box club," also occurred during this period. Some organizations appeared as early as the 1630s and 1640s, such as the United General Sea Box of Borrowstounness Friendly Society and the Sea Box Society of St. Andrews. The formative stages of devel-opment were almost wholly local in character. "Affiliated societies" with multiple lodges, such as the Manchester Unity and the Ancient Order of Foresters, did not emerge until the early nineteenth century.[16]

Freemasonry and friendly societies differed greatly in terms of function and membership composition. The average Mason was either a merchant or a professional. Friendly society members, on the other hand, were more likely to be wage earners or artisans. In addition, Masonic mutual aid tended to be informal, secretive, and geared to special cases, while friendly societies focused unabashedly on insurance.[17]

The friendly societies framed their insurance programs long before the advent of modern actuarial tables. They relied on a primitive sys-tem of assessment under which each member, regardless of age or occupation, paid an identical premium. The Amicable Society of Patring-ton in the East Riding was typical in providing "that when a member is sick, lame or blind, and rendered incapable of working ... he shall be allowed eight shillings per week during his inability to work," and "that upon the death of every free member, notice must be given to the stewards, who, at the next monthly meeting, shall pay to the widow or executor ten pounds."[18]

Friendly societies enjoyed almost uninterrupted growth during the eigh-teenth and nineteenth centuries. Membership surged from at least six hundred thousand in 1793 to as many as four million by 1874. An ever-rising demand for burial insurance by members of the working and lower middle classes fueled much of this expansion. "A pauper funeral," notes

---

[15] Alvin J. Schmidt, *Fraternal Organizations* (Westport, CT: Greenwood Press, 1980), pp. 119–39; Stevenson, *The Origins of Freemasonry*, pp. 228–33.

[16] E. P. Thompson, *The Making of the English Working Class* (New York: Vintage Books, 1966), pp. 418–19; P. H. J. H. Gosden, *Self-Help: Voluntary Associations in the Nineteenth Century* (London: B. T. Batsford, 1973), pp. 6, 27–30.

[17] P. H. J. H. Gosden, *The Friendly Societies in England, 1815–1875* (New York: Augustus M. Kelley, 1967), pp. 71–93; Lipson, *Freemasonry in Federalist Connecticut*, p. 201.

[18] Gosden, *The Friendly Societies*, pp. 17, 230; Thompson, *The Making of the English Working Class*, p. 421.

historian E. P. Thompson, "was the ultimate social disgrace. And ceremony bulked large in folk-lore, and preoccupied dying men."[19]

V. American Fraternal Orders: Initial Development

Not surprisingly, many of these patterns of mutual aid also appeared in the American colonies. The first Masonic lodge opened in Boston in 1733, only sixteen years after the founding of the British grand lodge. Early growth was slow and largely confined to major coastal cities such as Boston and Philadelphia. As in Great Britain, lodges drew membership primarily from the higher social, political, and economic ranks of society.[20]

The Revolution marked a divergence in the evolution of American and British Freemasonry. The presence of prominent members, such as George Washington, John Hancock, and Paul Revere, greatly widened Freemasonry's popular appeal in America. Initiates flocked to special traveling lodges chartered for the troops. As historian Dorothy Ann Lipson puts it, the war served to "Americanize" Freemasonry. The colonial "brethren" reacted to changing events by staging their own war of separation from British Freemasonry. They organized grand lodges in each state which were independent from the British structure. American Freemasonry not only expanded in size and numbers but also in membership diversity. The Revolution accelerated a trend, already underway by the 1750s, to broaden the base beyond a narrow upper crust. By the end of the eighteenth century, artisans and skilled workers were important components of the membership. They even formed a majority in some lodges. While American Freemasonry still catered to an elite after the Revolution, it had become a much less exclusive one.[21]

The Revolutionary Era also brought changes in the methods of Masonic social-welfare assistance. In the colonial period, barely a pretense of cen-

---

[19] J. M. Baernreither, *English Associations of Working Men* (London: Swan Sonnenschein, 1889; reprint, Detroit: Gale Research Co., 1966), p. 162; Thompson, *The Making of the English Working Class*, p. 419.

[20] Lipson, *Freemasonry in Federalist Connecticut*, pp. 48–49.

[21] *Ibid.*, pp. 50–62; Conrad Edick Wright, *The Transformation of Charity in Postrevolutionary New England* (Boston: Northeastern University Press, 1992), pp. 106, 213–19; Steven C. Bullock, "The Revolutionary Transformation of American Freemasonry, 1752–1792," *William and Mary Quarterly*, vol. 47 (July 1990), pp. 360–63; Wayne A. Huss, *The Master Builders: A History of the Grand Lodge of Free and Accepted Masons of Pennsylvania, Volume 1, 1731–1873* (Philadelphia: Grand Lodge F. & A.M. of Pennsylvania, 1986), pp. 286–91.

Bullock argues persuasively that the schism between the "Modern" and "Ancient" factions of American Freemasonry speeded the occupational shift in the composition of the membership. The Moderns drew almost wholly from the mercantile and professional classes, while the Ancients attracted large numbers of artisans. The Revolution served to discredit the Moderns, who tended to be Tories, thus assuring the spread of the more-inclusive Ancients. The split had originated in England in the 1730s after the Ancients had accused the Moderns of corrupting the original meaning of the ritual. See Bullock, "The Revolutionary Transformation of American Freemasonry," pp. 348–49.

tralization had existed. Each lodge had enjoyed full authority to raise and disperse all money and to establish requirements for recipients. By the 1780s, modifications began to be introduced to this system. The state grand lodges established charity committees to supplement (although never supplant) the local lodges. In 1789, the Pennsylvania Grand Lodge established a fund which was financed through annual assessments of 65 cents per member. That same year, the Connecticut Grand Lodge began to deposit $3 of each initiation fee in a state charity fund.[22]

Although the full extent of Masonic charity will probably never be known, fairly detailed figures exist for selected periods and locations. The Pennsylvania Grand Lodge assisted about one hundred members between 1792 and 1809. It allocated between $57 and $155 annually for this purpose. Such amounts were still negligible compared to the combined totals raised through individual lodges. Between 1798 and 1800 (the only years for which complete figures exist for both the state and local lodges), Masons in Pennsylvania disbursed over $6,000 to needy members. This amount exceeded that of any other private charity in Philadelphia at the time.[23]

Researchers should be leery of drawing broad conclusions from these account-book tallies, no matter how complete they may seem to be. A sizable portion of Masonic mutual aid entailed intangibles such as employment information, temporary lodging, and character references. The underlying premise of such assistance was that brethren should favor their own in any social or economic situation. "You are not charged to do beyond your Ability," summarized an early tract distributed by the fraternity, "only to prefer a poor Brother that is a good Man and true, before any other poor people in the same Circumstances."[24]

American sickness and burial insurance orders, much like American Masonic lodges, first developed from British precedents. One clear parallel between the two countries was the early primacy of localism. In New England and the rest of the United States, it was rare for a "society" to encompass more than a single lodge. It was not until the 1820s that national sickness and burial insurance orders of any consequence appeared. A major difference between Britain and the U.S. was that the Americans lagged behind in numbers of organizations. Forty-one mutual insurance societies (including Masonic lodges) existed in Massachusetts at the beginning of the nineteenth century, compared to just nineteen societies thirty years earlier. This growth, while impressive, still left the Americans well behind the British, who at the time had a total of nearly nine thousand friendly societies.[25]

[22] Huss, *The Master Builders*, p. 61; Lipson, *Freemasonry in Federalist Connecticut*, p. 210.

[23] Huss, *The Master Builders*, pp. 62–63.

[24] Lipson, *Freemasonry in Federalist Connecticut*, p. 207; Steven C. Bullock, "A Pure and Sublime System: The Appeal of Post-Revolutionary Freemasonry," *Journal of the Early Republic*, vol. 9 (Fall 1989), p. 368.

[25] Wright, *The Transformation of Charity*, pp. 63, 66; Gosden, *The Friendly Societies*, p. 5.

One possible explanation for these differing levels of growth was the impact of industrialization and urbanization. Most historians agree that fraternal orders developed first, and most successfully, in towns and cities. According to this view, the migration to cities, combined with increases in disposable income, created a niche for these and other formal associations to form. Richard D. Brown's study of colonial and early national Massachusetts, for example, concluded that voluntary associations did not generally arise until communities reached population thresholds of between one thousand and two thousand. Another precondition for the emergence of associations, according to Brown, was for one-fourth or more of adult males to be employed in nonagricultural pursuits. The necessity for an urban threshold has been seconded by more recent research for New England as a whole by Conrad Edick Wright.[26]

For many who joined, a lodge affiliation was a means to enhance older, and more stable, forms of mutual aid based on blood ties, geography, and religion. Hence, as Don Harrison Doyle has asserted, fraternal orders "acted to reinforce, rather than supplant, the family as a social institution. They also supplemented the extended kinship networks that supported the nuclear family." Mary Ann Clawson also stresses the "familial" features of lodges: "Fraternal association provided the ritualized means by which ... members could define one another as brothers; biologically unrelated individuals thus used kinship to construct the solidarity necessary to accomplish a variety of tasks."[27]

Much like the older kin and geographical networks, early American fraternal societies were often loose and informal in their methods of providing help. A survey of the bylaws and constitutions of six important societies in Boston during the eighteenth century showed great reluctance to guarantee specific cash benefits for working days lost or for funerals. Only one, the Massachusetts Charitable Mechanic Association, named an exact sum for burial, and this was $40.[28]

---

[26] Richard D. Brown, "The Emergence of Voluntary Associations in Massachusetts, 1760–1830," *Journal of Voluntary Action*, vol. 2 (April 1973), pp. 69–70; Wright, *The Transformation of Charity*, pp. 55–56.

[27] Karel Davids, *Towards an Ecology of Associations*, Working Paper Series, Number 54 (New York: New School for Social Research, November 1987), p. 47; Don Harrison Doyle, *The Social Order of a Frontier Community: Jacksonville, Illinois, 1825–1870* (Urbana: University of Illinois Press, 1978), p. 189; Mary Ann Clawson, *Constructing Brotherhood: Class, Gender, and Fraternalism* (Princeton, NJ: Princeton University Press, 1989), p. 25.

[28] The six societies were the Scots' Charitable Society of Boston, the Massachusetts Charitable Mechanic Association, the Charitable Irish Society of Boston, the Boston Marine Society, the Episcopal Charitable Society of Boston, and the Massachusetts Charitable Society. Copies of the original bylaws from the eighteenth century can be found in *The Constitution and By-Laws of the Scots' Charitable Society of Boston* (Boston: Press of Farrington Printing Company, 1896), pp. 36–40; Joseph T. Buckingham, *Annals of the Massachusetts Charitable Mechanic Association* (Boston: Press of Crocker and Brewster, 1853), pp. 6–9; *The Constitution and By-Laws of the Charitable Irish Society of Boston* (Boston: James F. Cotter and Company, 1876), pp. 22–26; William A. Baker, *A History of the Boston Marine Society, 1742–1981* (Boston: Boston Marine Society, 1982), pp. 302–3, 308–9; "The Articles and Rules of the Episcopal Charitable Society in Boston" (1724), in Clifford K. Shipton, ed., *Early American*

It was the usual practice of these societies to consider applications for aid on a case-by-case basis. The Scots' Charitable Society, for instance, allocated funds for such diverse purposes as ship passage, prison bail, and an old-age pension. It also paid regular stipends to a widow who lost her husband at sea. All of these societies showed little regard for consistency in the amounts they paid in each situation. Extant records of these organizations invariably classified any cash dispersals as "charity" and "relief" rather than "benefits."[29]

The Americans may have been informal in matters of money, but they were models of clarity in formulating sanctions for misconduct. The Boston Marine Society levied specific fines and other punishments for a multitude of offenses, including fines for failure to attend funerals of deceased members or for any who would "blaspheme the Name of Almighty GOD." The Society provided the ultimate punishment of expulsion for the "common Drunkard" and those who "shall at monthly meetings play, or promote the playing of any Cards, Dice, or other Gaming whatsoever."[30]

In some respects, the exactitude of the American societies in the punishment of behavioral infractions and the societies' ambiguity on guarantees of benefits made good economic sense. Actuarial science was still at an embryonic level. Promises to pay uniform sickness and death benefits entailed much greater risk than levying fines for infractions such as drunkenness or lack of decorum at meetings. Behavioral restrictions also helped to weed out the poorer risks and to heighten feelings of solidarity. Many American societies, after all, had not advanced beyond the formative stage of groping for an identity. It was not a time for reckless new financial experiments.

Some historians have argued that American fraternal societies were more likely than their British counterparts to recruit their members from all economic classes. Clawson notes that "the American multi-class fraternal order, with its large membership and popularity among male wage-earners, represents a phenomenon for which there is no exact equivalent in European societies." This view may be only half right. On the one hand, it is certainly true that fraternal orders in the United States rarely discriminated, at least as part of official policy, on the basis of economic class. As early as colonial times, the most prominent groups in Boston, such as the Massachusetts Charitable Society, the Boston Marine Society, and the Hartford Charitable Society, attracted both skilled workers and merchants. As Wright has concluded, lodges in New England "tended to

---

Imprints, 1639–1800 (Worcester, MA: American Antiquarian Society, 1967–74); and Massachusetts Charitable Society, "Rules and Articles" (1762), in Shipton, ed., *Early American Imprints.*

[29] *The Constitution and By-Laws of the Scots' Charitable Society of Boston*, pp. 22, 24–25, 29.
[30] Baker, *A History of the Boston Marine Society*, pp. 302–3.

reflect the communities they served." He uncovered evidence that wage earners, primarily from skilled occupations, often represented one-third or more of all members.[31]

The working-class nature of British friendly societies should not be overstated, however. They too included representation from all economic classes. Historian P. H. J. H. Gosden has found that business-owners constituted a majority of over one hundred principal leaders of the Manchester Unity of the Independent Order of Odd Fellows and the Ancient Order of Foresters, the two leading affiliated orders in Great Britain during the nineteenth century. It may be true that wage earners were better represented among the rank-and-file in the British societies, but even this remains unproven.[32]

VI. THE ODD FELLOWS: THE FIRST NATIONAL INSURANCE ORDER

Much like Freemasonry, the Odd Fellows began in the United States as a British import. In 1819, an immigrant opened a lodge in Baltimore of the Manchester Unity of the Independent Order of Odd Fellows. It formed the basis for the first "affiliated order" in the United States. Eleven years later, lodges of the Odd Fellows had appeared in four states and lodge membership had increased to over six thousand. The American lodges seceded from the British organization in 1843 and formed a wholly separate organization called the Independent Order of Odd Fellows. Although other British friendly societies, such as the Foresters, Rechabites, and Druids, also had entered the fray by this time, their impact was much more limited in the U.S. when compared to Britain.[33]

It is not too difficult to find evidence of continuity in the practice of American sickness and burial insurance orders between the colonial and the antebellum periods. Historical studies of Albany, Providence, and Kingston, New York, have confirmed that American Odd Fellowship, much like its eighteenth-century predecessors, drew liberally from all economic classes. Moreover, a substantial segment of skilled workers, in Albany and perhaps elsewhere, obtained leadership positions. According

---

[31] Clawson, *Constructing Brotherhood*, p. 107; Wright, *The Transformation of Charity*, pp. 209, 213–19.

[32] Gosden, *The Friendly Societies*, pp. 88–93, 224–28.

[33] Albert C. Stevens, *The Cyclopaedia of Fraternities* (New York: E. B. Treat and Company, 1907), p. 113; Brian Greenberg, *Worker and Community: Response to Industrialization in a Nineteenth-Century American City, Albany, New York, 1850–1884* (Albany: State University of New York Press, 1985), pp. 89–93; James L. Ridgely, *History of American Odd Fellowship: The First Decade* (Baltimore: James L. Ridgely, 1878), p. 234; Schmidt, *Fraternal Organizations*, pp. 243–45.

American Freemasonry never fit the definition of an affiliated order. State lodges were the highest level of authority, and proposals to establish a national grand lodge after the Revolution never advanced beyond the planning stage. It would be more proper to characterize Freemasonry in the United States as a confederacy of state grand lodges rather than as a distinct organization.

to Stuart Blumin, Odd Fellowship in the United States during these years was "a distinctively working-class movement" which only later solicited recruits from middle-class and professional ranks.[34]

The Independent Order of Odd Fellows was a fraternal trendsetter for the United States in several respects. It initiated the first major departure from the often haphazard grants of previous societies by using a clear schedule of guaranteed benefits. Under this new system, each member when taken sick could claim a regular stipend per week (usually $3 to $6) to compensate for working days lost. For many members, these benefits offered a much-needed financial cushion. The average daily wage of a typical skilled worker at the end of the antebellum period was about $1.62.[35]

In addition, the Odd Fellows helped to revise the language of American fraternalism. Prior to this time, most societies had favored the words "charity" and "relief" to describe the aid they provided. The Odd Fellows, by contrast, preferred the terms "benefit" and "right." Hence, as one member declared, money was "not paid or received as charity: it is every Brother's right, and paid to every one when sick, whether he be high or low, rich or poor." This was not a philosophy of unconditional entitlement, however. The Odd Fellows followed in the footsteps of colonial fraternal societies in vowing to withhold aid from individuals who engaged in excessive drunkenness, profanity, adultery, or disruptive behavior.[36]

The decades before and just after the Civil War were ones of sustained expansion for the Independent Order of Odd Fellows. Between 1830 and 1877, the membership rose from about 3,000 to 456,000. Total aid dispensed during these years amounted to over $69 million (at least $500 million by today's standards). Sickness and funeral benefits constituted a majority of this spending, but lodges also devoted substantial sums to

---

[34] John Gilkeson, *Middle-Class Providence, 1820–1940* (Princeton: Princeton University Press, 1986), p. 156; Greenberg, *Worker and Community*, p. 93; Stuart M. Blumin, *The Emergence of the Middle Class: Social Experience in the American City, 1760–1900* (Cambridge: Cambridge University Press, 1989), pp. 223–25.
At the same time, Blumin warns against too readily labeling American Odd Fellowship during its subsequent history as "middle class." He finds no evidence that "bourgeois values were brought to the order by businessmen and taught to workers" and asserts that "it is possible to find within the repeated assertion of a class-free brotherhood and hierarchy of merit a hint of the old working-class radicalism, if not of the Ricardian then at least of the 'Jack's as good as his master' variety" (*The Emergence of the Middle Class*, p. 225).
[35] U.S. Department of Commerce, Bureau of the Census, *Historical Statistics of the United States: Colonial Times to 1970*, part I (Washington, DC: U.S. Government Printing Office, 1975), p. 165.
[36] Albert Case, "The Principles of Odd Fellowship," *The Gavel*, vol. 1 (January 1845), p. 128. Expanding on this point in the second installment of this article, Case commented that "by observing the rule of life prescribed by Odd Fellowship, we shall be honest, frugal, temperate, and industrious, and thereby be most likely to secure enough to enable us to be as charitable as others, aside from our dues to the Lodge." See Albert Case, "The Principles of Odd Fellowship" (Concluded), *The Gavel*, vol. 1 (February 1845), p. 154.

other purposes. In 1855, for example, the Grand Lodge of Maryland provided aid to nine hundred orphans of deceased members.[37]

The geographically extended structure of the Odd Fellows allowed mobile members to retain benefits throughout the country. It also facilitated a kind of "coinsurance" to mitigate local crises such as natural disasters or epidemics. In 1855, members in Massachusetts contributed over $800 to relieve lodges in Pittsburgh which had exhausted their funds because of a fire, while ten years later they provided $400 of aid to lodges in Virginia during an outbreak of yellow fever.[38]

At the same time, the greater reliance on national systems also opened the door to abuse and fraud. By the antebellum period, publications of American Odd Fellowship began to warn of traveling imposters who would file false claims. This problem had been less prevalent among sickness and burial insurance orders during the eighteenth century, which could more readily rely on local knowledge to root out suspicious characters. To cope with these dangers, the national organization required that members who moved first obtain transfer or "clearance" cards. Within individual states, grand lodges established boards of relief to carefully investigate itinerants who petitioned for aid. According to an article in *The Emblem*, a leading voice of American Odd Fellowship, each state board was a "sort of detective police force" and "scarecrow" to frighten off imposters, thus leaving more aid for the deserving.[39]

Another device used by the Odd Fellows to short-circuit fraud was the ritual itself. "Pass-words and signs," asserted G. W. Clinton, a onetime Grand President in New York, "the latter common to the whole Order, and the former ever-changing and ever-circulating, guard against the impositions of the unworthy, assure us our rights, and open the hearts of our brethren to us." The increasingly elaborate amalgam of grips, degrees, regalia, and pageantry, was a world apart from the Spartan ritualistic forms of eighteenth-century sickness and burial insurance orders. In certain respects, the successful climb up the degree ladder was the antebellum equivalent of building a good credit rating. As a corollary, of course, the attention to degrees served to reinforce those *fraternal* bonds of trust and solidarity which could cut across community, class, or ethnic ties.[40]

---

[37] Ridgely, *History of American Odd Fellowship*, pp. 16, 233; "Editor's Table," *The Gavel*, vol. 2 (September 1845), p. 64; "Educating the Orphan," *The Emblem: An Odd Fellows Magazine*, vol. 1 (May 1856), p. 444; "I.O.O.F. Orphan Asylum," *The Gavel*, vol. 2 (May 1846), pp. 284–86.

[38] "The Order of Odd Fellows, and the Pittsburgh Sufferers," *The Gavel*, vol. 2 (May 1846), pp. 287–88; "Editorial," *The Emblem*, vol. 1 (November 1855), p. 201.

[39] "Board of Relief of Boston Lodges," *The Emblem*, vol. 1 (August 1855), pp. 53–54.

[40] G. W. Clinton, "Objections to Our Order Answered," *The Gavel*, vol. 2 (September 1845), p. 29. As might be expected, of course, the widespread appeal of ritualism during this period was multifaceted and defies simple explanations. For a provocative discussion of the role of psychological factors, including gender, see Mark C. Carnes, *Secret Ritual and Manhood in Victorian America* (New Haven: Yale University Press, 1989).

VII. The National Life-Insurance Order

The formation of the Ancient Order of United Workmen (AOUW) in 1868 signaled the onset of a new phase in American fraternal development. The AOUW was the first notable national life-insurance order. Its founder, John Jordan Upchurch, a master mechanic on the Pennsylvania Railroad and an ardent Mason, certainly had not planned it that way. Instead, he had envisioned the AOUW as a forum which would unite "through the medium of the lodge affiliation employer and employee and under solemn bond of helpful co-operation, adjust differences that might arise between them and avoid strikes." Had Upchurch achieved his original goal, the AOUW would have become a kind of conservative version of the Knights of Labor.[41]

The AOUW's life-insurance plan, which had started as an incidental feature to attract members, quickly moved to center stage. Adopted in 1868, it guaranteed a death benefit of $1,000 (later raised to $2,000). Funding came from a $1 per capita assessment on each member. It would have been beyond the capacity of antebellum societies to pay out this kind of money, because no individual lodge had the necessary resources. The AOUW responded to this problem by spreading the burden. It centralized the dispersal of funds into state (and later national) organizations. As a result, the membership of the AOUW expanded rapidly and finally crested at 450,000 in 1902.[42]

Before the Civil War, sickness insurance had been the major focus of fraternal societies. Individual lodges had paid death benefits, but the amount in each case had rarely exceeded $150, roughly the cost of a funeral. The AOUW reversed these priorities. Although many AOUW lodges also provided sickness benefits, this feature was never more than a secondary concern.[43]

The next three decades brought a full flowering of similar national life-insurance orders. Hundreds of new organizations, such as the Royal Arcanum, the Knights of Honor, the Order of the Iron Hall, and the Modern Woodmen of America, sprang up across the county. Many older societies, which had specialized in sickness and burial policies, such as the Knights of Pythias and the Improved Order of Redmen, followed suit

---

[41] M. W. Sackett, *Early History of Fraternal Beneficiary Societies in America* (Meadville, PA: Tribune Publishing Company, 1914), p. 25.

The Knights of Labor was founded in 1869, only a year after the AOUW. For a discussion of some similarities between these organizations, see Clawson, *Constructing Brotherhood*, pp. 138–43.

[42] Sackett, *Early History of Fraternal Beneficiary Societies in America*, pp. 27, 130–33; Walter Basye, *History and Operation of Fraternal Insurance* (Rochester, NY: Fraternal Monitor, 1919), pp. 10–14.

Beginning in the 1870s, the AOUW slowly shifted away from an assessment approach in favor of graded rates for *new* members. Not until the turn of the century, however, did it complete the transition; see Sackett, *Early History of Fraternal Beneficiary Societies in America*, pp. 147–96.

[43] Abb Landis, *Life Insurance* (Nashville, TN: Brandon, 1914), pp. 105, 107.

with their own national life-insurance plans. By 1908, the two hundred leading societies had paid well over $1 billion in death benefits.[44]

Membership in these societies grew rapidly during these years. According to *Everybody's Magazine*, the ranks of fraternalism had become nothing less than an "enormous army." The foot soldiers of this army were "the middle-class workman, the salaried clerk, the farmer, the artisan, the country merchant, and the laborer," all attempting to "insure their helpless broods against abject poverty. Rich men insure in the big [commercial life insurance] companies to create an estate; poor men insure in fraternal orders to create bread and meat. It is an insurance against want, the poorhouse, charity, and degradation."[45]

The combined membership of fraternal organizations in the United States during this period will never be known for sure. The constituent organizations of the National Fraternal Congress (NFC), the major clearinghouse for life-insurance societies, had a combined membership of a half million in 1886; by 1920, their membership was over nine million. The U.S. population in 1920 was just over one hundred million people. Even in its best years, however, the NFC failed to reach significant segments of the fraternal population, including blacks and many of those who subscribed to local sickness-benefit organizations. In 1920, about eighteen million Americans belonged to lodges, that is, nearly 30 percent of all adults over age twenty.[46]

The life-insurance order was a peculiarly American institution, although it soon spread throughout Canada. Nothing quite like it appeared in Great Britain until much later, and then in a very limited form. During the late nineteenth century, friendly societies continued to specialize in sickness and burial insurance, much like American fraternal organizations had in the past. Moreover, commercial companies in Great Britain still thoroughly dominated the life-insurance market after the 1860s, while in the United States they faced stiff competition from fraternal organizations.[47]

---

[44] *Fraternal Monitor*, vol. 18 (February 1, 1908), p. 22; Basye, *History and Operation of Fraternal Insurance*, p. 16; J. Owen Stalson, *Marketing Life Insurance: Its History in America* (Bryn Mawr, PA: McCahan Foundation, 1969), p. 553.

[45] Harris Dickson and Isidore P. Mantz, "Will the Widow Get Her Money? The Weakness in Fraternal Life Insurance and How It May Be Cured," *Everybody's Magazine*, vol. 22 (June 1910), p. 776.

By this time, large commercial legal reserve companies, such as the Equitable and Metropolitan, had been well established for decades.

[46] David T. Beito, "Mutual Aid, State Welfare, and Organized Charity: Fraternal Societies and the 'Deserving' and 'Undeserving' Poor," *Journal of Policy History*, vol. 5 (1993), pp. 420–21.

The NFC had been formed in 1886 at the instigation of the Ancient Order of United Workmen and eventually represented the leading life-insurance orders. Some other early members were the Knights of Columbus, the Royal Arcanum, and the Knights of Pythias. The NFC did not include representatives from secret orders, such as the Masons and the Elks. See Basye, *History and Operation of Fraternal Insurance*, pp. 71–72.

[47] Landis, *Life Insurance*, p. 107; Abb Landis, "Life Insurance by Fraternal Orders," *Annals of the American Academy of Political and Social Science*, vol. 24 (November 1904), p. 481; Abb Landis, *Friendly Societies and Fraternal Orders* (Winchester, TN: Abb Landis, 1900), pp. 67, 71;

American fraternal life-insurance societies had the good fortune to arrive on the scene at a time when commercial companies faced especially
bad publicity. A spate of bankruptcies associated with financial panics in
the 1870s had shaken consumer confidence. By one estimate, the unrecov-
ered losses suffered by policyholders in commercial companies during
this period totaled $35 million. In addition, the assessment approach of
fraternal organizations allowed rates low enough to undercut commercial
insurance companies—that is, at least initially. Most members paid a flat
premium which did not vary on the basis of age or health. Many societies
avoided the common commercial practice of accumulating a sufficient
reserve. Instead, they levied extra assessments on members to meet any
deficiencies caused by payment of death claims. While most fraternal
orders eventually abandoned the crude assessment method as untenable,
it gave them a leg up in the market in the meantime. By 1895, half the
value of all life-insurance policies in force were on the fraternal plan. As
one commentator put it at the time, the United States had entered an
unprecedented "golden age of fraternity."[48]

The interest shown by fraternal orders in life insurance, while certainly
considerable, never became all-encompassing. At the local level especially,
sickness and burial societies still predominated. In 1891, a detailed study
conducted by the Connecticut Bureau of Labor Statistics found that there
were 494,322 members of fraternal insurance societies in the state. More
than 60 percent belonged to sickness and burial orders, compared to 28 percent in life-insurance societies. Almost all the life-insurance orders were affiliates of centralized national organizations, such as the Royal Arcanum
and the Legion of Honor. Over 70 percent of these societies entrusted the
payment of death benefits to an office outside the state. By contrast, an
amazing 99 percent of sickness and funeral benefit societies assigned this
responsibility to local or state lodges. Even the national sickness and burial
orders, such as the Ancient Order of Foresters, the Ancient Order of Hi-
bernians, the Independent Order of Odd Fellows, the Grand United Order
of Galilean Fishermen, and the Deutscher Order Harugari, relied almost
wholly on local and state affiliates to raise and disperse benefit money.[49]

Life Insurance Independent, vol. 16 (October 1904), p. 235; *Life Insurance Independent*, vol. 17
(March 1905), p. 93; Basye, *History and Operation of Fraternal Insurance*, p. 26.

After the turn of the century, some leading British friendly societies experimented with
life insurance (as opposed to simple burial insurance). By 1908, for example, the Manchester
Unity offered a policy which was equivalent to 1,000 U.S. dollars. Even so, such examples
were fairly rare. See *Fraternal Monitor*, vol. 19 (September 1, 1908), p. 20.

[48] Richard de Raismes Kip, *Fraternal Life Insurance in America* (Philadelphia: College Offset
Press, 1953), pp. 30–31; Stalson, *Marketing Life Insurance*, pp. 451–52, 553; Basye, *History and
Operation of Fraternal Insurance*, p. 29; R. J. Myers, "The Effect of the Social Security Act on
the Life Insurance Needs of Labor," *Journal of Political Economy*, vol. 45 (October 1937), pp.
682–83; "The Cheapest Insurance," *World's Work*, vol. 11 (April 1906), p. 7398; Landis, *Life
Insurance*, p. 88; Viviana A. Rotman Zelizer, *Morals and Markets: The Development of Life
Insurance in the United States* (New Brunswick, NJ: Transaction Books, 1983), p. 93; Carnes,
Secret Ritual and Manhood in Victorian America, p. 1.

[49] Connecticut Bureau of Labor Statistics, *Annual Report* (1892), part III, pp. 71, 617.

The aforementioned study by the Connecticut Bureau of Labor Statistics found that the membership of all fraternal insurance orders relative to the general population (men, women, and children) was 15 percent. It calculated that "if to the membership reported should be added the number in the Masonic societies, the Elks, the Patrons of Husbandry, and other societies, not co-operative benefit, and therefore not included herein, the total would be in excess of the total male adult population of the state." This figure, however, is as large as it is because it does not eliminate individuals who had multiple memberships. A fairly safe bet is that membership in fraternal organizations encompassed one-third or more of the voting-age male population at the time.[50]

The success of fraternal societies coincided with an intense American fascination with ritualism. No class or ethnic group was immune. Ritualistic trappings, including grips, degrees, and passwords, were used by groups as diverse as the Knights of Labor, the Knights of the Ku Klux Klan, the Farmer's Alliance, the Union League, the American Protective Association, the Tammany Societies, the Church of Latter Day Saints, and the Patrons of Husbandry. Most were variants on the Masonic model; the linkage was especially close in the Knights of Labor, the Patrons of Husbandry, and the modern Ku Klux Klan, which had been founded by Masons.[51]

VIII. Conclusion

At the beginning of the twentieth century, fraternal societies seemed headed for a bright future. They had achieved a level of development which was striking when compared to the past. In 1800, the fraternal scene (with the possible exception of Freemasonry) had been characterized by small and localized societies with meager budgets and haphazard schedules of benefits. In 1900, Americans increasingly flocked to far-flung national organizations, characterized by multiple lodges and hefty death and sickness benefits. Observers had good reason to be optimistic about the prospects for fraternalism in the coming decades of the twentieth century. As Charles Moreau Harger commented in the *Atlantic Monthly*, "so rapidly does [the

[50] *Ibid.*, pp. 71, 617. The national estimate is based on an extensive, but nevertheless incomplete, tabulation of fraternal membership by Albert C. Stevens in 1907; see Stevens, *The Cyclopaedia of Fraternities*, p. 114.

[51] Stevens, *The Cyclopaedia of Fraternities*, pp. vi–vii, 70–72, 388–94; Carnes, *Secret Ritual and Manhood in Victorian America*, pp. 6–9; Noel P. Gist, "Secret Societies: A Cultural Study of Fraternalism in the United States," *The University of Missouri Studies*, vol. 15 (October 1, 1940), pp. 32–33, 48; Schmidt, *Fraternal Organizations*, pp. 38, 197; Clawson, *Constructing Brotherhood*, pp. 136–38; Robert C. McMath, *American Populism: A Social History, 1877–1898* (New York: Hill and Wang, 1993), pp. 58–59, 63, 70.

Historian Michael W. Fitzgerald writes that the ritual of the Union League, an organization dedicated to protecting the civil rights of blacks in the South during Reconstruction, "resembled that of the Masons from which it clearly derived; like those of many fraternal organizations, it extolled civic virtue, universal brotherhood, and other worthy causes." See Michael W. Fitzgerald, *The Union League Movement in the Deep South: Politics and Agricultural Change during Reconstruction* (Baton Rouge: Louisiana State University Press, 1989), p. 114.

fraternal order] increase in popularity that it shows little indication of ever wielding less power over men's destinies than it does today."[52]

While this fraternal golden age continued for a time, it ended much sooner than Harger had expected. In 1906, member societies of the National Fraternal Congress represented 91,434 lodges; by 1925, this figure peaked at 120,000 lodges. After that, the number of lodges leveled off and fell. The pace of descent accelerated rapidly during the Depression and continued unabated after World War II. An impressive 52,655 lodges still remain, but their emphasis on mutual aid has been greatly reduced. Many now exist primarily as social organizations.[53]

While it is not the goal of this essay to examine the reasons for the decline of fraternal societies, several possibilities immediately come to mind. Among these were changing social tastes, restrictive governmental regulation, commercial and employer competition in the provision of services, and the opposition of medical societies which fought fraternal efforts to offer health care. There was another, much more subtle, factor at work: the rise of the modern welfare state. Mutual aid, throughout history, had been a creature of necessity. Government, by taking away social responsibilities that were once the purview of voluntary institutions, undermined much of this necessity. Much was lost in the exchange that transcended monetary calculations.

There have been notable exceptions to this story of decline, however. Some all-black societies in the South, such as the United Friends, the Mississippi Jurisdiction of the International Order of Twelve Knights and Daughters of Tabor, the United Order of Friendship, and the Afro-American Sons and Daughters, underwent significant expansion during and after the Depression. All of these societies opened hospitals which served thousands of members. In some cases, they operated newspapers, built apartment houses, and founded credit unions. Nevertheless, even most of these enterprises soon declined.[54]

Although the overall role of fraternal societies has diminished, a few continue to be important service providers. One of the most significant is Mooseheart. This extensive orphanage, which has a current population of over two hundred children, has been successfully maintained by Moose International for over eight decades. Despite a few provocative examples of this kind, however, there has yet to arise a modern analogue to the fraternal society, either as a provider of services, such as low-cost medical care, or as a device to encourage the spread of the survival values of thrift, neighborhood cooperation, and individual responsibility.

History, University of Alabama

---

[52] Charles Moreau Harger, "The Lodge," *Atlantic Monthly*, vol. 47 (April 1906), p. 494.

[53] *Statistics of Fraternal Benefit Societies* (National Fraternal Congress of America, 1906–86).

[54] See also David T. Beito, "The 'Lodge Practice Evil' Reconsidered: Medical Care through Fraternal Societies, 1900–1930," *Journal of Urban History*, vol. 23 (July 1997).

TWO CONCEPTIONS OF WELFARE:
VOLUNTARISM AND INCORPORATIONISM

By Stephen Davies

I. Introduction

The history of the welfare state is not only or even primarily a story of men and measures but also one of concepts and social ideals. Over the last hundred and twenty years or so, the body of policies, rules, and practices which we collectively term the welfare state has become the most prominent feature of politics and state activity in every developed country. This reflects not only institutional and procedural pressures on the political process during this period, but also the gradual permeation (to use a term employed by one prominent advocate of the welfare state)[1] of all parties and arguments by a particular conception of welfare which has determined and limited the range and terms of debate. Both theoretical debate and concrete measures reflect pervasive assumptions and generalized arguments about the nature and content of collective and individual welfare, their preconditions, and their consequences.

If we look at the intellectual history of the welfare state, we can see that a crucial part of its origins lies in the period between about 1870 and 1914, when this particular set of arguments and assumptions came to gradually dominate debate. This happened initially and most prominently in Imperial Germany, but the rest of Europe soon followed suit. The Anglo-Saxon countries proved the most resistant, but Britain had succumbed by the 1900s and the United States by the 1920s. In both cases the shift in actual policy followed soon after, with David Lloyd George in Britain and Franklin Roosevelt in the United States. Until recently, there was a strong tendency among historians to see this as an inevitable process, part of the onward and unstoppable march of progress. This whiggish style of historiography interpreted the history of social policy and thinking as a seamless web from the 1800s through to the present day, with arguments and events leading inexorably to the modern welfare state.[2] The idea that this was not inevitable, that there was a real practical and intellectual

---

[1] The advocate in question was, of course, Sidney Webb. For the strategy of "permeation," see George Bernard Shaw, ed., *Fabian Essays* (London, 1889).

[2] Among British historians, "whiggish" or "whig history" means a historiography in which the present state of affairs, seen as both desirable and the end or goal of history, is taken as the starting point and the past is seen as an inevitable process by which the present came to be. The study of history then becomes the study of the past in order to justify either the present or a particular hoped-for and expected future, rather than looking at the past in its own terms. Among the alleged features of whig history are a tendency to anachronistic

alternative, was not considered until recently and has still not been accorded any serious attention. Nor was much credence given to the idea that there was a radical shift or discontinuity in thinking toward the end of the last century. This meant that many important intellectual and cultural figures were either ignored or, if they were too prominent, misunderstood because they could not easily be fitted into the traditional narrative.

However, recent historiography has become increasingly critical of this particular account. In part this reflects the impact of work by the new generation of labor historians since the 1960s who have uncovered details of working-class beliefs and practices from the nineteenth century which cannot easily be squared with the older view. There is also increasing skepticism about the entire notion of progress, particularly when this is linked to a benevolent view of the state. Consequently, there is an increasing amount of attention being paid to the debate on poverty which took place between about 1870 and 1900. The influence of ideas drawn from literary criticism has also made historians more aware of the way that shifts in argument and intellectual hegemony are often effected through a change in vocabulary or discourse, whereby the pattern of thinking about a particular subject changes as terms and concepts are invented, discarded, or redefined so that the same word will come to have a fundamentally changed meaning in its public usage.[3]

More attention is now being paid to movements and ideas about welfare which stand opposed to the dominant conception referred to earlier. What is gradually being recovered is a different discourse of welfare, a radically distinct set of ideas and beliefs which implies a way of thinking about welfare issues that is completely different from the currently dominant one. This is the discourse or vocabulary of voluntarism, which was the determining way of thinking about such issues for much of the nine-

---

moral judgement and the evaluation of past persons and events as progressive or reactionary according to their perceived part in bringing about the ideal present. The classic original of this was the history of the British constitution as recounted by Thomas Macaulay and Henry Hallam; see Macauley, *History of England from the Accession of James II*, 4 vols. (London: Longmans, 1855–61), and Hallam, *The Constitutional History of England* (1827; reprint, London: Garland, 1978). For the most famous critical account, see Herbert Butterfield, *The Whig Interpretation of History* (London: Bell, 1931). Some of the many works which show a whiggish approach to the history of the welfare state are David Roberts, *Victorian Origins of the British Welfare State* (New Haven, CT: Yale University Press, 1960); Derek Fraser, *The Evolution of the British Welfare State: A History of Social Policy since the Industrial Revolution* (Basingstoke: Macmillan, 1984); and Pauline Gregg, *The Welfare State: An Economic and Social History of Britain from 1945 to the Present Day* (London: Harrap, 1967).

[3] The outstanding example of this is the work of the late Geoffrey Finlayson, *Citizen, State, and Social Welfare in Britain, 1830–1990* (Oxford: Oxford University Press, 1994). See also, for example, Anne Digby, *The Poor Law in Nineteenth Century England and Wales* (London: Historical Association, 1982); Michael Rose, *The Relief of Poverty, 1834–1914* (London: Macmillan, 1972); Karel Williams, *From Pauperism to Poverty* (London: Routledge, 1981); and Gareth Stedman Jones, *Outcast London: A Study in the Relationship between Classes in Victorian Society* (Harmondsworth: Penguin, 1976).

teenth century and remained an influential part of popular belief for a long time thereafter. Historically, the voluntarist conception of welfare was opposed both to an older view, which it rejected, and to the contemporary one which replaced it in academic and political debate.

The two conceptions of welfare I shall be concerned with here, then, are the voluntarist one and the rival one which I shall term, for reasons to be set out later, the "incorporationist" model. These two ways of thinking about collective and individual welfare lead to profoundly different conclusions about what constitutes welfare and how it can best be achieved. In other words, there is disagreement over not only means but ends, over the very definition and content of the term "welfare." One point to grasp is that key terms such as "liberty" and "poverty" are used in both discourses, but with opposed or different meanings. This makes the understanding or recovery of one discourse very difficult when viewed from the standpoint of the other. In the last analysis, these divergences derive from opposed notions of such basic matters as the nature of the self and of human society. In terms of institutions and practice, they produce results which have almost nothing in common.

II. The Voluntarist Conception

The voluntarist conception of welfare, although once influential, has been so misinterpreted and misunderstood that its essential doctrines are now hardly comprehended or even known. Its leading exponents have also been either traduced or misunderstood, or else, even more frequently, simply forgotten. Although there is now a move toward rehabilitation of leading figures (such as Samuel Smiles) and more serious consideration of their ideas, this has still not gone far, and a multitude of other figures remain neglected. One difficulty is that much of the voluntarist conception derived from and employed the vocabulary of Dissenting Protestant theology (the theology of sects which dissented from the authority of the Anglican Church), and contemporary historians often do not recognize this kind of argument as being about welfare or social policy. However, there is no shortage of sources or material evidence, as both the theory and the practice of voluntarism have left a huge deposit of records for the historian to study, much of it virtually untouched.

The central focus of my investigation will be the two elements of the voluntarist conception which determine the concrete practices which it prescribed: the ideas of self-help and mutual aid. In order to understand their content, however, more-fundamental elements must also be considered. The sources for this kind of investigation are, as I have said, varied and rich. Although reference will be made to the experience of other countries, for practical reasons the primary focus will be on Britain and, to a lesser extent, the United States. The British case is also important because, for a variety of reasons, nineteenth-century Britain was seen as the nation which had pioneered both the theory and the practice of voluntarism. The United States, for its part, was widely perceived by both hostile and friendly observers as the country where the voluntarist principle was most fully articulated and practiced.

The source material for the study of the voluntarist ideal includes a huge range of writings on self-help, often incorrectly identified with the different genre of success literature. Among the authors of these writings are both well-known figures such as Smiles, Emerson, Franklin, and William Ellery Channing, and other now obscure ones such as Elbert Hubbard, Joseph Barker, and George Jacob Holyoake. There are also more specifically didactic works, such as the advice manuals which were a prominent part of popular reading throughout the last century from William Cobbett onward. Among these are works specifically about work, character, and their relation to welfare, along with expositions of the popular version of political economy by authors such as Harriet Martineau. From the later part of the nineteenth century, there are many early studies of the institutional application of the voluntarist principle, often by active participants, but also increasingly by scholarly polemicists such as Thomas Mackay. Throughout the whole of the nineteenth century, there are many works which articulate the voluntarist conception of welfare and society and attack rival conceptions, works which come from both practicing politicians such as Richard Cobden and from activists such as Edward Miall and Edward Baines, Jr.

In Britain there are a huge number of works which argue the case for religious voluntarism, while making it clear that this is only one application of a wider social ideal. In addition to works which advocate voluntarist ideas, the practice of voluntarist welfare has left a rich deposit in the form of the records of friendly societies, self-improvement societies, trade unions, clubs, and educational institutes. There are also a large number of periodicals produced both by individuals and by organizations. Among the most significant British examples are *Eliza Cook's Journal*, *Household Words*, *The Penny Magazine*, and *The Working Man's Friend and Family Instructor*. In America an early and important example was Benjamin Franklin's *Poor Richard's Almanac*. Last but not least are literary works, both fictional and nonfictional, which are explicitly concerned to exemplify the voluntarist idea. Among the former one could cite as examples *The Manchester Man* by Mrs. Linnaeus Banks or *John Halifax, Gentleman* by Mrs. Craik. More significant as sources, however, are the many exemplary lives and autobiographies, in which the life of an outstanding person is held up for emulation and as a source of encouragement.[4]

---

[4] Samuel Smiles, *Thrift* (London: John Murray, 1897); Smiles, *Character* (London: John Murray, 1872); Smiles, *Duty* (London: John Murray, 1887); Smiles, *Self-Help*, 2d ed. (London: John Murray, 1910); Ralph Waldo Emerson, *Complete Works* (Edinburgh: Nimmo, Hay and Mitchell, 1897); Max Farrand, ed., *Benjamin Franklin's Memoirs* (Berkeley, CA: University of California Press, 1949); William Ellery Channing, *Self Culture* (Boston, MA: Dutton and

With such a wide range of sources to draw on, it is little short of astounding that the ideal contained and articulated within them should be so misunderstood, yet such is the case. The essential elements of the voluntarist ideal are, however, easy to discern. The first is an individualist conception of society. Human society and community are seen as composed of free-standing and independent individuals, and as consisting of, and arising out of, the free cooperation and interaction of those individuals. However, the individual is not seen as asocial or self-sufficient, but as the product of his or her relations with others. Yet these relations should be, so far as possible, freely chosen. The reason for this is the second foundational element of voluntarism, the idea that the self, the identity and nature of the individual human being, is to a great degree self-made or self-determined and the product of the choices and free actions of the person. This leads to the doctrine of the moral responsibility of the individual for his actions and to the important belief that virtue is only possible where, and to the extent that, actions are freely chosen. It also implies that the self can be improved by choice and actions. These ideas and notions derive in large part from the theory and practice of radical Protestantism, with its ideal of the self-governing congregation and the belief in the importance of individual calling and awakening for salvation.[5]

The third foundational element of voluntarism, and the most important element for our purposes, is the belief that the key to general welfare is the welfare and happiness of individuals. In other words, the situation of actual, concrete individuals is taken as the starting point, while the wider welfare of the collective is seen as consequential. The general welfare of society is determined by, and a consequence of, the welfare of the individuals composing it. The only way to achieve social reform, therefore, is through the reform and improvement of individuals, which must mean improvement by freely chosen actions on their part. It is not possible to take actions which will improve the collective welfare of society and, as a consequence, improve the welfare of its constituent individuals. As we shall see, this does not mean that collective action is ruled out, only that it must be voluntary if it is to be effective. The next, closely related, assumption is that the key to individual welfare is personal independence, while its great enemy is dependency and servility. Welfare is seen

---

Wentworth, 1838); Elbert Hubbard, *The Philosophy of Elbert Hubbard* (Boston, 1898); Joseph Barker, *Teachings of Experience: Or Lessons I Have Learned on My Way through Life* (Leeds, 1869); George Jacob Holyoake, *Self-Help a Hundred Years Ago*, 2d ed. (London, 1890); Thomas Mackay, *Methods of Social Reform* (London: Sonnenschein, 1892); Dinah Craik, *John Halifax, Gentleman* (London: Collins, 1856); Isabella Banks, *The Manchester Man* (Manchester: Heywood, 1896).

[5] For a short but instructive account of Dissenting voluntarism, see Ian Bradley, *The Optimists: Themes and Personalities in Victorian Liberalism* (London: Faber, 1980). For a typical example of its arguments, see John Briggs and Ian Sellars, eds., *Victorian Nonconformity* (London: Edward Arnold, 1973), pp. 62–63.

in highly moralistic terms and is taken to be intimately connected with virtue and only secondarily with material resources. Personal independence, "standing on one's own feet" in the well-known phrase, means economic independence, being able to support oneself, and is therefore incompatible with being a recipient of charity or relief, or with being in any kind of economic position which can be construed as unfree. This could, and often did, lead to highly radical conclusions. It could mean, for example, the rejection of wage labor as being partly servile, and hostility to large-scale industrial organizations, particularly joint-stock companies. It frequently led to the advocacy of a social order dominated by many independent, small producers, both farmers and artisans.

The ideal of personal independence meant much more than this, however. It also encompassed the notion of independence of mind, of refusal to be swayed or governed by authority or collective passions and excitements, but rather the ability to consider and decide freely. This explains why the image of Martin Luther, defying Charles V and the Roman Catholic Church at the Diet of Worms in 1521 and insisting on his own opinions with the words "Here I stand, I can do no other," was a popular one among apologists. This is also why sharp attacks on "priestcraft and priestly authority" were a staple of much voluntarist argument. Thus, personal independence also meant free moral judgement, where moral choices were made by free agents who were then personally responsible for them. A popular theme in much of the literature was that of the man who holds to a moral conviction in the face of social pressure or government persecution.[6]

All this was part of a distinctly realistic, or even sober, view of the world and the human condition. One misconception, which cannot survive even a brief study of the literature, is that voluntarist and self-help literature promises an easy way to happiness. The truth is precisely the opposite. One constant theme is the way the natural world and misfortunes impose ineluctable limits on the possibilities open to human beings. This means that there is no *right* to happiness, that happiness and contentment do not come easily but have to be won by hard effort and struggle. The paradoxical proposition is that it is only by giving up the idea of a right to be happy that true happiness is to be found. Happiness, authors such as Smiles and Franklin never tire of repeating, is far more a consequence of fortitude and a cheerful disposition than wealth and conventional good fortune. It is only by abandoning optimism that the virtue of hope can be practiced. In this way of thinking, which can be traced back to authors such as the theologian Jonathan Edwards, optimism means the feeling or belief that everything is improving and that there are no ultimately inescapable tragedies. The virtue of hope, in contrast, is to

[6] For just one very clear statement of this, see William Ellery Channing, *Thoughts on Power and Greatness Political, Intellectual, and Moral* (Boston, 1828).

accept that tragedy exists, but to refuse to simply accept it, and above all, to refuse to accept that tragedy and wrong, while part of the world, are its defining features. A related theme is the belief that one can have a life which is too easy, that affluence and wealth are in fact suspect and morally enervating. The reason is that true virtue, and hence real welfare and happiness, is the product of struggle and difficulty, which develop the heroic qualities and deepen the reserves of character, in particular the quality of perseverance. This is one of the primary purposes of exemplary biography and autobiography: to highlight the triumph over adversity and the way in which that struggle made the person better and stronger.[7]

Along with fortitude and perseverance, the other personal quality which was seen as crucial to personal welfare and happiness was temperance, the restraining and controlling of appetite and desire. In other words, in this way of thinking, happiness was to be found not in the unlimited satisfaction of wants and desires but in their restraint and limitation. It is hard to imagine anything further removed from the contemporary cult of hedonism and self-gratification. The cultivation of self-discipline and determination is thus a key part of the voluntarist approach. A person who is unable to control or check his passions and desires will be unable to improve himself or to find true happiness, because he will be constantly chasing a receding will-o'-the-wisp of gratification. This way of thinking means that, in the voluntarist conception, frugality and sufficiency rather than affluence is the dominant social ideal. It also means that sexual continence and prudence is highly valued. This also explains the close connection between self-help and temperance in the narrow sense of the term, and the constant argument against the evils of drink.[8]

The other main consequence of the picture of the human condition as subject to stringent limits was the emphasis on the necessity of work. This in itself, however, was not new or even distinctive. What was a peculiar and vastly important part of voluntarism was the perception of work as a positive good and as essential for the full development and flourishing of human beings. The advocates of voluntarism saw work in elevated terms, as a calling and as a basic duty incumbent upon all human beings, to employ the talents and capacities which they had been given by God. Work was thus seen neither in the traditional way as a curse and a sad necessity, a consequence of the Fall, nor as a disutility which has to be

---

[7] See, for example, Smiles, *Character*, ch. 8, "Temper," pp. 216–34. Another classic statement is James Freeman Clarke, *Self-Culture: Physical, Intellectual, Moral, and Spiritual* (Boston: J. R. Osgood, 1880), pp. 399–411.

[8] For a recent discussion of the importance of continence to Victorians and its relation to other ideas, see Michael Mason, *The Making of Victorian Sexuality* (Oxford: Oxford University Press, 1994); and Mason, *The Making of Victorian Sexual Attitudes* (Oxford: Oxford University Press, 1994). The definitive work on the temperance movement in Britain is Brian Harrison, *Drink and the Victorians: The Temperance Question in England, 1815–1872* (London: Faber and Faber, 1972).

compensated for by money, the view of modern economics and social thought. Idleness and wasting of time were therefore seen both as grievous faults and, if involuntary, as a terrible and demoralizing curse. Work was also seen in Promethean terms, as a heroic activity and as the most important element in the formation of character and in self-improvement.[9]

This view of work has a number of important consequences for the voluntarist conception of welfare, consequences which serve to distinguish it further from both the older ideal and the contemporary way of thinking. It means that everyone should work regardless of social station. This marks a radical departure from the older idea that work was part of the fate of the lower orders in society but not of the elite, who could be defined as elite and better precisely because they did not work. It also leads to a total rejection of the ideal of the gentleman of leisure as the ideal social type. In contrast, the dignity of labor is advanced as a social ideal, the belief that all people are elevated and ennobled by productive labor. There is no distinction made between one kind of work and another; all are seen as equally valuable, and no kind of work is thought to be demeaning or ignoble. In particular, manual labor is seen to be every bit as honorable and noble as other types of work. In contrast to the modern way of thinking, work is seen almost as an end in itself and certainly as a means to moral improvement rather than as being about gaining income, "getting on," or participating in society.[10] One important point is that in voluntarist writings no distinction is made between domestic and outside work, or, as we would say, waged and unwaged work. Both are seen as forms of work and as equally valuable; there is no notion that only paid work is true work.

All this means that the voluntarist conception of welfare implies a form of egalitarianism, but one very different from that prevalent today. Equality, in this way of thinking, means that all people have equal moral value and standing, so that no one should be socially or politically inferior to another. Thus it means the absence of a social or political hierarchy, and the existence, as an ideal, of a public culture in which all can participate.[11]

---

[9] For an extended treatment of this, see Timothy Travers, *Samuel Smiles and the Victorian Work Ethic* (New York: Garland, 1987). See also Asa Briggs, "Samuel Smiles and the Gospel of Work," in Briggs, *Victorian People* (Harmondsworth: Penguin, 1990), pp. 116–39. For a more recent discussion of the historical development of the whole concept of work, see Patrick Joyce, ed., *The Historical Meanings of Work* (Cambridge: Cambridge University Press, 1987). For a clear and typical statement of the principle of the moral value of work, see Clarke, *Self-Culture*, p. 31.

[10] See, for example, William Ellery Channing, *Lectures on the Elevation of the Labouring Portion of the Community* (Manchester, 1840).

[11] The idea of equal moral standing could be seen as implying, and often did mean, a rejection of the Calvinist notion of an "elect." In this connection, it is worth pointing out the strong influence on voluntarist ideas of the part of Dissent Protestantism which rejected predestination or which espoused some form of Arminianism. Even those who continued to hold to predestinarian ideas of salvation rejected the idea that there was a visible body of the elect, and therefore held that all had to be treated on a presumption of equal moral worth.

It does not imply uniformity of material circumstance or of capacity or even opportunity. For many voluntarist authors, however, this conception did imply that there should be no great disparity of fortune or circumstance among people, and that ideally all should have a certain minimum, the amount necessary for personal independence and autonomy.

As I mentioned above, the voluntarist ideal was not one which saw human beings as selfish or isolated atoms, entirely dependent upon their own efforts. The voluntarists argued that human needs are met through a variety of means. These include personal, private effort, trade and agreement, friendship and benevolence ("neighborliness" in the American diction), and free cooperation. The point is that all of these are voluntary relations, based upon free choice. On this view, other kinds of relationships, which involve dependency and subordination, are not seen as conducive to human welfare. One of the most important ways of providing for human needs in this way of thinking is, of course, the family, and a great deal of space is devoted in voluntarist literature to the role and importance of the family. Marriage is construed, in the fashion which can be traced back to seventeenth-century authors such as John Locke, as a voluntary and companionate relationship between two individuals, of equal worth but with different roles. The role of the mother in shaping the character of the child is of crucial importance. The relationship between parent and child, the only one seen as both involuntary and good, is described in terms of trusteeship on the parents' part—again, an idea which can be traced back to a number of seventeenth-century theorists.[12]

A. Self-help

The active part of voluntarism, its conception of the means by which human welfare may be realized, has two aspects: self-help and mutual aid. The once powerful social ideal of self-help is now portrayed in such a caricatured form as to be almost unrecognizable to any person who has bothered to read examples of it. Indeed, an account of the concept of self-help has to spend as much time defining what it is not, as describing what it is. The most famous exponent of self-help was, of course, Samuel Smiles, and his five major works in this area—*Self-Help, Thrift, Character, Duty*, and *Life and Labour*—still turn up regularly on the shelves of secondhand book dealers. Some idea of his influence can be gained from the commercial success and sales of his books. *Self-Help*, published in 1859, had gone through fifty-four reprintings by 1908. Twenty thousand copies had been sold by the end of the first year, and fifty-five thousand by the end of five years. By 1905, it had sold over a quarter of a million—all of this only in Britain. It was highly successful in the United States and was translated into many languages, achieving popularity in all of them, and

[12] See Smiles, *Character*, pp. 31–35, 299–342.

particularly so in Japan. To put this into context, these sales were larger than those of the great classics of Victorian literature.[13] In America, Emerson was perhaps the most prominent exponent of the self-help ideal, particularly in works such as *Self-Reliance*, *Heroism*, and *Character*.

Perhaps the most frequent misrepresentation of self-help is to present it as being about success. Even perceptive and careful studies, such as those by Asa Briggs and J. F. C. Harrison,[14] fall into this error. Smiles emphasizes that simple worldly success is not the goal of self-help and not conducive to the individual's welfare:

> Worldly success, measured by the accumulation of money, is no doubt a very dazzling thing; and all men are naturally more or less the admirers of worldly success. But though men of persevering, sharp, dexterous, and unscrupulous habits, ever on the watch to push opportunities, may and do "get on" in the world, yet it is quite possible that they may not possess the slightest elevation of character, nor a particle of real goodness. He who recognizes no higher logic than that of the shilling, may become a very rich man, and yet remain all the while an exceedingly poor creature. For riches are no proof whatever of moral worth and their glitter often serves only to draw attention to the worthlessness of their possessor, as the light of the glow worm reveals the grub.

The literature of success is a product of the end of the nineteenth century and does not fully supplant self-help until the 1920s. Many of the works commonly cited as examples of success literature, such as the McGuffey readers or the works of Samuel Goodrich, are nothing of the kind.[15]

The goal of self-help is, rather, the making of character, and particularly the key quality of self-discipline. "Character is human nature in its best form," Smiles writes. "It is moral order embodied in the individual. Men of character are not only the conscience of society, but in every well governed state they are its best motive power; for it is moral qualities in the main which rule the world." To achieve this requires constant effort.

---

[13] Travers, *Samuel Smiles*, pp. 360–63. For the interesting case of Japan, see Earl Kinmouth, "Nakamura Keiu and Samuel Smiles: A Victorian Confucian and a Confucian Victorian," *American Historical Review*, vol. 85 (1980), pp. 535–56.

[14] J. F. C. Harrison, *Learning and Living, 1790–1960: A Study in the History of the English Adult Education Movement* (London: Routledge, 1961); Briggs, "Samuel Smiles and the Gospel of Work."

[15] The quoted passage is from Smiles, *Self-Help*, pp. 364–65. For the general point, see Harrison, *Learning and Living*. For the distinction between the two literatures (self help and success), see Travers, *Samuel Smiles, passim*, and esp. pp. 330–48. For Goodrich, see Samuel Griswold Goodrich, *Recollections of a Lifetime* (New York: Miller, Orton, and Mulligan, 1856). The McGuffey readers were a series of popular works widely used in nineteenth-century America for both education and moral instruction. Most contained accounts of exemplary lives, fictional and nonfictional.

"The best sort of character, however, cannot be formed without effort. There needs the exercise of constant self-watchfulness, self-discipline and self-control. There may be much faltering, stumbling, and temporary defeat; difficulties and temptations manifold to be battled with and overcome; but if the spirit be strong and the heart be upright, no one need despair of ultimate success."[16]

If self-help is not about success, it has even less connection with wealth. A common theme, in fact, is that of the corrupting and enervating effects of wealth and luxury (or "affluence," as we would now say). "Riches are oftener an impediment than a stimulus to action; and in many cases they are quite as much a misfortune as a blessing." Also emphasized is the relative social unimportance of wealth compared to other factors:

> The truth is, that we very much exaggerate the power of riches. Immense subscriptions are got up for the purpose of reforming men from their sinful courses, and of turning them from evil to good. And yet subscriptions will not do it. It is character that can do the work; money never can. Great changes in society can never be effected through riches. To turn men from intemperance, improvidence, and irreligion, and to induce them to seek their happiness in the pursuit of proper and noble objects, requires earnest purpose, honest self-devotion, and hard work. Money may help in many respects; but money by itself can do nothing.[17]

The point of self-help as a practice is not to achieve wealth but to achieve economic independence and sufficiency, so as to free the individual from the condition of servility and dependence. The two keys to this are the acquisition of what was known as a "competency" and the virtue of thrift. The term "competency" commonly meant two things: having enough savings and resources to be independent, and having a skill which would enable one to make one's own way in life. The virtue of thrift meant not miserliness, seen as a vice, but frugality, restraint, and control—above all, the avoidance of debt. On the voluntarist view, thrift is seen to be the source not only of independence but of self-respect and virtue. On the other hand, luxury and lavish living on the part of the rich is seen not as beneficial but as positively harmful, and income above a certain point is seen as having no use to the individual other than to be saved (so as to increase the stock of productive capital) or to be spent on socially useful ends. One important consequence of this approach is that while poverty per se, in the sense of a lack of income, is regrettable, it is not the main threat to human welfare. The peril to be avoided and to be

[16] Smiles, *Self-Help*, p. 450; Smiles, *Character*, p. 11.
[17] Smiles, *Thrift*, pp. 288–89.

removed by welfare strategies such as thrift and self-help is not poverty but pauperism, the state of economic dependency.[18]

Another misconception, which arises from reading contemporary social ideals back into the past, is to identify self-help with the meritocratic ideal of social mobility, and to suppose that the goal of self-help is to enable the individual to rise in society to a higher social position. Although the literature argues that this may happen, and is more likely if self-help is practiced, it is not the main point. The true gentleman may be found in any social position and is worth far more than the person of higher status but less moral worth. The aim of self-help is not to raise a few individuals but to bring about a general improvement in the quality of all the population. In particular, it aims at bringing about a state of moral and cultural equality, in which all people have equal access to knowledge and culture and participate in the public sphere as equal citizens. Self-help also stresses the idea of the dignity of labor and its inherent virtue and value, no matter how humble.[19]

Finally, to address the last common misconception, self-help is not about selfishness, nor the modern concept of self-realization which sees obligation as a form of constraint. Along with thrift goes the notion of duty. People have duties and obligations, and one of the reasons for self-help is to enable individuals to better discharge them; at the same time, the performance of duty is an important part of self-help. The carrying out of duties is one of the main mechanisms which connects individual improvement to collective betterment. One duty is the practice of benevolence or philanthropy, for, as Smiles writes, "[i]t is a duty that belongs to men as individuals, and as members of the social body. As individuals, because we are enjoined to help the widow and the fatherless in their affliction; and as members of the social body, because society claims of every man that he shall be a helper in the cause of progress and of social well-being." This is one reason for the virtue of thrift, for "[m]an must be thrifty in order to be generous." However, as we shall see, in the voluntarist way of thinking, charity had to take a particular form to be effective rather than corrupting.[20]

A major part of the self-help movement was self-culture or self-improvement. This obviously included self-education, reading, and an

---

[18] See Channing, *Lectures on the Elevation of the Labouring Portion of the Community*, for a forceful statement of this. For another typical statement of this view, see Goldwin Smith, "What Is Culpable Luxury?" in *Lectures and Essays* (New York: Macmillan, 1881). For one of many statements by Smiles, see his *Character*, p. 7.

[19] See Smiles, *The Education of the Working Classes* (Leeds, 1845), quoted in Briggs, "Samuel Smiles and the Gospel of Work," and in Harrison, *Learning and Living*, p. 56. See also Channing, *Lectures on the Elevation of the Labouring Portion of the Community*. For a historical survey and a powerful restatement of this, see Christopher Lasch, *The Revolt of the Elites and the Betrayal of Democracy* (New York: Norton, 1995), ch. 3.

[20] Smiles, *Thrift*, pp. 286–87.

emphasis on the "company of books." It meant more than this, however, since it included the acquiring of all sorts of skills and knowledge and not merely book learning. In fact, a common theme of self-help literature is deprecation of purely academic learning and of the separation of knowledge from the practical world of work. This often takes the form of sharp attacks on the intellectual as a social type and on the intellectual professions and their pretensions. Abraham Lincoln claimed to have been "educated by littles," but it is also clear that he saw the informal nature of his education as an advantage rather than a hindrance.[21]

The concept of self-help, as articulated in this way, had a number of implications for social thought and social policy. It implied a critique of the older, aristocratic ideal of the gentleman and the related notion of a hierarchical society, where each person was born into a particular station or position in life with attendant rights and duties. As I have already mentioned, this meant rejection of the older notion of work as pertaining to, and necessary for, the lower orders only. The aristocrat who did not work became an object of obloquy rather than respect. This also meant rejection of the ideal and practice of paternalism. Consequently, self-help and voluntarism were commonly linked to a particular theory of class, a theory which distinguished between the "productive" or "working" classes on the one hand, and the nonproductive on the other. The latter category included aristocrats, rentiers, and, frequently, the clergy, but also the non-working poor. The former included artisans, farmers, laborers, and also merchants and entrepreneurs, and, according to authors such as William Ellery Channing and Daniel Webster, made up about nine-tenths of the population. The term "capitalist" was commonly used in a restrictive fashion to mean only rentiers or stockholders and speculators.[22]

Moreover, in much of the earlier self-help literature, particularly in the United States, there was an aversion to wage labor, which was seen as servile and as at best a temporary expedient before one became economically independent. This was held to be the case even when the money returns from wage labor were higher. As the nineteenth century passed, it became clear that wage labor was going to be the only option for many people, and thus there came to be a defense of the status of wage laborer and an argument that it was not incompatible with economic independence. In the United States, this grew out of the debate between critics of, and apologists for, slavery. The defenders of slavery, such as George Fitzhugh, had argued that the position of the wage laborer was in some

---

[21] Harrison, *Learning and Living, passim*, but esp. pp. 43–56.

[22] Channing and Webster are discussed in Lasch, *Revolt of the Elites*, pp. 56–58. For an example of a British work based on this analysis, see John Wade, *The Extraordinary Black Book; or, Corruption Unmasked* (London: Effingham Wilson, 1831). For an account of the French origins of this analysis, see Élie Halévy, *The Era of Tyrannies: Essays on Socialism and War*, ed. and trans. R. K. Webb (Garden City, NY: Doubleday, 1965), pp. 21–104.

ways inferior to that of a slave, and in response anti-slavery writers had defended the essential dignity and free status of wage labor. In Britain, such arguments often took the form not of a simple defense of wage labor tout court, but of what was called "free labor," meaning a kind of halfway house between self-employment and wage labor where workers were paid on a profit-sharing basis. This view of wage labor, along with the anti-aristocratic aspect of voluntarism, meant that voluntarism was linked to a specific social ideal, that of a society made up of a large number of independent small producers with no great disparity of wealth or condition.[23]

Not surprisingly, therefore, self-help was also connected to a species of radical politics: for example, Chartism during the 1830s and 1840s in the British case and, in the United States, Populism during the later nineteenth century, or radical Republicanism before and immediately after the Civil War. Popular radicalism in general in nineteenth-century Britain was thoroughly imbued with the values of self-help, along with other ideas such as the iniquity of the income tax. Many modern historians find this combination of views disconcerting and hard to explain, since it does not fit contemporary notions of radicalism. One frequent theme in the writings of such historians is that the supposed adoption of self-help in the 1850s marked a retreat from radicalism to reformism on the part of the working class and on the part of individuals such as Smiles who had supported Chartism in the 1840s. Work such as that of Timothy Travers shows that this was simply not the case, and that self-help ideas were an important part of early nineteenth-century radicalism and had not lost their radical qualities and implications after 1850; there was a change perhaps of method but not of ideals.[24]

In terms of social policy, self-help as a strategy was strongly opposed to two others. On the one hand, it led to rejection of benevolent assistance directed to the lower orders from above, by organizations such as the Society for the Diffusion of Useful Knowledge. This was an organization set up in Britain by a number of Whig worthies, most notably Lord Brougham, to improve the educational and moral standing of the working population by such means as lectures, the giving out of tracts and pamphlets, and the support or creation of educational institutions. Although the ends of such bodies were very much those of voluntarism, the

[23] Very little has been written about either the critique of wage labor by nineteenth-century radicals or the idea of "free labor." For the most extensive recent discussion, see Christopher Lasch, *The True and Only Heaven: Progress and Its Critics* (New York: Norton, 1991), esp. pp. 203–16. For a discussion of Fitzhugh's argument, see Eugene Genovese, *The World the Slaveholders Made: Two Essays in Interpretation* (London: Allen Lane, 1970).

[24] Travers, *Samuel Smiles, passim*. On the general issue, see E. F. Biagini and A. J. Reid, eds., *Currents of Radicalism: Popular Radicalism, Organised Labour, and Party Politics in Britain, 1850–1914* (Cambridge: Cambridge University Press, 1991); for the contrary view, see Robert J. Morris, "Samuel Smiles and the Genesis of Self-Help: The Retreat to a Petit-Bourgeois Utopia," *Historical Journal*, vol. 24 (1981), pp. 89–109; and Neville Kirk, *The Growth of Working Class Reformism in Mid-Victorian England* (London: Croom Helm, 1985).

means, of benevolent assistance from the rich to the poor, was seen as not ultimately conducive to those ends. This was because such assistance was seen as degrading and reflecting a relationship not of equality but of servility, and because true improvement had to arise from the choice of the people involved. The very idea that there might be a *right* to assistance was rejected as impugning the independence and freedom of working men. As one author put it in 1869, "[t]he human appendage to the soil had a *right* to maintenance from his lord. But the free man feels that he has no such claim. He knows that for him and his, there can exist no real liberty which is not founded upon self-dependence" (emphasis in original). In his essay on Smiles, Asa Briggs cites a passage from a letter to Smiles from Richard Cobden in 1853: "Depend upon it, there is a spice of despotism at the bottom of all this intervention by combined bodies in the affairs of individuals. . . . I think we shall not get right till there is a revolt against all such organizations, whether on one side or another, in the interests of liberty—personal liberty."[25]

Self-help, while encouraging philanthropy, led to a critique of what was termed "indiscriminate charity," meaning the giving of aid to the undeserving or those who would not mend their ways and giving money without ensuring it was well spent. "The charity which merely consists in giving, is an idle indulgence—often an idle vice. The mere giving of money will never do the work of philanthropy." The type of charity advocated by voluntarists was that which encouraged and enabled self-help.[26]

While rejecting upper-class benevolence from high to low, the self-help movement was also naturally opposed to state action. In nineteenth-century Britain, the voluntary principle was the basis for resistance to state education and to moves toward the provision of state old-age pensions. The limited form of state relief of poverty under the Poor Law was accepted, but only as a regrettable necessity, and a constant theme was that of the need to strictly enforce the provisions of the 1834 Poor Law Amendment Act, particularly the banning of "outdoor relief." While insurance and saving were encouraged and advocated, compulsory state insurance, of the kind introduced in 1911, was firmly rejected.[27]

---

[25] Briggs, "Samuel Smiles and the Gospel of Work," p. 124. Harrison, *Learning and Living*, p. 51, describes the distinction made by nineteenth-century observers between three routes to social improvement: by the state; by help from the upper and upper middle classes (e.g., via mechanics institutes and the Society for the Diffusion of Useful Knowledge); and by self-improvement on the part of the working classes. The 1869 quote is from Charles Hardwick, *The History, Present Position, and Social Importance of Friendly Societies* (Manchester, 1869), p. 18.

[26] Smiles, *Thrift*, pp. 302–6; the quote is from p. 303.

[27] The Poor Law was the minimal system of state relief of poverty in Britain, originally set up on a parish-based system in 1601 and funded out of a local property tax (the poor rates). In the early nineteenth century, concern grew over the rising cost of poor relief and the perception that the operation of the system was encouraging pauperism, i.e., welfare dependency. This led to the establishment of a commission of enquiry and, following its report,

Thus, the practice of self-help meant above all the adoption of a particular kind of lifestyle, marked by the cultivation of certain qualities. This was an "art of living" which was centered on the home and the family, and after that the locality. One thing which the advocates of this principle rejected was too much physical mobility (Emerson was particularly scathing on this point). The outcome of this "art of living" was to be both economic independence and moral growth, since the two were seen as intimately related to each other. The person who followed this principle was assured of respectability, a status which was earned rather than inherited and was not connected to money or wealth.[28]

One particular form of self-help worth mentioning, since it has attracted some attention recently, was small-scale enterprise or "penny capitalism," to give the title of a recent study. In 1977, Elizabeth Roberts found that in several working-class communities between 1890 and 1914, the population was generally in good health and enjoying a sound diet despite earning wages near or even below a poverty line of the sort developed by social reformer Seebohm Rowntree; i.e., they were earning a wage which was not enough to provide a minimal subsistence-based standard of living. The reason for this disparity between recorded incomes and living conditions was widespread small-scale entrepreneurship to supplement low wages. John Benson's pioneering study of working-class entrepreneurs looks at a whole range of activities, from small-scale farming and horticulture, through household manufacture, to services of various kinds and even moneylending. Small retailing was especially important, and historians such as Geoffrey Crossick have made the historical profession more aware of how many artisans and small businesses survived the supposed move to large productive units and proletarianization in the later nineteenth century.[29]

---

to the passage in 1834 of the Poor Law Amendment Act, which provided (1) that the condition of a person in receipt of relief should always be worse than that of the lowest paid laborer (the principle of "less eligibility"); (2) that the administration of relief should be handled by large unions of parishes; and (3) that in order to get relief a person would have to enter an institution—the workhouse—with relief outside the workhouse (outdoor relief) being abolished. In practice, this third provision was not applied. The National Insurance Act of 1911 introduced a system of state insurance against sickness and unemployment, paid for by deductions from wages and compulsory contributions from employers. For a selection of extracts from original sources relating to this and the related question of state old-age pensions, see Eric J. Evans, ed., *Social Policy 1830–1914: Individualism, Collectivism, and the Origins of the Welfare State* (London: Routledge, 1978), esp. pp. 161–73, 272–82.

[28] See Smiles, *Thrift*, ch. 16, "The Art of Living," pp. 358–78; and Smiles, *Character*, pp. 31–62. For Emerson's views, see, e.g., his *Complete Works*, pp. 29–30.

[29] John Benson, *The Penny Capitalists: A Study of Nineteenth-Century Working-Class Entrepreneurs* (Dublin: Gill and Macmillan, 1983); Elizabeth Roberts, "Working Class Standards of Living in Barrow and Lancaster, 1890–1914," *Economic History Review*, vol. 30 (1977); Geoffrey Crossick, *An Artisan Elite in Victorian Society: Kentish London, 1840–1880* (London: Croom Helm, 1978); Geoffrey Crossick and Heinz-Gerhard Haupt, *The Petite Bourgeoisie in Europe, 1780–1914* (London: Routledge, 1995).

B. *Mutual aid*

The voluntarist concept of welfare did not rely simply on individual self-help, however. There was also the second active element of voluntarism, the practice of mutual aid. As Edward Baines, one leading exponent, put it, this encompassed a huge range of activities:

> Let me first define what is meant by the voluntary system. It seems needful to inform some that it is not confined to charity; still less does it mean Dissent. The voluntary system includes all that is not governmental or compulsory—all that men do for themselves, their neighbours or their posterity of their own free will.

In other words, there was a great variety of organizations and bodies, formed by free association among individuals to meet common needs. They were typically self-governing and independent, with a rule of equality of status and rights among the members, and they frequently practiced a form of active participatory democracy.[30]

So numerous and varied were voluntary mutual aid organizations that only the briefest outline of the most prominent kinds can be given here; to do full justice to the subject would require a large book—or several such. All originated as clubs of one kind or another—a club, it may be remembered, was defined by Samuel Johnson as "an association of good fellows joined together for a common purpose." Many of these organizations were ephemeral, lasting only as long as there was a felt need by the members, but others became large, established institutions, complete with written rules and constitutions. Many were educational, intended to impart skills or to encourage the shared and communal acquisition of knowledge and learning. One common form of penny capitalism was the dame school or common day school, which provided cheap but surprisingly effective education for the poor. There were also many charitable schools or ones run by educational societies. The clearest case of mutual aid in education was that of mutual improvement societies. These generally had a small number of members who would meet in each other's homes or in a hired room and would instruct each other and participate in a program of shared learning. Subscriptions would be used to buy a small stock of books and to pay for outside lectures. Many working-class autobiographies contain references to societies of this kind, and in the 1840s it was estimated that every small town in Yorkshire had at least one such society. It was the lectures given to such a society in Leeds that Smiles later put together to make *Self-Help*. Many of the friendly societies and trade unions also had an active educational function, not least through the provision of libraries, reading rooms, and journals. In Leeds in 1849,

---

[30] Edward Baines, Jr., *Education Best Promoted by Perfect Freedom* (Leeds, 1834), quoted in Briggs and Sellars, *Victorian Nonconformity* (*supra* note 5), pp. 131–34.

the Odd Fellows, one of the largest of the affiliated-order type of friendly societies, had a library of over fifteen hundred volumes, and many lodges and branches had reading rooms and stocks of educational books.[31]

Other significant institutions were savings clubs and working-class savings banks. Again there was a great variety of forms. A common one was the terminating society, in which members made contributions to a fund for a fixed period of time, after which the accrued savings were divided up among the surviving contributors. A popular variant of this, which is still widely found today among immigrant communities in both Britain and the United States, was the revolving fund. Under this arrangement, each member would undertake to pay at least a certain amount into a fund for a given number of weeks. At any one time during the cycle, he could draw out an amount equal to his contribution multiplied by the allotted number of weeks. The most extensive development of voluntary cooperative banking, however, took place in Germany with the invention by Hermann Schulze-Delitzsch and F. W. Raiffeisen of the Genossenschaften, or credit cooperative. This developed into a nationwide network of localized credit unions, made up of voluntary associations of workers and farmers. These associations were imitated elsewhere in Europe and also in the United States, but for a number of reasons did not take root in Britain before 1900. This was not for lack of advocacy; Thomas Mackay, one of the leading theoreticians of voluntarism toward the end of the nineteenth century, was one of several prominent advocates of the idea. Today there are many such organizations in Britain, usually known as credit unions.[32]

There were also many specialized voluntary organizations, designed to provide particular services. These included building societies and freehold land societies, which in their original form provided housing for their working-class and artisan members. Other organizations provided pharmacies and dispensaries, while many hospitals were built and funded through the establishment of voluntary savings schemes within a town or locality. However, by far the most significant mutual aid institutions were friendly societies. These were associations which, in return for a membership fee, provided a whole range of services, but in particular protection against loss of income through sickness, accident, or old age. Their activities are sometimes confused with philanthropy but were fundamentally different in nature. "The mutual benefit association was not run by one set of people with the intention of helping another separate group, it

---

[31] Harrison, *Learning and Living*, pp. 50–57. See also Phil Gardner, *The Lost Elementary Schools of Victorian England* (London: Croom Helm, 1984). An affiliated order, such as the Odd Fellows or Foresters, was a national friendly society made up of local branches (lodges), all affiliated to a national governing body.

[32] See J. W. Mason, "Thomas Mackay: The Anti-Socialist Philosophy of the Charity Organisation Society," in *Essays in Anti-Labour History: Responses to the Rise of Labour in Britain*, ed. Kenneth D. Brown (London: Macmillan, 1974), pp. 290–316.

was an association of individuals pledged to help each other when the occasion arose."[33]

The number of such societies and their membership grew steadily throughout the nineteenth century in Britain and for longer in the United States. In 1801, Sir Frederick Eden estimated that in Britain there were roughly 7,200 societies with 648,000 adult male members (at a time when the total population was about 9 million). By 1911, 9 million people belonged to registered and unregistered friendly societies. In 1910, 6.6 million had belonged to registered societies alone, with as many belonging to unregistered ones. The work of P. H. J. H. Gosden and the records kept by the government registrar of friendly societies show that not only were societies growing throughout the nineteenth century, the rate of growth was increasing right up to 1910. Moreover, contrary to some allegations, the societies had by 1910 overcome earlier financial problems by a more scientific use of actuarial principles. The work of David Beito shows a similar pattern in the United States, but with the growth persisting for longer. In the U.S., membership in friendly societies—or fraternal orders, as they were commonly known—was particularly widespread among immigrants and minority groups. There was an especially strong tradition of mutual aid and fraternity among freedmen in the years following the Civil War and Emancipation.[34]

Although friendly societies provided many of the same services which the welfare state would provide later, they did so in a different way. The detailed personal knowledge which lodge or branch officials had of applicants for assistance meant that they were able to avoid the moral hazards associated with state benefits. This also made possible follow-up work and informal assistance on a case-by-case basis. Above all, these were organizations of working men, by working men, and for working men. There was no question of dependency, only of mutual support. They also explicitly aimed at producing and enhancing the same qualities as those advocated by self-help, and, by virtue of their internal democracy, they acted as schools of citizenship.[35]

In fact, all of these organizations were intended to promote and support individual independence and welfare. Their voluntary and self-governing nature was, to their advocates, precisely the reason they were able to do this where charity and state action could not. They were seen explicitly as part of a process of social reform and betterment, but one

[33] David Green, *Reinventing Civil Society: The Rediscovery of Welfare without Politics* (London: Institute of Economic Affairs, 1993), p. 30.

[34] *Ibid.* See also J. M. Baernreither, *English Associations of Working Men* (London: Sonnenschein, 1889); P. H. J. H. Gosden, *The Friendly Societies in England, 1815–1875* (Manchester: Manchester University Press, 1961); Gosden, *Self-Help: Voluntary Associations in Nineteenth Century Britain* (London: Batsford, 1973); and David Beito's essay in this volume.

[35] See Baernreither, *English Associations of Working Men*, pp. 5–9, 142–51. See also William Ellery Channing, *Remarks on the Disposition which Now Prevails to Form Associations to Accomplish All Objects by Organized Masses* (London, 1830).

based on the voluntary principle and driven by the self-determined improvement of individuals rather than by action upon those individuals, whether by the state or private charity. This ideal of voluntary social reform was also found in the temperance movement, most notably in organizations such as the Band of Hope. (Several of the leading friendly societies, such as the Rechabites and the Order of the Sons of Temperance, were explicitly committed to temperance and abstention.) In the voluntarist way of thinking, this was the only feasible route to social improvement. Voluntarists in general had great faith in the reformative and character-building capacity of self-help and mutual aid and believed strongly that adoption and execution of their principles would bring about a transformation of the character and quality of the people. In voluntarism's heyday, there was little or no notion of a class of unredeemable delinquents.[36]

C. Origins of voluntarism

Where, though, had the voluntarist idea come from? In one sense it was simply a continuation and elaboration of long-established practice going back to the burial clubs of ancient Rome—if not beyond. As an elaborated theory, however, it clearly originated in Britain from the theory and practice of Dissent, that is, the various Protestant sects which dissented from the authority of the established Anglican Church, including Quakers, Baptists, Congregationalists, and Unitarians. The earliest formulations of the conception can be seen in writers such as Daniel Defoe. More generally, there is the Dissenting ideal of religious liberty, articulated in the nineteenth century by a number of figures, including Edward Baines, Edward Miall, R. W. Dale, and C. H. Spurgeon. Religious liberty meant more than just civil and political equality between different denominations. It derived from the fundamental independence and autonomy of the individual believer. This meant that the Church as a body consisted of a multitude of individuals who chose to freely associate in self-governing congregations, which could then, in turn, combine freely among themselves. This was explicitly contrasted with the Anglican system, whereby (in theory at least) one was born into a particular denomination by virtue of being a citizen of the state. By virtue of being born, or living, in a particular parish, one was automatically part of a specific congregation, with no choice in the matter and no say in the choice of priest, since the parish itself was part of a hierarchical structure in which authority flowed downward from above. Because of the persisting tendency to identify church and society, it was easy for voluntarist theorists to apply the voluntary model of church government to society in general and also to

---

[36] See Mackay, *Methods of Social Reform* (*supra* note 4), passim; Channing, *Remarks, passim*; and Baernreither, *English Associations of Working Men*, pp. 228–96.

apply the critique of Anglicanism to all involuntary and hierarchical social arrangements.[37]

One important point to realize is that voluntarism was not a social ideal associated with a specific political ideology, such as classical liberalism or conservatism. Many socialists, such as Robert Blatchford, were ardent admirers of Smiles's *Self-Help,* and key parts of the labor movement, such as trade unions and the cooperative movement, should be seen as part of, and inspired by, the voluntarist ideal. There was also throughout the nineteenth century the now almost forgotten tradition of voluntary socialism, as articulated by figures such as F. D. Maurice, James Hole, and F. D. Tandy. Even later figures such as R. H. Tawney and G. D. H. Cole owed a great deal to this intellectual tradition, and thus much socialist thinking on welfare issues took place within the voluntarist conception of welfare.[38]

On the other side, many of the sharpest critics of voluntarism were conservatives, such as James Fenimore Cooper and Francis Parkman in America, and we can observe how it proved easy for Tories to move from a traditional and paternalist view to the modern one. Both Parkman and Cooper argued for a patrician view of society and politics, one aspect of which was the continuation of a paternalist relationship between the upper and lower orders and a rejection of voluntarist principles, particularly the social ideal of the "self-made man" and the notion of personal independence. As George Watson has pointed out, early conservative thought as found in people such as John Calhoun and Benjamin Disraeli has a positively Marxist tone, and this underlying hostility to market society and its social ideals led to strong support from many conservative politicians for measures to check individualism. In Britain, figures such as Joseph Chamberlain, Stanley Baldwin, Neville Chamberlain, and Harold MacMillan all certainly played a major part in the development of the welfare state.[39]

How successful had voluntarist welfare strategies been, in their own terms, by the end of the nineteenth century? The straightforward answer

[37] There is a large and extensive literature on Dissent and its historical impact. The best survey by far is the monumental work of Michael R. Watts, *The Dissenters,* vol. 2, *The Expansion of Evangelical Nonconformity, 1791–1859* (Oxford: Oxford University Press, 1995). See also Bradley, *The Optimists* (*supra* note 5). For one of Miall's many works, see Edward Miall, *The Bearing of Religious Equality on the Right of Individuals and Spiritual Communities* (Manchester, 1873). One typical work from Dale is R. W. Dale, *The Politics of Nonconformity* (Manchester, 1871).

[38] On Hole, see Harrison, *Learning and Living,* pp. 119–37. For voluntary socialism, see W. H. Greenleaf, *The British Political Tradition,* vol. 2, *The Ideological Heritage* (London: Methuen, 1983), pp. 412–63.

[39] For the views of James Fenimore Cooper and Francis Parkman, see John G. Cawelti, *Apostles of the Self-Made Man: Changing Concepts of Success in America* (Chicago: University of Chicago Press, 1965), pp. 75–80. For the role of conservatives in creating and sustaining the British welfare state, see Greenleaf, *The Ideological Heritage,* pp. 196–262. See also George Watson, *The Idea of Liberalism: Studies for a New Map of Politics* (London: Macmillan, 1985).

is that they had been highly successful, according to a number of indi-cators. Between 1850 and 1900 in Britain, crime, delinquency, illegitimacy, and drunkenness all fell markedly, while savings increased. Most social observers of the 1880s and 1890s commented on the increased virtue, sobriety, and restraint of working people in particular and of society in general. This fitted in with a way of thinking about progress which was often found in the voluntarist literature. According to this view, progress consisted of the moral improvement of individuals and the growth of economic independence among members of the community, along with the more general access of the mass of the public to culture and the growth of public opinion as a factor in politics.[40]

At the end of the last century and the start of this one, however, the voluntarist conception of welfare was replaced in public discourse by another one, which made incorporation of the poor into the wider com-munity (rather than individual independence) the key goal of welfare. It is important to realize the degree of continuity and overlap between the old, voluntarist ideal and the new, incorporationist one, most notably as regards the belief that moral improvement was a crucial element of wel-fare. However, the way that central concepts and analyses were changed meant that the whole nature of the argument for welfare was altered.

III. THE INCORPORATIONIST CONCEPTION

What, then, are the main features of this other conception of welfare? Since it is much more familiar, there is less need to defend it from mis-representation, although both theory and practice have undergone an evolution over time which would probably have startled many of its earlier advocates such as Beatrice and Sidney Webb. The starting point of this conception is an organic model of society in which the social unit is seen as an entity with a real existence independent of the individuals who compose it. The identity or selfhood of these individuals is largely deter-mined by the network of social relations of which they are elements, so that factors and forces outside the individual or outside his control play a great part in determining his character and actions. People are born into positions which, in the absence of democratic control of social processes, they have little if any influence over. The central argument of this con-ception is that the key welfare consideration is the ability to participate fully in the social unit of which one is a part. This, in turn, has led to the idea of a generalized collective responsibility for the welfare of others and to the perception that a moral wrong or poverty in one part of society imposes a duty upon all, due to what Beatrice Webb, in an arresting

---

[40] See the references and remarks in Baernreither, *English Associations of Working Men*, pp. 5–9.

phrase, called "collective consciousness of sin."[41] This is very different from the idea of personal and specific duties found in the work of Smiles and other authors.

This approach meant that the purpose of active measures to promote welfare was not primarily the improvement of individuals (although it was hoped this would happen) but rather the lifting up or incorporation of large classes of people into the social whole. On this view, the poor, and especially the lowest section of them, were in some sense excluded or outcast from society by the workings of the economic system. The historical works of authors such as Arnold Toynbee and Barbara and John Hammond presented this as being the consequence of industrialization and the move to market society—a view previously associated with Tory authors such as Disraeli. The difference was that in the Tory view the need was to restore a stable mutual relation between the higher and lower classes, whereas for the Fabians and the New Liberals, the need was to incorporate the working classes by a move to a more egalitarian society. The negative aspect of this was the idea that there should be a floor or safety net, a minimum level of comfort below which no one should fall, so as to ensure that the poor remained part of society. This was very different from the idea lying behind the New Poor Law of 1834, where the metaphor of the safety net was used in a very different (and more literal) way, as a mechanism for "catching" those who had fallen.

This incorporationist way of thinking generated a great variety of proposed active measures, from state old-age pensions and insurance, to a guaranteed income, to some which have fortunately been forgotten, such as eugenics measures to eliminate the unfit, and forced-labor colonies to retrain the "unemployable." Proposals of this last kind were put forward by many of the early advocates of the welfare state, often under the heading of "national efficiency." Among their advocates were such figures as the Webbs, William Beveridge, and Havelock Ellis. Such notions and proposals remained a major part of most welfarist thinking well into the 1930s, although some such as Beveridge had reversed their views by then; and such proposals were only completely removed from the scope of political acceptability with the coming of World War II. One significant point is that initially the distinction between deserving and undeserving poor was retained, but the undeserving (the "residuum," to use the contemporary term) were to be brought back into society, by harsh measures if necessary. The principle was the Augustinian one of "compel them to come in," in the same way that heretics and unbelievers had been coerced into becoming members of the Church. This is arguably a more pessimistic view of the prospects for many of the poor than the voluntarist view

---

[41] Beatrice Webb, *My Apprenticeship* (Cambridge: Cambridge University Press, 1979), p. 147.

described above, and may be reviving in some contemporary discussions of the "underclass."[42]

At least initially, the incorporationist model was every bit as moralistic as the voluntarist one. However, moral improvement and virtue were now seen in collective terms, as pertaining to the whole of society—hence the possibility of "collective sin." For individuals, the key to virtue was to be a full and productive member of society. Moreover, a key idea was that moral degradation was caused by poverty and that therefore the way to moral reform was to remove or relieve poverty. Voluntarists agreed that poverty had a demoralizing effect, but because of their moral philosophy they maintained that trying to relieve it by involuntary collective action would only make things worse.

On the incorporationist view, the problem facing the lower classes is poverty rather than pauperism, lack of money rather than dependency. The cure, therefore, in crude terms, is money; or as it was more commonly put, money was a necessary condition for any cure. Since the collective rather than the individual is primary, effective relief of poverty means action on all of the poor or even on the whole of society, and this inevitably means action by the state—the active agency of society. This also meant action by experts, those with a special knowledge, rather than by the objects of that action themselves.

The incorporationist view also redefined progress to mean the moral improvement and development of society as a whole, with a move toward greater complexity, more conscious direction and control, and more collective and less individual action. Progress also came to mean a move toward greater comfort and affluence, but this was a later development and hardly figures in early incorporationist writings. Another element which only appears later is the contemporary notion of self-realization, defined as the removal of obstacles to self-expression and the satisfaction of wants. (The Webbs, for example, would have been aghast at the idea that this was a part of welfare.) However, these later developments, along with the decline in the moralistic elements of the ideal, are inevitable consequences of its logic, and they are particularly consequences of the undermining of the notion of personal responsibility. Once society is seen as having an overall responsibility for the welfare of all, it is natural to combine this with the traditional liberal idea of individual flourishing and development (as found in Wilhelm von Humboldt and J. S. Mill) and to believe that there is a collective responsibility to help individuals fulfill themselves.

---

[42] See W. H. Greenleaf, *The British Political Tradition*, vol. 1, *The Rise of Collectivism* (London: Methuen, 1983), pp. 269–72, for discussion of the role of eugenics. See also Finlayson, *Citizen, State, and Social Welfare* (*supra* note 3), pp. 149–52. For contemporary discussions of the "underclass" and its growth, see, for example, Myron Magnet, *The Dream and the Nightmare* (New York: William Morrow, 1993), and Lawrence M. Mead, *The New Politics of Poverty* (New York: Basic Books, 1992).

It must be emphasized that almost all contemporary debate over welfare issues now takes place within the terms, and using the vocabulary, of the incorporationist model. Arguments between left and right, over particular measures and strategies, are about the effectiveness or ineffectiveness of various means of achieving the goal of incorporating everyone into a collective entity. The contemporary arguments about the underclass, and about the effects of programs such as Aid to Families with Dependent Children, focus on the way the underclass is excluded and outcast. There are still arguments made about moral hazards and the corrupting effects of welfare, but these are framed in terms of the way perverse incentives create or aggravate poverty rather than in terms of the undermining of autonomy and independence. There is discussion of dependency as an effect of welfare programs, but again this is seen as a problem because it prevents full participation. There is almost no argument made that dependency is bad because it prevents moral growth and the formation of character, much less that honest poverty is preferable to dishonest affluence.

This may seem a strange line of argument given recent arguments and developments in the United States (though not in Britain). Surely the developing critique of the welfare state in the U.S. is articulated in voluntarist terms, in terms of the morally corrupting effects of welfare and its crippling consequences for personal autonomy and development. Indeed, such arguments are found and their reappearance is significant. However, such claims are subordinated to other arguments: ones about the effects of state welfare on the functioning of the entire economy; about the perverse effects of welfare on personal happiness, defined as the realization of goals; about the relation between the effects of state welfare and a functioning society; and above all, the argument that state welfare has failed because it has not met the goal of incorporating all sections of society into some kind of common experience. American conservatives are perhaps less influenced by such arguments than before, but the arguments still shape much of the language in which debates take place. One reason for this is the utility-maximizing model of human motivation, which is not to be found at all in the vocabulary of voluntarism but has now come to be accepted on both sides of the debate and is particularly influential on conservatives. Another reason is the assumption, all the more powerful for being often unarticulated, that lack of money, or having only a little of it, is a crippling state because it prevents people from doing what they want and thus fulfilling themselves, and from being able to share in the collective life of society. The idea of honest poverty is still not a common one for American conservatives.[43]

---

[43] A recent work which looks at the changing debate is David Green, *Community without Politics: A Market Approach to Welfare Reform* (London: Institute of Economic Affairs, 1996).

IV. Explaining the Shift from Voluntarism to Incorporationism

An obvious question is why this shift of discourse and vocabulary took place. It is worth pointing out that more than the concept of welfare changed around the turn of the century. There was also a fundamental redefinition of work and of leisure, and the two are clearly related. It is important to realize that the shift of both discourse and vocabulary and actual practice did not take place without debate—quite the contrary. A furious argument did take place, in which both sides were well aware of the kinds of issues at stake. In Germany, for example, the Liberal politician Ludwig Bamberger described Bismarck's social welfare measures as effecting a fundamental alteration in the nature of the state and its relation to the individual.[44]

In both Britain and the United States, the later nineteenth century saw a movement to address welfare problems, by making charity and philanthropy more effective in promoting personal independence and less "dangerous," and by devising collective action intended to empower individuals by making it easier and more practicable for them to practice the ideal of self-help. Examples of this in Britain were the housing strategy of Octavia Hill and the idea floated by Joseph Chamberlain of providing the urban poor with allotments and giving the rural poor access to land. The main form which this phenomenon took was the charity organization movement, organized in Britain via the Charity Organisation Society and its provincial counterparts. Its aim was to ensure that charity was an enabling and not an enervating force, by coupling charitable giving with the practice of detailed investigation of individual cases by trained investigators. The Society was a major player in the debate at the end of the nineteenth century, articulating an individualist and voluntarist case. However, the Society faced a problem, identical to the one facing earlier middle-class reformers such as the Society for the Diffusion of Useful Knowledge: there was an inherent contradiction, in terms of its own principles, between the voluntarist ideal of personal independence and the perception, which motivated many of its actions, that there was a large group of poor who had to be helped or trained to help themselves. To combine these two, while possible, was always difficult and became more so as time went on. Moreover, while some of the movement's leading lights, such as Thomas Mackay, continued to advocate the voluntarist position, others, such as Helen and Bernard Bosanquet, came to argue for a particular variant of the incorporationist model; and by the time of the Royal Commission of the Poor Laws of 1905 (which led to the production of two reports in 1909, one broadly reflecting the views of the Bosanquets, the

---

[44] For an outstanding survey of the change and the related debate, see Finlayson, *Citizen, State, and Social Welfare*.

other those of the Webbs), the argument had become, as it is now, essentially one between different strategies within the same (incorporationist) model.[45]

There are a number of possible explanations that can be put forward for this. The simplest is that the voluntarist way of thinking about welfare had proved to be inadequate and unable to account for social problems or provide effective strategies for dealing with them, even in its own terms. The big problem with this argument is the evidence that mutual aid and self-help were both flourishing as never before and becoming more effective rather than less at the time when the shift in argument took place. However, it is possible that voluntarism was perceived to have failed even if that were not the case, and in history it is often perceptions that matter. One serious problem for most observers was the belief that there existed a substantial residuum, a class of incorrigibles who were immune to the ideal of self-help. It also came to be thought that, while welfare needs might be met by voluntary action, there was a substantial minority of poor people who were unable to participate in voluntary action because of their circumstances. A belief which had great impact was that friendly societies and other mutual aid institutions had proven incapable of dealing with the growing burden of providing for the aged—a belief that was probably incorrect but nonetheless influential. Most serious, however, was the growing perception that a great deal of hardship was due to impersonal forces beyond the control of any individual and therefore not amenable to the strategy of self-help. It was the work of social observers such as Charles Booth and Seebohm Rowntree which did the most to popularize all of these perceptions and the idea that social problems now required some kind of collective social response.[46]

Another type of explanation of the shift in argument is purely intellectualist, relating the demise of voluntarist ideas to wider intellectual developments. The most important of these was scientism, the (mistaken) application of concepts and methodologies derived from the physical sciences to the study of social life. F. A. Hayek and others have argued that this played a major part in the shift to collectivism at the end of the last century, and part of this was the rise to intellectual dominance of collectivist and organicist notions of society and the corresponding decline of individualist ways of thinking, which came to be seen as unscientific and hence invalid. Others have pointed to the impact of Hegelian idealism as found in the works of T. H. Green and his pupils, or to the

[45] On the Charity Organisation Society, see Charles Loch Mowat, *The Charity Organisation Society: Its Ideas and Work, 1869–1913* (London: Methuen, 1961). On the majority and minority reports of 1909, see A. M. McBriar, *An Edwardian Mixed Doubles: The Bosanquets versus the Webbs: A Study in British Social Policy, 1890–1929* (Oxford: Clarendon Press, 1987).

[46] On the social investigators and their impact, see Gertrude Himmelfarb, *Poverty and Compassion: The Moral Imagination of the Late Victorians* (New York: Knopf, 1991).

gradual spread of a form of sentimental Christianity derived from earlier Victorian Evangelicalism. Both of these led to the assertion of the notion of social and collective responsibility for others. Initially, this took the form of a renewed paternalism and an emphasis on the duty of the better off to engage in philanthropic activity, but it soon led to the idea of collective social action through the state.[47]

One idea that can be rejected is that the demise of voluntarism reflected the growing political importance of the working classes, and working-class discontent with, and rejection of, the ideal. As Henry Pelling and Pat Thane have pointed out with regard to Britain, the reality was exactly the opposite. The working class was strongly committed to self-help and deeply suspicious of, and hostile toward, state welfare, which was seen as a denial of working-class independence. The anti-statism and voluntarism of working-class leaders such as Steven Reynolds was common rather than otherwise. It was rather the middle classes who came to support the new ways of thinking, and middle-class politicians who advocated and instituted the welfare state. The same is true of the United States, where mutual aid was strongest, and state help most resisted, among the working class and particularly among blacks and immigrant groups. Such groups saw moves to introduce social insurance and other state welfare schemes as an attack on their own status as free and independent citizens—a feeling which helps to explain the form the welfare state actually took in America under the New Deal, with major programs presented as being enabling and linked to work or contributions. Although some fraternal orders, such as the Eagles, supported moves toward state welfare, the majority were strongly opposed.

All of this should lead us to reject the theory that a move away from voluntarism was the result of the extension of the franchise down the social scale, leading to demands from the newly enfranchised workers for a new kind of welfare system. (In Britain, the shift in argument happened when the franchise was still restricted, before 1918). Rather, the change in belief took place among the middle and upper classes first, and the change in policy was, at least initially, one mandated by those classes rather than the mass of voters.[48]

Another possibility, however, is that the theory and practice of voluntarism were incompatible in a different way with the nature and reality of

---

[47] See Friedrich A. Hayek, *The Counter-Revolution of Science: Studies on the Abuse of Reason* (Indianapolis: Liberty Press, 1979); Andrew Vincent and Raymond Plant, *Philosophy, Politics, and Citizenship: The Life and Thought of the British Idealists* (Oxford: Basil Blackwell, 1984); and Stefan Collini, *Liberalism and Sociology: L. T. Hobhouse and Political Argument in England, 1880–1914* (Cambridge: Cambridge University Press, 1979).

[48] Henry Pelling, *Popular Politics and Society in Late Victorian Britain* (London: Macmillan, 1979). Pat Thane, "The Working Class and State 'Welfare' in Britain, 1890–1914," *Historical Journal*, vol. 274 (1984), pp. 877–900. For a typical response from a fraternal order in the United States, see "The Menace of Social Insurance," *The Fraternal Monitor*, vol. 30 (1919), pp. 4–9.

democratic politics as they emerged at the end of the nineteenth century. It may be that the shift of thinking from one ideal to another reflected the material interests of particular social groups who were able to use the political process to benefit themselves. On this view, derived in part from the theory of public choice, the shift reflected successful rent-seeking by groups such as the professions, particularly doctors. A version of this thesis is put forward by Harold Perkin in his book *The Rise of Professional Society*, where he argues that the growth of the welfare state and its ideology are driven by the interests of the professional section of the middle classes—the experts held up by the Webbs. The incorporationist conception is seen by Perkin as part of what he calls the "class ideal" of the professionals.[49]

Another related argument is that the change was driven by the competition between nation-states and the need to generate loyalty and commitment on the part of the masses to the state—a necessity in the age of mass conscript armies. This was undoubtedly a motive, particularly in Germany, but also in Britain and the United States. Bismarck, who can be seen as the founding father of the modern welfare state, certainly saw it in these terms. One gloss on this is the radical left-wing view that the welfare state is actually a capitalist plot, and a necessary institution of late capitalism, thus making incorporationist beliefs part of the ideology of that stage of capitalist development.[50]

The final hypothesis, and perhaps the most suggestive, is that the actual historical development of capitalism, as opposed to its expected evolution, undermined the plausibility and social basis for the ideal of voluntarism and self-help. The relative decline of the artisan class and the growth of a large proletariat, along with the appearance of large firms, undercut the social foundations of voluntarism. Increased dependence upon employment and the diminution of alternative ways of making a living, when coupled with a trade cycle which seemed autonomous and uncontrolled, made the goal of individual welfare through self-sufficiency increasingly implausible to many people, particularly the lower middle classes, who underwent a substantial change in composition, social position, and aspirations at the end of the nineteenth century. The growth of a mass market and of modern consumerism also worked against the moral beliefs which were such an important part of the voluntarist ideal. In particular, they undermined the idea of personal independence and the related belief in the need to strive for happiness. This was reflected in the move in popular literature from self-help to success as the dominant theme, a transformation which was complete by the late 1920s. Suburbanism and commuting, which became central features of urban life from

---

[49] Harold Perkin, *The Rise of Professional Society: England since 1880* (London: Routledge, 1990).

[50] Richard A. Cloward and Frances Fox Piven, *Regulating the Poor: The Functions of Public Welfare* (New York: Pantheon, 1971).

the 1880s onward, were also blamed by contemporary observers for undermining the social networks which had sustained the practice of mutual aid. Many theorists of voluntarism, while vehemently supporting private property, markets, and individual enterprise, had been deeply critical of many aspects of emerging modern capitalism. Thus, for example, many had opposed limited liability and the growth of large corporations, the development of advertising, and the increasing domination of industry by pure capital. This opposition may have been farsighted and correct.

V. CONCLUSION

We now appear to be at a turning point similar to the one arrived at a hundred years or so ago. Now, as then, a way of thinking about the question of welfare is under attack and is increasingly seen, even by some of its supporters, as incoherent. One possible response may well be to return to other ways of thinking. Part of the argument of this essay has been that at present the incorporationist way of conceiving of social problems is still structuring debate, but there are signs that voluntarist ideas are reviving—in Britain on the left as well as the right. There is more awareness of the issues of morality and character raised by welfare policy and of the need to promote individual independence. Perhaps more significant is the practice of individuals and groups confronted with the growing fiscal crisis of the welfare state. Events such as the recent "Million Man March" in the United States show a revival of support for voluntarist ideas and practice. A revival of voluntarism may come, therefore, not from the thinking of intellectuals but as a product of the actual concrete actions of many people. There is also a growing feeling among the public and among commentators that a new turn in policy is needed to undo the social damage which is now so clearly visible. The historical record in both Britain and the United States supports the belief that a voluntarist approach is more likely to succeed. We should avoid the kind of historical thinking which sees the history of ideas as a one-way street in which there is a steady movement from one kind of thinking to another with no returning to older ways of thinking. Actual history shows that ideas and ways of thinking which have long appeared dormant or moribund can suddenly revive.

History, Manchester Metropolitan University

STANDARDS VERSUS STRUGGLE: THE FAILURE OF PUBLIC HOUSING AND THE WELFARE-STATE IMPULSE

By Howard Husock

I. Standards versus Struggle: Definition

In considering the development and course of the American welfare state, there are some places which are better starting points than others. One such place is the State Street corridor, the series of high-rise Chicago Housing Authority public-housing projects which loom over Lake Michigan. Most Chicagoans, like their counterparts in other cities, have become inured to conditions there: a murder rate far in excess of that of the city as a whole,[1] a society of unemployed single mothers, deferred maintenance that makes stairwells, plazas, and elevators places of danger. Author Alex Kotlowitz decribes the situation of a mother of two boys in Chicago's Henry Horner Homes: "She lived in daily fear that something might happen to her young ones. . . . Already that year, 57 children had been killed in the city, five in the Horner area, including two, aged eight and six, who died from smoke inhalation when firefighters had to climb the 14 stories to their apartment. Both of the building's elevators were broken."[2]

There is a tendency, to be sure, to ascribe conditions such as these simply to the personal and social problems of residents; and there is a tendency simply to view such conditions as inevitable, a function of life among the poor. But the projects in Chicago cry out to be viewed as another sort of phenomenon. The names of the Chicago housing projects point up the nature of that phenomenon. Robert Taylor—namesake of the infamous Robert Taylor Homes—was an African-American banker and student of architecture, dedicated to encouraging black home-ownership. Other namesakes of Chicago housing projects were equally distinguished. Jane Addams was a Nobel Peace Prize winner and the linchpin of the settlement-house movement, with its belief that the affluent had a duty to help the poor improve their lot. Ida Welles, former Illinois governor Henry Horner, Julia Lathrop, even Harold Ickes, a member of Franklin Roosevelt's cabinet and a key architect of the New Deal—were reformers all, in the

---

[1] "Poverty's Foundation," *The Economist*, April 11, 1993, p. 27. Although the Taylor Homes, located in the State Street corridor, house one-half of one percent of Chicago's population, they account for 11 percent of its murders.

[2] Alex Kotlowitz, *There Are No Children Here* (New York: Anchor Books, Doubleday, 1992), p. 17.

Progressive Era tradition. They were members of a movement which, as described by Chicago architectural historian Devereux Bowly, Jr., "saw public housing as a major component in the effort to rid the city of slums, and transform those at the bottom of the social spectrum into healthy, upwardly mobile citizens." Instead, he writes with great understatement: "There is no evidence that the housing has helped to make the residents more self-sufficient or contented, in fact the opposite may well be the case."[3] That the names and, indeed, the life's work of serious civic leaders and dedicated reformers are now associated with places casually considered to be among the most abject in Chicago, and even the most abject in the United States, is an irony so profound that it demands the deepest sort of consideration.

Many theories have been advanced to explain this incongruous outcome. Design is prominently mentioned, although there are many low-rise public-housing projects with problems as great as those of the State Street corridor's high rises.[4] Incremental public policy decisions are cited, as well—such as legislation which placed a ceiling on the rent paid by project tenants, and thus led to a limit on funds available for maintenance. Perhaps these and other factors have, in fact, played their role. But the difference between utopian vision and tragic reality is so great in the projects of Chicago that these factors seem unlikely to have mattered much. This is to suggest that, indeed, the failure of Chicago public housing is among the best symbols available of how far the reach of the welfare state has exceeded its grasp. It is a reach, I will assert, which, at its core, is based in beliefs which we have yet to confront fully, notwithstanding the failures which the welfare state has bequeathed to us—beliefs which share a key philosophical foundation with the socialist experiment which so devastated those countries which undertook it.

A. A link between welfare-state programs and "real socialism"

The collapse of socialism has not settled the social policy debates in the West over the content and form of the welfare state. In part, this is the result of the belief that the democratic welfare state, whether that of Bismark's Germany, Sweden, the New Deal—or public housing in Chicago—has differed in key respects from the sort of real socialism which evolved in Eastern Europe and the Soviet Union. The distinction is an understandable one. In contrast to the Soviet system, the Western welfare state has coexisted with democratic political institutions and a

---

[3] Devereux Bowly, Jr., *The Poorhouse: Subsidized Housing in Chicago, 1895–1976* (Carbondale: Southern Illinois University Press, 1978), p. 221.

[4] The National Commission on Severely Distressed Public Housing, *Final Report* (Washington, DC: National Commission on Severely Distressed Public Housing, 1992); see also Lawrence J. Vale, "Beyond the Problem Projects Paradigm: Defining and Revitalizing 'Severely Distressed' Public Housing," *Housing Policy Debate*, vol. 4, no. 2 (1993).

predominantly free market. Thus, it is tempting to say that the welfare state is unrelated to the systems which collapsed in 1989 and soon thereafter—especially because, for the most part, the Western welfare state did not adopt state planning and public ownership of the means of production, the hallmarks of the Soviet system. (There were exceptions, of course, such as national health-care systems and public housing. Even in these cases, however, Western democracies did not publicly manufacture medical equipment, pharmaceuticals, or construction materials; nor did government agencies themselves actually construct public-housing projects.) The distinction is important enough that any assertion that welfare-state programs are a "step on the road to socialism" can be characterized as extremism in contemporary political debates. No one who hopes to win policy debates suggests that mere expansions of the welfare state—whether in the form of health-care guarantees, credit allocations for inner cities, or increases in the minimum wage, all of which are issues of some currency—should be likened to socialism. Indeed, even in those cases in which the public sector did take a more classically socialist-style role (such as public housing), policy has tended to evolve in new directions (such as direct cash or voucher payments to individuals, or delivery of "social services" through nongovernmental, nonprofit organizations)— directions which, according to their advocates, constitute "reinventions" that have transcended past mistakes, and certainly have nothing in common with socialism.

There is, however, an impulse which discredited "real socialism" does have in common with the liberal public-policy initiatives which shaped the Western welfare state—and which it continues to pursue. It can be described as the impulse to favor standards over struggle. By "standards" I do not refer to the term as it is used in contemporary cultural debates, as in standards of education or morality, meaning higher standards of behavior or expectation. I refer instead to the belief that there must be certain minimums, whether of income, goods, or services, which policy must enshrine as law and use as a means to guarantee citizens a minimum level of overall economic security. This contrasts with the idea of struggle—by which I mean the gradual improvement (with the possibility of decline) of living conditions through the efforts of individuals and their private enterprises. Western welfare-state programs may not inevitably lead to full-blown socialist regimes, but they do share the impulse to minimize struggle, an impulse at the root of the problems which have plagued programs such as public housing.

B. The impulse to minimize struggle

In this essay, I will argue that we have not resolved our welfare-state debates because we have not come to grips with the tension between standards and struggle—which is to say that we have not been able to accept the fact that struggle is an inevitable part of the human condition and that no attempts to repeal it, through the disbursement of individual benefits, can long be sustained. To truly examine and evaluate the welfare state, we must confront the fact that efforts to substitute standards for struggle may—and often do—lead to short-term increases in comfort (as the newly opened public housing projects of Chicago surely did) but also consistently lead to problematic long-term outcomes.

As important as it is to evaluate the shortcomings of individual programs, however, it is even more important for us to come to terms with the (often unspoken) impulses and beliefs within ourselves which cause us to seek somehow to "repeal" struggle—to spare population groups from it, thus (ironically) exacerbating their social and personal problems. Insulation from struggle can, in effect, confine "beneficiaries" to a far worse form of struggle, a purgatory in which there is struggle without hope of improvement. Surely, barring dramatic change, that is the current fate of thousands of those living in Chicago Housing Authority properties. We must find ways of thinking which will allow us to resist the impulse to seek to suppress struggle. But what is that impulse about? Why does it arise?

The idea of a society in which struggle is somehow to be repealed, or minimized, is implicit in the vision of a society in which each can be assured of living not only according to his abilities but also "according to his needs." Needs imply minimal standards—a floor below which one must not fall. One can be said to *need* a certain number of bedrooms in a family apartment, a certain amount of time off from work, a certain level of medical care. In the socialist societies of the old Soviet bloc, the security offered by such standards was to be attained by creating a sort of steady-state society, one in which the same industries and technologies would indefinitely provide for needs defined by the state: numbers of shoes, apartment houses, automobiles. Ultimately, of course, such societies could not be buffered from the innovations of the West; the potential for change, improvement, and upheaval seeped across borders. In short, neither change, nor struggle in response to it, could be repealed.

The possibility, indeed the probability, of gradual change and improvement, is central to a life of hope, and is certainly an underpinning of free-enterprise economies. Perhaps if it were somehow possible to manufacture the same products in the same way to serve the same wants and needs in perpetuity, the case for socialism might be more persuasive. Instead, Western society accepts, as a fundamental, the belief that the creative impulse—harnessed to the production of better goods and services, and exchanged for personal rewards—makes change constant and inevitable. Put another way, we believe that struggle with hard problems can lead to improvement. As Jane Jacobs, an analyst of urban economies, has written of economic improvement: "All innovations, all new ways of economizing on materials, are, inescapably, masses of improvisations and

experiments, some successful and some not. . . . The practice of impro-
vising fosters delight in pulling it off and faith in the idea that, if one
improvisation doesn't work out, another likely can be found that will."[5]

And yet, as we consider the structure and reach of the contemporary
welfare state—something we do every time we debate what are called
social policy issues—we appear to be loath to integrate that core assumption about gradual improvement into our examination of public policy.
Instead, there is consistent pressure to favor standards over struggle,
especially as related to policy toward those of low income. Most often, an
argument based on the need for standards is advanced—and the potential
for gradual, but more enduring improvement through struggle is unacknowledged or unimagined. As Thomas Sowell has observed: the idea
of self-reliance is "mundane and unfashionable in our time."[6] What follows should by no means be seen as a criticism of all forms of altruism
and charity; I will cite examples of charitable efforts that are consistent
with the idea of assisting those who struggle. Nor should it be seen as an
absolutist bar on some sort of government role in arranging for such
assistance. Government, with its functions/charges to enforce contract
law and provide for public order, is a crucial foundation for those who
would struggle and achieve. At the same time, legally mandated minimum income levels, or de facto income standards, by diminishing the
incentive to struggle, risk pauperizing (i.e., permanently impoverishing)
the poor and robbing them and society of the fruits of their labor.

II. Examples in Which Standards are Favored over Struggle

To begin to understand the impulse to suppress struggle, I shall first
examine three aspects of social policy, all related to members of lower-
income groups and to their environs: public and subsidized housing;
"community reinvestment," i.e., mandated credit allocation to low-income
neighborhoods; and the legally prescribed minimum wage. These will
serve both as a demonstration of the rejection of struggle implied in such
policies and as a prelude to a broader discussion that attempts to come to
grips with the roots of the anti-struggle impulse.

A. Public and subsidized housing

The reformers who put forward the idea of public housing, and their
policy descendants who have insisted on the need for a variety of suc-
cessor subsidy programs, have been intent on providing poor tenants,
primarily, with ways of meeting at least two standards: (1) a "decent"
home in (2) a good, or "better," neighborhood. In practice, this has meant
a variety of things. Reformers—beginning with Jacob Riis, muckraking

---

[5] Jane Jacobs, *The Economy of Cities* (New York: Random House, 1969), p. 150.
[6] Thomas Sowell, *Race and Economics* (New York: McKay, 1975), p. 238.

author/journalist (*How the Other Half Lives*) in New York during the 1890s, and Lawrence Veiller, secretary of the National Housing Association during the first two decades of the twentieth century—first emphasized physical standards to which private-sector builders must conform. (These were codified in model building codes, proposed by reform groups and widely adopted by municipal governments.)[7] By the 1930s, however, crusader/writers such as Edith Elmer Wood and Catherine Bauer were convinced that the private construction and housing industries would inevitably produce "slums" for those of lower income. First at the state level, and later through the National Housing Act of 1937 (and generations of amendments to it), they succeeded in using the public-finance process to build apartment buildings that offered more and larger rooms, private baths, appliances, and other amenities than tenants could themselves afford. Rents were to be kept low both by raising capital through the sale of tax-exempt bonds and by operating the apartments through a not-for-profit public authority. The concept of standards was central to the reform vision: "By minimum standard of housing is here meant not minimum existing standard, nor minimum legal standard, nor minimum attainable-under-existing-conditions standard, but minimum health-and-decency standard. This should be the standard provided for in wage scales or health-and-decency budgets."[8]

Reformers explicitly despaired of the notion of incremental, individual-based improvements in housing and dismissed evidence that it was occurring. During the period from 1890 to 1930, for instance, truly vast amounts of new working-class housing were being built in American cities. In Philadelphia during that period, for instance, some 299,000 brick row homes were built—many of which have stayed in use. Data from the period show that a significant percentage of residents of poor neighborhoods lived, not in tenements owned by rapacious absentee landlords, but in small homes which they either owned themselves or in which the owner lived on the premises, renting out one or more units in addition to that in which he lived. As early as 1894, more than a third of residents in the poorest neighborhoods of Chicago lived in their own homes or rented homes in which the owner was also an occupant.[9] By 1930, census data for twenty-three poor Chicago neighborhoods showed that the percentage of homes owned by their occupants was fully double that of 1894.[10] It is noteworthy that, by 1940, Chicago had more than twice as many

---

[7] See, e.g., Lawrence Veiller, *Housing Reform: A Handbook for Practical Use in American Cities* (Philadelphia: William F. Fell Co., 1910). For Jacob Riis, see his *How the Other Half Lives: Studies among the Tenements of New York* (1890; New York: C. Scribner's Sons, 1903).

[8] Edith Elmer Wood, *Recent Trends in American Housing* (New York: The Macmillan Company, 1931), p. 39.

[9] *Slums of Great Cities: Seventh Annual Report of the United States Commissioner of Labor* (Washington, DC: Commissioner of Labor, 1894).

[10] Edith Abbott, *The Tenements of Chicago, 1908–1935* (Chicago: University of Chicago Press, 1936), p. 371.

housing units in two-, three-, and four-family houses (382,028) as it had single-family homes (164,920). In contrast to the public housing that would be built largely after World War II, the world of modest, owner-occupied residential structures can be said to imply a struggle-based vision of housing improvement. One could rent an apartment, or even a room (reformers called this "the lodger evil").[11] One could save money to buy a modest "workingman's cottage" (small single-family home) or small "tenement" (two to four units), improve it (perhaps helping to pay for it through rental income), then sell it and move up to a better home in a slightly more affluent neighborhood. Thus were new and better neighborhoods being built, such as those described by pioneering sociologists Robert Woods and Albert Kennedy, in their 1915 study of immigrant upward mobility in the U.S., as "zones of emergence" into the mainstream of American economic life.[12] It was a system in which—and here lies the sharpest, most central contrast to public housing—struggle helped forge social fabric: homes were cared for by owners, often with an incentive to maintain them for tenants, whose rental income they needed. Even some conditions which have been made to seem incontrovertibly bad— e.g., "overcrowding"—can also be seen as a way extended families marshaled their financial resources as part of the effort of upward mobility. There can be no doubt that there were difficult conditions but that incremental improvement was taking place, coincident with (and helping to spur) the growth of the U.S. economy.

Nonetheless, reformers explicitly dismissed the struggle of poor homeowners. Nathan Straus, appointed by Franklin Roosevelt to head the United States Housing Authority, the agency responsible for purchasing the bonded indebtedness of local housing authorities and thereby supporting public housing construction, wrote: "It is the truth that the purchase of a house on the installment plan cannot be recommended to families of small income. Government policies directed toward encouraging or facilitating such action are of very dubious wisdom."[13] Univer-

---

[11] *Ibid.*, p. 343.

[12] Robert A. Woods and Albert J. Kennedy, *The Zone of Emergence: Observations of the Lower Middle and Upper Working Class Communities of Boston, 1905–1914* (Cambridge, MA: Joint Center for Urban Studies of the Massachusetts Institute of Technology and Harvard University, 1962), p. 151. Writing about the large numbers of frame three-decker homes being built in Boston, Woods and Kennedy observe: "One cellar, one water and gas main, one plumbing shaft for three families, divide the cost of these by three for each family. The number of tenants that can be accommodated is, of course, multiplied by three and this is what has made possible such a large outpouring from the city proper."

[13] Nathan Straus, *The Seven Myths of Housing* (New York: Alfred A. Knopf, 1945), p. xi. It is worth noting that long-term mortgages did not come into widespread use until after the Depression; it had previously been common for payments to be made over a relatively short time period—perhaps five years—after which the owner would owe one large "balloon payment" to the lender (a payment which the buyer often could not afford). The development of federal institutions, such as the Federal Housing Administration, to encourage home ownership and the development of mortgage banking, is a reflection of the fact that housing reformers were only one of the interest groups influencing New Deal policy.

sity of Chicago sociologist Edith Abbott, writing in 1936, drew special attention to what she viewed as the problem of the "tenement landlord," decrying traits that others might find positive. Home-owning families, wrote Abbott, often took the least desirable units for themselves and rented out the better units. Resident owners, moreover, saw themselves as joining a "superior social group."[14] Not only struggle—accepting inferior units so as to accumulate capital—but the satisfaction that comes with a sense of status, offended the reform impulse, with its emphasis on egalitarian settings such as housing projects in which various income groups lived together.

The tragic results of the public-housing experiment have not inspired our present generation of reformers to accept the incremental progress of struggle over the cure-all promised by policy standards. Instead, they have opted for different strategies to minimize struggle. These include the use of "vouchers" which reduce the rental payments of lower-income tenants renting accommodations in privately owned buildings. Again, the goals of this subsidy policy are both to provide "decent" housing and to place lower-income families in "better"—i.e., safer, more affluent—neighborhoods. Housing and Urban Development department secretary Henry Cisneros has urged such an effort to minimize what HUD terms "spatial separation" of income groups. This philosophy shares many of the flawed assumptions of public housing—i.e., the inevitability of poor neighborhoods' being "slums," the inability of the private sector to provide adequate low-cost homes for those of low income. In addition, however, it can be seen as indifferent to another struggle: the dynamic of the formation of that part of civil society known as the neighborhood. In his 1979 book *Residential Patterns in American Cities*, the geographer Philip Rees found, based on census data, that "socioeconomic status is a universal sorting principle in American cities."[15] Rees found that people of similar incomes and educational backgrounds choose overwhelmingly to live together. Families strive to improve their economic position—to climb the ladder of upward mobility to a higher rung. They fear neighborhood deterioration and work to forestall it—to avoid falling to a lower rung. Conversely, moving to a more expensive neighborhood is one of the rewards for the economically successful. Whether one hopes to move up or simply to stay put in a good neighborhood, keeping a neighborhood safe and well-kept is in all residents' interests. Maintaining neighborhood property values is a key part of the glue that helps hold neighborhoods together, and draws citizens into community activities. Vouchers, in contrast, reward need—that open-ended term linked to standards—rather than achievement. In so doing, they can be seen as signaling to recipients

---

[14] Abbott, *The Tenements of Chicago*, p. 38.
[15] Philip H. Rees, *Residential Patterns in American Cities* (Chicago: University of Chicago, Department of Geography, Research Paper no. 189, 1979), p. 47.

that struggle is unnecessary and signaling to voucher holders' potential neighbors that their struggle is, to say the least, unappreciated. Thus, one can infer a key element of standard-setting: the undermining and/or invalidation of the efforts of those who do struggle. At the same time, housing subsidies ignore the ways in which struggle forges character by forcing those who would move to better neighborhoods to take the risks and initiatives necessary to rise.

B. Community reinvestment

The reform impulse in housing has not, however, been limited to the policy of public subsidies for housing construction and rentals for individuals. It has, more recently, led to a policy designed to ensure private-sector investment in poor neighborhoods. Typically, this investment is not the direct loaning of money to private owners or developers. Rather, it involves investments made in exchange for tax credits, in housing renovation projects which also receive various other forms of subsidy, such as rent payments for residents. All in all, this has led to what is arguably a new form of public housing, one in which banking regulation and the tax code are used to create subsidized apartment buildings run by nominally private nonprofit community groups.

The roots of this policy lie both in the failure of public housing and the search for an alternative. More broadly, it is linked to the population exodus from American cities after World War II and the subsequent physical decline of older, urban residential neighborhoods, which has been accompanied, inevitably, by diminished investment in such neighborhoods by financial institutions. Beginning in the mid-1970s, a variety of advocacy groups advanced the idea that the decline in credit directed to older neighborhoods was not so much a symptom of their decline but the cause of it. A sort of conspiracy, called "redlining" was alleged. As one account has put it: "Consumer groups focused particularly on [what they viewed as] the ... deliberate but unacknowledged policy of denying loans to lower-income, inner-city neighborhoods by banks situated in those neighborhoods."[16] To some extent, these charges were based in concerns about racial discrimination in lending, which, of course, cannot be defended. Nor, however, was it likely to persist, if there were financial gain to be realized in making loans to members of racial minorities in these areas. At any rate, the 1977 Community Reinvestment Act (CRA) went well beyond a concern with racial discrimination in lending, asserting, rather, that "regulated financial institutions have a continuing obligation to help meet the credit needs of the local communities in which

[16] David Jernigan, "The Community Reinvestment Act," Kennedy School of Government Case Study C14-80-336.0, Harvard University, 1980.

they are chartered."[17] As noted above, the term "needs" is an implicitly subjective and open-ended term—one that invites minimum standards. In practice, it has meant that banks which seek somehow to expand must demonstrate to regulators that either their existing branches in poorer neighborhoods, or the branches of banks they might acquire, have met the standard implied in "serving credit needs."

Although initially intended to assure that banks made investments in neighborhoods in some level commensurate with deposits drawn from those neighborhoods, the CRA has, in practice, worked as a source of pressure on major banks to invest in poor neighborhoods per se, as a demonstration of "social responsibility." Community groups, using the wedge of CRA requirements—as well as the lure of tax reductions for investors made possible by the 1986 Low-Income Housing Tax Credit— have forced financial institutions to provide capital for the renovation of abandoned apartment complexes, to be run by the community groups themselves as nonprofit ventures. As with public housing, it is far from clear that such nonprofit management will serve these communities well in the long run. An early study by the New School of Social Research of building maintenance in such properties, for instance, has found incipient problems not dissimilar to those found in public housing.[18] Examining the condition of thirty-four such developments, the authors of the study noted that "beyond [an] initial snapshot of relative well-being loom some major problems which, if unaddressed, will threaten the stock of afford-able housing included in this study." The study examined the buildings' exteriors, interiors, and systems (e.g., security, plumbing) and found that 62 percent of the properties had problems in at least one of these areas.

Why are we making such a substantial public investment in such "community reinvestment"? Again, the reform impulse toward minimum standards underlies it. It is assumed that neighborhoods deserve some sort of minimum credit allocation, regardless of the demand for housing in that locale. This means, of course, that directing capital to such neighborhoods is judged to be more important than a bank's maximizing return on its investment for its stockholders and depositors, a return which would almost undoubtedly be made greater through some other investment strategy. (If demand for housing in a neighborhood is low then, by definition, home values are not likely to rise and may, in fact, fall, jeopardizing the bank's investment in the event of foreclosure.) Just as significant as the issue of return on investment, however, is the message which the Community Reinvestment Act sends to individuals. In effect, it seeks to assure seekers of credit who live in specific neighborhoods that their loan requests will be approved because banks have an obligation to make the

---

[17] *Ibid.*, p. 2.

[18] Rachel Bratt, Langley Keyes, Alex Schwartz, and Avis Vidal, *Confronting the Management Challenge: Affordable Housing in the Non-Profit Sector* (New York: Community Development Research Center, Graduate School of Management and Urban Policy, New School for Social Research, 1994), p. 106.

requisite numbers of loans in that neighborhood. Just as the sheer fact of employment qualifies jobholders for a minimum wage, the fact of residence or desire for residence in a given neighborhood would, by the standard of the CRA, help to qualify credit-seekers for loans. One's zip code could matter more than one's creditworthiness.

The struggles overlooked and/or discounted in the thinking behind community reinvestment policy relate both to individuals and to their work together as neighbors. First, it is a far different matter for an individual, or a housing developer, to assert that he deserves credit on the basis of residence (census tract or zip code) than to assert that he deserves it on the basis of the accomplishments which are implied in traditional lending criteria: tenure of employment and credit history, for instance, for individuals; or business plan and capitalization for developers. Saving money for down payments or exerting effort to hold a job are the sorts of struggles which have great value for individuals but which are, inevitably, deemphasized by the standards of community reinvestment. Still, one must acknowledge that it may be possible for creditworthy individuals to be denied credit because banks are dubious about a neighborhood as an investment vehicle. Individual struggle and accomplishment may pale before the lack of demand on the part of potential buyers of housing in an overall area. To counteract such possibilities, individuals must struggle together to create neighborhoods which are attractive to others—and therefore can be attractive to lenders. One would be naive or insensitive not to recognize this as a burden and a challenge; but this is among the most important kinds of work which one can do in civil society—creating a social fabric. This is the work which is too often not done in public housing, because of an ownership structure which provides no incentive to do it. (Other forms of housing subsidy are no better at offering such an incentive.) There is no doubt that the task of creating a social fabric is complicated for individuals in poor neighborhoods because of the fact that there are, in their midst, so many whose incomes are subsidized through welfare payments of various sorts—payments granted to support child-rearing (Aid to Families with Dependent Children), the purchase of food (food stamps), and medical care (Medicaid). In the absence of struggle to attain these goods, one can be robbed of the incentive to improve one's situation, or, indeed, of the belief that it can be improved.

Still, it is only the prospect of the employed, law-abiding creditworthy poor, working together to create good (if modest) neighborhoods, that can be viewed as the long-term path to attracting "reinvestment." Credit allocations, fixed to a standard, may create the illusion that such work to build social capital is not needed; and such allocations will lead to protracted suffering when it becomes clear that improved physical surroundings—attained through subsidy—do not a neighborhood make.

It is worth considering, as well, whether public support for existing structures and residents of declining neighborhoods may stand in the way of those locales' finding new purposes—perhaps even nonresidential purposes. As Jane Jacobs has observed, the economics of new ideas means that new enterprises need old buildings, with their cheap rents, as places in which to start up.[19] Such approaches might be considered akin to the approach of "benign neglect" once advocated by Daniel Moynihan (an idea greeted by no small amount of public ridicule). But this view— essentially that neighborhoods might best be left to adapt on their own to changed market conditions—may, like struggle in general, offer the better path to enduring accomplishment and prosperity.

C. *The minimum wage and low-wage employment*

The impulse to protect those of modest means from the passages of struggle goes well beyond such matters as housing policy, of course. Income policy—the attempt to assure those of modest means that they can somehow attain more in wages or other forms of assistance than the labor market would itself provide—is a bedrock of social policy as well. The fact that some forms of employment pay very modest wages has, historically, led to calls that such wages be augmented, either through state subsidies (the earliest of which goes back to eighteenth-century England)[20] or through a legally prescribed minimum wage, designed to transfer greater wealth from employer to employee. The 1996 congressional session in the United States saw the minimum-wage issue, somewhat unexpectedly, take center stage.[21] The proposal that there be an increase to $5.15 an hour from the former $4.60 relied on a classic standards-based argument, based in the belief that the rate of pay for any job must meet at least a specific level. The arguments for such an increase were presented as both moral and practical: only an increased wage will allow the working poor to afford what are said to be the necessities of life (another commonly cited standard). The impulse to increase the minimum wage was based, in part, on the view that denying employees such protection leaves them open to exploitive employers who will pay them less than a "living wage," a term recently cited by the city council of New York, which has sought to mandate a $12 minimum wage for employees of city contractors. "People who work should not be poor," insists Balti-

---

[19] Jane Jacobs, *The Death and Life of Great American Cities* (New York: Modern Library, 1993), p. 244.

[20] See Gertrude Himmelfarb, *The Idea of Poverty: England in the Early Industrial Age* (New York: Knopf, 1983), pp. 160–63, for a description of the so-called Speehamland system of government-paid wage supplements. In this system, wages were supplemented by public funds so that they would meet "a minimum level of subsistence, determined by such objective measures as the price of bread and the size of the family" (*ibid.*, p. 163).

[21] The issue had been simmering for some time, however. In his first State of the Union address and again in his 1995 address, Bill Clinton deplored the fact that the U.S. minimum wage of $4.60 had gone without increase for more than a decade and proposed that it be raised.

more mayor Kurt Schmoke, echoing a common belief.[22] Such contemporary arguments resemble those advanced by Supreme Court Justice Charles Evans Hughes, in his 1937 opinion upholding state minimum-wage laws for women and children:

> The exploitation of a class of workers who are in an unequal position with respect to bargaining power and are thus relatively defenseless against the denial of a living wage is not only detrimental to their health and well-being, but casts a direct burden for their support upon the community. What these workers lose in wages the taxpayers are called upon to pay. The bare cost of living must be met.[23]

On this view, one standard implies another: failure to provide standard wages means that some minimum income or basic food and lodging would have to be provided by some other means.

As with any standards-based claim, there is a countervailing possibility, which is implicitly discounted. In this case, minimum-wage advocates ignore the possibility that the minimum-wage-earner will, over time, improve his status: by struggling to perform well, to augment his skills and marketability, to find better-paying work. Those willing to countenance struggle have understood the incremental nature of such improvement. Minimum-wage laws, Milton Friedman has written, penalize the poor (and poor minority group members in particular) by preventing them from gaining experience through working at low-wage jobs: "On-the-job training—the main route whereby the unskilled have become skilled—is thus denied them."[24] Moreover, getting such training may require a series of jobs which, on a variety of levels, offend, by their nature, the sensibilities of those who would raise the minimum wage: sweeping floors, shining shoes, cleaning bathrooms.

Indeed, minimum-wage advocates have been content to see lower-wage, entry-level jobs simply disappear. As retail grocers have noted: "In ours and other service industries, there are plenty of jobs to be done that are no longer done because the minimum wage has made their cost prohibitive. Service station attendants, grocery store bag boys, soda fountain workers, carhops, all manner of errand-runners and clerks have been greatly reduced in number or eliminated entirely because of the higher minimum wage."[25] The impulse to buffer the poor from the struggle of modest employment and incremental gains is, by all appearances, a pow-

---

[22] From a report on the minimum wage, broadcast on the Cable News Network, January 8, 1996.

[23] *West Coast Hotel Co. v. Parrish*, 300 U.S. 379 (1937).

[24] Milton Friedman, *An Economist's Protest* (Glen Ridge, NJ: Thomas Horton and Company, 1972), pp. 144–45.

[25] Quoted in Vlad Jenkins, "The Urban League and the Youth Subminimum Wage," Kennedy School of Government Case Study C15-86-720.0, Harvard University, 1986, p. 4.

erful one—one which, indeed, transcends the strategy of minimum wages to the point of prohibiting certain kinds of work outright. Consider the story of the municipal garbage dump in Manila, capital of the Philippines, where some fifteen thousand squatters were, in September 1995, said to support themselves by sifting through trash for items of value. That notwithstanding, the specter of families thus making their living led to pressure on the Philippine government to announce plans to level the dump and seek to redevelop it for industrial purposes. According to one account, this effort was undertaken despite the opposition of the scavengers themselves,[26] who had effectively organized an integrated salvage operation, wherein some found iron, tin, or plastic and sold it to others who acted as go-betweens to wholesalers, providing materials to manufacturers. In the confrontation between standards and struggle, theirs was a rare, organized voice asserting that struggle—its difficulty and unattractiveness notwithstanding—holds the promise of long-term improvement.

Of course, there will be some beneficiaries of a minimum-wage increase. Some number of lower-skilled persons will be hired, in effect, for more than their market worth. Even those fortunate minimum-wage employees, however, may be viewed as having been denied the chance to struggle, the chance to savor the achievement of attaining a higher wage, a struggle which tests and may expand individual capacities.

There are myriad other issues affecting people of low income which can be seen through this prism. There is the concept of a minimum income, even for those who do not work, for instance, which was once a topic of lively debate during the Nixon administration: Would it ensure access to a market basket of "basic needs," or would it, like a minimum wage, undermine the incentive toward incremental improvement? There is the question of whether government should use tax revenues to guarantee a standard level of old-age retirement income. Might the struggle to save and invest better serve individuals in the long run? Should affirmative action guarantee places in graduate schools or government contracts for African Americans? Or might struggle with the residue of racism—in the absence of legal discrimination—be the best way, or the only way, ultimately to expunge it? On the international level, does "development assistance" assure equity among nations, or does it undermine the struggle toward modernization taking place in poorer countries?

Similarly, there are other public policies which seek to mandate a minimum legal level of quality for specific commodities, at the risk of diminishing overall supply of such goods, much as the minimum wage dampens the supply of jobs. Indirectly, these policies may deny individuals the chance to struggle to move up from cheaper to more expensive versions of that good. This can be true of housing, where minimum room-size standards or rent controls may discourage construction of dwellings; or it can be true of child-care centers, where high education requirements for

[26] "The Philippines: Smoking Mountain Blues," *The Economist*, September 9, 1996.

staff members force up salaries and fees. In both cases, such standards then lead, inevitably, to calls for cross-subsidies funded by tax revenues, as has been the case with the provision of health care. The push for higher standards, as opposed to minimalist, basic medical-insurance plans, has led to calls for public financing of the entire health-care system. Implicit in such calls is the belief that people should not have to struggle to maintain their health (or that it is beyond their control)—or that they would not be willing to do so in order to save money.

Strong arguments can thus be made that public policies which seek to minimize struggle have predictably bad side-effects, that they offer powerful disincentives to self-improvement (welfare payments, minimum wage), to the stewardship of property and the accumulation of wealth (housing subsidies), to the development of informal institutions of civil society that bind neighborhoods (community reinvestment programs). My aim here, however, is not to analyze these various policies only in order to highlight these sorts of undesirable side-effects. Rather, assuming that such side-effects exist, that they have been powerfully demonstrated in such policies as public housing, we must next seek answers to a series of crucial questions: What prompts people to advocate policies which prefer standards to struggle? What assumptions about the world do they make? Can those assumptions be influenced so as to make struggle more palatable to those who would seek to minimize it?

III. Motivations of Those Who Favor Standards over Struggle

In this section, I shall describe and critique a series of beliefs—i.e., ways of seeing the world—which would lead one to favor standards over struggle. These are assumptions which have both ideological and psychological bases and which—although I shall try to advance reasons for viewing them as erroneous—have a strong hold on many adherents. I want to suggest that, to consistently favor standards over struggle, one must subscribe to one or more of the following viewpoints.

A. Snapshot theory

Housing reformers—beginning with Jacob Riis, who literally photographed the poor of New York's Lower East Side near the end of the nineteenth century—based their prescriptions (ultimately, public housing) on a view of the world formed by images of those they considered to be living in abject conditions. Implicit in their response is the assumption that, absent intervention, the conditions observed in a snapshot will continue indefinitely. Incremental improvement does not show up in photographs or succinct descriptions of conditions at a given moment. The process by which families decided to take in boarders, to seek extra income, or to take any of the other steps necessary to leave the nineteenth-century Lower East Side for one of the expanding outer boroughs, such as Brooklyn or the Bronx, can pale, in its emotional impact, beside the mental image of the family currently living in "substandard" conditions. There is a general point in this. To subscribe to the snapshot theory, one must believe that, absent public measures, conditions simply will not improve. This is an assumption contradicted by the economic expansions of the twentieth century and the growth of the middle class. But it retains a power, perhaps magnified by film and television, which portray immediate situations in emotional terms, effectively inviting one to seek a happier ending to the story.

Those who respond to snapshots turn naturally to minimum standards. If one is emotionally affected by images of people who are sick but lack health insurance, one may turn to a standard mandating such insurance. If one is touched by the plight of employees who have lost their jobs, one may advocate standards of government support for businesses that are major providers of employment. In both cases, the snapshot ignores the churning that comes with struggle: the person who chooses not to buy health insurance when he has no dependents and is trying to save money, but who later obtains it; or the new businesses which are born as older ones are dying. The attempt to ameliorate problems portrayed in a snapshot inevitably ignores the kind of self-correcting processes which are the result of human endeavor.

B. Too great a challenge

One may believe in the possibility of change and improvement—i.e., that the snapshot need not be permanent—but still believe that the challenge of rising is too great for those at the lower end of the income spectrum. This, in effect, is a patronization/infantilization of the poor: the belief that permitting those of modest means to struggle is wrong because they are not up to it, or because the task is too hard (e.g., working and raising children with only minimal health insurance). Surely this risks being a self-fulfilling prophecy. For how can one be sure of such a judgment? Is it really one's place to decide such a matter for others? The establishment of social policy standards inevitably draws populations into systems in which struggle may be explicitly discouraged. In public housing, for instance, those who earn higher incomes must pay higher rent. Similarly, U.S. public assistance recipients who amass savings can disqualify themselves for benefits. In such circumstances, floors (minimums) can become ceilings.

C. Not in their shoes

Another possible motivation for favoring standards over struggle may lie in the social and economic distance between those who favor standards and those who are engaged in struggle. The middle-class reformer who supports liberal, standards-based policies may simply shrink from the reality of struggle as experienced by the poor. In part, this is a response based in imagining himself falling from grace—i.e., suddenly finding himself in a situation with many fewer comforts and amenities. He may be motivated, then, by the belief that he himself could not be successful in reduced circumstances. Imagining that he would want to be spared such a fate, the reformer is inspired to spare others similarly. Such an impulse ignores perspective: if one perceives oneself—or one's children—to be climbing upward, a modest station is far more acceptable than if one has experienced a fall.

Of course, not everyone is climbing upward; but the fact that someone lives a life of modest, even quite modest, economic means is not a prima facie case for public policy intervention. The middle-class reformer may be hard-pressed to imagine life at a modest station: as a day laborer living in a single room, or a member of a low-income family which never takes out-of-town vacations. Again, the middle-class reformer shrinks at such a prospect and finds it difficult to imagine others finding satisfaction—through family, neighbors, social clubs, mass media—in such a life.

D. The generational issue

A serious objection to the idea of incremental improvement through struggle is one that can be characterized as generational. If today's sacrifice leads to tomorrow's greater wealth, what of the lives of those who are sacrificing? The efficiency of a corporation may be enhanced by reducing its workforce—but some of those who lose their jobs may experience a decline in their own standard of living, which may never be reversed. Rural peoples uprooted from inefficient farms and drawn to the cities—whether to Dickens's London or present-day Sao Paulo or Lagos—may be caught up in a process of modernization which will ultimately transform and improve their countries; but their own lives may well be made worse.

It can, in such circumstances, seem just to seek to ameliorate, through income redistribution, the condition of those who suffer. Put another way, one may believe that if the struggle of some is a hopeless one, there is an ethical obligation on the part of others to help in a continuing, systematic way. On reflection, however, a solution to the generational issue can be seen as a point on a horizon which may never actually be reached. Consider what happens when one moves to provide generous pensions for the present-day elderly poor. There is no doubt, of course, that doing so provides near-term improvement in their lives. At the same time, however, it takes capital away from those who are currently active wage earners. Lacking those funds to invest, or having diminished incentive to earn, those currently active in the economy will produce less wealth. Funds transferred as pensions to the elderly only have meaning in a productive economy. (The examples of German hyperinflation of the 1930s and the pensions of elderly Russians today are sobering.) Absent the context for enjoying pension benefits, they become nothing but scrip—paper money without value. More broadly, the impulse to suppress struggle because its benefits, inevitably, lag behind its costs, overestimates the possibility of distributing real—i.e., valuable—benefits. To the extent that the redistribution of income curtails or inhibits economic growth, standardized benefits only appear to ease the struggle of beneficiaries. In the long run, if the overall wealth of the society diminishes or does not keep pace with population growth, a steady stream of apparent benefits will not prevent pensioners from being left disappointed and vulnerable. Pensioners, in other words, must rely on the productivity of subsequent generations; to the extent that the distribution of standardized benefits inhibits productivity, the "benefits" enjoyed by pensioners may be meaningless. This is not to rule out the idea that there should be an attempt to ameliorate the situation of those in abject circumstances; the point is that attempts to use public funds to help individuals attain minimum standards of living will likely be self-limiting. As Jane Jacobs has written:

> It seems unfair that programs undertaken out of compassion or to combat the injustice of poverty in regions that remain obdurately poor should unwittingly work as instruments for spreading stagnation and deepening poverty. But one might as well say that it isn't fair for unfertilized soil to deplete itself when it is exploited to feed the hungry rather than for less defensible purposes. The soil doesn't know the difference; neither do economies being drained of the nourishment they need to remain creative and productive. . . . Subsidies . . . are economic time bombs. They help buy tranquillity as long as they can be afforded—but not longer. When they must be drastically curtailed, or when inflation renders them meaningless, societies that have depended on them become distraught socially and politically.[27]

E. System failure

One may sincerely believe that within a market-based economic system, struggle is futile, and that there will inevitably be an unemployed (and/or underemployed) labor force whose situation is an aspect of "the system," and not due to a failure of will. One may then believe, for moral reasons (e.g., no one should starve, no one should freeze) that a minimum-income standard is required. Or one may believe that such a standard is needed to protect those who benefit from the economic system from a revolt from below. (One might well believe the latter and publicly assert the former.) The minimum-income system may not be called that: it may combine in-kind provision of goods and services, public employment, and direct income transfers. But whether benefits are cobbled together

---

[27] Jane Jacobs, *Cities and the Wealth of Nations* (New York: Random House, 1984), p. 194.

from various parts or not, the belief in "system failure" leads to the call for a minimum-income standard.

Calling for such a standard, however, requires one to ignore notable historical trends. Consider, for example, the work of early sociologist Robert Hunter, who, in 1904, calculated the percentage of Americans living in poverty at that time, using an annual income of $460 (a cutoff he acknowledged to be low) as the dividing line between poor and nonpoor. By that standard, Hunter calculated that at least 20 percent (ten million people) of the United States population could be classified as living in poverty. Contemporaries of Hunter agreed that a cutoff anywhere from $600 to $750 a year might have been a more accurate figure, a change which would likely have doubled Hunter's poverty estimate. Hunter himself conceded that he had "endeavored to be as conservative as possible in [his] estimate of the extent of poverty."[28] In estimating the number of poor today, no analogous advocate for public measures to reduce poverty makes a claim in Hunter's ballpark. For instance, in his 1988 book *Poor Support*, economist David Ellwood estimates the poverty population (those whose income *before government support* places them below the poverty line, set at approximately one-third of the median income for a comparable family) at *no more than 11 percent*.[29] (It is difficult to compare, via calculation, the Hunter and Ellwood poverty lines. It seems clear, however, from Hunter's own arguments, that he set the nonpoverty threshold at a point he considered very low. Thus, it is quite likely that the overall level of economic improvement since Hunter's time has been even greater than that suggested by comparing a 20 percent poverty rate to an 11 percent rate.)

If one accepts the apparent long march toward economic improvement, one can, of course, still believe that there will be a sector of the population immune to such change. But that alone is not a case for a social policy — for efforts to substitute standards for struggle. In order to justify creating the sort of alternative economy that standards imply — one of continuing minimum income and benefits for many who are not working — one must believe further that, absent intervention, the excluded population will remain so over time; one must believe that there is a class of physically healthy unemployables who must simply be comfortably maintained. Absent such assumptions, there is no convincing rationale for a system of open-ended benefits, based on relative need. If many members of the lowest economic groups are likely to rise, why risk the system of disincentives, which have given us the State Street corridor in Chicago — a world largely without property ownership, without personal achievement, and without the behavioral norms that these things necessitate? Certainly, one can maintain that public assistance will provide the leg up

---

[28] Robert Hunter, *Poverty: Social Conscience in the Progressive Era* (New York: Harper and Row, 1965), p. 350; see also the introduction by Peter d'A. Jones, p. xix.

[29] David T. Ellwood, *Poor Support: Poverty in the American Family* (New York: Basic Books, 1988), p. 89.

that will allow the poor to struggle successfully; but such an argument discounts a powerful idea: that without the pressure to struggle, one is far less likely to do so. In this light, the data developed by David Ellwood and Mary Jo Bane—who found that one quarter of U.S. public-assistance recipients receive welfare payments for ten years or more and consume some two-thirds of all benefits—is sobering.[30]

F. Rewards of altruism

The beliefs described above—the "snapshot fallacy" and the others—may all be considered to be good-faith errors, steps taken in the belief that society will improve because of them. There are, however, other motives underlying the middle-class reform impulse which one can identify, which are less benign in motivation, even if they are not consciously expressed. In thinking along these lines, we must consider what might be called the origins of altruism—the act of helping others. Genuine, interpersonal altruism is, to be sure, a deep-seated and complex aspect of human nature. As Lauren Wispe, a specialist in communications and psychology at the University of Oklahoma, has observed in considering the emotion of sympathy, a precursor to altruistic action: "[T]he most difficult question to answer about sympathy is why? Why would people willingly make themselves unhappy? Why would people do for others ... ?"[31] Wispe posits two possible answers to such questions. One is biological: concern may stem from an instinct for species survival, or what social psychologist Leonard Berkowitz has called a "norm of social reciprocity."[32] On the other hand, notes Wispe, such concern "must compete with the drive for self-preservation, which is stronger." Thus, she notes, altruism depends on social support and social norms, which develop what Kant refers to as the impulse to "dutiful helping."[33]

We are familiar with the interrelatedness of such norms. Persons of wealth have, historically, in supporting charitable projects, had in mind their enlightened self-interest (preservation of the social order, diminution of health threats and social chaos), but they have also no doubt enjoyed the recognition and status rewards that come with charitable activity. Indeed, it is standard operating procedure for the parvenu to

[30] See David T. Ellwood, *Targeting "Would-Be" Long-Term Recipients of AFDC*, Report to the U.S. Department of Health and Human Services (Princeton, NJ: Mathematica Policy Research, 1986); and Mary Jo Bane and David T. Ellwood, *The Dynamics of Dependence: The Routes to Self-Sufficiency*, Report to the U.S. Department of Health and Human Services (Cambridge, MA: Urban Systems Research and Engineering, 1983).

[31] Lauren Wispe, *The Psychology of Sympathy* (New York and London: Plenum Press, 1991), p. 135.

[32] Leonard Berkowitz, "Social Norms, Feelings, and Other Factors Affecting Helping Behavior," in Leonard Berkowitz, ed., *Advances in Experimental Social Psychology* (New York: Academic Press, 1964), vol. 6, pp. 63–106, quoted in Wispe, *The Psychology of Sympathy*, p. 166.

[33] Immanuel Kant, *Groundwork for the Metaphysics of Morals*, trans. H. J. Paton (London: Hutchinson, 1956), quoted in Wispe, *The Psychology of Sympathy*, p. 167.

gain social standing by using a portion of his new-found wealth for charitable purposes. Even at the middle-class income level, charitable contributions and voluntarism combine both the enlightened self-interest and status rewards: the ability to devote discretionary time and income to unpaid works denotes a level of achievement and status. As Reinhold Niebuhr remarked: "We love what is weak and suffers. It appeals to our strength without challenging it."[34]

The ego gratification and social reward promised by altruism/compassion are significantly complicated by the growth of the welfare state. The use of the public purse to institutionalize/standardize "compassion" raises an ominous possibility: the opportunity for those of higher incomes (middle class and above, perhaps) to gain social status by associating themselves with advocacy for "programs," without making the sacrifice of charitable giving and without having interpersonal contact with those who are actually struggling. Garrett Hardin, in his 1977 attack on the idea of development assistance to poorer nations, has, in a phrase borrowed from Dickens, called such a possibility "telescopic philanthropy." Hardin pointedly observes that "[t]elescopic philanthropy is especially appealing because we are unlikely ever to hear of the mistakes we make. We can enjoy believing we are behaving altruistically without being forced to probe deeper into our motivation."[35] It follows that members of the liberal middle class—and even those with an interest in seeking a higher social status—have an incentive to associate themselves with advocacy for government programs for the poor. Making the image of altruism costless (i.e., no explicit marginal cost is involved, beyond tax payments) creates a reason for advocates of social programs to continue to support them, regardless of the programs' perverse incentives and undesirable side-effects. Thus, even those who are not social-service professionals employed directly or indirectly by welfare-state programs have an interest in continuing to support them. As political scientist Edward Banfield has written: "By far the most effective way of helping the poor is to keep profit-seekers competing vigorously for their trade as consumers and for their services as workers; this, however, is not a way of helping that affords members of the upper classes the chance to flex their moral muscles. . . ."[36] Put another way, there is ego satisfaction to be found in thinking of oneself as humane and liberal, in contrast to the purely greedy and self-interested.

An even darker possibility is that advocates of social programs are, unconsciously, acting in ways to protect their own interests (favoring self-preservation over species preservation). The poor can be troubled and dysfunctional—but they can also be ambitious, with much to prove and great reserves of energy. In that way, they can be a threat to existing

[34] Reinhold Niebuhr, *Beyond Tragedy* (New York: Scribner's, 1937), p. 155.
[35] Garrett Hardin, *The Limits of Altruism* (Bloomington and London: Indiana University Press, 1977), p. 127.
[36] Edward Banfield, *The Unheavenly City* (Boston: Little, Brown, and Co, 1968), pp. 250–51.

orders. In this context, social programs which provide minimal standard benefits—and reduce the incentive to strive—can be seen as an aspect of what economist Milton Friedman has called "the tyranny of the status quo."[37] This argument is a variation of one advanced, to make the case for relatively generous and easy-to-obtain public assistance, by sociologists/ welfare-rights advocates Frances Fox Piven and Richard Cloward. Piven and Cloward assert that welfare payments have varied historically in order to minimize "civil disorder and to regulate labor."[38] (Their assumption is that order is maintained in times of high unemployment by increasing relief payments; a shift in the business cycle would then dictate a reduction in benefits in order to push those on public assistance back into the workforce.) Piven and Cloward are undoubtedly on to something, though the system they attack can actually be seen as defensible: shrinking public-assistance payments (e.g., the decline in the real value of Aid to Families with Dependent Children over the course of the past ten years, because it is not indexed to inflation) has undoubtedly "regulated" the poor—but by keeping payments low, the system might actually encourage struggle and self-improvement. Were payments to be increased, as Piven and Cloward would favor, the incentive for struggle would diminish still further. Welfare-rights advocates such as Piven and Cloward would view measures to minimize struggle as a matter of moral duty. There is also another possibility they ignore, however: that there are reasons for those who favor higher standards to keep them high even in good economic times. Organized labor, for instance, might have guild-like reasons to restrict the labor supply. This impulse can be seen as related to the high-minimum-wage strategy: once effectively barred from the labor market by high minimum-wage rates, the poor receive the sop of public assistance.

Such policies, then, may have psychological as well as political appeal because of a deep-seated and widespread ambivalence about struggle, an ambivalence which extends beyond policy toward the poor. Those in business are willing to use government to shelter themselves from the vagaries of product markets; those in unions are willing to use their power to shelter themselves from the vagaries of labor markets. It may be natural to project—and to try to deliver—a life to the poor in which struggle is minimized. If struggle is the way we define ourselves, it still may never be something we will choose.

So it is that those who countenance struggle are vilified for what is said to be a lack of compassion, but those who believe compassion and the welfare state are synonymous can be seen as using public policy to protect their own social and economic positions. As implied in the foregoing

[37] Milton and Rose Friedman, *The Tyranny of the Status Quo* (San Diego: Harcourt Brace Jovanovich, 1984).

[38] Frances Fox Piven and Richard A. Cloward, *Regulating the Poor: The Functions of Public Welfare* (New York: Random House, 1971), p. 342.

discussion of altruism, my aim is not to argue against all forms of helping, or against public policy initiatives designed to ameliorate poverty. In considering such actions, however, we must seek to assist those who struggle, rather than seeking to repeal struggle itself.

IV. ASSISTING STRUGGLE: ALTRUISTIC EXAMPLES

The goal of assisting rather than discouraging struggle is a noble one, but one which is difficult to define. Does Aid to Families with Dependent Children assist struggle by giving poor children better nutrition and clothing than they would otherwise have? Or does it subvert struggle by luring recipients into an alternative economy whose floor becomes a ceiling? In general, I take the point of view in this essay that it is far preferable to assist the poor through means other than de facto income (direct payment, goods and services). Moreover, methods can be crafted to marry the impulse toward altruism with the benefits that emerge from personal struggle. Here follow two examples of approaches which would seem to do so.

A. The settlement house

Settlement houses were a major phenomenon associated with the waves of immigration to the U.S. during the period from 1880 to 1920. Although many of the leading lights in the settlement-house movement went on to become advocates for and architects of the welfare state during the New Deal, the settlement house itself can be seen quite differently. Named for the fact that many of their volunteers moved, or "settled," into poor neighborhoods, settlement houses—or what might today be called community centers—sought to broaden the horizons of the poor, providing social, recreational, and educational programs, and simple exposure to the milieu and values of middle-class volunteers. In Philadelphia in the 1890s, for example, the offerings of the College Settlement Association (so named because it drew volunteers from elite Eastern colleges) commonly included a "penny provident bank" to encourage children to save, as well as "hero clubs" in which members would discuss the lives of successful persons and how they had risen from humble circumstances. One good symbol of settlements at their best: Benny Goodman got his first clarinet from the staff of Hull House in Chicago. Settlement houses were privately supported and were generally nonsectarian. They were founded and run by the affluent and/or their offspring and offered everything from classes in child nutrition to "fresh-air" summer camps for entire families.

The scale of the settlement-house movement was significant: the *Handbook of Settlements*, published in 1911, listed no fewer than 413 such institutions in thirty-two states of the U.S.[39] (The movement was popular in Britain, as well.) In a single week in 1904, for instance, the annual report of Pittsburgh's Kingsley House from that year indicates that the settlement house served no fewer than 1,680 children and teenagers. Privately endowed, and staffed largely (though not exclusively) by volunteers, the settlement houses proved that a social policy can be crafted which is neither based on income standards nor operated by government.

It is noteworthy that settlements were not focused only on those residents of poor neighborhoods who had identifiable problems—a common aspect of "categorical grant" programs which serve poor neighborhoods today. Rather than seeking to serve and categorize people on the basis of dysfunction, settlements sought to provide uplift to those of modest means. Many settlement houses survive today, and though a large number are simply "multiservice centers" where a variety of government-supported "treatment" programs (e.g., counseling, drug and alcohol programs) are housed, others continue to serve as community centers offering everything from late-night basketball to college admission test tutoring. Enough of that aspect of the movement remains that it could, through relatively modest private support, be revived and expanded to significant effect.

B. Habitat for Humanity

There is no doubt that the settlement impulse, moreover, is extant. Consider, for instance, the growth of the volunteer-based organization Habitat for Humanity. The idea that a volunteer-based, nonprofit organization could grow to such a scale as to become a significant social policy force may seem fanciful in the welfare-state era. Nevertheless, coincident with the disillusionment with welfare-state practices—and with public and subsidized housing in particular—Habitat for Humanity has grown and spread to such a point. Its combination of altruism and encouragement for struggle takes the form of the construction of very-low-cost homes for poor families—built through contributions, volunteer labor, and the labor of the beneficiaries themselves. Founded in 1978 but virtually unknown until the early 1980s, "Habitat" has grown to have more than 1,100 local chapters and has erected more than 35,000 homes.[40]

In stark contrast to the public-housing impulse, Habitat emphasizes ownership. Families who qualify for Habitat homes get an implicit subsidy—the cost of the home is lowered through the work of volunteers and the use of donated materials—but they must still pay off a twenty-year mortgage on homes which would likely be valued at $50,000 but

[39] Robert A. Woods, *Handbook of Settlements* (New York, 1911). See also Judith Ann Trolander, *Professionalism and Social Change: From the Settlement House Movement to Neighborhood Centers* (New York: Columbia University Press, 1987).

[40] See Howard Husock, "It's Time to Take Habitat for Humanity Seriously," *City Journal*, vol. 5, no. 3 (Summer 1995).

which Habitat generally sells for around $30,000. (The recipient families involved—the overwhelming majority of whom hold low-paying jobs but do not receive public assistance—earn roughly $8,000 to $25,000 annually.) Moreover, in contrast to the workings of standards-based programs, need is not sufficient for a family to qualify for a Habitat home. Not only must they volunteer to help build their own home but they must have helped build another's, as well—and they must have passed what amount to character tests administered by local screening committees. Such committees scrutinize work history, housecleaning, even the behavior of children. Moreover, once Habitat's "partner families" become home-owners, they do not receive continuing assistance: the struggle to make their payments and maintain their homes is theirs, as is the achievement of ownership. Could the free market obviate the need for Habitat if building codes were relaxed so that the construction of extremely modest and inexpensive houses could be undertaken for those of modest means? This is a possibility. At the same time, there is a case to be made, as with settlement houses, that persons of limited horizons or sophistication may need a helping hand, and that society as a whole is better off if they are assisted in—but not relieved of—their struggle.

As Habitat for Humanity founder Millard Fuller has observed:

> The idea had been for the government to do everything. First we gave them highrises; then we just gave them money. They were nothing but clients, subjects. The people who devised these programs were people of good will. But they were basically saying there are a bunch of poor slobs who are barely human; let's just give them a few bedrooms and they'll be fine. [In my view], it is the greater blessing to give than to receive; recipients must also be allowed to give.[41]

It may not be possible, in the abstract, to convince those who would continue to favor standards over struggle that allowing the poor to struggle is not heartless. The building of real-world models which marry altruism and struggle, and produce results on a significant scale, may be the only way fundamentally to alter the course of the debate.

V. CONCLUSION

There is little likelihood, nor should we want there to be, that the private, nonprofit sector will come forward to replace public funding of social programs on a *one-to-one* basis. Rather, the withdrawal of public funding for various forms of income transfer should be accompanied by the emergence of a different sort of "poor support," one in which institutions help people on occasion, at key moments and in crises, but do not

[41] Millard Fuller, quoted in *ibid.*, p. 38.

provide continuing financial support. Moving toward such a world requires not only that model institutions be developed to serve as demonstrations and reminders of what a nongovernment social policy might look like, but that *humane ways of disengaging* from the present system be devised—both for moral reasons and to reduce the likelihood of political backlash. Further, it will require that the concept of struggle and incremental progress gain a renewed foothold in the public imagination. This is a slow, long-term process, one which requires that aspects of the standards or security-oriented mind-set be highlighted and understood as problematic. One could imagine that something like the "snapshot fallacy" might come to be viewed as akin to NIMBY (not in my backyard), the opposition of local communities to the placement of public facilities in their neighborhoods. Those who oppose the construction of such facilities in their area must now take pains to show that they are not simply indulging in NIMBY. Would that proponents of income standards and similar initiatives were at pains to show that they would not ultimately harm the prospects of "beneficiaries." Indeed, the crucial question may be this: How do we convince a society changed by the advent of the welfare state to change anew—and begin again to countenance struggle?

Can government itself create and operate programs which allow altruism and struggle to coexist? It may be difficult, if not impossible. It is difficult for government to say that some should receive help and others should not, as Habitat for Humanity does. It is difficult for elected officials to resist the pressure to "solve" problems—that is, to deliver near-term benefits which raise the short-term comfort level of those in relative need. This is not to assert that there are no functions related to social welfare in which government should play a role. Those whose struggle must be judged so great as to require standards of assistance for them—the severely disabled, for example—may not be able to rely solely on private support. This is not to say that government must operate the facilities and programs which support them. Similarly, government seems to be the logical institution to ensure that education will be available to all children—lest they be robbed of the tools that will aid them in their struggles. Again, this is not to say that government must itself operate the schools. Most important, it is government which, by giving form to the idea of a society of law, allows labor and investment to bear fruit. The temptation of the welfare state lies in imagining a government which purports to do more—and leads us, both as individuals and societies, to do less.

Public Policy, Kennedy School of Government, Harvard University

THE G.I. BILL AND U.S. SOCIAL POLICY, PAST AND FUTURE*

By Theda Skocpol

I. Introduction

The fiftieth anniversary of the death of President Franklin Delano Roosevelt arrived only months after the 1994 U.S. elections brought to power conservative Republican congressional majorities determined to reverse key legacies of Roosevelt's New Deal. At this juncture of special poignancy for many of those assembled at the "Little White House" in Warm Springs, Georgia on April 12, 1995, President Bill Clinton offered remarks on "Remembering Franklin D. Roosevelt."[1] "Like our greatest presidents," Clinton eulogized, Roosevelt "showed us how to be a nation in time of great stress" and "taught us again and again that our government could be an instrument of democratic destiny."

Suitably for the occasion, President Clinton spoke in broad thematic terms, mentioning just a few specific pieces of Rooseveltian legislation (including "the very emblem of the New Deal, Social Security"). Yet there was one enactment upon which he dwelt at surprising length. Roosevelt's "most enduring legacy," Clinton claimed, was a post–World War II "generation prepared to meet the future, a vision most clearly embodied in the G.I. Bill which passed Congress in June of 1944 just a few days after D-Day. . . ."

Clinton was referring to the Servicemen's Readjustment Act of 1944, popularly known as the "G.I. Bill of Rights."[2] This comprehensive piece of social legislation authorized generous educational and training vouchers, family allowances, up to a year's worth of transitional unemployment payments, and low-interest, federally guaranteed loans for homes, farms, and businesses. All of these benefits were made available to millions of soldiers returning from World War II, and subsequent "little G.I. bills"

* This essay was written with support from a 1995-96 Arthur Schlesinger, Jr. Fellowship from the Franklin and Eleanor Roosevelt Institute.

[1] All quotes from this speech are from Office of the Press Secretary, The White House, "Remarks by the President at 'Remembering Franklin D. Roosevelt,' 50th Anniversary Commemorative Services," The Little White House, Warm Springs, Georgia, April 12, 1995, 5 pp. typescript.

[2] For an overview of the 1944 G.I. Bill and basic facts about it, see Michael J. Bennett, "The Law That Worked," and Keith W. Olson, "The Astonishing Story: Veterans Make Good on the Nation's Promise," both in *Educational Record*, vol. 75, no. 4 (Fall 1994).

recapitulated similar though less generous entitlements for veterans of the Korean and Vietnam conflicts.[3]

The G.I. Bill, Clinton explained at Warm Springs, "gave generations of veterans a chance to get an education, to build strong families and good lives and to build the nation's strongest economy ever, to change the face of America. . . . The G.I. Bill helped to unleash a prosperity never before known." In Clinton's view, Franklin Roosevelt promoted the G.I. Bill because he "wanted to give returning G.I.s a hand up. He really captured the essence of America's social compact. Those people that served, they had been responsible, and they were entitled to opportunity." In "the '50s, the '60s, and the '70s all kinds of Americans benefitted from the economy the educated veterans and their fellow Americans built. . . . [W]e grew, and we grew together."

If the Franklin Roosevelt of Clinton's April 1995 commemorative speech comes off seeming suspiciously like a member of today's Democratic Leadership Council wing of the Democratic Party, we should not be surprised. People take inspiration from history to address perceived dilemmas and possibilities in the present. Although (for reasons I shall shortly explain) Franklin Roosevelt would surely be startled to hear that the G.I. Bill was his "most enduring legacy," from the vantage point of America's preoccupations today, the G.I. Bill is in many ways a model worth pondering. This remarkable landmark of U.S. social legislation does indeed have lessons to teach, provided that we are astute enough to make creative analogies across very different historical times and national challenges. In this essay, I first discuss the accomplishments and origins of the G.I. Bill, and then consider its possible relevance as a model for contemporary U.S. policymaking.

II. Historic Accomplishments that Resonate Today

Millions of Americans today worry acutely about getting the training and education they need to compete for good jobs in a national economy increasingly unforgiving toward the less formally educated, and toward those without adaptable, up-to-date skills. Against this backdrop it is easy to understand nostalgia for the G.I. Bill of 1944. Through that law some $14.5 billion in federal funds was spent between 1944 and 1956 to subsidize training for approximately half of those who returned from World War II (the 16.3 million who served, minus around 400,000 who died). Returning veterans were helped to obtain vocational training or higher education, preparing for occupations ranging from skilled industrial trades

---

[3] See Sar A. Levitan and Karen A. Cleary, *Old Wars Remain Unfinished: The Veteran Benefits System* (Baltimore, MD: Johns Hopkins University Press, 1973); and Educational Testing Service, *Final Report on Educational Assistance to Veterans: A Comparative Study of Three G.I. Bills*, submitted to the Committee on Veterans' Affairs, United States Senate, September 20, 1973 (Washington, DC: U.S. Government Printing Office, 1973).

to engineering, medicine, law, and business.[4] Overall, training or educational benefits went to some 7.8 million people, most of them young men (for less than 3 percent of those who served in the World War II military were women). Unlike previous federal expenditures on education—such as the Morrill Act of 1862, which subsidized the creation of land-grant colleges—educational spending under the G.I. Bill flowed directly to individuals in the form of grants for tuition, supplies, and living expenses. Individual veterans could choose the best kinds of training or education to which they could achieve admission. As a result, many sharply raised their aspirations, compared to expectations they had expressed in surveys during the war.[5]

Of the 7.8 million World War II veterans who received G.I. educational benefits, nearly two and a quarter million used them to attend colleges and universities. Compared to the share of college-goers they had previously attracted, America's top private and public institutions enrolled an unusually large share of the veterans who enrolled under the G.I. Bill.[6] About 20 percent of these veterans, and perhaps more, would not otherwise have achieved higher educations; and others would have had to settle for enrollment at less challenging institutions.[7] Without having to call on the resources of their parents, or compete with siblings in large families, many working-class and lower-middle-class young men gained access to even the best colleges and universities for the first time in U.S. history.[8] The G.I. Bill authorized tuition for up to $500 a year, which was at that time sufficient to pay for the most prestigious private colleges, such as Harvard.

Some elite college presidents were concerned about the influx of a broader cross-section of American society, fearing, as University of Chicago President Robert Hutchins put it, that "colleges and universities will find themselves converted into educational hobo jungles."[9] But the veterans proved to be unusually serious and successful students.[10] Their huge inflow in the late 1940s permanently transformed the U.S. univer-

---

[4] Bennett, "The Law That Worked"; and Raymond Moley, Jr., *The American Legion Story* (New York: Duell, Sloane, and Pearce, 1966), p. 281.

[5] Keith W. Olson, "The G.I. Bill and Higher Education: Success and Surprise," *American Quarterly*, vol. 25, no. 5 (December 1973), p. 601.

[6] Olson, "The G.I. Bill and Higher Education."

[7] The 20 percent estimate comes from the leading historian of the G.I. Bill. See Keith W. Olson, *The G.I. Bill, the Veterans, and the Colleges* (Lexington, KY: University Press of Kentucky, 1974), p. 102.

[8] Jere R. Behrman, Robert A. Pollak, and Paul Taubman, "Family Resources, Family Size, and Access to Financing for College Education," *Journal of Political Economy*, vol. 97, no. 21 (1989), pp. 398–419.

[9] Robert Hutchins, "Threat to American Education," *Collier's*, vol. 114 (December 30, 1944), pp. 20–21.

[10] Benjamin Fine, "Educators Praise Their G.I. Students: Colleges throughout the Nation Agree That Standards Have Been Raised by Veterans," *New York Times*, October 11, 1949, p. 35. A key study was Norman Frederiksen and W. B. Schrader, *Adjustment to College: A Study of Ten Thousand Veteran and Nonveteran Students in Sixteen American Colleges* (Princeton,

sity system into an avenue for mass mobility rather than gentlemanly certification.[11] Only about nine out of a hundred young people attended college in 1939, but that rate almost doubled (to sixteen out of a hundred) by 1947–48. "The higher education system was pushed through an irreversible expansion, and when veterans re-entered the labor force after further education, many did so in professional and technical fields. . . ."[12] Recent statistical studies conclude that the educated veterans personally benefited from increments to their incomes of up to 10 percent over what people with similar characteristics might in any event have earned.[13]

At the twilight of our century, U.S. citizens and policy experts alike worry about the difficulties of "family formation" for young adults. Setting up a stable, two-parent household has become increasingly difficult as real wages for young workers, especially men, have declined over the past two decades; as homes have become more difficult to afford; and as low-wage or entry-level jobs increasingly come without social benefits relevant for families.[14] Against this backdrop, the G.I. Bill once again looks retrospectively attractive.

In addition to funds for tuition and supplies, modest family allowances were provided under the G.I. Bill while veterans pursued their studies for between one and four years. About half of the veterans who attended college were married and a quarter had children, so families became a fixture on many U.S. campuses for the first time. Other provisions of the 1944 legislation authorized loans for purchasing homes or farms or setting up new businesses. G.I. loans helped some 4.3 million veterans purchase residences in the decade after World War II.[15] Under the 1944 G.I. Bill and its successors, some one-fifth of postwar mortgages for single-family homes became available at lower interest rates because of subsidies and guarantees by the Veterans' Administration; and practices in the long-term mortage market were changed in ways that opened up loans to many nonveterans as well.[16]

Overall, various provisions of the G.I. Bill served to make it easier for young families to form and to achieve sustained economic security in the

---

NJ: Educational Testing Service, 1951). For a full discussion and citations to many other studies, see Olson, *The G.I. Bill, the Veterans, and the Colleges.*

[11] Clark Kerr, "Expanding Access and Changing Missions: The Federal Role in U.S. Higher Education," *Educational Record*, vol. 75, no. 4 (Fall 1994), pp. 27–31.

[12] Paul Starr, *The Discarded Army* (New York: Charterhouse, 1973), p. 233.

[13] David O'Neill, "Voucher Funding of Training Programs: Evidence from the G.I. Bill," *Journal of Human Resources*, vol. 12, no. 4 (Fall 1977), pp. 425–45; Joshua D. Angrist, "The Effects of Veterans' Benefits on Education and Earnings," *Industrial and Labor Relations Review*, vol. 46, no. 4 (July 1993), pp. 637–52.

[14] On these contemporary conditions, see Richard B. Freeman, ed., *Working under Different Rules* (New York: Russell Sage Foundation, 1994); and Katherine S. Newman, *Declining Fortunes: The Withering of the American Dream* (New York: Basic Books, 1993).

[15] *Veterans' Benefits in the United States: A Report to the President by the President's Commission on Veterans' Pensions* (Washington, DC: U.S. Government Printing Office, 1956), pp. 300–306.

[16] *Ibid.*; and Moley, *The American Legion Story*, p. 282.

immediate postwar period. By the middle of the 1950s, almost half of Americans were veterans or members of their families. These (mostly younger) adults and their children were doing better educationally and occupationally than other Americans of their generation (in part because of help from veterans' benefits, yet also because those who fought in World War II were preselected for characteristics that helped survivors to succeed later).[17] As President Clinton stressed in his commemorative speech, the economic successes and social achievements of those directly aided by the G.I. Bill probably spilled over to fuel postwar economic trends that helped many more American families as well.

Lest the picture painted here seem too rosy, I should note two important problems with postwar veterans' benefits. First, while the G.I. Bill of 1944 may have helped millions of American men go to college, it set back female participation in higher education. This happened, of course, because over 97 percent of the World War II veterans were men. As they used G.I. benefits to crowd into the colleges, there was less room for nonveteran applicants, including females. Although absolute numbers of women students and graduates continued to increase with the overall expansion of higher education, the proportion of women compared to men declined in baccalaureate and postgraduate education, just as a huge expansion in the ranks of faculties and other professional occupations was occurring.[18] Women's presence in universities and in professional life therefore became less weighty than it might otherwise have been.

Arguably, trends since the 1960s have corrected the relative shrinkage of female presence in higher education temporarily occasioned by the G.I. Bill. But another problem area from the 1940s persists in U.S. economic and institutional life even today. Most who write or speak about the G.I. Bill of 1944 stress its beneficial impact on college attendance and mobility opportunities for veterans to move into managerial and professional occupations. Less often mentioned is what happened to the 5.6 million (71 percent) of claimants of G.I. educational benefits who undertook vocational rather than college training. Many of these veterans enrolled in programs that may not have done much to enhance their skills, or may only have provided training that could have been received through employers. During the late 1940s, fly-by-night commercial vocational "schools" often sprang up to collect G.I. tuitions, and the G.I. Bill provided no federal oversight adequate to ensure the quality or effectiveness of such enterprises.[19]

Federal benefits given to millions of individuals left free to choose how to allocate them work best when a suitable institutional infrastructure is

[17] *Veterans' Benefits in the United States*, ch. 3. For the continuity of this comparison into the 1970s, see Michael Taussig, *Those Who Served: Report of the Twentieth Century Fund Task Force on Policies toward Veterans* (New York: Twentieth Century Fund, 1974), pp. 51, 55.

[18] Susan M. Hartmann, *The Home Front and Beyond: American Women in the 1940s* (Boston, MA: Twayne Publishers, 1982), pp. 105–7.

[19] Starr, *The Discarded Army*, pp. 236–37.

already in place. America in the 1940s already had a nationwide network of excellent colleges and universities, which could, if necessary, expand and adjust to an influx of veteran students. But the United States did not then have—nor does it have now—an adequate nationwide infrastructure of vocational training arrangements, ready to do an effective job of preparing high school graduates for good jobs that really exist in actual local or regional labor markets. Recently some efforts have been made to stimulate closer, more effective links among employers, community colleges, public job-placement institutions, and assorted job-training ventures. Should more U.S. money end up being poured into training for those who are not college-bound, it would be vital for such institutional efforts to have made headway in advance. Otherwise, the earlier shortcomings of the G.I. Bill for the non-college-bound would be recapitulated in any future U.S. program of investment in job training.

III. An Unusual Kind of Social Policy

Despite a few shortcomings, the G.I. Bill was basically very successful. What is more, from a larger historical perspective it stands out as a most unusual kind of American social policy. Breaking the mold of both earlier and later federal undertakings, the G.I. Bill invested in young men and families at the inception of their prime years as workers and parents.

Prior to the 1930s and the 1940s, the most important efforts in U.S. social-welfare provision across all levels of government helped aging men and "dependent" mothers and children. As I have elaborated in my 1992 book *Protecting Soldiers and Mothers: The Political Origins of Social Policy in the United States*, elderly veterans of the Union Civil War effort received generous help around the turn of the twentieth century under the terms of the Dependent Pension Act of 1890.[20] In addition, from the 1910s onward, some American mothers and children received bits and pieces of help through pensions for survivors of Union soldiers, and through state-level mothers' pensions for needy widowed mothers. Between 1921 and 1929, moreover, the federal Sheppard Towner program offered subsidies to states and localities to pay for health workers to offer advice to pregnant women and mothers of newborns, advice that was in principle open to all American mothers. Meanwhile, though, working-aged men were left out of the early stages of nationwide social provision in the United States.

Even the Social Security Act of 1935 did relatively little for wage-earners at their prime (unless they later lost work in occupations covered by unemployment insurance). Thus, the G.I. Bill broke sharply even with the fledgling "New Deal tradition" by focusing on investments in young men right at the start of their occupational and breadwinner ca-

---

[20] Theda Skocpol, *Protecting Soldiers and Mothers: The Political Origins of Social Policy in the United States* (Cambridge, MA: Belknap Press of Harvard University Press, 1992).

reers. Yet the G.I. Bill was cohort-bound in the benefits it delivered: once the young veterans of World War II (and, to a lesser degree, those of Korea and Vietnam) had passed through the system, the investments of U.S. social provision in young men and their families dissipated too. Social Security and Medicare for all retirees, plus welfare aid for very poor mothers and children, were what remained in late-twentieth-century U.S. social provision.

Not surprisingly, as the United States approaches the turn of the twenty-first century, commentators of various partisan and intellectual stripes complain loudly about "generational bias" in U.S. social provision.[21] Meaning very different things, both the Children's Defense Fund and insurgent conservative Republicans call for America to legislate on behalf of "our children and grandchildren."[22] Urged on by investment bankers and insurance interests who want to privatize retirement savings, the fiscally conservative Concord Coalition complains that working-aged taxpayers have to cover the costs of allegedly overly generous social programs for America's elderly.[23] In the immediate postwar decades, U.S. federal social provision was much more balanced in its impact across the life cycle. Now that the investments authorized by the G.I. Bill are gone, the problem may not so much be that America is doing "too much" for the elderly. The real problem could equally well be that too little is being done through government to invest in young workers and families.

Soon I will return to the question of whether the G.I. Bill could serve as an inspiration for more generationally balanced social provision for the future. But first let us look back at why the G.I. Bill of 1944 happened in the first place. How did this exceptional program of large-scale investments in young workers and families come to be enacted in a U.S. policy that, both before and after the postwar conjuncture, has much more readily generated and sustained generous social benefits just for the elderly?

IV. The Politics of the G.I. Bill

Why the G.I. Bill of 1944 happened might seem obvious: millions of Americans volunteered or were drafted to serve in the U.S. armed forces during World War II, and afterwards they "had to" receive generous social benefits from a grateful nation. But this is, at best, an incomplete explanation.

[21] Further discussion appears in the conclusion to Theda Skocpol, *Social Policy in the United States: Future Possibilities in Historical Perspective* (Princeton, NJ: Princeton University Press, 1995).

[22] Children's Defense Fund, *Wasting America's Future: The Children's Defense Fund Report on the Costs of Child Poverty* (Boston, MA: Beacon Press, 1994); Newt Gingrich, *To Renew America* (New York: HarperCollins, 1995).

[23] Peter G. Peterson, *Facing Up: How to Rescue the Economy from Crushing Debt and Restore the American Dream* (New York: Simon and Schuster, 1993). On the groups pushing privatization, see Julie Kosterlitz, "Touching the Rail," *National Journal*, December 23, 1995, pp. 3136–40.

To be sure, the moral theme of benefits in return for service was central to the nation's understanding of the G.I. Bill—just as this principle has been crucial to all of America's great undertakings in social provision. Following the Civil War, pensions and other benefits were understood as justly given to the "Saviors of the Union."[24] In the early twentieth century, mothers' pensions and health services for mothers and babies were seen as legitimately given to homemakers, women who were then understood as serving the community and the nation by giving birth to children and properly caring for future American citizens.[25] Similarly, since 1935, Social Security benefits have been understood as returns for the "contributions"—not just of taxes but also of work—that employed Americans make over a lifetime prior to retirement.[26] In terms of their moral justification as rewards for loyal service to the nation, therefore, G.I. benefits nicely fit into a well-worn groove in U.S. political culture.

Even so, there are several problems with treating the G.I. Bill of 1944 merely as an automatic response to mass participation in World War II itself. True, the United States has a long history of remarkable generosity to veterans and survivors of its major wars. But where benefits for able-bodied veterans have been concerned, they have usually been granted long after the war in question was over—not until the veterans had become elderly, or else had accumulated sufficient political clout at home to tap significantly into the federal treasury. Peak portions of federal spending on veterans came some forty years after the end of the Revolutionary War, twenty-eight years after the end of the Civil War, and a decade and a half after the end of World War I. The usual kinds of general benefits for able-bodied veterans were straightforward payments—either pensions or "bonuses." Before the 1940s, U.S. generosity to veterans did not take the form of educational benefits or investments in youthful family formation.

The experience of veterans in the aftermath of World War I did not seem to bode well for soldiers returning from World War II. Very promptly in 1919, U.S. officers and soldiers from the World War I Expeditionary Force launched the American Legion, a nationwide voluntary federation. Over time, the Legion enrolled between 15 and 25 percent of all World War I veterans, and it spread more than ten thousand local posts across cities, towns, and rural areas in all of the U.S. states (though the Legion was weakest in the South).[27] Despite such strong and widespread organization, however, the American Legion ended up waging protracted and often frustrating political battles over benefits for veterans of World War I.

[24] Skocpol, *Protecting Soldiers and Mothers*, ch. 2.

[25] *Ibid.*, ch. 9.

[26] Skocpol, *Social Policy in the United States*, ch. 4.

[27] William Pencak, *For God and Country: The American Legion, 1919–1941* (Boston, MA: Northeastern University Press, 1989), p. 82; Richard Seelye Jones, *A History of the American Legion* (Indianapolis and New York: Bobbs-Merrill Company, 1946), chs. 15 and 27.

Veterans' organizations clashed horns repeatedly with both Republican and Democratic presidents of the 1920s and 1930s.[28]

Because pensions for Union veterans of the Civil War had become so generous and costly by the early twentieth century, fiscally cautious U.S. elites and reformist professionals became obsessed with heading off further "raids" on the federal treasury, whether by ordinary citizens or by World War I veterans.[29] World War I benefits were deliberately designed to feature aid and training for the disabled, along with government-subsidized life insurance *but not direct payments* for able-bodied veterans.[30] When the frustrated war veterans demanded more, Congress had to override a (second) Republican presidential veto to enact in 1924 a grant of promissory certificates for "adjusted compensation," or a "bonus" payment to able-bodied veterans.[31] Later, veterans would react to the economic crisis of the Depression by agitating for early full payment of the bonus certificates (which were supposed to be fully payable only after twenty years).[32]

During the 1930s, Democratic president Franklin Roosevelt was even more reluctant than his Republican predecessors to accept more expenditures on veterans. To help cut federal costs in response to the Depression, Roosevelt trimmed expenditures on veterans in 1933. Subsequently, he vetoed bills calling for advance payments of the bonus, until Congress overrode him in 1936. Extra help for World War I veterans was not a desirable priority in the eyes of President Roosevelt and many of those who advised him during the New Deal.

Boldly appearing before the American Legion national convention in 1933, Franklin Roosevelt explained his philosophy, which stressed building general social provision rather than providing "special" aid to able-bodied veterans. While "the Government has a responsibility for and toward those who have suffered injury or contracted disease while serving in its defense," Roosevelt declared to the assembled Legionnaires,

> no person, because he wore a uniform must thereafter be placed in a special class of beneficiaries over and above other citizens. The fact of wearing a uniform does not mean that he can demand and receive from his Government a benefit which no other citizen receives. It does not mean that because a person served in defense of his country,

---

[28] William Pyrle Dillingham, *Federal Aid to Veterans, 1917–1941* (Gainesville, FL: University of Florida Press, 1952).

[29] Skocpol, *Protecting Soldiers and Mothers*, discusses early-twentieth-century U.S. elite reactions against open-ended spending on federal social or veterans' benefits.

[30] Dillingham, *Federal Aid to Veterans*, chs. 1 and 2; and National Industrial Conference Board, *The World War Veterans and the Federal Treasury* (New York: National Industrial Conference Board, 1932), chs. 1 and 2.

[31] National Industrial Conference Board, *The World War Veterans and the Federal Treasury*, ch. 3.

[32] Dillingham, *Federal Aid to Veterans*, ch. 13.

performed a basic obligation of citizenship, he should receive a pension from his Government because of a disability incurred after his service had terminated, and not connected with that service. . . .[33]

In his May 22, 1935 veto message in response to a bonus bill, President Roosevelt became even more explicit about his New Deal philosophy. "[G]reater and broader concerns of the American people have a prior claim for our consideration at this time," he firmly declared. "They have the right of way." Roosevelt continued:

> There is before this Congress legislation providing old-age benefits and a greater measure of security for all workers against the hazards of unemployment. We are also meeting the pressing necessities of those who are now unemployed and in need of immediate relief. In all of this every veteran shares. . . . The veteran who suffers from this depression can best be aided by the rehabilitation of the country as a whole. . . .
>
> I am thinking not only of the past, not only of today, but of the years to come. In this future of ours it is of first importance that we yield not to the sympathy which we would extend to a single group or class by special legislation for that group or class, but that we should extend assistance to all groups and all classes who in an emergency need the helping hand of their Government.[34]

Once the New Deal of the 1930s was overtaken by mobilization for World War II, President Roosevelt adjusted his views about benefits for veterans, acknowledging that steps would need to be taken to compensate for the disruptions in education and employment suffered by millions of young draftees.[35] Yet as plans for postwar demobilization were developed by the Roosevelt administration and its liberal allies, these strategies consistently sought to address the needs of veterans along with those of war workers in general.[36] New Deal planners wanted to link benefits for veterans to an expanded and nationalized welfare state for all Americans. Equally important, in their minds every social issue during the war was viewed through the prism of the Depression-born expectation that the postwar U.S. economy might sink again into mass unemploy-

[33] Quotes are from "Address of President Roosevelt," *Proceedings of the Fifteenth National Convention of the American Legion*, Chicago, Illinois, October 2–5, 1933 (Washington, DC: U.S. Government Printing Office, 1934), pp. 15–17.

[34] "The President Vetoes the Bonus Bill, May 22, 1935," in *The Public Papers and Addresses of Franklin D. Roosevelt*, vol. 4 (New York: Random House, 1938), pp. 189, 190, 193.

[35] See Roosevelt's "Statement on Signing the Bill Reducing the Draft Age," November 13, 1942, in *The Public Papers and Addresses of Franklin D. Roosevelt*, vol. 11, compiled by Samuel I. Rosenman (New York: Russell and Russell, 1950), pp. 470–71.

[36] This account draws especially upon Olson, *The G.I. Bill, the Veterans, and the Colleges* (*supra* note 7), ch. 1; and Davis R. B. Ross, *Preparing for Ulysses: Politics and Veterans during World War II* (New York: Columbia University Press, 1969).

ment, unless federal planning and unemployment benefits were used to head off such a calamity.

New Dealers hoped to retain after the war a national system of unemployment insurance, plus a unified United States Employment Service designed to match workers to available jobs across the country. The idea was to use these federal programs, along with planned conversions of businesses from war to domestic production, to smooth manpower transitions for ex-soldiers and domestic workers alike. Meanwhile, two overlapping executive planning groups commissioned by the president—the National Resource Planning Board's "Postwar Manpower Conference" of July 1942 through June 1943, and the "Armed Forces Committee on Postwar Educational Opportunities for Service Personnel" (the Osborne Committee) of January through July 1943—both approached possible educational benefits for World War II veterans as tools for heading off unemployment and guiding men toward employment opportunities after the war.[37]

Acting on the recommendations of these commissions, the Roosevelt administration did not initially propose such broad educational benefits as those eventually embodied in the G.I. Bill. In alliance with elite educators from America's major colleges and universities, the Roosevelt administration and its congressional partners called during 1943 for a general veterans' educational benefit limited to one year, with only a minority of veterans selected for further university training. A combination of merit criteria, quotas distributed across the states, and federal planners' estimates of needs for specific kinds of trained manpower were to be used to select the lucky minority of G.I.s who could go on for more than one year of higher education. This would have been an elitist and centrally managed approach to educational grants, had it survived in Congress.

But of course very little New Deal "planning" of any kind survived in Congress after substantial Republican gains in the 1942 elections.[38] The president's advisory board for research and economic planning, the National Resources Planning Board, was voted out of existence by Congress during 1943. After that, the Roosevelt administration retained little capacity for overall planning and legislative steering, and it was riven by administrative rivalries. Would education benefits for veterans be administered by the Department of Education or the Veterans' Administration? Would the Labor Department retain a nationalized Employment Service, or would this function be reduced, broken up, and passed back to the states? On the domestic front, these were the issues that engaged officials of Franklin Roosevelt's late wartime administration most avidly during

[37] Olson, *The G.I. Bill, the Veterans, and the Colleges*, ch. 1.

[38] For an overview, see Edwin Amenta and Theda Skocpol, "Redefining the New Deal: World War II and the Development of Social Provision in the United States," in *The Politics of Social Policy in the United States*, ed. Margaret Weir, Ann Shola Orloff, and Theda Skocpol (Princeton, NJ: Princeton University Press, 1988), pp. 81–122.

the 1943–44 period. Meanwhile, congressional committees and alliances moved to the fore in shaping a variety of policies for late wartime and postwar America, including veterans' benefits.

Many observers have viewed the G.I. Bill of 1944 as a simple product of congressional conservatism, substituting special benefits for veterans for the comprehensive welfare state and full-employment guarantees for all Americans that liberal New Dealers had hoped to achieve. This view has much to recommend it, because the Roosevelt administration was frustrated in its efforts to achieve other national social policies during the 1940s. What is more, as proposals for veterans' benefits made their way through Congress, New Deal liberals (who held a bit more sway in the Senate) did end up compromising with congressional conservatives (who had more leverage in the House).[39] The compromises and modifications in Congress took the usual form for successful 1940s legislation: possible executive controls were removed, leaving benefits and subsidies going directly to individuals and to state and local interests. Thus, the final G.I. Bill mainly authorized grants and loans for individual veterans, to be delivered through any college or vocational school licensed by the states, or through private lenders.[40]

Yet in the final analysis the G.I. Bill of 1944 was no more a simple product of congressional conservatism than it was just a result of President Roosevelt's sponsorship. The very idea of a comprehensive bill for World War II veterans came neither from the Roosevelt administration nor from the Congress, but from the American Legion, which unveiled an omnibus proposal in January 1944 and dubbed it the "Bill of Rights for G.I. Joe and G.I. Jane"—an appellation soon shortened to "G.I. Bill of Rights" as a national publicity campaign was mounted.[41] Introduced by supporters in Congress, the Legion's comprehensive bill uniquely combined provision for the disabled, a full year's worth of unemployment benefits, up to four years of educational benefits open to virtually all veterans, and generous provisions for low-interest loans for homes, farms, and businesses.

Not only did the Legion initiate a bold omnibus approach, it stimulated the national publicity and grassroots pressure on Congress that moved legislative decision-making over many obstacles during 1944. Legion posts throughout the land bombarded their congressmen with letters and telegrams, mounted a national petition drive that garnered a million signatures, and targeted crucial committee chairs for special scrutiny and

---

[39] Ross, *Preparing for Ulysses*, ch. 4.

[40] The overall pattern is discussed in Amenta and Skocpol, "Redefining the New Deal."

[41] For the Legion's work on the G.I. Bill, see Moley, *The American Legion Story*, ch. 16; Jones, *A History of the American Legion*, pp. 217–20; and David Camelon, "I Saw the GI Bill Written," in 3 parts, *American Legion Magazine*, vol. 47, nos. 3–5 (September, October, and November 1949).

pressure.[42] As historian Davis Ross has concluded, the G.I. Bill needed the "general blessing" of President Roosevelt, but the American Legion "provided the constant pressure to bring the bill through to enactment."[43]

How are we to understand the American Legion's place in the story of World War II veterans' benefits? The Legion has often been portrayed by commentators and scholars as a reactionary lobbying group of privileged militarists. Led by businessmen, professionals, and other middle-class men, and inspired by what may seem a parochial understanding of patriotism, the American Legion of the 1920s and 1930s was virulently opposed to leftists, civil libertarians, and labor unions.[44] Although the Legion was officially nonpartisan, in effect it often operated in partnership with Republicans and conservative Democrats in Congress. The Legion passed information to the FBI and encouraged congressional anticommunist witch hunts, while pushing schools, businesses, and voluntary organizations toward what often amounted to outright repression of unionists and leftists of any variety.

Still, the Legion was also a grassroots voluntary civic organization that engaged popular loyalties in towns and cities across America.[45] Particularly when the needs and aspirations of military veterans were at stake, the Legion espoused a populist version of conservatism rather than a fiscally stingy one. The Legion denounced greedy businessmen and tight-fisted Republicans, as well as leftists and unionists. What is more, having decided in 1942 to open its ranks to World War II as well as World War I veterans, the Legion was suddenly very attentive to the needs of all young soldiers returning from World War II.

The usual pattern in U.S. politics before the 1940s was for each major war to generate a new set of veterans' organizations; and it usually took a couple of decades for each major veterans' federation to build up political clout on behalf of the survivors of its war.[46] In the 1940s, by contrast, the American Legion was already well-established as a nationwide federation with enormous political leverage, and it had an acute interest in proving to World War II veterans that it could address their needs. Only in this way could the Legion hope to attract millions of new members, competing effectively with other veterans organizations of the day, and replenishing its own ranks as veterans of World War I aged and died. (The efforts paid off with a sharp upturn in Legion membership starting in 1945.)

---

[42] Ross, *Preparing for Ulysses*, pp. 121–22.
[43] *Ibid.*, p. 123.
[44] Pencak, *For God and Country*.
[45] *Ibid.*, ch. 10; Jones, *A History of the American Legion*, chs. 15–18.
[46] For a good overview, see William Pencak, "Veterans' Movements," in *Encyclopedia of American Political History: Studies of the Principal Movements and Ideas*, ed. Jack P. Greene (New York: Charles Scribner's Sons, 1984), vol. 3, pp. 1332–47.

While building upon established organizational strengths, leaders of the American Legion also learned from past experience. They had spent much of the 1920s and 1930s engaged in disputes over bonus bills with U.S. presidents. Not wanting to repeat this sad history, they downplayed the usual focus on simple income supplements, orienting their planning for World War II veterans toward ideas about education and postwar economic stimulation that resonated with concerns of the Roosevelt administration. Those at the American Legion who prepared a draft proposal for the G.I. Bill in effect stretched the Roosevelt administration's ideas in a populist direction, while at the same time calling for many kinds of veterans' benefits to be packaged in one bold, omnibus bill and administered as exclusively as possible by the Legion's favorite executive agency, the Veterans' Administration.

Ideas and pressures from the Legion also prodded congressional conservatives in new directions. For example, John Rankin of Mississippi, the chairman of the crucial House Veterans' Affairs Committee, was loath to accept generous transitional unemployment benefits for all veterans. He also tended to favor quick payments of severance bonuses and limited educational grants, suspecting that many southern and western boys would not need or want four years of education. Rankin was reluctant to send millions of G.I.s to become "overeducated and undertrained" by studying with "red" professors in "certain" colleges and universities. "I would rather send my child to a red schoolhouse than to a red school teacher," he explained.[47] Rankin had a point. Why, after all, would it be in the interests of congressional conservatives to subsidize the expansion of U.S. higher education after World War II?

American Legion pressure on many conservative congressmen, Republicans and southern Democrats alike, surely helped to overcome reservations such as those held by Democratic representative Rankin. The Legion also outmaneuvered Rankin himself at the very end, when his delaying tactics and unwillingness to compromise with the Senate version of the G.I. Bill threatened to scuttle the legislation in the House-Senate conference committee. Legionnaires in the state of Georgia took extraordinary steps to transport ailing congressman John S. Gibson back to Washington, D.C. in time for him to break a tie in the conference committee and send the G.I. Bill to the floor of the Senate and the House, where it passed overwhelmingly on June 12 and 13, 1944.

As much as Franklin Roosevelt, therefore, the American Legion of the 1940s deserves credit for the huge federal investments in higher education and youthful family formation that were embodied in the Service-

---

[47] *Hearings before the Committee on World War Veterans' Legislation*, House of Representatives, Seventy-Eighth Congress, Second Session, on H.R. 3917 and S. 1767 (Washington, DC: U.S. Government Printing Office, 1944), pp. 162–63.

men's Readjustment Act of June 22, 1944. Melded together in Congress—
that crucial institutional arbiter of all U.S. policy—an unusual blend of
populist conservatism and New Deal liberalism brought about the G.I.
Bill. The populist conservatism came from the Legion, a widespread federation with local community roots and an unusual ability to persuade
anti–New Deal congressmen who would not usually support generous
social benefits, especially not those likely to strengthen elite or liberal
institutions. Meanwhile, New Dealers in and around Congress and the
Roosevelt administration proved willing to compromise on what were,
from their perspective, non-optimal forms of social-welfare spending.
Their bottom line was to use federally funded education and unemployment benefits to help head off postwar unemployment.

Generous educational grants and other benefits open to masses of World
War II veterans thus turned out to be the meeting point in 1944 of disparate, even somewhat politically contradictory, streams of support. For
once, the U.S. federal government was drawn in a big way into the
business of investing in young breadwinners and their families. The usual
mold of U.S. federal social provision was broken, and the result was one
of the best-loved and most successful social programs ever sponsored by
the American national government.

V. Reinventing the G.I. Bill for a New Era?

Not surprisingly, the model of the G.I. Bill has inspired more than just
nostalgia in recent U.S. politics, particularly among Democrats of various
stripes. A service-oriented strategy for reinventing the G.I. Bill has been
championed by the conservative Democratic Leadership Council (DLC),
while liberal groups and thinkers have looked for a way to renew large-
scale federal investments in training and higher education. President Bill
Clinton has tried to synthesize themes from both camps. Yet to some
degree, the moral and the economic legacies of the G.I. Bill have become
sundered.

Always on the lookout for ways to push the party away from what it
sees as dead-end "liberalism," the Democratic Leadership Council adopted
in 1988 a plan for giving federal aid to students in return for either
military or domestic "national service."[48] Young people could either serve
in the military at lower rates of pay than regular volunteers, or else they
could participate in nonprofit or public sector jobs such as child care,
serving the elderly, or building needed infrastructure. Domestic service
activities were supposed to be undertakings of clear community or national value not readily provided through the market or existing govern-

[48] Democratic Leadership Council, *Citizenship and National Service: A Blueprint for Civic
Enterprise* (Washington, DC: Democratic Leadership Council, May 1988).

ment agencies. In return for one or two years of such military or domestic service, former volunteers would receive generous vouchers to pay for future training, education, or home loans. Such a bill was introduced into Congress in early 1989 under the sponsorship of DLC stalwarts Senator Sam Nunn of Georgia and Representative Dave McCurdy of Oklahoma.

Core ideas of the DLC/Nunn-McCurdy plan came from Northwestern University sociologist Charles Moskos, who had worked for a decade to champion a vision of a new kind of G.I. Bill. "The GI Bill following World War II was a nation's way of expressing its gratitude for those who served in its military," argued Moskos. "It is time to extend this principle to those who perform civilian service as well."[49] Moskos hoped to revive a sense of duty among American young people of the 1980s. As a proponent of communitarian ideals, Moskos positioned himself between "big-government" liberals and individualist, free-market conservatives. He was uncomfortable with a purely mercenary "all-volunteer" military; nor did he like the existence of billions a year in federal educational expenditures not tied to service. "We have created, really, a GI Bill without the GI. We now pay people *not* to serve their country," Moskos told the 1988 annual convention of the Democratic Leadership Council.[50] (Ideally, Moskos would like to require all young Americans to serve the nation, either in the military or in domestic service. In practice, though, he and the Democratic Leadership Council have had to settle for proposals for voluntary service.)

The Nunn-McCurdy bill of 1989 proposed to make federal educational benefits conditional on prior service by low-income or middle-class young people. "Freedom and democracy are not free," declared McCurdy.[51] The Nunn-McCurdy bill did not, however, fare very well in Congress, where it ran into strong opposition from liberals and educational lobbyists concerned that it would displace previous federal educational spending and require only the less privileged to do service as a prerequisite for access to college. The worry was that children of rich families would be able to pay their own way, avoiding any need to contemplate service.

If Charles Moskos and the Democratic Leadership Council were looking for a moral equivalent of war in their 1980s effort to reinvent the G.I. Bill, Barry Bluestone took a different approach in an article called "Generational Alliance: Social Security as a Bank for Education and Training" that appeared in the summer 1990 issue of *The American Prospect*, an outlet for socially conscious liberal thinking. Bluestone proposed to link revi-

---

[49] Charles C. Moskos, *A Call to Civic Service: National Service for Country and Community* (New York: Free Press, 1988), p. 160.

[50] As quoted in Steven Waldman, *The Bill: How the Adventures of Clinton's National Service Bill Reveal What Is Corrupt, Comic, Cynical—and Noble—About Washington* (New York: Viking, 1995), p. 4.

[51] As quoted in "Nunn-McCurdy Plan Ignites National Service Debate," *Congressional Quarterly*, March 25, 1989, p. 645.

sions of two great Franklin Roosevelt initiatives, the Social Security Act of 1935 and the G.I. Bill of 1944, using tax funds accumulated for the elderly to help young people as well.

Today the surpluses in the Social Security Trust Fund are used to cover federal government debt. They are not "invested" in private securities that might produce higher rates of return. In Bluestone's vision, though, the Social Security Trust Fund would be taken "off budget," and partially invested in long-term educational loans to working-aged adults.[52] Either young people or adults in mid-career could borrow directly from the federal government for job training or college education. Later, they would repay over several decades at a rate set in relation to their incomes (thus, people in lower-paid occupations would pay back less overall than people fortunate enough to be highly paid). Working-aged Americans would get funds at rates more affordable than bank loans when they really need them; and older Americans would benefit from the long-term contributions that better-educated workers would make from their enhanced incomes.

In response to critics who argue that Social Security should be trimmed because it is "going bankrupt" and unfairly taxes younger workers, Bluestone argues that federal policy "can create a positive link between those coming of working age and those coming of retirement age." His approach seeks to achieve "generational equity not by retrenching on the elderly, but by putting our reserves for the elderly to work for the entire society."[53]

So far, Bluestone's ideas for using the Social Security Trust Fund as an educational bank have not been taken up. (Politicians of all stripes fear to touch Social Security, and its current surpluses remain vital for covering federal indebtedness.) Yet elements of both the Bluestone vision of direct federal lending for education and the DLC stress on public service have been sponsored by Bill Clinton. As he typically does, Clinton has tried to synthesize a conservative Democratic emphasis on "values" and "personal responsibility" with a more traditional Democratic effort to deliver needed material benefits to middle-income and lower-income families.

---

[52] Other voices today are also calling for investing the Social Security Trust Fund in something more remunerative than low-yield government debt. See, for example, Barry Bosworth, "Putting Social Security to Work: How to Restore the Balance between Generations," *Brookings Review*, vol. 13, no. 4 (Fall 1995), pp. 36–39. It would be possible, of course, to combine Bosworth's call for institutionally managed market-investments of Social Security funds with Bluestone's call to devote part of the Trust Fund to investments in income-contingent educational loans. The latter invests in human capital and in future enhanced tax returns, while the former invests in the stock market, both without breaking Social Security into individualist private-investment pools. Together, Bosworth's and Bluestone's ideas are a cogent alternative to current calls, urged on by Wall Street, to "privatize" Social Security, hence destroying it as a source of mildly redistributive social insurance for all of America's elderly.

[53] Barry Bluestone, "Generational Alliance: Social Security as a Bank for Education and Training," *The American Prospect*, no. 2 (Summer 1990), p. 29.

The full story is told in Steven Waldman's book *The Bill: How the Adventures of Clinton's National Service Bill Reveal What Is Corrupt, Comic, Cynical—and Noble—About Washington.*[54] During the 1992 campaign, Clinton made extravagant promises about guaranteeing access to post-high-school education to all Americans, using a combination of direct federal loans, income-contingent repayments, and voluntary public service as one way for students to earn, or repay, educational expenses. Faced with budgetary constraints, the Clinton administration had to greatly retrench on this campaign promise, along with many others. Nevertheless, during his first year in office President Clinton persuaded the 103d Congress to establish his AmeriCorps national service program, a modest and purely voluntary version of the original Moskos/DLC proposal. At the same time, Clinton and his congressional allies successfully battled fierce opposition from the banking industry to establish direct government lending and income-contingent loans for a portion of federal higher-education spending.

The first part of the Clinton presidency thus appeared to further G.I. Bill–like ideas, both domestic public service and expanded federal educational spending. But then came the conservative Republican triumphs in the 1994 congressional elections. After that, insurgent Republican conservatives arrayed behind the generalship of Speaker of the House Newt Gingrich were determined to roll back rather than enhance the domestic role of the federal government. And they deliberately took aim at both the Clinton AmeriCorps and direct federal educational lending.

AmeriCorps has been criticized by conservatives because it competes with their stress on unpaid voluntarism and private charity. Conservative intellectuals denounce AmeriCorps as nothing more than "government make-work," and call instead for huge cuts in federal programs and taxes—reductions that will, supposedly, clear the way for an automatic flowering of unrecompensed voluntary efforts by families and churches.[55] Meanwhile, the Republican attack on direct lending proceeds more quietly in congressional committees, where representatives of the private banking industry seek to rein in a federal program that threatens their profits. Prior to the advent of direct lending, federal educational loans actually functioned as a form of guaranteed profit for bankers, because the federal government promised to repay student loans with interest, regardless of possible defaults by the former students themselves.[56] Direct lending, according to its supporters, could channel more federal resources to students, while improving collection rates through the Internal

---

[54] Waldman, *The Bill* (*supra* note 50).

[55] See, for example, John Walters, "Clinton's AmeriCorps Values: How the President Misunderstands Citizenship," *Policy Review*, no. 75 (January–February 1996), pp. 42–46.

[56] For the scope and structure of federal student loan programs in the mid-1980s, see Denis P. Doyle and Terry W. Hartle, "Washington: Student-Aid Muddle," *The Atlantic*, vol. 257, no. 2 (February 1986), pp. 30–34.

Revenue Service. In the process, however, America's bankers would lose a safe source of profits.

VI. A National Challenge for Today

Where does all of this leave possibilities for reinventing the G.I. Bill at the turn of the twenty-first century? I conclude that those who want to revisit this historical model need to think in bold moral as well as material terms about the real national challenges that Americans face today. Ironically, the Democratic Leadership Council's effort to find a moral equivalent to World War II ends up falling a bit flat—and proving very vulnerable to outflanking on the right—precisely because it does not seem to call upon all Americans to address a shared national crisis. The Bluestone vision of a "generational alliance" might hold more promise for the nation and the Democratic Party, but only if it were to receive a clearer moral articulation as a response to one of the major challenges facing the nation today.

I do not want to be misunderstood here. The sincerity of Charles Moskos's vision of public service cannot be questioned, because he calls for as many young Americans as possible to engage in socially important work in communities, gaining educational benefits in return for nationally important service, just as the G.I.s of World War II once did. The trouble comes when this ideal has to be put into legislative practice. Congress cannot agree on what counts as socially vital public employment. Conservatives refuse to grant that any such work needs to be done outside of either the market or purely voluntary efforts by families, churches, and charities. And there remains a pervasive sense in the population at large that government employment is inherently inefficient, and possibly corrupt. The contemporary federal government is simply too delegitimated, and too riven by ideological wars, to serve as a stimulator and funder of socially important work on a large scale. A scaled-down version of Clinton's AmeriCorps program seems to be surviving, supported by Democrats and what is left of moderate Republicans in Congress. This program alone, however, will not reinvent the G.I. Bill or serve as a channel for large federal investment in the education of young workers.

Barry Bluestone's 1990 *American Prospect* article reads like most current liberal contributions to public policy debates. It uses a rational tone and lots of tables to prove the technical feasibility of using Social Security to fund educational investments. Missing is any more than a hint of a moral argument. True, Bluestone talks about a "generational alliance" rather than zero-sum generational conflict. But there is no direct appeal to the elderly to contribute to the future, no highlighting of the contributions the young would provide in return for Social Security–financed loans, no call for a national endeavor comparable to Moskos's stirring "call to civic service."[57]

There could be such a call, however. Preserving Social Security and Medicare is going to require contributions from all Americans. If the Social Security Trust Fund were taken off-budget and partially invested in educational loans, this would require moral understanding and political support from today's elderly. What is more, loans would have to be given to students contingent on a democratically articulated moral understanding about the future. Those who get national help now should be prepared to more than repay the nation in the future. Some might repay through participation in public service. But most would develop their own abilities, contribute to the national economy, and then repay their loans through payroll contributions tailored to their ability to pay over a lifetime. Ability-to-pay loans would necessarily be repaid at rates that would more than replenish the Social Security Trust Fund into the twenty-first century. Social Security would give to working-aged Americans, and they would give back to enhance the nation's capacity to care for the elderly. This is a morally compelling exchange. Why not openly feature both the personal responsibility and the social solidarity it would imply?

Educational loans as well as youthful public service are possible keys to public investment in national needs, just as Barry Bluestone and Charles Moskos have suggested in their visions for reinventing the G.I. Bill. But Bluestone's "generational alliance" has to become more than a technical plan, taking on some of the moral fervor of Moskos's public service. And why not? Why do Americans care so much about investing in the training and education of young workers for the future? Not only because we want these young people to be happy, have good jobs and nice incomes, and care for their children. We want these things, of course; but we also want today's young people to be able to build a more productive and just national economy, and to contribute taxes to meet national needs in the future. Not least among these national needs is preserving and replenishing social protections for the elderly.

VII. Looking Back and Looking Forward

Anyone who studies the serendipitous history of the G.I. Bill of 1944 can easily reach a pessimistic conclusion about the possibilities for recapitulating its best features. In some ways, this remarkable bill was a departure from usual patterns in U.S. social provision, because it enabled the federal government to make massive tax-financed investments in young adults and families. We might conclude that only a global war made this possible, so it is unlikely to happen again (barring disastrous world developments for which no one could wish, still less plan).

[57] See Moskos, *A Call to Civic Service* (*supra* note 49).

In another way, though, the G.I. Bill fits the mold of many success-ful U.S. social policies: it encompassed both more- and less-privileged Americans; and it joined benefits with service, citizenship rewards with citizenship responsibilities. Americans who believe that the federal gov-ernment can be "an agent of democratic destiny" must articulate a clear message about the real shared challenges the country needs to address. Then it may be possible to come up with bold new ways to marry benefits and service, entitlements and responsibilities. Only now this must be done apart from war, in genuinely new ways that speak to the very different national challenges that America faces today.

Government and Sociology, Harvard University

CAN OLD-AGE SOCIAL INSURANCE BE JUSTIFIED?*

By Daniel Shapiro

I. Introduction

While in America most people think of "welfare" as means-tested programs such as Aid to Families with Dependent Children, in reality in the United States and other affluent democracies the heart of the welfare state is social insurance programs, such as health insurance, old-age or retirement pensions, and unemployment insurance. They are insurance programs in the sense that they protect against common risks of a loss of income if and/or when certain events come to pass (illness, old-age or retirement, unemployment); they are "social" because unlike market insurance they are not run on a sound actuarial basis, the premiums are not voluntarily incurred but compulsory, and there is very limited choice or flexibility concerning the type of policy one can purchase. Why have social insurance rather than market insurance? In this essay, I take up this question with regard to old-age or retirement pensions, which at present absorb around 9 percent of the gross domestic product (GDP) and 25 percent of government spending of the affluent industrial countries comprising the Organization for Economic Cooperation and Development (OECD).[1] My aim is to show that old-age or retirement social insurance (henceforth "SI") is worse in virtually every relevant normative respect than its alternative, some form of market or private pensions. By relevant normative respect, I mean those values or principles which are used by contemporary political philosophers in their discussions and justifications of welfare-state policies, and which are applicable to assessments of different systems of old-age or retirement pensions. (Although they are

* I wish to thank N. Scott Arnold, Lawrence M. Mead, Christopher W. Morris, Ellen Frankel Paul, and the other contributors to this volume, for comments on earlier drafts of this essay. I presented this paper to the philosophy department at Bowling Green State University in April 1996, and I wish to thank the participants for their comments as well. Earlier drafts of this essay were written while I was a Visiting Scholar at the Social Philosophy and Policy Center at Bowling Green State University, and I am greatly indebted to the directors of the Center, Fred D. Miller, Jr., Ellen Frankel Paul, and Jeffrey Paul, for their support and encouragement, as well as for providing a wonderful place to work.
[1] These figures for OECD countries refer to the years 1986 through 1991 and are taken from the World Bank Policy Research Report, *Averting the Old Age Crisis: Policies to Protect the Old and Promote Growth* (New York: Oxford University Press, 1994), pp. 358–60. Unless significant structural changes are made, expenditures on pensions as a percentage of GDP are expected to double from 1990 to 2050 in the OECD countries (*ibid.*, p. 7). See also E. Philip Davis, *Pension Funds: Retirement-Income Security and Capital Markets* (Oxford: Clarendon Press, 1995), p. 46.

applicable, almost no contemporary political philosophers have in fact applied them[2]—an amazing state of affairs which I hope to remedy here.)

In Section II, I describe the different systems: SI versus private pensions. Private pensions can be compulsory or voluntary, but for purposes of this essay, I will focus only on compulsory pensions, such as those that exist in Chile. In Section III, I argue that a system of compulsory private pensions (henceforth "CP") is better in every respect than SI. I believe that voluntary private pensions are preferable to compulsory private pensions, but that argument requires another essay and will have to wait for another occasion.

It is worth emphasizing that unless I say otherwise, my focus here is not on any particular country, such as the U.S. There are enough similarities among different countries' pension systems that one can meaningfully abstract from the differences.

II. The Institutional Alternatives

A. The central features of old-age social insurance

Old-age or retirement SI has two central features: first, it is a pay-as-you-go scheme (henceforth "PAYG"), rather than being fully funded; and second, in many cases the management and financing of the system reflects both insurance and welfare (i.e., needs-based) principles.

In a fully funded pension,[3] a certain percentage of the recipient's wages or the recipient's contributions is invested, and the assets plus the interest finance the retirement pension. In PAYG systems, the source of the retirement pensions is not investment in the capital market but the power to tax: pensions are funded by taxes on the present generation of workers, rather than by the pensioners' contributions or their past taxes. In a pure PAYG system, the level of benefits paid out to pensioners determines the taxes present workers must pay; that is, present workers' taxes go directly and almost immediately to pensioners. Most PAYG systems are not pure, but have some degree of partial or advance funding,[4] meaning that some of the taxes taken from present workers are invested, usually in govern-

---

[2] One cannot find such a discussion by liberal defenders of the welfare state, such as John Rawls, Ronald Dworkin, Thomas Nagel, Will Kymlicka, or David A. J. Richards, or by communitarian advocates, such as Michael Walzer, Charles Taylor, or Daniel Bell. Robert Goodin and Brian Barry do provide a defense of social insurance and income-replacement programs, but they do not discuss old-age insurance in any detail, and their defense of these programs rests crucially on the claim that the market cannot provide certain kinds of insurance—a claim which is clearly false in the case of pensions. See Brian Barry, "The Welfare State versus the Relief of Poverty," *Ethics,* vol. 100, no. 3 (April 1990), pp. 503–29; and Robert Goodin, "Stabilizing Expectations: The Role of Earnings-Related Benefits in Social Welfare Policy," *Ethics,* vol. 100, no. 3 (April 1990), pp. 530–53.

[3] A fully funded pension is usually, but not always, a private pension. A few countries do have government-managed, fully funded pensions. See note 25.

[4] See World Bank, *Averting the Old Age Crisis,* pp. 110–12; and Carolyn L. Weaver, "Controlling the Risks Posed by Advance Funding—Prospects for Reform," in *Social Security's*

ment bonds, and thus a portion of the money paid out to pensioners is accumulated from interest. However, the reserves in these "trust funds," as they are sometimes called, do not make the system fully funded, for the taxes invested plus the accumulation of interest falls far short of the amount needed to fund all the benefits that have been promised to existing workers and beneficiaries. One way to appreciate this point is that a *genuine* trust fund which promises to pay benefits over a specified number of years keeps its promise by using the assets in the fund plus the interest accumulated; that is, it should not need any infusion of assets or subsidization from another source to keep its promises. For an SI system to function in this way, its "trust fund" would have to be large enough that, if the program were to end today and no future taxes were to be collected, and therefore no future entitlements accumulated, the assets in the fund (the portion of the taxes on present workers that were not paid out immediately) plus the interest could pay all the benefits to which existing workers and beneficiaries were entitled.[5] In *no* case of SI is this true or even close to being true; even in the PAYG systems with considerable surpluses at present, such as Sweden, Japan, and the U.S., the implicit public pension debt—the liability for future expected or promised benefits—is as large as and often larger than the GDP, which in turn is *considerably* greater than the reserves in these "trust funds."[6] Furthermore, as I shall discuss later, in PAYG systems these surpluses turn to deficits in a fairly short time, and depending on the structure of the budgetary process, these surpluses may be only an accounting device which does not reduce the liability of the government for future expected benefits (this seems to be the case with the "trust fund" in the U.S.).[7]

Looming Surpluses: Prospects and Implications, ed. Carolyn L. Weaver (Washington, DC: American Enterprise Institute, 1990), pp. 167–84.

[5] On the misleading idea that PAYG systems have genuine trust funds, see Peter J. Ferrara, *Social Security: The Inherent Contradiction* (Washington, DC: The Cato Institute, 1980), pp. 49–51.

[6] In the OECD countries, the implicit public pension debt in 1990 ranged from 90 percent of the GDP (the U.S.) to almost 250 percent of the GDP (Italy). Sweden at that time was the country with the greatest degree of advance funding, with a "trust fund" of about 30 percent of the GDP. Japan's reserve was 18 percent of the GDP, and the U.S. reserve was around 5 percent (it has since gone up to almost 10 percent). On the implicit public pension debt, see World Bank, *Averting the Old Age Crisis*, pp. 139–40. On Sweden and Japan, see Alicia H. Munnell and C. Nicole Ernsberger, "Foreign Experience with Public Pension Surpluses and National Savings," in Weaver, ed., *Social Security's Looming Surpluses*, pp. 85–118. I obtained the figures on the U.S. from *Statistical Abstracts of the United States* (Washington, DC: U.S. Government Printing Office, 1995), pp. 334, 379, 451. But see note 7 on why the U.S. trust fund is probably just an accounting device that does not reduce future SI liabilities.

[7] To see why the "trust fund" in the U.S. may very well be an accounting device that does not reduce the implicit public pension debt, one needs to understand how advance funding can actually reduce that debt. This happens when payroll taxes are used to purchase outstanding government debt held by private investors, and then those investors substitute new private securities for government debt they relinquish. That action by private investors allows for increased capital formation and ultimately higher future incomes to meet the cost of retirement benefits in coming decades. Payroll taxes can be lower than otherwise in the meantime, because of substantial interest accruing to the trust funds. And income taxes that

Before proceeding, I need to address an important claim made by the economist Nicholas Barr: that fully funded and PAYG systems are basically similar, because in both systems the consumption of a group of pensioners is produced by the next generation of workers. "From an *aggregate* viewpoint, the economic function of pension schemes is to divide total output between workers and pensioners, i.e., to reduce the consumption of workers so that sufficient output remains for pensioners."[8] However, all Barr is looking at is the relationship between the two classes (workers and pensioners) and *ignoring* what happens to the income or assets the pensioners previously surrendered. In a fully funded scheme, all of the income the workers save—their forgone consumption—to provide for their pensions is *invested*; this does not happen in a PAYG scheme. This investment expands the productive capacity of the economy and provides for the future consumption of the pensioners.[9] Barr's aggregate analysis looks at retirement pensions like a black or opaque box:

---

finance the payment of the interest need not be any higher, because there is no change in the government's total indebtedness—only a change in the ownership of the debt from the public to the trust funds (in other words, money that would have gone to private investors goes to the trust funds instead). Thus, with increased capital formation, lower payroll taxes, and no increase in income taxes, the burden of SI on present and future workers decreases.

The crucial assumptions in the above scenario are (1) that payroll taxes are used to purchase outstanding government debt held by private investors; that is, there is net government savings; and (2) that this leads to private investors substituting private securities for the government debt they previously held, which in turn increases national savings. The first condition fails to obtain when taxes raised for the purpose of advance funding are used to finance the general operations of the government's budget and/or if these taxes loosen fiscal restraint in the sense that the government's budget deficit increases. The second condition fails to obtain if the net government savings is offset by a decrease in private savings. Condition (1) may have been met in Japan and Sweden, as the taxes raised by partial funding were placed in a separate account which was not allowed to be used to finance the general operations of the budget; and the partial funding did not seem to loosen fiscal restraint, at least in the sense that budget deficits did not increase (though since we do not know whether or not deficits would have increased in the absence of partial funding, the effects of that funding on budget deficits are hard to determine). In the U.S., however, there is little if any reason to believe that the first condition has been met. Under current law, all tax revenues not needed to meet current benefits are "invested" in new special-issue government bonds. The trust funds are credited with a bond—an IOU from one part of government to another—and the Treasury gets the cash. From the Treasury's viewpoint, this cash is available to finance the general operations of the federal government. We do not know whether it is being used to retire outstanding publicly held debt, that is, whether it has produced any net government savings. To determine that, either we would have to know what the size and composition of the budget would have been in the absence of trust-fund buildup, or the budget excluding Social Security would have to be in balance. For a clear exposition of the problems with advance funding in the U.S., see Weaver, "Controlling the Risks Posed by Advance Funding," in Weaver, ed., *Social Security's Looming Surpluses*, pp. 168–72. On the special conditions in Japan and Sweden that may have helped advance funding to genuinely reduce future SI liabilities, see Munnell and Ernsberger, "Foreign Experience with Public Pension Surpluses and National Savings," in *ibid.*, pp. 90–106, 114–18.

[8] Nicholas Barr, *The Economics of the Welfare State* (Stanford: Stanford University Press, 1993), p. 220, emphasis in original.

[9] I have been aided here by Norman P. Barry, "The State, Pensions, and the Philosophy of Welfare," *Journal of Social Policy*, vol. 14 (1985), pp. 479–80.

he looks only at the income in (reduction in workers' wages) and the income out (pensions), without looking at what happens to the former in order to transform it into the latter (what happens inside the black or opaque box, as it were). It is true, however, that a long-term economic disaster could prevent a significant amount of savings from workers' paychecks from being invested and then retrieved to pay for pensioners' later consumption; and if one thought the market subject to systematic and significantly long-term discoordination, then the extent to which the savings for pensions would fund pensioners' future consumption would be significantly lessened. That is a separate issue, however; and in any event, modern economies are not repeatedly subject to semi-permanent economic depressions.[10]

The second feature of SI systems, that they frequently incorporate aspects of both an insurance and a welfare system, is reflected in the method of financing and the payout of benefits. Virtually all SI systems are financed, at least in part, by a payroll tax, and in many systems the more taxes paid, the more benefits received: both of these are appropriate for an insurance scheme. They are, however, inappropriate for a welfare scheme, since payroll taxes are a regressive method of finance (they are a flat tax on earnings and typically there is a ceiling on the earnings taxed) and since need, not taxes paid, should determine benefits in a welfare scheme. However, some SI systems have progressive benefit formulas, so that those with low earnings histories get a higher percentage of their past incomes in benefits than those with high earnings histories; some systems have a means-tested component that awards benefits completely independently of one's earnings history (a component which is sometimes financed out of general revenues and not by a payroll tax); and some SI systems withhold benefits to pensioners who work after reaching the official retirement age. All of this reflects the idea of awarding or denying benefits based on need, and is appropriate for a welfare scheme, but not for an insurance scheme.

The connection between the PAYG feature of old-age SI systems and the way such systems combine insurance and welfare elements is historical-empirical, not logical or conceptual. These systems began by paying out benefits to current retirees who had put nothing or very little into the

---

[10] That modern economies are not subject to repeated depressions is a fact; the explanation for this fact is a matter of controversy, which revolves around the extent to which various government policies are or are not responsible for the depression-free record of modern economies. It might seem that this controversy is relevant for the evaluation of SI versus CP, for if CP were to threaten the ability of modern economies to prevent long-term depressions, then that would be an excellent argument against CP. However, the government policies that are often claimed to be the defense against economic depressions—such as preventing bank failures and the shrinkage of the money supply, keeping world trade reasonably free, the existence of automatic "stabilizers" (programs that transfer income to the unemployed during economic downturns), etc.—have no necessary connection with an SI system, and could perform their function within a CP system, as will become clear from the description of CP that occurs within the text.

system, but who were considered entitled to considerable benefits. Such a justification had to be based on need, not earnings history or the amount of taxes paid, and it guaranteed that the system would have to be financed on a PAYG basis. Indeed, many old-age SI systems did not begin with an earnings-related component at all, but paid a flat rate and/or a means-based benefit: the earnings component, with benefits based in part on one's earnings history, came later. It would have been *possible* for a PAYG system to pay no benefits to current retirees and to delay paying benefits until the system matured, but the system never would have acquired support or been instituted under such circumstances.[11]

B. The early stage of pay-as-you-go systems

PAYG systems have a typical, indeed virtually universal, life cycle.[12] The early stage of a PAYG system is marked by high benefits for retirees—much higher than they would have received had they invested their contributions in the market—and low costs or taxes for the workers. This is due to three types of reasons or causes: (1) those inherent in a PAYG system; (2) those due to contingencies that were present during PAYG's early stages; and (3) those which are in all likelihood necessary in order for the introduction and development of PAYG to receive support. (As I note below, the second and third factors overlap.)

1. The essence of PAYG is that pensions are funded by taxes on present workers; thus, retirees who receive pensions during the early years of the system have not paid into the system for very long, certainly not their whole working lives, and therefore they get a great "rate of return" (the phrase is in quotes, since there is no return in any market sense).

2. During the early stage of PAYG, there was a lower life expectancy than exists today; and this, combined with a period of high population growth at this early stage, helped to produce a high support ratio—the ratio of workers to pensioners—in the range of fifteen-to-one to eight-to-one. Lower life expectancy reduced the number of beneficiaries (and the total cost of the benefits), while high population growth increased the stream of workers and taxpayers, which reduced the cost per taxpayer. In many cases, the system's early phase also coincided with high wage growth, which, while not affecting the support ratio, made the collection of payroll taxes more painless and increased the total amount of benefits.

3. Major political programs or policy changes are usually introduced gradually, and in this case PAYG's gradual emergence kept costs low and the support ratio high. The former occurred because the full range of

---

[11] World Bank, *Averting the Old Age Crisis*, pp. 102–5; Ferrara, *Social Security: The Inherent Contradiction*, pp. 5–7, 53–55.

[12] World Bank, *Averting the Old Age Crisis*, pp. 315–16. The World Bank uses a more fine-grained analysis, dividing PAYG into three stages instead of two, but for my purposes, such detail is not necessary.

benefits was not available to the first retirees[13] (which is why the biggest winners in PAYG are not the first retirees but those who were thirty to fifty years old at the time the system was founded); and the latter occurred because as benefits were expanded, so was coverage (thus, for example, agricultural workers and members of small firms who were originally excluded were later added to the system). This point overlaps with point (2) because benefits and coverage typically underwent their greatest expansion during the period beginning shortly after World War II and running through the 1960s, when population and/or wage growth were quite robust.[14]

Since the "rate of return" is high, and taxes are still relatively low, it is not surprising that the system is enormously popular at this stage. Few people pay attention to the implicit public pension debt—the liability for the present value of the future stream of expected benefits—that is quietly building up.

C. The later or mature stage of pay-as-you-go systems

At this stage, typically when the system is over forty years old, all the conditions that led to the rate of return being high and costs low have been reversed.

1'. At this point, almost all people receiving benefits have paid into the system for most or all of their working lives, and thus the terrific "rates of return" that PAYG gives in its early stages cannot be replicated.[15]

2'. The support ratio has dropped significantly at this stage: it is less than six-to-one and falling. This is due to the aging of the population, which increases the number of retirees, and the slowing of population growth, which lessens the flow of new workers to support the burgeoning retiree population. Thus, the level of taxes increases significantly. In many cases, wage growth also slows (which may be due in part to the increased burden of payroll taxes), and therefore the increased cost of the system becomes more noticeable.

3'. Since the system is obviously no longer being phased in, virtually everyone is covered and entitled to full benefits; indeed, in the beginning of the mature stage, benefit levels are likely to have increased due to the increased political clout of retirees. Thus, for example, early retirement may be allowed, benefits may be indexed to wage growth and/or price increases, etc. However, as the mature stage continues, the recognition

---

[13] For example, disability and survivors' benefits were often added later. That SI schemes combine retirement pensions with these benefits is a complication which for the most part I shall ignore in this essay, as it does not affect my central arguments.

[14] World Bank, *Averting the Old Age Crisis*, p. 105.

[15] That later retirees cannot get the windfall that early retirees receive is a separate matter from whether the former can get a greater-than-market "rate of return," an issue I shall discuss shortly.

that the implicit public pension debt is at least as large if not larger than the GDP, and that expenditures are climbing up to almost 10 percent of GDP, may lead to a scaling back of benefits: raising the retirement age, taxing benefits, reducing indexing, etc. The increased expenditures and rising public pension debt also lead to deficits in the "trust fund" and a dipping into general revenues to cover them, or a further increase in payroll taxes to create some advance funding.[16] The latter, however, only postpones the problem, as the demographics of a worsening support ratio mean that these surpluses will lead to deficits unless a breathtaking level of taxation is imposed.

The end result of these increased taxes for people who will be paying most or all of their lives for the system in its mature stage is that their "rate of return" is far worse than what they would get in the private capital market. And things promise to look even worse down the road, as people who are just entering the system can only look forward to further reduction of benefits and increased taxes, as the trends in the mature stage toward slow population growth and an increase in life expectancy do not seem reversible and reduction in the number of retirees covered by the system seems politically unimaginable.

Since some of the reasons PAYG moves from its early stage to its mature stage are due to contingent factors, it is not strictly speaking *necessary* that PAYG move from an early stage to a mature stage, in the sense that it could continue to have a "rate of return" greater than the market rate for everyone, as the economist Paul Samuelson has proven.[17] The argument goes as follows. Suppose population growth is zero and the rate of growth of real wages on covered employment is greater than the rate of return on capital. If there is a constant payroll tax, then the total taxes collected and benefits paid would increase by the rate of growth in payrolls, which is greater than what the individual would have gotten on his own if he had invested the taxes. Or suppose there is zero growth in real wages but population growth is greater than the return on capital investment. The increase in population will cause a similar increase in workers, and with a fixed tax on payrolls, total taxes collected will also increase at this rate; thus, the individual will again be better off than if he had invested his contribution. Therefore, if either population growth or growth in real wages is greater than the return on capital investments, then PAYG can

---

[16] If the payroll-tax increase is sizable, and the taxes are actually invested and not used to cover other government spending, the surpluses created at this point can be considerable, but they still do not come even close to eliminating the public pension debt, as I discussed in note 6.

[17] Paul Samuelson, "An Exact Consumption-Loan Model of Interest with or without the Social Contrivance of Money," in *The Collected Scientific Papers of Paul Samuelson*, ed. Joseph Stiglitz (Cambridge, MA: MIT Press, 1966), vol. 1, pp. 219–34. Samuelson's argument is explained, minus the complex mathematics, in Ferrara, *Social Security: The Inherent Contradiction*, pp. 293–94; and Gordon Tullock, *The Economics of Income Redistribution* (Boston: Kluwer-Nijhoff Publishing, 1983), pp. 111–22.

continually provide a "rate of return" greater than one could obtain by investing the money on one's own.

However, Samuelson's proof is of little relevance for the type of comparisons that I am concerned with here—comparisons of real institutions. Neither of the two contingent conditions required to sustain a "rate of return" above market returns is one which exists for any significant period of time. Except during periods of unanticipated inflation, interest rates and the return on capital investments are higher than the growth in wages;[18] and population growth drops as living standards increase. Now, since the existence of high population and wage growth that produces a greater than market rate of return will not last long (if it exists at all), and since the other conditions that keep the "rate of return" high in the early stage—the phasing in of benefits and coverage, the windfall gained by retirees who have paid nothing or almost nothing into the system—will also disappear with time, in the real world the early stage of PAYG leads, almost inevitably, to the later or mature stage.

D. Redistributive effects of old-age social insurance

The progress, or perhaps one should say regress, from the early to the late stage of PAYG entails a significant redistribution of wealth from the later generations to the earlier generations. This intergenerational effect is clear and needs little elaboration; its normative significance will be the heart of my argument in Section III. What may be less obvious is that the intragenerational effect, that is, the transfers of expected lifetime income among those born around the same time, is regressive or at least not progressive.[19] Upper-income people tend to enter the work force later than the poor, and to live longer after retirement, and thus they contribute less[20] and receive more than lower-income people over a lifetime. Nor do the progressive benefit formulas found in some systems, such as in the

[18] From 1971 to 1990, the average annual rate of return for a portfolio containing half stocks and half bonds was around 3 percent above the growth in real wages, and for a portfolio containing only stocks, the difference is considerably greater. This data is from the World Bank, *Averting the Old Age Crisis*, pp. 299–302, 355. During the same period, population growth was slow—indeed, in many OECD countries the growth rate was (and continues to be) barely above the replacement rate. Since SI's "rate of return" declines as the mature stage progresses, one suspects that the advantage of equities over PAYG would look even better if the period from 1980 to the present were used. Note also that with capital becoming more mobile, an international portfolio is likely to do better than a national one, and is likely to provide advantages to those living in countries with sluggish economies, which should give an additional advantage to equities over PAYG in the future.

The point about unanticipated inflation comes from Gordon Tullock, *Welfare for the Well-to-Do* (Dallas: Fisher Institute, 1983), p. 54. He provides no data, but since the point is an obvious one, data is probably unnecessary.

[19] World Bank, *Averting the Old Age Crisis*, pp. 131–34.

[20] The World Bank's *Averting the Old Age Crisis* does not indicate whether "contribute less" means less total taxes or less proportionately. Either way, however, the result is not a progressive intragenerational redistribution.

U.S., the UK, the Netherlands, and Sweden, change matters. Obviously, the formulas do not prevent the affluent from living longer, or affect the poor's earlier entrance into the work force. Furthermore, the method of financing PAYG systems, which relies largely upon a payroll tax, is regressive: there is often a ceiling on taxable earnings in systems with payroll taxes, and even if the benefit schedule is weighted somewhat toward those with low lifetime earnings, it is still the case that those who earn more will get more benefits. While financing such programs solely through general revenues could eliminate the regressive financing in a PAYG system, the fact of the affluent's longer life expectancy and later entrance into the workforce are ineliminable obstacles to progressive intragenerational income redistribution in such a system.

E. Private pensions

Private pensions are either "defined-benefit" or "defined-contribution." In defined-benefit pensions, the sponsor promises to pay a pension related to career earnings (e.g., a certain percentage of final or average salary) or a flat rate (per years of service). Recipients thus trade a portion of their wages for pensions, while sponsors (usually employers) bear the investment risk. (SI pensions might seem to be an example of defined benefit; however, since the level of benefits is frequently redefined by the vagaries of the political process, no set benefit is promised.)[21] In defined-contribution pensions, contributions are fixed and benefits vary with market returns; the risk is borne by the recipient, not the provider. Defined-benefit pensions run a risk of not being fully funded, since employers may not invest sufficiently to guarantee the benefit, while defined-contribution pensions do not run this risk, since there is no benefit guaranteed.[22] In many countries, tax laws and regulations have biased pensions toward occupational pensions,[23] many of which are defined-benefit, but it is probably safe to say that, given the problems with labor mobility inherent in occupational defined-benefit pensions, in a free market defined-contribution pensions would play a very large if not dominant role.[24]

---

[21] On the spotty record of SI systems keeping their promises, see World Bank, *Averting the Old Age Crisis*, pp. 112–13.

[22] It was the belief that a significant amount of defined-benefit occupational pensions were not being fully funded by U.S. employers that helped to produce the Employment Retirement Income Security Act (ERISA) in 1974. The act provided both tax incentives and legal penalties for failure to fund pensions adequately and created a set of regulations governing employee participation and the vesting of benefits (i.e., the conditions under which employees could leave the company without losing their pensions). For further information, see Barbara J. Coleman, *Primer on ERISA* (Washington, DC: Bureau of National Affairs, 1985). Laws similar to ERISA exist in many of the OECD countries. See World Bank, *Averting the Old Age Crisis*, pp. 193–97.

[23] World Bank, *Averting the Old Age Crisis*, pp. 167–69, 182–83.

[24] Partly for these reasons, and partly because some employers consider the ERISA regulations burdensome, occupational pension plans in the U.S. have been shifting from

Pensions of both types can be converted at retirement age to annuities, or can be received in a lump sum or in phased withdrawals.

In a compulsory private (CP) pension system the government requires one to save for one's retirement, but the management and financing of these pensions are left largely to the free market. If CP systems require that one set aside a certain percentage of one's wages, then they are defined-contribution pensions; if they require that, no matter what savings one has put aside, the pension at retirement must be a certain amount, then they are defined-benefit. As my model for a CP system, I shall use Chile,[25] which combines elements of both defined-contribution and defined-benefit. Employees are required to contribute at least a certain percentage of their wages and invest them in individual pension savings accounts managed by private investment companies. In addition, workers must purchase private disability and life insurance. After retirement, workers must either purchase (indexed) annuities or make phased withdrawals from their pension savings accounts. However, if one's pension (or disability and survivor benefits) does not meet a certain minimum benefit when one retires, the government makes up the difference; and for those not covered by pensions, the government provides pensions funded by general revenues. Thus, the Chilean system has two aims: to force retirement savings, and to provide a safety net for those whose pensions do not meet a certain minimum.

Though I will use Chile as my model, not all aspects of the Chilean system need be the benchmark for comparison. The pension system in Chile is heavily regulated in a number of respects. The investment companies which manage the pension savings accounts must provide a certain minimum return; workers are allowed to invest in only one of these companies at a time (though they may switch their accounts among the companies once a month); these companies, whose sole function is to manage pension savings accounts, are required to hold a diversified portfolio with minimum risk (which has entailed that the portfolio contain a

---

defined-benefit to defined-contribution. That trend also exists in some other OECD countries, such as Australia and Switzerland. For the U.S., see Karen Ferguson and Kate Blackwell, *Pensions in Crisis* (New York: Arcade Publishing Company, 1995), pp. 168–69, 173; for the OECD countries, see World Bank, *Averting the Old Age Crisis*, pp. 198–200.

[25] My information about the Chilean system was obtained from Davis, *Pension Funds* (*supra* note 1), pp. 250–53; World Bank, *Averting the Old Age Crisis*, ch. 6; and Peter J. Ferrara, John C. Goodman, and Merrill Matthews, Jr., *Private Alternatives to Social Security in Other Countries*, NCPA Study No. 200 (Dallas: National Center for Policy Analysis, 1995), pp. 13–23.

A system that is intermediate between SI and CP is a system called "provident savings," found in a number of countries, and most effectively run in Singapore. Here employees and/or employers are required to save, but the savings must be deposited in a government-managed system which invests primarily in government securities. The system is fully funded—one gets back one's contribution plus interest—and contributors do have a property right in their accounts, but since the government manages the system, it would be too large a stretch to place this in the category of *private* pensions. On Singapore, see Davis, *Pension Funds*, pp. 253–55; World Bank, *Averting the Old Age Crisis*, ch. 6; and Ferrara et al., *Private Alternatives to Social Security in Other Countries*, pp. 7–13.

significant percentage of government securities); until recently, foreign investment was not allowed; there is a minimum age of retirement; and so forth. Since these features reduce the sense in which there is a free market in pensions, and are not essential to the aims of forced savings and the provision of a safety net, I will not include these features in my comparison of SI and CP. All I will assume for CP is that the government requires a certain minimum contribution toward one's retirement, and provides some kind of safety net for those whose pensions at retirement are below a certain minimum, either because their wages were too low to finance an adequate pension or because they were not wage earners. Arguably, the aim of providing a safety net may require that on retirement one cannot receive a lump-sum payment but must purchase annuities or make phased withdrawals, so perhaps that could be included as a necessary feature of CP as well.

Since CP systems are fully funded, they lack the significant intergenerational transfers of SI systems. As a result, early generations do not do well at the expense of later ones, and the poor returns that later generations get in a PAYG system are absent in CP systems.[26] Indeed, fully funded pensions do not redistribute across persons, but only across different portions of a person's life.[27] However, CP's safety net does involve redistribution to the elderly poor. But if this redistribution is financed out of general revenues, it is likely to be more progressive in its income effects than the intragenerational redistribution in SI, which, as we saw, has various forms of regressivity built into the system (since it gives larger lifetime benefits to the affluent than to the poor, and is financed in large part by payroll taxes).

III. WHY COMPULSORY PRIVATE PENSIONS BEAT SOCIAL INSURANCE

I shall now evaluate the choice between SI and CP using four values or principles that are central to contemporary political philosophy and are applicable to old-age pensions: justice and fairness, positive rights and

[26] How much larger the rate of return will be in a CP system as compared with what later generations get in an SI system will depend upon the particular country as well as the degree of maturity of the SI system (for the longer an SI system goes on, the worse its "rate of return"). It is worth stressing that all that my arguments in Section III will require is that CP has a nontrivial advantage here, an advantage which grows as SI matures (see note 18 for the advantage that investing in equities has over PAYG). It is also worth stressing that my arguments will not rely upon the extremely impressive 13 percent average annual rate of return that the Chilean system has had since its inception in 1981. See Davis, *Pension Funds*, p. 252; and Ferrara et al., *Private Alternatives to Social Security in Other Countries*, p. 21.

[27] Note that if one views these different stages as different selves, in the manner of Derek Parfit's theory of personal identity, then the distinction between (1) transfers between different parts of a person's life and (2) transfers between different persons is not metaphysically significant. For purposes of this essay, however, Parfit's views are not relevant, since whether or not they are true, they are not *politically* significant, as people generally view "redistribution" across different stages of a life as belonging in a vastly different category than redistribution across different persons. For Parfit's views, see his *Reasons and Persons* (New York: Oxford University Press, 1985), pp. 199–347.

security, negative rights and freedom, and public justification of basic political institutions.

A. Justice and fairness

I am concerned here with principles of justice that are not primarily rights-centered or rights-based, for I shall discuss those matters separately. Many of these principles are often described as egalitarian; unfortunately, there is no univocal usage of this term. Strictly speaking, egalitarian principles of justice are those which value equality *as such*, that is, consider it a noninstrumental value.[28] Thus, an egalitarian, when asked to compare (1) a redistribution from the better off to the worse off (however these terms are defined), and (2) identical gains for the worse off with equal (or even greater) gains for the better off, will rank the former as better, since there is less inequality between the better and worse off. (Since egalitarians need not—and if their view is to be sensible, will not—consider equality as the *only* value, this ranking is defeasible.) However, "egalitarian" is commonly predicated of principles of justice, such as John Rawls's difference principle, which states that social and economic inequalities are to be arranged so that they are to the greatest benefit of the least advantaged.[29] The difference principle would be indifferent between the two alternative distributions described above, since the absolute position of the worst off (least advantaged) in both cases is identical. To accommodate the tendency to describe the difference principle as egalitarian, I shall distinguish between strong egalitarianism, which considers equality a noninstrumental value, and weak egalitarianism, which requires that significant weight be given to improving (at the limit, maximizing) the plight of the worst off, and is only concerned with equality per se as a means to improving the lot of the worst off.

Three other conceptual points about egalitarianism need to be made. First, any egalitarian theory must answer the question: Equality of *what*? That is, in what aspect of people's lives should people be made more equal or should the position of the worst off be improved? Most egalitarian theories are either *welfarist*, which means that the relevant metric of equality is happiness, satisfaction, or some desirable psychological state of the person, or *resourcist*, which means that the relevant metric of equality is resources, opportunities, capacities, and the like.[30] Second, most egalitarian theories incorporate some kind of responsibility or choice condition, so that being badly off or being unequal in welfare or resources calls for rectification only if one's condition has not come about through

[28] On this conceptual or terminological matter, I have been influenced by Larry S. Temkin, *Inequality* (New York: Oxford University Press), pp. 7–8.

[29] John Rawls, *A Theory of Justice* (Cambridge: Harvard University Press, 1971), p. 302; Rawls, *Political Liberalism* (New York: Columbia University Press, 1993), p. 291.

[30] Two helpful summaries of the "Equality of what?" literature are G. A. Cohen, "On the Currency of Egalitarian Justice," *Ethics*, vol. 99, no. 4 (July 1989), pp. 906–44; and Amartya Sen, *Inequality Reexamined* (Cambridge: Harvard University Press, 1992).

some fault or choice of one's own.[31] Third, egalitarian theories differ on whether justice is relativized to time or not: some theorists believe that there are obligations of justice owed to those of later generations and some deny this. But even those who deny it admit special obligations to one's children as well as a concern for one's descendants, even if they are not yet born.[32]

With these distinctions out of the way, the egalitarian argument which favors CP over SI is pretty simple: The latter places significant burdens upon later (but overlapping) generations which the earlier generations did not have. These burdens include a low "rate of return" and a high level of taxes and implicit public pension debt—conditions which reduce the later generations' resources and most likely their welfare compared with what would exist if CP were in place. Furthermore, the nonaffluent or poor of the later generations are the most burdened, and since in all probability there will be a significant connection between those who are worst off in welfare and/or resources and those who are poor,[33] it follows that the most burdened are the worst off of the later generations. These burdens and inequalities, of course, could hardly be said to be due to the later generations' fault or choices. Since CP does not have these effects,

---

[31] John Rawls's difference principle is the great exception here: his conception of the worst off does not incorporate a responsibility or choice condition. But post-Rawlsian egalitarianism invariably incorporates such a condition, for two reasons. First, it is quite implausible that persons or institutions have stringent obligations to rectify an inequality or a burden if it is voluntarily incurred or if one can be held responsible for incurring it. Second, many egalitarians also defend some basic individual rights, and such a defense almost inevitably involves accepting the principle that one has a right to act in accordance with (certain of) one's choices. That principle would be difficult to reconcile with the view that voluntarily acquired inequalities or burdens require rectification, or so I argue in "Liberal Egalitarianism, Basic Rights, and Free Market Capitalism," *Reason Papers*, vol. 18 (Fall 1993), pp. 171-73.

Ronald Dworkin's writings are probably most responsible for the presence of a responsibility or choice condition in contemporary egalitarianism. For Dworkin's theory, which he calls "equality of resources," see his "What is Equality? Part I: Equality of Welfare," *Philosophy and Public Affairs*, vol. 10, no. 3 (Summer 1981), pp. 185–262, and "What is Equality? Part II: Equality of Resources," *Philosophy and Public Affairs*, vol. 10, no. 4 (Fall 1981), pp. 283–345.

[32] Another way to put this is that those who reject obligations to future generations, i.e., who relativize justice to time, are primarily rejecting such obligations for *strangers*.

[33] It might seem that there is not just a "significant connection," but that necessarily or by definition the worst off are the poorest. But that is not so. First, as I noted earlier, some egalitarians are concerned with inequalities in welfare, and there is no necessary connection between being unhappy or lacking satisfaction and being poor (though extreme poverty, over the long run, considerably reduces happiness and satisfaction). Second, measuring poverty simply in terms of low income, as is often done, omits some important considerations that affect the quality of people's lives. For example, two people can have equal incomes but not be equally well off because of different capabilities of converting that income into resources: e.g., someone with a high metabolic rate, a large body size, or a parasitic disease that wastes nutrients may have a much harder time meeting minimal nutritional requirements with her income than someone who does not have these characteristics. See Sen, *Inequality Reexamined*, ch. 7, for more discussion of this last point.

Thus, although there are obvious connections between the poor and the worst off, egalitarians cannot and do not equate them. The best one can say here is that when concerned with policy or institutional choices, poverty is a plausible but not completely reliable marker for being badly off.

and maintains a safety net for the elderly poor, CP appears to rank far better in terms of egalitarian values. Notice also that the ones burdened and made worse off are the children and descendants of the earlier generations, and thus the argument applies also to those who reject obligations to future generations, since such people do admit special obligations to their children as well as a concern for their descendants, even if they are not yet born.

I can think of three egalitarian replies to my argument.

1. Some egalitarians believe that *natural* as well as social inequalities are an injustice that should, subject to trade-offs with other values, be rectified. Since being old in many ways makes one worse off than being young, SI's redistribution from young to old is a positive feature, not a negative one.[34] This response, however, ignores the fact that CP also "redistributes" from young to old, in that income is saved for old age and a safety net is provided for the elderly poor; and more importantly, the reply does not justify an SI system's making those who are very young during the early years of the system worse off when they become old as compared with those who are old during the early stages of the system.

2. My response to (1) may produce the following counterargument: Even though later generations do worse vis-à-vis SI than earlier generations, *all things considered* later generations will be better off—due to the effects of economic growth, science and technology, etc.—than earlier generations.[35] This inequality between generations is prima facie objectionable (at least when it occurs in societies that are already affluent),[36] since it is largely due to circumstances which no one chose (i.e., when one was born). Accordingly, the redistribution within SI, but not within CP, from later to earlier generations is not an objection against SI, but, on the contrary, is exactly what egalitarians want: to mitigate the extent to which the lives of members of later generations will be better than those of members of earlier generations. This argument, it should be noted, will almost certainly be made by strong egalitarians who object to inequality as such, rather than by weak egalitarians, since for the latter the fact that later generations are better off than earlier ones is probably a plus, not a minus, at least to the extent that the increase in living standards or quality of life makes the worst off of the later generations better off than they otherwise would be and does not occur at the expense of the worst off of earlier generations.

[34] Larry S. Temkin makes this argument about the justifiability of transfers from the young to the old in "Justice and Equality: Some Questions about Scope," *Social Philosophy and Policy*, vol. 12, no. 2 (Summer 1995), pp. 96–97, although he makes no mention of SI.

[35] Loren E. Lomasky raised this objection (which he does not, incidentally, endorse). After Lomasky raised this objection, I discovered that Davis, *Pension Funds*, pp. 38–39, makes a similar point, as does Temkin in "Justice and Equality," pp. 93–94, although Temkin does not do so in the context of a discussion of SI.

[36] I add this because it is inconceivable to me that any egalitarian would object to later generations being better off than earlier ones in situations where grinding poverty is the norm.

However, even if egalitarians should favor redistribution from later to earlier generations, the way this redistribution occurs within SI is objectionable on egalitarian grounds. Even though in a growing economy the average member of a younger cohort will have a higher lifetime income than the average member of an older cohort, people who survive to old age are not a random sample of their cohorts. They generally come from higher socioeconomic groups, whose expected longevity is higher. A larger proportion of people who are young will have shorter lifetimes and lower lifetime annual incomes than people who are old.[37] Thus, the redistribution from later to earlier generations is not really from those who are better off to those who are worse off; in a significant respect, the redistribution goes the other way. What a strong egalitarian should favor, perhaps, is a system which redistributes from the better off members of later generations to the worse off members of earlier generations; however, since neither SI nor CP does this, while CP avoids the perverse redistribution from the worst-off members of the later generations to the better-off members of the earlier generations, CP is in that respect preferable to SI on egalitarian grounds.

3. Egalitarians who believe that there are no obligations of justice to those not yet born, but who acknowledge obligations to one's children (and grandchildren), might argue that members of earlier generations can mitigate the negative effects of SI by gifts and bequests. However, if one believes that the negative effects of SI on one's children (and grandchildren) should, as a matter of fulfilling one's parental obligations, be *mitigated* by gifts and bequests, it would make more sense to avoid these negative effects in the first place by having a system of CP instead of SI—especially since SI by its coercive transfers guarantees these effects, while gifts or bequests, which are voluntary transfers, do not necessarily mitigate them, as some parents will not and/or cannot provide substantial gifts or bequests.

Thus, none of the egalitarian counterarguments I have discussed come to grips with the anti-egalitarian effects of SI (as compared with CP) or show how the problems can be remedied (without having a CP system). Counterargument (1) focused on the egalitarian virtues of transfers from young to old, but ignored the fact that the old of later generations do much worse vis-à-vis SI than the old of the earlier generations. Counterargument (2) tried to make a virtue of the fact that later generations do worse than earlier ones on the grounds that this mitigated the extent to which later generations are (involuntarily) better off than earlier ones, but ignored the fact that transfers go from the worse-off members of the later generations to the better-off members of the earlier generations. Counterargument (3) at least acknowledged the redistributive problems with SI, but its solution of parental gifts and bequests was a weak remedy for the problem, as compared with having a CP system which avoided these

[37] World Bank, *Averting the Old Age Crisis*, pp. 78–80.

effects. There seems to be no way around it: CP is better on egalitarian grounds than SI.[38]

I have focused my attention so far on egalitarian views of justice, but I believe the same considerations apply to nonegalitarian views. Such views usually understand justice in terms of reciprocity or mutual advantage. The primary injustice for such accounts is exploitation, or taking unfair advantage. We need not go into details about various accounts of exploitation: very roughly, the idea is that exploitation or taking unfair advantage occurs when there is a failure of reciprocity or one fails to get the value of one's contribution, and when one has no alternative to participating (or is forced to participate) in the relationship or exchange where reciprocity fails. Given what I have argued so far, it seems clear that SI is more unfair or exploitative than CP. SI burdens later generations with a tax liability that is very difficult for them to escape, and gives them a rate of return far inferior to what they could obtain from CP. SI is thus less fair to future generations than CP; and if there are no obligations of fairness to future generations, but there are such obligations with regard to one's

---

[38] Since there is a paucity of discussion of SI by egalitarian philosophers, I should mention one other argument that might seem germane to this topic. Political theorist Albert Weale argues that although a flat-rate form of SI, which provides the same modest pension to everyone, may appear to be more egalitarian than one with an earnings-related component (since the latter increases benefits with increased earnings), in fact the opposite is true. The reason resides in the different incentives the two systems give to the nonpoor or middle class. In the former, the incentive is to supplement the modest flat-rate pension with a private pension which is expected to produce returns which are as lucrative as possible for oneself and one's family; one would try to avoid any pension scheme which redistributes income or includes poor risks (as occurs in some occupational pensions). Indeed, to the extent to which your taxes for the flat-rate scheme reduce your ability to purchase an advantageous private pension, you will resist any attempts to expand the level of coverage. In an SI system with an earnings-related component, on the other hand, the incentive is to expand the level of coverage. Doing so will not be a pure loss, since while benefits are not proportional to earnings, they will rise with earnings to some extent. And there will be little incentive to resist the redistribution that is often a part of earnings-related schemes, since such collective action would be extremely costly. The result of these incentives is that more money from the pension funds reaches the worse-off members of society in an earnings-related scheme than in a pure flat-rate scheme, even though the latter is more egalitarian per unit of resources. In effect, spillover from the larger amount of tax funds expended on earnings-related systems means that there is more *total* redistribution in such a scheme than in one which is more egalitarian per unit of resources.

Suppose Weale's argument is sound. Does his argument about the egalitarian merits of different forms of SI have any application to the subject at hand, the egalitarian merits of SI versus CP? Could CP be a stand-in for a flat-rate form of SI? No, because CP is a fully funded pension, rather than being PAYG, and it is the PAYG nature of SI, plus its regressive financing, that produces its anti-egalitarian effects, as compared to CP. The logic of Weale's argument is to favor forms of SI which absorb a greater share of GDP on the grounds that more of that money will spill over to the poor than in more modest forms of SI; but even if this is true, it ignores the intergenerational effects of SI. An SI system which absorbs a lot of the GDP means a greater burden for later generations—particularly the poor of those generations, for reasons already discussed. See Albert Weale, "Equality, Social Solidarity, and the Welfare State," *Ethics*, vol. 100, no. 3 (April 1990), pp. 480–81. Since Sweden is Weale's model for the type of SI system he favors, it is worth noting that even if Sweden's system is more egalitarian than a pure flat-rate system would be, it does not have progressive intragenerational transfers. See World Bank, *Averting the Old Age Crisis*, p. 133.

children and descendants, then the same conclusion applies vis-à-vis children and descendants.

B. Positive rights and security

A major dispute in rights theory concerns the status of basic[39] positive rights, that is, basic rights which require that someone (other than the right-holder) perform some positive action, rather than merely refrain from certain actions, as negative rights require. The classical-liberal view of rights is that positive and negative rights have a very different status: the only positive rights are special rights, rights that arise from a special relationship between the parties, such as contractual rights or rights between parents and children, whereas negative rights are usually general or universal rights, rights which all persons have. Sometimes welfare state programs are justified by arguments that this classical-liberal view of rights is mistaken, that positive and negative rights have the same status. A common way of attempting to show this is by reference to basic needs. Sometimes it is argued that just as one can ground negative liberty rights as a requirement or need of moral agency—the idea being that in order to be a moral agent capable of making choices and pursuing a conception of the good, one needs a certain sphere of noninterference or liberty—so one can argue that moral agents need certain minimal conditions of well-being. Or it is argued that if negative liberty rights are to have value or to be effectively exercised, then one needs certain (material) goods and services.[40] Whatever the contours of the argument, however, a needs-rights link seems like an unpromising way to ground any form of *insurance*, whether social or private. Insurance grounds a right to a pension based on contribution, not on need. Of course, both SI and CP incorporate some criterion of need into their systems: SI to a greater extent, CP to a lesser extent. The point, though, is that a pure means-tested or needs-tested program would seem to best fit a positive-rights argument, rather than SI or CP.

However, political theorist J. Donald Moon has attempted a reconciliation of positive rights with SI.[41] He argues that a necessary condition for the justification of basic rights is that their legal instantiation not undermine self-respect, by which he means the belief that one is a person of

[39] A basic right is a moral right that has a considerable degree of weight, so that it typically defeats perfectionist considerations (claims about individual well-being or virtue) and claims of societal or aggregate well-being.

[40] Both arguments have been given by a variety of philosophers. For a helpful summary and critique, see Lesley Jacobs, *Rights and Deprivation* (Oxford: Oxford University Press, 1993), ch. 6.

[41] See J. Donald Moon, "The Moral Basis of the Democratic Welfare State," in *Democracy and the Welfare State*, ed. Amy Gutmann (Princeton: Princeton University Press, 1988), pp. 30–36, 41–46; and Moon, "Introduction: Responsibility, Rights, and Welfare," in *Responsibility, Rights, and Welfare: The Theory of the Welfare State*, ed. J. Donald Moon (Boulder, CO: Westview Press, 1988), pp. 4–8. See also Jacobs, *Rights and Deprivation*, pp. 198, 200–202.

worth who lives up to certain standards, who is entitled to respect. In a
society where markets are the predominant form of producing and allo-
cating goods and services, people are expected to be able to support
themselves through productive activity, and positive rights based purely
upon need run the serious risk of undermining self-respect. This problem
is avoided by delivering state services upon the basis of universal provision and social insurance. Universal provision means that these services
are provided to every citizen, so that no stigma is attached to receiving
them; and social insurance means that one's positive rights are based
upon having contributed to their provision. Since one's contributions
help to fund one's benefits,[42] one is viewed as an independent person, not
someone purely dependent upon others for meeting one's needs, or "on
welfare" as it is often pejoratively put, at least in the U.S. Another way
Moon puts his argument is that these social insurance programs help to
balance welfare rights with the notion of responsibility, which is inherent
in the notion of a moral agent. The principle of individual responsibility
implies that relations among adults will be based on reciprocity; they will
not be asymmetrical relations of dependence. That one's right to a pension is based on contributions means that it is no threat to this norm of
reciprocity.

The upshot of this argument is that the best way in a market society to
meet needs is *indirectly* through a program that is not exclusively or
primarily needs-based. Of course, this is not always possible, given the
inability of some people to work, which is why, Moon says, some purely
needs-based or means-tested programs are necessary. In the case of old-
age or retirement pensions, however, it is possible; and thus a social
insurance program is better than a pure needs-based or means-tested
program.

I shall not take issue with Moon's argument that SI is better than pure
means-tested programs as a way of protecting positive rights without
threatening self-respect or the norm of reciprocity. But one can also use
his argument to compare SI with CP, and in that regard CP wins deci-
sively on three counts. First, in an SI system one does not get the result of
one's contribution, while in a CP system everyone (except those needing
a safety net) gets the result of her contribution (plus interest). Second, SI
is a serious threat to the norm of reciprocity because of its severe intergenerational transfers, while in a CP system there are few if any harmful
transfers between generations. Third, the indirect way SI meets needs is
quite harmful for the poor of later generations, while CP does not have

---

[42] In "The Moral Basis of the Democratic Welfare State," p. 46, Moon says that recipients
of social insurance benefits have in fact contributed their fair share, but in "Introduction:
Responsibility, Rights, and Welfare," p. 7, he merely says that "at least in theory" the
recipients have contributed the resources that make the benefits possible. Hence, it is unclear to what extent Moon really believes that in an SI system one's pension is funded by
one's own contributions.

this feature. Thus, rather than indirectly meeting needs in a way that does not violate the norm of reciprocity, old-age SI is a significant threat to that norm and is a poor way of meeting needs, while CP does not violate the norm of reciprocity and is a comparatively better way of meeting needs.

I will assume that Moon would have to concede the points mentioned above—that in CP, but not SI, (most) everyone gets the result of his contribution (plus interest), that CP lacks the severe intergenerational transfers present in SI, etc. I can think of two strategies Moon could employ to reply to my argument despite admitting these facts. One strategy is to argue that although SI is objectionable on the grounds that it violates a norm of reciprocity or contribution, CP is objectionable because of its paternalism: by forcing a person to save for her own retirement, CP treats sane adults as if they were children who must be protected from harming themselves, thus undermining their self-respect. On the other hand, SI forces workers to save for *others'* retirement, and therefore does not face this problem of paternalism. Thus, CP and SI are on a par as far as balancing positive rights with self-respect, which, after all, was Moon's main concern. CP has a comparative advantage because it is no threat to a norm of reciprocity or contribution, while SI has a comparative advantage on the issue of paternalism.

Now, as Joel Feinberg has pointed out,[43] whether a law or policy is paternalistic is a matter of its (predominant) justification. Since the issue here is the citizens' sense of self-respect, we have to ask how the citizens understand the justification of CP and SI. However, there are often multiple justifications for a law or policy, and this muddies the waters. CP clearly can be justified nonpaternalistically: I have already indicated how one could argue that it is a fairer and more just system than SI. And SI can be justified on paternalist grounds: for one might wonder why workers must save for other people's retirement, and the answer one might supply is that these others cannot be trusted to save for their own pensions.[44] Furthermore, in a number of respects CP involves greater trust of the citizenry than SI: citizens have much more freedom within the system to choose their own particular type of retirement plan, how much to invest (provided it is not below a minimum), where to invest, when to retire, etc. Thus, I conclude that an argument that CP is more paternalistic than SI,

---

[43] Joel Feinberg, *Harm to Self* (New York: Oxford University Press, 1986), pp. 16–17.

[44] One might argue that this cannot be a paternalist argument, since the persons who cannot be trusted to save are not the persons being required to save. However, as Feinberg suggests, paternalism is a matter of the justification of a law or policy, and if the justification for forcing A to save for B is that otherwise B will harm B (rather than, say, that B will harm A), then the rationale for the law is indeed paternalistic. While this is a rather indirect way of meeting a paternalistic objective, it is paternalistic nonetheless so long as the aim is to prevent B from harming B. Furthermore, as I shall argue later, PAYG systems are not infrequently misunderstood, and workers come to think that their taxes are being invested for their own retirement, in which case they may view the justification of SI as paternalistic in the more obvious sense.

and in that regard, more potentially destructive of self-respect, is speculative at best. If one wants to avoid all taint of paternalism, the best way to do so is to avoid any system of forced savings.

A different strategy that Moon might employ is to argue that my criticisms of SI are irrelevant to his main concern. That concern, he might remind me, is that the legal protection of positive rights not undermine self-respect, and since self-respect depends on one's *beliefs*, not on whether these beliefs are true, it follows that whether recipients of SI get the result of their contributions or whether in fact SI is a threat to a norm of reciprocity is not of crucial importance. What is of crucial importance is that the system be widely perceived as embodying or being compatible with the principle of contribution or reciprocity, and that it not be viewed pejoratively as "welfare." In this regard, Moon might continue, old-age SI has generally been a resounding success. The point of this rebuttal by Moon is not to show that SI is better than CP, but, as before, to show that it is no worse as regards embodying positive rights to a pension without undermining self-respect. This rebuttal, however, has three problems.

First, one may wonder how long the belief that SI is compatible with a norm of contribution or reciprocity will last or even whether it is still widespread; recent developments in the U.S. certainly throw doubt on this claim.[45] It would hardly be surprising to see this belief collapse, since it is based upon an illusion. And as I shall discuss in the section on public justification, there is something very troubling about a program whose support depends crucially upon an illusion.

Second, the *value* of self-respect is diminished if it is based upon an illusion. After all, presumably the reason why Moon thought it important to argue that the legal instantiation of positive rights should not undermine self-respect was that self-respect is supposed to be an extremely important value, and if there is a threat that its value will be diminished by SI, but this is not true for CP (since the latter is founded on a genuine insurance principle of getting one's contribution back plus interest), then this is a reason to favor CP.[46]

---

[45] Recent polls show that a large majority of those under thirty-five and those over sixty support a proposal to allow people to direct part of their Social Security taxes to a financial institution of their choice and to receive less in Social Security benefits. See Peter J. Ferrara, *A Plan for Privatizing Social Security* (Washington, DC: Cato Institute, 1997). The bipartisan Social Security advisory panel, appointed by President Clinton in 1994, has recommended three different plans for reforming Social Security, all of which involve investing at least part of Social Security taxes in the stock market, and two of which endorse taxpayers doing their own investing. See "A Consensus Emerges: Social Security Faces Substantial Makeover," *Wall Street Journal*, July 8, 1996, pp. A1, A4. While these results do not prove the collapse of the belief that Social Security embodies some norm of reciprocity or contribution, they certainly suggest it, for it would be hard to explain these results if Social Security were viewed as embodying that norm.

[46] The strength of this reason is unclear. It is difficult to say to what extent the value of self-respect is diminished if it is based on illusions. Furthermore, the sources of self-respect

Third, and perhaps most important, Moon's point was that a *necessary* condition for the justification of positive rights is that their legal instantiation not undermine self-respect; but clearly a *sufficient* condition is that there be a solid basis or rationale for these rights. Recall that I began this discussion of positive rights and SI by noting that need would seem to be the most promising way to ground a positive right, but that Moon argued that grounding these rights by reference to contribution was preferable, since it would not threaten the notion that one was an independent person worthy of self-respect, and since it would not divide society into two classes, one needy and dependent, the other providing the support for the needy. But if, as I have noted, contribution is a suspect way of grounding rights to one's pension in an SI system, and if need as a basis for supporting positive rights is tainted because of its threat to self-respect, then there seems to be no plausible way to ground SI within the realm of positive-rights arguments. Since CP does have a legitimate ground in that realm, i.e., contribution, it follows that conceding that SI may lack such a ground is indeed relevant, to put it mildly.

Closely related to the question of positive rights is the value or importance of security. Old-age SI is often justified in terms of creating economic security for the elderly, or more realistically, in terms of minimizing economic insecurity during retirement. One's security is a function of (1) a guarantee or high probability of an income, and (2) the amount of income guaranteed. In the early stage of PAYG, present retirees and workers who will retire within fifteen to thirty-five years have a greater degree of security than they would have under any private alternative. SI in that stage has a higher degree of security regarding (2) than CP, while it is no worse in terms of security regarding (1), because at this stage, the redefinition of benefits is in the retirees' favor and the changes in tax rates are only mildly to the workers' disadvantage. However, in the later stages retirees and workers have a lower degree of security regarding both (1) and (2) than they would have in a CP system. The "rate of return" is lower, worries about whether promises will be kept are widespread, and redefinition of benefits and contributions to the disadvantage of both retirees and workers is common.

Another way to put this comparison is that SI *redistributes* security over time. The early generations are made more secure at the price of reducing security for later ones. On the other hand, CP keeps all generations at an even keel of fairly high security.[47] I assume that the value of security

---

are multiple, and it is unclear to what extent the self-respect of recipients of SI is linked with a view that they are entitled to their pensions or are not harming later generations.

[47] It might be objected that this is false, because in the beginning of a CP system those who had not saved much on their own voluntarily, or who invested imprudently, would have little security when they retired. But all this means is that in the beginning of a CP system, the safety net may have to be larger than in the later stages. It does not negate the point that a CP system does not redistribute security through time.

lessens if it is achieved at the expense of others, and therefore I conclude that CP is better than SI on this score. The same conclusion would be reached if one were concerned with overall security over time; while there is no way to even semi-precisely aggregate this, a fairly high level of security over time seems to beat a very high level followed by a decreasing level.

C. Negative rights and freedom

There is little controversy that there are basic negative rights, such as rights over one's mind or body (sometimes described as rights of self-ownership, or the right to physical security and integrity), rights to freedom of speech and freedom of religion, and rights to privacy. There is also considerable common ground concerning the type(s) of arguments that ground negative rights. The core of many of these arguments is that these rights provide the right-holder with the freedom to pursue a wide variety of peaceful plans and projects which reflect and constitute his higher-order values and which help to shape his identity, etc., and that such freedom must be protected as a way of showing respect for, or expressing the proper kind of value for, persons of the sort we are. Controversy does exist, however, concerning whether robust private property rights (which include rights to exchange and rights to exclude) should be included in the list of basic negative rights, as classical liberals maintain, or whether the only property right that belongs in that list is a right to have exclusive use of personal property, as modern liberals maintain.

If there are robust private property rights, then CP is far less of an infringement or interference with such rights than is SI. Both arguably do infringe or interfere with such rights, since they compel contributions (in the absence of any plausible relation between these forced contributions and the need to protect others' rights), but CP gives one far more control or choice over where and how to invest these contributions. However, even if one does not believe that there are robust private property rights, one should acknowledge that the kind of values protected by negative rights apply to retirement decisions. Clearly, the freedom involved in choosing what kind of retirement to have, when to cease working, how much to put aside for one's retirement at various times in one's life, etc., are all intimately involved with one's self-definition, one's higher-order plans and projects, etc. Indeed, retirement decisions are part of other sorts of major life decisions: one's occupation, the trade-off between work and leisure, one's time preference, the extent to which one is concerned with or plans for one's future, etc., and these decisions constitute and reflect one's conception of the good, one's higher-order plans and projects, etc. While CP does restrict one's freedom to choose how and when to invest one's retirement savings by forcing one to save a certain minimal amount throughout one's working years, it is obviously much less restrictive than

SI, which gives one no freedom to determine how one's contributions are to be utilized.

Thus, whether one focuses on the freedom to choose how to invest one's retirement income, or on robust private property rights as basic rights, CP unequivocally is less of a restriction or threat to either.

D. Public justification and epistemic accessibility

Many contemporary political philosophers, particularly those defending some form of liberalism, argue that basic political principles and institutions must be publicly justified.[48] There are two parts to this idea: the "public" part and the "justification" part. The former means that political institutions and principles must be supported by public reasons, reasons which are widely and openly accessible to citizens with normal reasoning powers. These reasons must be seen by citizens to be good reasons, to offer rationales or arguments which make sense to them and which provide for them a plausible basis for supporting or endorsing (or at least not objecting to) basic political institutions and state programs. This notion of public reasons is based upon or is an outgrowth of a notion of respect for persons. This respect is for that which we share in common as persons, namely certain powers of reasoning and judgment; generating public support for political institutions or major social programs in a way which bypasses or subverts such powers manifests disrespect.

As for the justification side of the notion of public justification, the fact that an institution is supported by public reasons does not entail that it is publicly justified, because even conscientious and thoughtful people make invalid inferences and accept bad arguments.[49] What is needed to link public reasons with public justification, or what is needed for something to count as a *good* public reason, is quite controversial. It is easier to state negative requirements, such as the following. Suppose a political institution or major social program has the following features: (a) it blocks or makes it difficult to obtain reasonably accurate or reliable information about the nature or evolution of that institution or program, and/or (b) it is so complex that it is unlikely that anyone but experts can monitor its effects or evolution. Suppose further that there is a feasible institution of the same type which does not have feature (a) and/or feature (b), or has them to a lesser extent. Then the institution or program that has (a)

---

[48] For an argument that public justification is central to liberalism, see Stephen Macedo, *Liberal Virtues: Citizenship, Virtue, and Community in Liberal Constitutionalism* (Oxford: Clarendon Press, 1990), pp. 40–48. Liberal theorists differ concerning the subject matter of public justification: sometimes it is principles of justice; at other times it is the social order or basic social and political institutions. I shall assume that a state program or institution like SI, in virtue of its far-reaching effects and the relevance of questions about its justice and fairness, is an institution that falls within the subject matter of public justification.

[49] Gerald Gaus makes this point, citing much empirical evidence to support it, in Gaus, *Justificatory Liberalism* (New York: Oxford University Press, 1996), pp. 130–36.

and/or (b), or has them to a greater extent than its feasible alternative, is, *ceteris paribus*, unjustified. The rationale for this principle of epistemic accessibility, as I shall dub it, is that, whatever counts as a good public reason for endorsing institution X, if the public is seriously misled or misinformed about the nature of X, then its endorsement of what it takes to be X may in fact be an endorsement of something different from X, and thus we lack grounds for saying in this case that public support implies public justification. If all feasible institutions of type X would produce these epistemic obstacles, then we might have to acknowledge that public justification of institutions of this type is a requirement we cannot meet; but if there is a feasible alternative which does not produce these epistemic obstacles, then we have a solid basis for preferring the one that is more epistemically accessible.

The principle of epistemic accessibility implies support for CP over SI, for a variety of reasons. First, the PAYG nature of SI makes it very difficult for the typical person to monitor or understand its actuarial status and the relation between the taxes he pays and his expected benefits.[50] This is because (1) an SI system's "rate of return" is heavily dependent upon population trends and the growth in wages, (2) there are fairly frequent changes made in the rate and level of taxation and in the benefit levels and schedules, and (3) in general the system's status is subject to frequent political maneuvering. Second, many SI systems are funded, at least in part, by a payroll tax, split between employer and employee. This makes it difficult for the taxpayers to know the cost of the system; most people are likely to be unclear about who really pays the tax. Also, the payroll tax gives the impression or the illusion that one is contributing a premium that will be invested. Third, this impression is compounded by descriptions of the system as social *insurance*, references to trust funds, etc. Fourth, typically the system does not allow any exit, and thus faces no direct competition, and therefore there is little or no information provided by the managers of the system concerning how it is doing relative to other pension plans. Of course, people have private pensions in most countries with SI, and they understand, at least in a vague sense, that government SI does not operate just like a private pension, but they have little or no basis for making direct comparisons. Related to this is a fifth point, namely that one has no genuine private property right in an SI system, and thus those who operate the system have no duty or incentive to provide accurate information to their "shareholders" concerning the way the system is being run, its likely future, its performance, etc.

In all these respects, CP is fundamentally different. CP, except for the minimum pension guarantee, is a defined-contribution system, and therefore the premiums or contributions are well understood (and, beyond the

---

[50] It is worth noting that in the first thirty years or so of Social Security in the U.S., most citizens had an extremely hazy and poor idea of how it worked. See Martha Derthick, *Policymaking for Social Security* (Washington, DC: Brookings Institution, 1979), pp. 188–90.

minimum contribution, are under the control of the contributor). Private pension plans have both the incentive and the obligation to provide information about their actuarial status and their rate of return, and as a result the investor or participant has a good basis for understanding the system. With the exception of the definition of the minimum contribution and minimum retirement pension, CP is not inherently subject to political manipulation; and one has a genuine property right in the system, which adds further incentive to follow and monitor the progress of one's investment or contribution. Thus, CP is pellucid compared with SI, and by its very nature information about CP's status and evolution is widely available.

One response to my argument that SI is at a comparative disadvantage to CP vis-à-vis epistemic accessibility is that SI could be modified so that it is closer to market insurance and thus more comprehensible and less subject to misinformation:

1. SI need not be subject constantly to political maneuvering. It could be placed in a separate budget; rules could be established to prevent it from being influenced by the normal budgetary maneuvering; changes in tax rates and benefits could be subject to a supermajority rule; and so on.

2. SI could be financed exclusively by an employee payroll tax, so as to avoid disguising its costs to present workers.

3. Advance funding could be increased to limit the PAYG nature of the system, with the taxes invested in whatever would lessen the implicit public pension debt with the least risk (e.g., some combination of private and government securities).

4. Partial opting-out could be allowed, as it is in a number of countries,[51] thus creating some direct competition between SI and its private alternatives.

5. Though genuine private property rights are incompatible with SI, the government could provide to individuals the equivalent of accurate quarterly or annual reports, and could make widely available accurate information about SI's actuarial status, expected rates of return, etc. Doing so would probably compel governments to make the benefit schedules simpler and easier to follow.

The problem with this reply is that the issue is not one of "coulds," of whether something is empirically possible, but of probabilities; and the probability of these reforms of SI, taken collectively, is fairly remote. Governments, as the ultimate organizations of coercive enforcement, have grave difficulties binding themselves to a set of rules and procedures—particularly outside of the constitutional setting, which is SI's location—and therefore there is a low probability that rules will be promulgated and followed that keep the SI budget separate, disseminate accurate in-

---

[51] This is allowed, e.g., in Britain and Japan. See Davis, *Pension Funds*, pp. 64–65; and Ferrara et al., *Private Alternatives to Social Security in Other Countries* (*supra* note 25), pp. 1–2, 25–28.

formation about its status, etc. The incentives and obligations of a government system, even if partial opting-out is allowed, to act more like a private pension fund are obviously fewer and weaker than those which would exist in an actual private pension fund. The fact that these suggested changes, taken collectively, have not been instituted in real SI systems is testimony to the improbability of these alterations to SI.[52] Furthermore, even with advance funding, SI remains a PAYG system. This means that the ratio of taxes paid in to benefits payed out is heavily influenced by such factors as demographics, which in turn implies that there will be no set contribution or benefit, and that determining one's rate of return, the actuarial status of the system, etc., will necessarily remain difficult compared with CP. Even if the reforms were enacted, then, CP would still be superior to SI as far as epistemic accessibility is concerned.

A different and almost opposite way of reducing the inability of the average citizen to comprehend SI would be to increase the PAYG nature of the system and to make this change explicit. SI systems could be redescribed as "old-age assistance" programs or something to that effect, and advance funding and references to trust funds could be abandoned. The system could be financed largely or completely by general taxation, thus helping to eliminate confusion between a tax and a genuine investment. Adding a healthy dose of means-testing to the system (e.g., prohibiting those in the top quintile of income from obtaining public pensions) could also facilitate breaking the comparison of SI to market insurance.

However, while in one sense these suggested reforms would make SI more easily comprehended by the average citizen—by making it clear that SI has nothing to do with market insurance—in other respects they would make SI *less* epistemically accessible. That is because if SI—now called "old-age assistance" under these proposed reforms—becomes completely integrated into other government programs (by being financed by

---

[52] Philosopher Michael Robins has objected to this statement, maintaining that the existence of pension plans for state employees in the U.S. (or for certain state employees, such as teachers) shows that a government-run pension system can be close to being fully funded, give quarterly or annual reports to its recipients, and not be subject to political maneuvering. However, these pensions systems are not nationwide systems, while my concern in this essay is with systems that cover (virtually) all citizens in a country; thus, the operation of pension plans for these state employees does not negate my point that no existing SI system has adopted all the reforms mentioned in the text that would make it operate more like market insurance. More importantly, pension plans for state employees are defined-benefit plans. Defined-benefit plans that rely upon taxpayers for funds, even if they are not subject to political maneuvering, have a stronger incentive than private occupational defined-benefit plans not to fund adequately. This is because the former use the power to tax to make up for any mistaken actuarial projections, while private occupational plans that make mistakes are at a competitive disadvantage (since wages for younger workers will have to be lowered to meet the unfunded pensions promised to retirees). Indeed, many pension plans of states and municipalities in the U.S. are in trouble because in the late 1980s and early 1990s, overly optimistic assumptions about future rates of return made them cut their required contribution rates, and as a result, it is estimated that almost one in three of these plans have less than 75 percent of the assets required to meet their liabilities. See World Bank, *Averting the Old Age Crisis*, pp. 188–89.

general revenues, abandoning analogies to market insurance, etc.), it becomes even more subject to political maneuvering. As such, changes in benefits payed and taxes required might become more, not less, frequent, and the cost of the system would become harder, not easier, to comprehend.

There is, perhaps, an even deeper problem with both of the responses I have been considering. Recall that the problem at hand is that public support does not translate into public justification if it is difficult for the public to comprehend the institution it supports. The reforms I have discussed are designed to make it easier to obtain accurate information about SI. But if making that information available would eliminate or drastically reduce public support for SI, then the issue of the relationship between public support and public justification would not arise in the first place for SI. Were governments to advertise loudly, clearly, and persistently that the system is PAYG, this would mean letting citizens know that there are significant intergenerational transfers that harm later generations, that one's taxes are not being invested in a genuine trust fund, and that the system should not be confused with market insurance (for even with partial funding the analogy is strained). In the U.S., there is evidence that equating SI with fully funded market insurance (or viewing them as closely analogous) has been crucial to its support,[53] and while one cannot rule out the possibility that, in different political cultures, such a system would be supported by a public knowledgeable of the nature of SI, such support does seem unlikely in light of the system's distributive unfairness, redistribution of security, and restrictions on negative freedom. On the other hand, since CP does not have these problems (or has them to a lesser degree), accurate information about its nature does not seem to be an obstacle to its obtaining public support.

IV. Conclusion

Old-age social insurance is one of the central institutions of the welfare state. I have shown that it is unjustified, in light of an alternative—compulsory private pensions—that is superior when judged by four central normative values or principles that are used by contemporary political philosophers in their discussions (and usually defenses) of the welfare state.[54] If my argument can be replicated for other forms of social insur-

---

[53] See Carolyn L. Weaver, The Crisis in Social Security (Durham, NC: Duke University Press, 1982), pp. 80–86, 123–24; and Derthick, Policymaking for Social Security, pp. 199–201, 204.

[54] Norman Daniels, Am I My Parents' Keeper? (New York: Oxford University Press, 1988), pp. 134–35, defends SI, but since his arguments do not fit neatly within any of the values or principles I have discussed so far, I have put them in this note. Daniels denies that later generations in an SI system have grounds for complaints despite their poor "rate of return" because (1) returns are indexed in an SI system and not in private pensions, (2) private pensions will give a variable return and thus subject the elderly to more significant risks than one gets with SI, and (3) SI reduces the financial burden of supporting one's parents. These

ance, such as health and unemployment insurance, then the central values and principles of contemporary political philosophy provide ample grounds for condemning the welfare state.

Though the results obtained here are clearly important, two limitations of my arguments should be noted, one retrospective in character, the other prospective. My argument does not necessarily support the view that when SI was introduced, its introduction was a wrong or unjust decision. To support that view, CP would have to have been a feasible alternative to SI when the latter was first introduced, and I have not addressed that historical-institutional question here. It may be that when some SI systems, or the earnings-related component of those systems, were first introduced in certain countries, the feasible private alternative to SI was voluntary savings or pensions plus a means-tested system for the elderly poor. I think such a system would also be superior to SI, but to demonstrate that would require arguments that would be beyond the scope of this essay. Thus, the retrospective implications of my argument are somewhat indeterminate.

As for prospective judgments, my arguments imply that measures should be introduced to phase out SI and introduce a CP system—subject, however, to a caveat that it is possible that the transition from SI to CP might end up being so bad that we would be justified to keep the present system. Though this is *possible*, it is very unlikely, since for reasons already discussed, the problems with SI will get worse as the mature stage of PAYG continues, in which case transition measures to get us to a CP system should be introduced sooner rather than later.[55]

Philosophy, West Virginia University

---

are weak arguments. The first argument is weak because SI's record of indexing benefits is spotty, and a CP system could incorporate indexed annuities into one's post-retirement choices, as Chile's system does. The second argument is weak because CP's safety net provides a minimum guarantee, thus limiting the degree of risk, while in an SI system all citizens are subject to the risk of redefined benefits, changing tax rates, etc. The third argument clearly fails, because CP also reduces the burden of children caring for their parents, and compared to the later stages of SI, CP does a better job of reducing that burden in virtue of its superior rate of return and safety net. On the question of indexing, see Davis, *Pension Funds*, p. 114; and World Bank, *Averting the Old Age Crisis*, p. 156.

[55] For an argument that the transition to CP would not be terribly difficult or costly, see Peter J. Ferrara, "Privatization of Social Security: The Transition Issue," elsewhere in this volume. Note that even if all the values or principles discussed in this essay imply support for a transition to CP, it does not follow that they all imply support for the same way of making that transition.

PRIVATIZATION OF SOCIAL SECURITY: THE TRANSITION ISSUE

By Peter J. Ferrara

I. Introduction

The possible privatization of Social Security has long been a matter of theoretical interest to those who ideologically favor free markets and maximum personal autonomy. But in the spirit of an age when the Berlin Wall fell and the totalitarian Soviet empire collapsed through a peaceful revolution from within, the politics of Social Security has been remade in recent years in a similarly dramatic fashion.

Suddenly, major national pollsters are finding huge majorities in the U.S. in favor of privatization and the freedom of workers to control their own funds.[1] Chile's wildly successful privatization in 1981 is now being copied across Latin America and elsewhere, most recently with the vigorous endorsement of the usually staid World Bank.[2] U.S. financial firms participating in these newly privatized systems see firsthand how well they work, and consequently have been transformed into vigorous advocates of doing the same in the U.S. Liberal writers and Democratic politicians are joining conservative writers and Republican politicians in advancing privatization reforms.[3] Major think tanks, grassroots activist groups, and trade associations are beginning to work to enact such reforms.

As a result, the possible privatization of Social Security is no longer a purely theoretical question, but a very practical one as well. Can the current public system be feasibly reformed into a private one? What would the costs be of the transition from the current public, pay-as-you-go system to a private, fully funded one? Would these costs be manageable and worthwhile? These are the issues discussed in this essay.

---

[1] A 1994 poll by Luntz Research found that 82 percent of adults under thirty-five supported the idea of "directing part of [their] Social Security taxes to a personal retirement account like an IRA which could be kept at any financial institution they would like, and receiving less in Social Security benefits from the government." A 1995 Luntz poll of all adults found the public supporting such an option by 77 percent to 14 percent. In 1996, McInturff and Associates conducted a nationwide poll for the Cato Institute which found the public supporting the idea by 68 percent to 11 percent. These poll results are reviewed in Peter J. Ferrara, *A Plan for Privatizing Social Security* (Washington, DC: Cato Institute, 1997).

[2] Peter J. Ferrara, John C. Goodman, and Merrill Matthews, Jr., *Private Alternatives to Social Security in Other Countries*, NCPA Study No. 200 (Dallas: National Center for Policy Analysis, 1995); World Bank Policy Research Report, *Averting the Old Age Crisis* (New York: Oxford University Press, 1994).

[3] See Ferrara, *A Plan for Privatizing Social Security*; and Peter J. Ferrara, "The New Politics of Social Security," *Wall Street Journal*, March 8, 1996, p. A19.

II. The Social Security System

A. Background

The Social Security system pays cash retirement benefits for those who have worked and paid into the system for at least ten years. Full retirement benefits are paid to those who retire at age sixty-five. The benefit amounts are based on past wages, but are skewed to pay a higher percentage of past earnings to lower-income workers than to higher-income ones. Actuarially reduced benefits are available to those who retire as early as age sixty-two.

The system also pays cash survivors' benefits to the spouse and children of a covered worker who dies, though a working spouse or one receiving his or her own retirement benefits is unlikely to be eligible. In addition, disability benefits are paid for a covered worker who can no longer work, as well as to his or her nonworking spouse and children.

The system is financed primarily by a payroll tax equal to 12.4 percent of wages up to a maximum taxable income equal to $62,700 in 1996. This maximum taxable income is indexed to increase with the rate of growth of wages each year. The tax is putatively paid half by the worker and half by the employer, but the employer's share probably comes out of wages the worker would have received otherwise. Another payroll tax of 2.9 percent finances part of the Medicare program.

Social Security operates on a pay-as-you-go basis. Most of the funds coming into the program are not saved and invested for the future benefits of today's workers. Rather, they are immediately paid out to finance the benefits of current retirees. The future benefits of today's workers are to be paid out of the future taxes of those working at the time.

In fact, any excess of Social Security taxes over expenditures is lent to the federal government and spent on the full range of other government programs. Social Security receives in return specially issued government bonds to be held in the Social Security trust funds. These bonds are just further national debt that will have to be paid out of general taxes or higher federal deficits and borrowing when the funds are needed to pay Social Security benefits.

B. The basic rationale for privatization

The reasons why Social Security should be privatized have been discussed in great detail in numerous books and publications.[4] Briefly, these reasons include the following.

---

[4] These include Peter J. Ferrara, *Social Security: The Inherent Contradiction* (Washington, DC: Cato Institute, 1980); Peter J. Ferrara, ed., *Social Security: Prospects for Real Reform* (Washington, DC: Cato Institute, 1985); Peter J. Ferrara, *Social Security Rates of Return for Today's Young Workers* (Washington, DC: National Chamber Foundation, 1986).

Bankruptcy. The current Social Security system is inevitably headed for bankruptcy. Based on the government's own latest projections, paying all the retirement benefits financed by the current 15.3 percent payroll tax to those entering the workforce today will probably require doubling or tripling that tax to 30 to 40 percent.[5] That level of taxation is neither economically nor politically feasible. Consequently, there is no prospect that today's young workers will receive their currently promised benefits. In a privatized system, this financial crisis would be avoided, as all future benefits would be fully funded by private savings and investment. Indeed, once the transition costs of a privatization reform were offset, the reform would start producing surpluses that would reduce the total federal deficit, providing the key to solving what is otherwise an intractable long-term budget crisis in the U.S. This is discussed in detail below (near the end of Section IIIA).

Bad deal for young workers. Even if Social Security did somehow manage to pay all its promised benefits, the taxes for today's young workers are already so high that the benefits would be a bad deal in return for those taxes. These benefits would represent a low, below-market rate of return, or effective interest rate, on the taxes workers and their employers had to pay into the system throughout their careers. Studies show that investing these tax funds instead in private savings and insurance would likely yield three or more times the benefits Social Security promises to today's young workers.[6] Investing through the private system and earning modest returns, the average two-earner couple would retire with a trust fund of over $1 million in today's dollars to support their retirement benefits. This trust fund would pay more than Social Security out of the continuing interest alone, while still allowing the couple to leave the $1 million to their children or other heirs. Alternatively, they could use the entire trust fund for an annuity that would pay them three times what Social Security promises.

Savings and economic growth. Social Security's pay-as-you-go system probably displaces private fully funded alternatives where the funds coming in would be saved and invested for the future benefits of today's workers. The result is a large net loss of national savings, reducing economic growth.[7] The payroll tax probably substantially reduces economic growth as well.

[5] Board of Trustees of the Federal Old-Age and Survivors' Insurance and Disability Insurance Trust Funds, *1996 Annual Report* (Washington, DC, 1996). For a thorough discussion of the basis of this long-term financing crisis, see Ferrara, *Social Security: The Inherent Contradiction*, chs. 2 and 5; and Mark Weinberger, *Social Security: Facing the Facts*, Cato Institute Social Security Paper No. 3 (Washington, DC: Cato Institute, 1996).

[6] Ferrara, *Social Security Rates of Return for Today's Young Workers*; William G. Shipman, *Retiring with Dignity: Social Security v. Private Markets*, Cato Institute Social Security Paper No. 2 (Washington, DC: Cato Institute, 1995). For a thorough discussion of the basis of this problem, see Ferrara, *Social Security: The Inherent Contradiction*, chs. 2 and 4.

[7] Martin Feldstein estimates that as a result of this effect, Social Security reduces national savings by 30 to 40 percent; see Martin Feldstein, "Social Security, Induced Retirement, and

Shifting to a private system, with hundreds of billions invested in individual retirement accounts each year, would likely produce a large net increase in national savings, depending on how the government financed the transition. This would increase national investment, productivity, wages, jobs, and economic growth. Replacing the payroll tax with private retirement contributions would also improve economic growth, both because the required contributions would be lower and because those contributions would be seen as a direct part of the worker's compensation, stimulating more employment and output.

Equity. Social Security pays widely differing benefit amounts for the same amount of past taxes paid into the system, depending on a wide variety of factors. A private, invested system, by contrast, would offer the same market returns to everyone.

Blacks and other minorities would be among the biggest gainers from a private system. That is because they tend to live fewer years in retirement and consequently collect less in benefits. In a private, invested system, by contrast, they would each retain control over the funds paid in, and could pay themselves higher benefits over their fewer retirement years, or leave more to their children or other heirs.[8]

The poor would be among the greatest winners for the same reason as well, despite the extra benefits for them in the Social Security benefit structure. Moreover, the higher returns and benefits in a private, invested system would be most important to the poor. Even without counting the lower life expectancy of the poor, a private, invested system would pay minimum-wage earners more than twice the benefits promised by Social Security.[9] The saved funds in the private system that could be left to the children of the poor would also greatly help families break out of the cycle of poverty.[10]

Freedom of choice and control. Privatization of Social Security would also give American workers direct personal control over the thousands and thousands of dollars they and their employers must presently pay into Social Security each year. The desire for such freedom of control is fueling much of the public support for privatization. Moreover, through the private market, people would be free to tailor their retirement and insurance benefits to their own personal needs and circumstances. They would have broader freedom to choose their own retirement age, for example, or the level of life and disability insurance protection appropriate for them.

Aggregate Capital Accumulation," *Journal of Political Economy*, vol. 82, no. 5 (September–October 1974); and Martin Feldstein and Anthony Pellechio, "Social Security Wealth: The Impact of Alternative Inflation Adjustments," Conference on Financing Social Security, American Enterprise Institute (Washington, DC, 1977). For a thorough discussion of this issue, see Ferrara, *Social Security: The Inherent Contradiction*, ch. 3.

[8] Peter J. Ferrara and John C. Goodman, *Social Security and Race*, NCPA Policy Report No. 128 (Washington, DC: National Center for Policy Analysis, 1987).

[9] Ferrara, *Social Security Rates of Return for Today's Young Workers*.

[10] For a more thorough discussion of these issues, see Ferrara, *Social Security: The Inherent Contradiction*, ch. 6.

III. A Concrete Proposal for Reform

To get a clear idea of how the transition to a privatized Social Security system would work, I shall set out and examine a specific, concrete reform proposal.[11] Under this proposal, for those who choose to participate in the optional private system, the worker and employer would each pay 5 percentage points of the current 6.2 percent Social Security tax on each into an individual private retirement-investment account for each worker, subject to the maximum taxable income limit calculated as it is today. It is not necessary to require the same amount of payments into the private system as is required for the old Social Security system, because the investment returns of the private system provide so much more in benefits. As indicated above, studies show that for today's young workers the private system can provide at least three times the benefits promised by Social Security for the same amount of payments. Financing for such a high level of benefits should not be mandatory. Workers and their employers would have the freedom to contribute more if they choose, up to some overall limit, perhaps 20 percent of wages as in the Chilean system.

The remaining 1.2 percent of the current tax on each employer and employee would continue to be paid for ten years after the worker opted into the private system, with the funds used to finance the reform's transition costs. After that, the worker and employer would each no longer have to pay this portion of the tax. As a result, this privatization proposal effectively provides for a 20 percent payroll tax cut along the way.

Part of the funds in each individual's investment account would have to be used to purchase private life and disability insurance covering at least the same survivors' benefits (pre-retirement) and disability benefits as Social Security. Workers would consequently be covered for these contingencies through the private system as they are through Social Security. Since Social Security only pays pre-retirement survivors' benefits to workers with children, workers without children would be free to forgo the life insurance and devote the funds to their retirement benefits. Similarly, workers would not have to buy disability insurance providing any greater benefits than Social Security would in their family circumstances.

The same rules, regulations, and restrictions would apply to the private retirement accounts as apply to individual retirement accounts (IRAs) today,[12] except that no withdrawals would be allowed before retirement. Employee contributions to the private accounts would not be tax deductible, just as employee Social Security taxes are not deductible. Employer contributions would be deductible as a business expense like wages, just as employer Social Security taxes are deductible today. Investment returns to the accounts over the years would be tax exempt until with-

---

[11] I set out the full proposal in *A Plan for Privatizing Social Security* (*supra* note 1).

[12] These rules allow broad investment choice among stocks, bonds, and other market vehicles, including foreign issues, but preclude the most risky, highly leveraged instruments, or non-interest-bearing commodities, such as gold.

drawal, just like returns in IRAs. In retirement, half the benefits would be included in taxable income and half would not, unless the worker made voluntary, nondeductible supplemental contributions. Then a formula would have to determine what proportion is taxable and what proportion is not.

Benefits at retirement would equal what the accumulated funds would support. The worker could use the funds to purchase an annuity paying promised benefits for the rest of the worker's life. Or the worker could make regular, periodic withdrawals. Regulations would limit such withdrawals so that the retiree could not use up all the funds early and then be left without retirement support. Workers in the private system could retire at any age after fifty-nine and a half. They could even retire earlier if their accumulated retirement funds were sufficient to satisfy a specified standard of benefits.

For workers who choose the private option, the government would pay into their accounts recognition bonds compensating them for past taxes paid into the Social Security system. The bonds would be credited with interest over the years. The amount of the bonds would be set so that with interest they would pay a proportion of future benefits equal to the proportion of lifetime Social Security taxes paid. At retirement, workers could turn in the bonds to the government over time for cash to finance their benefits, and could combine this income with the benefits payable from the private savings and investment accounts accumulated after the workers shifted to the private system. This system would give all workers a proportionally equal incentive to opt out for their remaining working years.

The government would guarantee all workers a minimum benefit as in Chile. This minimum benefit would be financed out of general tax revenues, supplementing private benefits to the extent necessary to reach the minimum benefit level. This would assure that no one would fall below a basic benefit level, with probably no significant cost to the government. That is because the high returns of the private system would likely leave almost all workers well above even a healthy minimum benefit level. Indeed, government assistance spending overall would probably be reduced, as the high returns and benefits of the private system left fewer people qualifying for such assistance.

Workers would have the complete freedom to choose to stay in the public Social Security system if they preferred. There would be no benefit reductions for anyone currently receiving Social Security benefits. But future benefits would be reduced by delaying the retirement age two months per year until the age reaches seventy. Early retirement would still be available at age sixty-two, with a full actuarial reduction in benefits. In addition, the Social Security benefit formula should be changed so that future benefits would grow over time at the rate of prices rather than wages. This would maintain the value of today's benefits in real terms, but would stop them from automatically growing higher in real terms. These benefit changes are justified to bring the system's expenditures into line with steady-state long-run revenues. They were proposed by the chairmen of the National Entitlement Commission in 1994, Senator Bob Kerrey (Democrat, Nebraska) and now-retired Senator John Danforth (Republican, Missouri). The proposals are included in legislation cosponsored by Kerrey and Senator Alan Simpson (Republican, Wyoming).

A. Managing the transition

Probably the key issue raised by this proposal for reform is how to finance the transition to the new system. More precisely, with workers paying into the private system rather than into Social Security, how will the government finance the benefit obligations of the old system until those obligations mostly end and future retirees are relying on the new system instead?

The advantage of a specific concrete proposal is that it allows analysts to map out exactly how the transition would work. Table 1 projects the fiscal effects of the specific proposal outlined above over forty years, assuming it was adopted at the start of 1997. These figures are meant to provide a general idea of the likely magnitude of each category over time, and not a precise estimate. They are calculated from the Social Security Administration's own projections of the future income and expenditures of Social Security, using the government's own assumptions.

To make these calculations, it was assumed that 50 percent of all workers would choose the private system over Social Security in the first year, continuing in the private system thereafter. An additional 25 percent of all workers, for a total of 75 percent, were assumed to choose the private option in the fourth year, continuing thereafter. Finally, an additional 15 percent of all workers, for a total of 90 percent, were assumed to choose the private option in the seventh year, continuing thereafter. All figures in the table are presented in 1996 dollars.

Column 1 shows the amounts that would be invested in the private retirement accounts each year instead of being paid into Social Security. The government would have to come up with alternative means of offsetting these shifted payments in order to continue to pay Social Security benefits during the transition.

Column 2 shows the total amount of invested funds that would be accumulated in the private retirement accounts each year. The private retirement investments were assumed to earn an average real rate of return of 4 percent, which is justified by market experience.[13] The retirement, survivors', and disability benefits paid from the private system were subtracted from these accumulations each year. The projections show

[13] Ferrara, *Social Security Rates of Return for Today's Young Workers*, p. 15.

that the total value of the private retirement accounts would grow quickly to almost $1 trillion after just five years (2001) and to over $2 trillion after just nine years.

Column 3 shows additional tax revenues that would be generated from the private retirement investments. The private system would be creating new savings and investment which would produce the full before-tax rate of return to capital. While the returns earned directly by the retirement accounts would not be taxed, substantial taxes would still be paid on the investments at the business level. Business enterprises would use the capital investments to generate, on average, the typical before-tax rate of return to capital. They would then pay their full income, payroll, and other tax assessments out of that return before paying the tax-exempt interest, dividends, and other returns to the investment accounts. This would still leave the investors with sufficient returns to receive the high benefits discussed earlier. At the same time, substantial new tax revenues would be generated for the government to help finance the transition costs of the reform and, eventually, to reduce the total federal deficit.

Harvard economics professor Martin Feldstein, chairman of the National Bureau of Economic Research, estimates that the full, real, before-tax return to capital is 9.3 percent.[14] Of that, he estimates that 3.9 percent would go to the government in taxes paid at the business level before remaining returns are paid to the retirement investment accounts. This is consistent with market investment data. It is also consistent with our assumption above that the accounts would directly receive a 4 percent real rate of return out of the full before-tax 9.3 percent return. With the private retirement account savings growing to huge amounts relatively rapidly, this would result in the generation of huge amounts of new tax revenue to offset the transition costs.

It should be noted that the private system can and should be structured in any event so that this proportion of the full before-tax return to capital is taxed away to help finance the transition. These full before-tax returns are so high that the private benefits would still be overwhelmingly higher than those paid by Social Security, as discussed above. Moreover, these full before-tax returns do not go completely untaxed in any other alternative savings vehicle. Consequently, this seems to be the least painful way to help finance the transition. It also follows a basic principle of successful privatization strategies in general—using some of the benefits of the reform to offset any costs.

Column 3 shows that this new revenue grows to large amounts over time, and will help to offset the transition costs in a major way. This is apart from any efficiency gains or supply-side spin-off effects multiplying

---

[14] Martin Feldstein, "The Missing Piece in Policy Analysis: Social Security Reform," *American Economic Review*, vol. 86 (May 1996).

TABLE 1. *Financing the transition (All figures in billions of 1996 dollars)*

	1 Revenues Invested in the Private System Instead of Social Security	2 Total Accumulated Funds Invested in the Private Retirement Accounts	3 Revenue Feedback from Private Investments	4 Replaced Social Security Benefits for Those Who Opt Out	5 Expenditure Savings Due to Reduced Benefit Growth	6 Extra Revenue Generated by Additional Economic Growth	7 Revenue Lost Due to Waiver of Continuing Taxes by Those Who Opt Out	8 Net Shortfall of Revenues to Pay Benefits after Prior Columns	9 Reductions in Other Government Spending	10 Sale of Government Bonds	11 Interest on Transition Bonds Sold to the Public
1997	154	156	7	9	—	—	—	-110	57	53	2
1998	157	312	14	17	—	—	—	-97	55	42	4
1999	159	466	22	26	1	—	—	-83	59	24	5
2000	241	704	32	36	1	—	—	-146	66	80	9
2001	245	944	45	47	2	—	—	-127	66	61	11
2002	248	1182	59	59	2	—	—	-103	58	45	14
2003	302	1475	74	72	3	—	—	-130	56	74	17
2004	306	1767	90	87	5	—	—	-104	63	41	19
2005	311	2073	109	88	6	—	—	-88	63	25	19
2006	318	2386	129	92	7	—	—	-72	62	10	19
2007	324	2717	149	95	9	—	43	-98	65	33	20
2008	329	3063	171	99	12	—	44	-77	64	13	20
2009	334	3427	196	102	15	—	44	-53	53	—	19
2010	338	3809	221	106	20	—	68	-49	49	—	18
2011	344	4179	245	112	23	—	69	-30	30	—	18
2012	349	4566	272	118	28	—	70	-8	8	—	17
2013	354	4969	299	125	34	—	85	+5	—	—	12

(continued)

TABLE 1. Continued

	1 Revenues Invested in the Private System Instead of Social Security	2 Total Accumulated Funds Invested in the Private Retirement Accounts	3 Revenue Feedback from Private Investments	4 Replaced Social Security Benefits for Those Who Opt Out	5 Expenditure Savings Due to Reduced Benefit Growth	6 Extra Revenue Generated by Additional Economic Growth	7 Revenue Lost Due to Waiver of Continuing Taxes by Those Who Opt Out	8 Net Shortfall of Revenues to Pay Benefits after Prior Columns	9 Reductions in Other Government Spending	10 Sale of Government Bonds	11 Interest on Transition Bonds Sold to the Public
2014	359	5390	327	131	41	—	86	+33	—	—	—
2015	363	5828	456	138	48	—	87	+64	—	—	—
2016	368	6236	382	148	57	—	88	+90	—	—	—
2017	373	6659	411	158	67	—	90	+119	—	—	—
2018	377	7095	440	167	77	—	90	+151	—	—	—
2019	381	7546	469	177	88	—	91	+185	—	—	—
2020	385	8010	500	188	98	—	92	+222	—	—	—
2021	389	8424	527	201	107	—	94	+251	—	—	—
2022	394	8849	554	215	115	—	95	+283	—	—	—
2023	399	9281	582	229	124	—	96	+317	—	—	—
2024	403	9722	610	243	134	—	97	+354	—	—	—
2025	406	10170	639	258	143	—	97	+392	—	—	—
2026	412	10545	663	275	153	—	99	+426	—	—	—
2027	417	10923	686	292	164	—	111	+450	—	—	—
2028	422	11303	710	310	174	—	112	+486	—	—	—
2029	426	11684	733	329	186	—	113	+525	—	—	—
2030	430	12067	757	346	199	—	115	+566	—	—	—
2031	436	12351	773	368	207	—	116	+599	—	—	—

154

2032	442	12632	789	389	218	—	118	+633	—	—
2033	447	12906	804	410	229	—	119	+669	—	—
2034	452	13172	818	433	239	—	121	+705	—	—
2035	457	13427	831	454	250	—	122	+740	—	—
2036	464	13564	836	479	261	—	124	+770	—	—

The figures in column 1 are based on the assumption that 50 percent of workers would opt out of Social Security in favor of the private system in the first year, that an additional 25 percent would opt out in the fourth year, and that an additional 15 percent (for a total of 90 percent) would opt out in the seventh year.

Column 2 presents the accumulation of the invested funds plus returns on the investments, assuming a 4 percent annual real rate of return. The benefits paid from the private system are subtracted from these accumulated funds each year.

Column 3 presents the new revenues produced from taxation of the full, before-tax real returns earned by the net increase in the private investments, after subtracting the amount of government bonds sold each year.

Column 4 presents the savings arising from replaced Social Security retirement, survivors', and disability benefits of those who opt for the private alternatives.

Column 5 presents the savings arising from delaying the retirement age and changing future benefit calculations from wage-indexing to price-indexing.

Column 6 reflects the conservative assumption that no extra revenues are generated by additional economic growth generated by the reform.

The figures in column 7 reflect the assumption that after ten years, employees and employers would only pay 5 percent of wages each into the private system and would no longer pay an additional 1.2 percent each into Social Security to help finance transition benefits, as they did for the first ten years.

The figures in column 8 include the effects of current Social Security surpluses and the continuing 1.2 percent of taxable wages paid by employees and employers each for the first ten years after the worker opts out of Social Security.

Column 9 shows the reductions in projected total federal spending that are needed to help finance the transition.

Column 10 shows the amount of money to be raised through the sale of bonds each year to pay continuing Social Security benefits. These can be either new government bonds or the already-existing bonds in the Social Security trust funds.

into broader economic growth and still further increased revenues to the government.

Such broader economic growth, however, would surely result from the reforms, as discussed in detail below (in Section IIIB). However, to be conservative, no estimate of the extra revenue and reduced government public-assistance spending likely to result from such increased economic growth and efficiency gains is included in the projections in Table 1. This is emphasized in column 6, which effectively leaves a blank for such effects. Sophisticated econometric studies could later provide some reasonable estimates of these effects.

Workers who choose the private option would receive fewer and ultimately no benefits from the old public system, receiving likely better benefits from the new private system instead. Column 4 estimates the savings from this effect that would help to reduce the costs of transition. The great majority of the savings shown in the early years results from sharp reductions in disability benefits and pre-retirement survivors' benefits paid by the old system. Workers who choose the private option would have all such benefits thereafter paid through private life and disability insurance rather than through the public system, producing this immediate savings. Over the years, savings from forgone retirement benefits would grow to large amounts, as more and more workers retired who had paid into the private system instead of Social Security for more and more years. Indeed, eventually this effect alone would completely eliminate transition costs.

Column 5 shows the savings that would result from delaying the retirement age under Social Security and changing the program's benefit-calculation formula from wage-indexing to price-indexing, as discussed above. This eventually grows to large amounts as well, as the amount that must be paid in recognition bonds for those who choose the private option is substantially reduced.

Column 8 shows the net shortfall in revenues to pay continuing Social Security benefit obligations, after all the previous changes to revenues and expenditures are taken into account. This shortfall is reduced over the next ten to fifteen years by the surpluses of Social Security taxes over expenditures that are projected for that time, which amount to about $20–$25 billion per year in constant 1996 dollars. This surplus creates a cushion that will partially offset the shortfall of revenue to pay Social Security benefits due to the private option. The shortfall in Column 8 is also reduced by the continuing payment of 1.2 percent of taxable wages each by employers and employees for the first ten years after the worker opts out; these funds would help finance the transition, as discussed above. Column 7 shows the revenues that would be lost when workers and their employers stopped paying this tax after the ten-year period.

One source of funds to help close this remaining shortfall is to cut other government spending. Much of this spending is wasteful and even counterproductive, and thus reducing it will not amount to a significant cost. To the extent that the money can at least be more efficiently spent in the private sector, cutting this spending will produce an efficiency gain that again will help to offset the transition costs. Column 9 shows specific dollar amounts of other government spending to be cut each year to help finance the transition. These amounts are equal to around $60 billion per year in constant 1996 dollars, or less than 4 percent of the entire federal budget, for each of the first twelve years of the reform, declining to only $8 billion by the sixteenth year, with no spending reduction required thereafter.

The final source of funds to meet the shortfall is to sell government bonds to the public. These could be either new government bonds or the already-existing bonds in the Social Security trust funds. Of course, the sale of these bonds would draw savings out of the private sector, reducing the savings increase resulting from the contributions to the private retirement accounts. But such bonds would also allow some of the costs of the transition to be spread out into future years. Thus, it can still be desirable to rely on a modest amount of money from the sale of such new bonds, which would offset only a small portion of the net savings increase.

Column 10 shows the amount of such bonds that would have to be sold each year to eliminate the net shortfall shown in column 8 (when combined with the spending reductions shown in column 9). The government would have to sell such bonds only for the first twelve years after the reform, totaling only about $500 billion in 1996 dollars. The sale of these bonds would, of course, reduce the total savings produced by the reform, but only by a small fraction. Moreover, as discussed further below, after another ten years the reform would produce sufficient surpluses to pay off and retire these previously sold bonds, restoring the savings that were lost by issuing the bonds in the first place.

Finally, column 11 shows the interest that must be paid on the government bonds sold to the public. This interest expense is reduced to $12 billion in 2013 and completely offset thereafter by the net surpluses produced by the reform (shown in column 8, which begins to show surpluses rather than shortfalls at this time). The government can completely avoid any outlay for this interest during the early transition deficit years by issuing zero coupon bonds that will accumulate the interest to maturity. This interest can then be paid later, out of the eventual surpluses generated by the reform. Alternatively, since the privatization reform would avoid the Social Security deficits that would otherwise start in about 2012, as discussed further below, the government would save a huge amount of interest expense on bonds it would otherwise have to issue under the current system to raise the funds to pay continuing Social Security benefits. This interest savings would be far more than enough to pay off the matured interest on the bonds sold to the public to finance the privatization transition.

Quite remarkably, the table shows that apart from the effective 20 percent payroll tax cut, the annual deficits due to the transition are actually eliminated by the fourteenth year of the reform. In that year (2010), $68 billion is lost due to the effective tax cut, while the total net shortfall of the reform before any spending cuts is only $49 billion. From that year forward, the spending cuts are needed only to finance the effective tax cut, with no need to sell any further government bonds.

Moreover, in the seventeenth year of the reform (in 2013), even the costs of the payroll tax cut are completely offset, and the reform starts producing net surpluses, without any continuing reductions in other government spending. Within a few years, these surpluses grow to large amounts. Indeed, after about six more years, roughly twenty-three years after the start of the reform, these surpluses will have been sufficient to pay off and retire all the government bonds previously sold to the public to help finance the transition.

After that, the net surpluses would reduce the total federal deficit. By that time, the annual surplus would be larger than the entire federal deficit today in 1996 dollars. Thirty years after the reform is begun, the surplus is equal to $426 billion in today's dollars, or about 3.5 percent of gross domestic product (GDP) in that year. Forty years after the reform starts, the annual surplus is equal to about 5.6 percent of GDP.

Moreover, the amount of these surpluses is sharply understated, for several reasons. First, as indicated above, the government bonds sold to finance the reform can be paid off and retired within a few years by the net surpluses generated by the reform. For the projections in Table 1, the initial sale of these bonds was assumed to reduce the net savings produced by the reform, and therefore reduced the resulting revenue feedback from taxation of the full returns to that savings. Similarly, later paying off and retiring these bonds would restore the lost savings and commensurately increase the revenue feedback. But this later effect was not counted in the projections given in the table, leaving the revenue feedback and total net surpluses resulting from the reform lower than they would actually be.

Second, under the current system, Social Security will start running a deficit of expenditures over tax revenues in 2012, based on the Social Security Administration's own latest intermediate projections.[15] That deficit will increase the total federal deficit, requiring the government to issue new bonds that will offset and reduce national savings. These Social Security deficits will just grow larger and larger over time, adding more and more to the federal deficit, and further reducing national savings.

However, the privatization reform would completely eliminate these Social Security deficits, as workers would be providing for their benefits through the fully funded private system rather than through Social Se-

---

[15] Social Security Board of Trustees, *1996 Annual Report*, table III.B.4.

curity. The projections in Table 1, in fact, show a surplus resulting from the reform starting in 2013, even while paying outstanding Social Security benefits. Eliminating these deficits through the privatization reform would result in a net increase in savings over our present course, since the government would not be issuing as much in government bonds that consume private savings in order to finance its deficits.

Indeed, these Social Security deficits will completely draw down and liquidate the Social Security trust funds by 2029 under the Social Security Administration's intermediate projections. During that time, Social Security will turn in bonds equaling more than $1.3 trillion in constant 1996 dollars, to obtain the cash to pay outstanding benefits. The government would then have to sell new bonds to the public as part of its deficit financing to obtain the cash to pay off the Social Security trust fund bonds. The Social Security privatization reform, however, would again avoid these deficits and this enormous draw down of the Social Security trust funds. Savings over this period would consequently be $1.3 trillion higher than otherwise.

The higher savings resulting from avoiding the long-term Social Security deficits and the massive trust-fund draw down would again result in a higher revenue feedback from the reform, due to the taxation of the full before-tax returns to that savings as discussed above. This would produce even higher long-term surpluses as a result of the privatization reform. Again, however, this effect was not counted in the above projections.

Finally, the long-term surpluses produced by the privatization reform, as shown in Table 1, would further reduce the total federal deficit each year. As discussed above, such reduced federal deficits would mean higher savings, higher revenue feedback, and higher surpluses from the reform than would otherwise occur. But this effect was also not included in the projections above.

These longer-term projections reveal a whole new benefit from privatizing the Social Security system. If, for the first dozen years or so of the reform, it is possible to maintain the fiscal discipline required to adopt the admittedly substantial but still feasible reductions in other government spending discussed above, then over the long run the reform would produce large and growing surpluses that hold the key to solving what is otherwise an intractable long-term budget deficit crisis facing the U.S. The Congressional Budget Office now projects deficits of 15 percent of GDP in 2030, compared to about 2 percent today.[16] Privatizing Social Security would remove the projected Social Security deficits from that future total federal deficit, and would also, at a minimum, reduce it by the amount of the surpluses resulting from the reform as projected in Table 1. This alone would reduce the projected total budget deficit by half. In

---

[16] Congressional Budget Office, *The Economic and Budget Outlook: Fiscal Years 1997–2006* (Washington, DC: U.S. Government Printing Office, May 1996), table 4-3, p. 77.

addition, the uncounted factors discussed above that would lead to much higher surpluses from the reform, along with higher general economic growth produced by the reform, would likely be sufficient to eliminate most of the remaining projected long-term federal deficits.

Consequently, the transition of Social Security to the private sector is not just a matter of dealing with transition deficits that create a budget problem in the short term. If the short-term sacrifices are made to close the initial transition deficits, the reform would produce much larger long-term and permanent surpluses that hold the prospect of solving what is otherwise an intractable long-term federal deficit crisis.

Finally, it should be noted that the higher economic growth that would undoubtedly result from the reform (discussed further below) would substantially lessen the reductions in other government spending that would be necessary to close the transition deficits over the first fourteen years or so. If after a few years this effect would reduce the necessary spending reductions by $10–$20 billion per year, the transition would be even more manageable.

B. Why the transition works

Opponents of privatization have argued that it would never be feasible because of a so-called double payment problem. They contend that the generation working at the time of the transition to a new system would have to pay for two retirements. They would have to finance their own retirement by paying for the investments in the private fully funded system. And they would have to continue to pay the promised benefits of the generation already retired on Social Security, who have no saved funds in the current pay-as-you-go system with which to finance their benefits.

Under the reform proposal discussed above, however, members of the first working generation at the time of the reform do not pay for two retirements. Indeed, after ten years they pay 20 percent less than under the current system, eventually receiving twice as much (or more) in benefits. How is that achieved? The answer is that the shift to the private system adds so much to production and national output that the transition costs can be entirely financed out of that additional output, while still leaving workers with much better benefits than under Social Security.

As discussed above, the new savings and investment in the private system would generate new income equal to the before-tax real rate of return to capital. Taxes on that return were in fact the largest factor in financing the transition in the above discussion. But the reform would also produce efficiency gains and increase economic growth in several other ways as well.

First, economic growth would be further enhanced by removing the burden of the payroll tax. Under the reform plan discussed above, the required payments into the private system would be almost 20 percent less than the Social Security payroll tax, providing an effective 20 percent payroll tax cut. This alone would significantly increase work, productive output, and economic growth. But the benefits from the privatization reform would go beyond that. Because Social Security benefits are not directly tied to the amount of taxes a worker pays into the system, but vary widely depending on a wide range of factors, the Social Security levy is seen by workers as a tax reducing their compensation. This reduces the incentive to work and to produce. In the privatized system, by contrast, benefits are directly tied to contributions, which are accumulated in each worker's own individual account. These contributions will consequently be seen as part of the worker's direct compensation, increasing work incentives, which will lead to greater employment and output.

Another major gain will result from more diligent and effective policing of disability claims. Government administrators have no direct economic incentive to control costs. As a result, experience shows that they are lax in denying benefits to claimants who are not truly disabled, or in ending benefits to those who have recovered. At the same time, some who seem to be truly disabled are lost in the bureaucratic maze or are victims of arbitrary rulings and are unfairly denied benefits. In the private system, by contrast, incentives and competition would produce vastly improved administration. Insurance companies who wastefully allowed bad claims would have higher costs and would not be able to compete with those who efficiently weeded out claimants who were not truly disabled. At the same time, insurance companies who developed a reputation for being too harsh and disallowing good claims would lose business to those who were more fair. The market, in the end, would produce the most fair and efficient balance, as desired by consumers.

Another efficiency gain would arise because the private benefits would not be subject to the Social Security earnings test, which reduces benefits to the extent that workers continue to work and earn wages after retirement. This discourages work, and reduces employment and output. Removing this limit would allow workers to choose the optimal level of continued work throughout their senior years.

Still another efficiency gain would result to the extent that the reform led the government to cut wasteful spending to finance the transition. The same would be true to the extent that the government was led to finance transition costs by selling government assets that would be more efficiently and productively utilized in the private market.

In addition, spin-off effects from the increased savings would likely produce greater economic growth as well. The increased savings and investment would increase production and wages, and create new jobs. The resulting higher incomes would support still higher growth.

All these gains would in fact be more than sufficient to finance the transition costs of the reform, while still leaving workers with far better benefits than those promised by Social Security. As discussed above, Feld-stein estimates that the before-tax real return to capital is about 9.3 per-cent in the U.S. Yet, for most young workers today, the real return paid by Social Security will at best be 1 percent or less.[17] The present value at retirement of a lifetime of contributions equal to Social Security taxes, accumulated at a real return of 9 percent, would be about ten times the present value of Social Security benefits paying a 1 percent real return on those taxes.

Consequently, taxing the full before-tax real returns on the private sys-tem's retirement savings to finance Social Security's outstanding obliga-tions at the time of the reform would reduce the total value of those accumulated savings at retirement by only about 10 percent at most.[18] This would still leave those workers with far higher benefits than those offered by Social Security. The other efficiency gains and enhanced eco-nomic growth discussed above would add still more to the net benefits of privatization after paying the transition costs.

Moreover, the above analysis does not include several other benefits of privatization which may not be quantifiable, but would still be highly valued by the general public. As indicated previously, the reform would greatly increase the freedom of choice and control that workers could exercise. Workers would retain control over their contributions in their own individual accounts, and could choose their own investments, within limits. They would also be free to choose to pay more into the system (and thus build up a larger retirement benefit), as indicated above. They would be free as well to tailor their retirement and insurance benefits to suit their personal needs and preferences. For example, single people could devote much less of their contributions to life and disability coverage, while married workers with large families could devote more. Workers could also choose to leave their accumulated retirement funds to their children or other heirs, unlike Social Security. They would also have much broader freedom to choose their own retirement age, retiring anytime after their funds reached a targeted level of benefits. Finally, in retirement, workers would be free to choose to return to work part- or full-time, again unlike Social Security.

The reform would, in addition, substantially equalize the distribu-tion of wealth. That is because each worker would be accumulating sub-stantial assets in his or her private account that would be more equally

---

[17] Ferrara, *Social Security Rates of Return for Today's Young Workers.*

[18] The Social Security benefits owed to the previous working generation at the time of the reform would be somewhat less than the amount calculated here, which was the future benefits to be paid to the current working generation at the time of the reform. Due to wage growth over time, the Social Security benefits for the current working generation would be higher than those for the previous working generation. Consequently, paying for the pre-vious generation's benefits out of the investment returns of the initial working generation at the time of the reform would reduce the total value of those accumulated investments and returns by less than the 10 percent calculated above.

distributed than current wealth holdings. Feldstein estimates that the concentration of national wealth could in fact be reduced by one-third as a result.[19]

As liberal activist Sam Beard has argued,[20] the reform would also provide particularly important benefits for the poor. It is they who are most in need of the higher retirement benefits and enhanced economic growth and opportunities that would result from the reform. The lower mandatory contributions required under the private system (as compared to Social Security) would also provide them with a sorely needed immediate increase in income. The personal wealth each worker would accumulate through the private system would provide special opportunities for the poor and their children to break out of the cycle of poverty by giving them control over some capital.

Finally, the reform would sharply reduce taxes and government spending while producing a major shift of economic functions from the public sector to the private sector.

IV. CONCLUSION

This essay shows that the transition from Social Security's public, pay-as-you-go system to a private, fully funded one is quite feasible and manageable. I have described a specific, concrete reform proposal and have projected the transition effects that would result. The projections showed that the transition can be financed without new taxes and without cutting benefits for today's recipients. Indeed, the reform plan I have described provided for an effective 20 percent cut in current payroll taxes after ten years.

The primary factors financing transition costs included:

(1) taxation of the full before-tax returns generated by the savings and investment in the private retirement system;

(2) continued payment of part of the payroll tax for ten years for those who opt out;

(3) reductions in future Social Security benefits;

(4) reductions in other government spending;

(5) Social Security surpluses currently projected for the next fifteen years or so;

(6) the sale of government bonds.

The projections of the transition effects showed the following:

(1) The transition deficits due to the privatization reform are completely offset after about fourteen years. From that point forward,

---

[19] Martin Feldstein, "Social Security and the Distribution of Wealth," *Journal of the American Statistical Association*, November 1976.

[20] Sam Beard, *Restoring Hope in America: The Social Security Solution* (San Francisco: Institute for Contemporary Studies, 1996).

the spending cuts are needed only to offset the revenues lost due to the effective 20 percent payroll tax cut, without selling any further government bonds.

(2) Three years later, or seventeen years after the reform is begun, the revenues lost due to the tax cut are completely offset as well. After that, the reform starts producing net surpluses, without any continuing reductions in government spending.

(3) Six years later, twenty-three years after the reform is begun, these surpluses will have been sufficient to pay off and retire all the government bonds previously sold to the public to help finance the transition.

(4) After that, the net surpluses would reduce the total federal deficit. By that time, the annual surplus would be larger than the entire federal deficit today in 1996 dollars. Thirty years after the reform, this surplus is equal to about 3.5 percent of GDP. After forty years, the surplus is equal to about 5.6 percent of GDP.

(5) Indeed, the full surpluses produced by the reform hold the key to solving what is otherwise an intractable long-term federal deficit crisis for the U.S.

The transition works because the privatization reform produces so much in additional production, output, efficiency gains, and economic growth. The transition costs can be entirely financed out of these gains, while still leaving workers with much better benefits than they would receive under Social Security, and ultimately leaving the government with large and growing surpluses.

Economics, Americans for Tax Reform

CAN DEMOCRACY PROMOTE
THE GENERAL WELFARE?

By James M. Buchanan

I. Introduction

To commence any answer to the question "Can democracy promote the general welfare?" requires attention to the meaning of "general welfare." If this term is drained of all significance by being defined as "whatever the political decision process determines it to be," then there is no content to the question. The meaning of the term can be restored only by classifying possible outcomes of democratic political processes into two sets— those that are general in application over all citizens and those that are discriminatory.

Analysis must start from the recognition and acknowledgment that "democracy," as this structure of politics is commonly understood, is not compatible with nondiscriminatory collective action. In Section II, I offer a summary treatment of the logical basis for this statement. We must also recognize, however, that democracy as a political process is observed to operate within constitutional constraints or rules, whether or not these are formalized in explicit and written documents. The elementary distinction between collective choices made by ordinary politics as constrained by a constitutional structure and collective choices among alternative elements of this structure itself is summarized in Section III.

After the introductory, but necessary, discussion in these sections, the question of whether democracy can promote the general welfare is addressed directly. In Section IV, I discuss the design of constitutional constraints that are consistent with (1) the common-sense meaning of generality, (2) the traditional principle of legal equality, at least as interpreted by jurists and philosophers in the pre-welfare-state epoch, and (3) what may have been the Founders' understanding when the "general welfare" terminology was introduced into the United States Constitution in 1787. It may be difficult to make any such constraints normatively persuasive to those who have subconsciously accepted the welfare-state mind-set. In Sections V through VII, the discussion shifts to what may prove to be a more acceptable set of limits, which allows for more familiar welfare programs, although, even here, the argument for "constitutionalization," as a means of checking the natural proclivities of majoritarian politics, may seem antidemocratic to those who remain philosophically naive. In these sections, the dominant welfare-state institutions, involving income transfers from the currently productive citizens to the aged and disabled, are examined in some detail. In Section VIII, I offer an assessment of the state of play in the late 1990s, as related to the question posed in the essay's title.

II. MAJORITARIAN POLITICS

Democracy—the single-word description of an institutional structure through which choices for the collectivity as an organized political community are made—is widely associated with majority rule. In the stylized model, each adult citizen holds the franchise, and alternatives for the whole community, and thereby applicable to everyone, are chosen by a rule of majority voting in elected representative assemblies. And majority rule has as its corollary, the minority as ruled. So long as members of prospective minorities are allowed full participation in the process, they are expected to acquiesce in the decisions made by the majority, even if these decisions are differentially burdensome.

Analyses of democratic political processes, modeled as the working out of majority voting rules, whether by traditional political scientists or by modern social-choice and public-choice theorists, have embodied the presumption that the mutually exclusive alternatives, among which political-collective choices are made, are themselves general in the sense that, once one alternative is chosen, this alternative becomes available to all members of the polity, and not only to the members of the dominating majority. Also, and importantly, the alternatives have been assumed to exist independently of the choosing process. If, however, the elementary logic of majority rule is exposed in a setting in which there are no constitutional limits on what majorities may do, it is evident that the alternatives for collective action may be endogenous; they may be constructed specifically by the members of the majority coalition with the purpose of exploiting the minority.[1] Any such construction must, of course, reflect a deliberate departure from general or uniform treatment of all citizens.

The simple point made here may be illustrated in the familiar two-by-two matrix (see Figure 1), with ordinal payoffs from cooperative behavior (c) and noncooperative behavior (d) assignable to two participants A and B. The interaction depicted becomes analogous to political-collective choice when we postulate that the outcome or solution in one of the four possible cells is to be explicitly chosen in one process rather than emerging as a result of separate but interdependent choices, as in the game-theoretic or exchange setting. Further, the analogue to majority voting is the assignment of authority to make decisions for the collectivity to one or the other of the two persons, A or B. The results are straightforward. If A is assigned the power to make decisions, a solution in Cell III will emerge,

---

[1] For elaboration of the analysis, see James M. Buchanan, "Foundational Concerns: A Criticism of Public Choice Theory," in *Current Issues in Public Choice*, ed. José Casas Pardo and Friedrich Schneider (Cheltenham, UK: Edward Elgar, 1995).

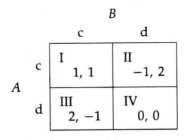

FIGURE 1

in which the payoff to A is maximized. (Contrariwise, if B is assigned the power to make decisions, a solution in Cell II will emerge.) Note that, in either case, the majority outcome lies "off the diagonal" in the sense that such outcome reflects differential or discriminatory treatment accorded to the two parties by the collective action chosen. The "on diagonal" outcome (Cell I) that is both general and to the benefit of both parties over the status quo (Cell IV) will not emerge.

This simple illustration exposes the basic logic; there is no need to introduce complex models with many alternatives and many persons. If a subset of those persons involved in an interaction that is collectivized is assigned the authority to select a collectively imposed outcome, then an outcome that is differentially beneficial to members of that subset will be dictated by the logic of the choice process itself. The general welfare will not be promoted by nongeneral choice-making.

III. Constitutional Limits on Majoritarian Democracy

The bare-bones analysis of the preceding section embodies the presumption that political majorities are not constitutionally constrained—a presumption that is not descriptive of historical reality. The authority of majority coalitions is, everywhere, limited by constitutional constraints or rules, even if these may, in some cases, be informal. A parliamentary or legislative majority, for example, is not allowed to abrogate the electoral process and to declare its members immune from competition in periodic elections. If this basic constitutional prerequisite of democracy is acknowledged, then the issue is not about the existence or appropriateness of constitutional limits but rather about what limits are desired. How much authority should legislative majorities be granted?

Confusion arises from a failure to appreciate the distinction between majoritarian politics, as it operates within a set of constitutional constraints or rules, and constitutional politics, which operates to determine these constraining parameters. There are two sets of choices in politics— choices that go on simultaneously, but that are directed to quite different ultimate purposes. Majoritarian politics within constitutional constraints, which we may call ordinary politics, involves the activities of legislatures that operate by majority voting and produces results that maximize the feasible payoffs to members of majority coalitions. Constitutional politics involves the choices among alternative sets of constraints or rules. This politics does not enter so directly into public consciousness, and, further, the process need not be closely associated with majority rule, as such. First of all, prospective payoffs to defined persons as members of groups are more difficult to estimate; and, secondly, there is something normatively repugnant about assigning a subset of participants the authority to choose the rules under which all must play.[2]

As I have suggested, however, historical experience in democratic politics has incorporated some recognition of the distinction between the separate levels of political choice. Choices among constraints—that is, constitutional rules—have been made by a more inclusive electorate and have been placed in a more deliberative and time-extended setting, than choices among legislative alternatives. My concern here is not particularly with how genuine constitutional choices are made, or should be made. My concern is more limited. Can constitutional constraints be designed that will allow legislative majorities to move beyond protective and productive state functions into the activities summarized under the "welfare-state" rubric, while, at the same time, holding in check the natural proclivity of majoritarian politics to promote particular rather than general interests? Is the welfare state in a democracy necessarily discriminatory in its operation?

IV. Generality as a Constitutional Constraint

One means of subverting the predicted results of majority rule, and especially as aimed at producing more generality, is to change the rule itself. If majority rule were replaced with a more inclusive assent requirement, say, two-thirds, three-fourths, five-sixths, or in the limit, unanimity, outcomes of legislative choice processes would necessarily become less discriminatory in impact. I shall not examine this avenue for political reform in this essay, since I have treated this subject matter in some detail elsewhere.[3] A further reason for shifting the focus away from this avenue is based on the recognition that the association between "democracy" as a political ideal and "majority rule" seems to be so well entrenched in public consciousness as to make serious challenge to the linkage futile.

For ordinary or in-period politics, therefore, I want to postulate majority-rule decision making in legislative assemblies. In this setting, an explicit

---

[2] For an extended discussion of arguments made in this section, see James M. Buchanan and Gordon Tullock, *The Calculus of Consent: Logical Foundations of Constitutional Democracy* (Ann Arbor: University of Michigan Press, 1962).

[3] *Ibid*. For the seminal analysis, see Knut Wicksell, *Finanztheoretische Untersuchungen* (Jena: Fischer, 1896).

constitutional requirement that political action, as authorized by a legislative majority, must be general in its effects over all members of the body politic, offers what seems to be an attractive prospect. In terms of the simple illustration in Figure 1 above, the off-diagonal outcomes (Cells II and III), each of which involves discrimination in treatment, would be placed out-of-bounds by constitutional mandate. The question then reduces to: What actions that might be taken by legislative majorities would be constitutionally prohibited under enforcement of a generality rule?

First of all, I should emphasize that existing constitutional understanding and interpretation does include elements of such a generality norm. Overt discrimination among persons and groups based on membership in majority coalitions would be considered unconstitutional in the United States and also in most modern democracies. The discussion here is directly informed by the United States political-legal environment, but the basic extension is applicable more generally to all liberal-democratic structures. Furthermore, elements of the generality norm go well beyond this strictly political limit. With some exceptions (e.g., affirmative action in the United States), legislative majorities cannot explicitly discriminate in the politically imposed treatment of persons based on criteria of race, religion, or gender. And such treatment, if attempted, would be declared unconstitutional by the understanding and traditional interpretation of equality before the law. By contrast, legislative majorities can discriminate among persons on criteria of geographical location, occupation, profession, industry or product category, economic status, age, family characteristics, productive capacity, and any number of other classificatory schemes. Extension of the generality principle to apply over all such categories of political activity would reduce the range of modern majoritarian politics dramatically, although it would not necessarily generate a reversion to government in its strictly night-watchman role.

As concerns political action in promoting welfare, however, which is the focus of this essay, would a generality rule eliminate the whole purpose of what is widely understood to be the welfare enterprise, described as the provision of income support to defined groups at the direct expense of other groups in the citizenry? Are welfare transfers compatible with any generality norm? In what follows, I suggest that it is possible to apply a generality norm to both the taxation and distribution sides of a system of social insurance.

A. Flat-rate tax

Any income transfer must be financed; the fiscal account has two sides, revenue and outlay. Consider, first, the application of the generality principle to taxation. An extreme libertarian (if he or she would acknowledge any taxation at all) might hold that only equal-per-head taxes would qualify and that any differentiation among persons would violate the generality norm. This argument incorporates an analogy between the private or market sector and the political sector. Persons face uniform prices in market transactions; the collective analogue is equal-per-head taxes. Such an argument must presume, however, that persons (families) can exist independently from collective association, that entry into and exit from each collective interaction is voluntary and attainable at relatively low cost and, further, that persons may purchase publicly supplied goods and services in quantities separately preferred. In a more comprehensive perspective, the political enterprise, inclusively considered, is scarcely voluntaristic in any market-analogue sense—entry and exit involve high threshold costs. There are elements of "publicness" that are necessarily present. Individuals cannot privately adjust desired quantities of politically supplied goods to tax prices. The generality principle would lose both meaning and its persuasive power if interpreted to imply equal-per-head taxation.

In the traditional public-finance literature, a tax is classified as general if it applies a uniform rate to a comprehensive base. The taxation of income at a proportional or flat rate meets the criterion of generality on almost any reckoning. The exemption, exclusion, or special treatment of any sort of income would represent violation of the generality norm. Also, and importantly, the taxation of some incomes at differentially higher rates or lower rates, including zero, would depart from generality. Only the taxation of all income, as received by all persons, and without exemption, deduction, or exclusion, at the same rate meets the standard here.[4]

Proposals advanced in the 1980s and 1990s aimed at modifying the United States federal tax structure through the introduction of some version of a flat rate of tax on income would, if enacted and treated as if they were constitutional, do much toward thwarting the majoritarian impulses toward discriminatory exploitation through the taxing process. However, most of these flat-rate tax schemes, as proposed, have failed to qualify as general because they have not eliminated all exemptions, such as income from investments as well as low-level incomes. Any exemption from the comprehensive tax must set up opportunities for majoritarian conflict which is, precisely, the primary result that the general tax should be aimed at avoiding. Generality, properly understood, would require that each and every dollar of income, by whomever received, be taxed at the same rate. With such a tax in place, members of prospective majority coalitions would operate in the knowledge that any change in the tax rate would impact on themselves in the same way that it impacts on others outside those coalitions. Membership, or the absence thereof, in the ma-

---

[4] For extended discussion of the political efficiency of general taxation, see James M. Buchanan, "The Political Efficiency of General Taxation," *National Tax Journal*, vol. 44, no. 4 (1994), pp. 401–10.

jority coalition, per se, would not affect tax liability, except indirectly through the composition of the tax base.

B. Demogrants

What is the outlay-side equivalent to the flat-rate tax on income in the context of the welfare enterprise? Justificatory argument in support of welfare transfers is beyond the scope of inquiry here. The discussion is limited to the question of possible reconciliation between welfare transfers and the generality norm. Here equal-per-head transfer payments, or demogrants, meet the criterion for generality. All citizens would secure equal payments, as financed from the flat-rate tax on income. In net, the combined fiscal process would redistribute income from those persons who earn higher-than-mean incomes, pre-tax, to those who earn less-than-mean incomes, pre-tax. Politically, however, on neither the tax nor the transfer side of the fiscal account would particular groups be singled out for differentially favored or disfavored treatment. The natural proclivity for majority coalitions to use their decision-making authority to exploit members of minorities would be attenuated.

In characteristic patterns of pre-tax income distribution, the median income tends to fall below mean income, pre-tax. (High income earners raise the average [mean] income but may leave the median income earner unaffected.) In this situation, there would be positive redistribution predicted under the operation of majority rule because the median income recipients would also be the median voters whose preferences on the issue would tend to be controlling as well as consistent. In public-choice terms, the preferences would be single-peaked; hence, majority voting yields consistent results. Individual preferences as to the height of the rate of tax, and, residually, as to the size of the demogrant, would vary inversely with pre-tax incomes. Those persons with below-mean incomes would prefer high rates of tax, while those with above-mean incomes, pre-tax, would prefer low rates. To this extent, distributional conflict would remain descriptive of majoritarian politics, even as constrained fiscally in the manner suggested here. The debates would be about the choice among positions "on the diagonal," however, and therefore would be categorically different from debates about alternatives that involve deliberate exploitation of any group.

C. Social insurance

I submit that a structure of equal-per-head transfer payments, or demogrants, financed by a flat rate of tax on all incomes, if effectively constitutionalized and removed from the agenda of ordinary majoritarian politics, would allow an affirmative answer, of sorts, to the question "Can democracy promote the general welfare?" Legislative majorities would be empowered to set the rate of the flat tax and, with that, the size of the demogrant, but specific actions aimed at discriminating favorably or unfavorably, on either the taxing or the transfer side of the account, would be out of bounds.

The rate of tax that would be predicted would depend on several factors: (1) the pattern of pre-tax income distribution; (2) the predicted response behavior of persons as taxpayers and as transfer recipients; (3) the predicted bureaucratic-administrative leakages in the fiscal process; (4) the predicted mobility of persons among income classes; (5) the predicted lengths of periods between changes in rates of tax; and possibly others. Any rate of tax above zero would, of course, be predicted to impact negatively on the rate of economic growth. In effect, this impact might be considered to be the aggregate cost of the scheme of social insurance that the flat-tax/demogrant system represents.

The positive political effects of this structure should not be overlooked. Majoritarian democratic process is preserved; it is not allowed to degenerate into the cross-group redistributive transfer absurdity that describes the "churning state."[5] The welfare state maintains legitimacy because it is seen to be basically nondiscriminatory in its operation. The structure would remain immune to some of the "end welfare as we know it" attitudes expressed by pundits, politicians, and philosophers in the 1990s.

V. Fiscal Transfers to the Elderly

Nonconstrained majoritarian politics would not generate the fiscal transfer structure outlined above; we should not, therefore, have observed such a structure in existence, because the constitutional requirement for generality has never been explicitly put in place. It may, then, seem surprising that a major transfer program of the modern welfare state has contained elements of generality in treatment among persons, despite the absence of an explicit constitutional precept. I refer to programs (such as Social Security in the United States) in which massive fiscal transfers are made between those persons who are currently productive and those who are defined to be beyond income-producing ages.

In the direct sense, of course, the generality norm is violated, since a particular group, the aged, is singled out for differentially favored fiscal treatment. And members of this recipient group are necessarily placed in political opposition to those who must finance the transfers through taxes. On the other hand, and indirectly, elements of generality are present, due to the elementary fact that (barring misfortune) all persons eventually grow old. Tax payments made by those who currently earn income be-

---

[5] Anthony de Jasay, *The State* (Oxford: Basil Blackwell, 1985).

come, in one sense, a part of an intergenerational reciprocal exchange, and such payments are justified by the expectation of benefits to be financed by future taxpayers in later periods.[6] In choosing a preferred rate of tax to finance transfers to the old, the income earner is, indirectly and expectationally, choosing her own preferred rate of income support in post-earning years. This effect surely attenuates the direct intergenerational conflict that would be present if transfers were to be made to some arbitrarily selected group.

In the Social Security system in the United States, direct money transfers are paid out to eligible recipients and are financed by a flat tax on payrolls up to a maximal limit. The tax is nominally imposed on both employees and employers, presumably aimed at fostering some illusion that a payroll tax paid by employers is not a cost of labor. Benefit payments are related to, but not closely correlated with, persons' separate payroll histories.

This old-age transfer structure has been plagued, from its inception in the 1930s, by confusion as to what it is designed to accomplish, even in its idealized operation. On the one hand, the system has been effectively "constitutionalized," as witness common references to keeping the system "off the table" of majoritarian politics. By contrast, however, the old-age tax-transfer structure, as it has existed, is best described as a mixture of collectivized social insurance, collectivized private insurance, and redistributional welfare transfers. It will be useful here to examine these three models, as separate idealized types, and to evaluate these in terms of the generality norm that might be broadly consistent with the viability of majoritarian democracy.

A. Social insurance for post-earning periods

Consider, first, the structure that would be designed exclusively to provide income support for persons who are beyond income-earning years. To meet the generality norm, this program would be best financed by a flat tax on all income. And the revenues from this tax would be paid out in demogrants, equal-per-head to all persons who meet the straightforward age requirement. The rate of tax would be selected through ordinary majoritarian politics, and this rate would residually determine the size of the demogrant, adjusted for the size of the recipient group. Or, conversely, the size of the demogrant might be selected, and then the rate of tax adjusted so as to balance the fiscal account.

Distributional conflict between recipients of transfers, the old, and all income earners would remain to be settled through the operations of

---

[6] For a formal analysis of intergenerational exchange, see Paul A. Samuelson, "An Exact Consumption-Loan Model of Interest with or without the Social Contrivance of Money," *Journal of Political Economy*, vol. 66, no. 6 (December 1958), pp. 467–82.

ordinary politics. But the opportunities for differential treatment, on either the tax or the transfer side, would be effectively minimized. Since all incomes are taxed at the uniform rate, there would be little incentive for groups to seek out special tax favors. And since all persons who meet the age requirement would get the same size transfer payment, there would be little scope for this or that group to demand differentially favorable treatment. Note particularly that, under this structure, computations as to private rates of return on taxes paid in, as if these were treated as investments in funded pension schemes, would be meaningless. Persons would be "purchasing," through the political process, "social insurance"; no elements of private insurance would be involved at all.

B. *Private insurance publicly funded*

The United States system contains elements of the general social-insurance structure sketched out above, but these are intermingled with at least two other models. It is not surprising that both public understanding and political argument have remained confused. Early advocates of the federal program used the rhetoric of private insurance, in which each person, separately, "contributes" during income-earning years, thereby accumulating personalized interest-bearing claims that are redeemed during years of retirement. In this stylized model, the redemptions, that is, benefit payments for each recipient, are directly related to the payments made into the system.

Despite the private-insurance rhetoric, however, the system has been realistically acknowledged, since its inception in the 1930s, to be financed on a pay-as-we-go basis, which necessarily implies political organization and operation, in which taxes are levied on current income earners with revenues collected paid out in transfers to current retirees. Social Security taxes have, broadly considered, met the generality requirement; these taxes have been assessed against payrolls and have been imposed at uniform rates up to an upper cut-off limit. Benefit payments have, to an extent, been separately related to individualized contributions, but these payments have not been related to rates of return that would be consistent with those that would be necessary to keep the pay-as-we-go structure financially viable. Almost from the start, transfer payments have been adjusted upward, both for directly political reasons and on some "as if" relationship to a funded system, in which rates of return on individualized accounts would be tied to rates of interest. In the pay-as-we-go system, fiscally feasible rates of return are necessarily affected by shifts in the age profile of the population, particularly by shifts in the ratio between the size of the income-earning group and the size of the post-earning group.

A collectively operated scheme of retirement income support, financed pay-as-we-go, with separable individual accounts yielding rates of return consistent with this organizational structure and effectively constitution-alized, could meet most of the criteria for generality. As the United States system has developed, however, there have been departures from this stylized model, used in the early advocacy rhetoric, in the direction of both the social-insurance scheme sketched out earlier and the direct-transfer scheme discussed below; and these departures have created op-portunities for discriminatory majoritarian politics.

C. Redistribution to the aged poor

The third, and quite distinct, model that has come to be increasingly descriptive of the United States system, is explicitly and openly discrim-inatory in its operation. In this conception, there is no pretense that the objective is to provide either social or private insurance. The objective is, quite simply, to provide income support for those persons who are poor, and who, at the same time, are old. There is no relationship between the size of transfer payments and any "contributions" that may or may not have been made, either individually or in the aggregate. Persons may qualify for supplemental income support solely on age and economic-status criteria, totally divorced from participation in the system during income-earning periods.

D. Fiscal crisis and means-testing

As noted, the United States system of income support for the aged has been and remains an institutional mixture of the three models discussed. The generality norm is violated to the extent that the third, or strictly redistributive, model has come to be a more important element. And changes in this direction occur more or less naturally as the system is faced with threatened fiscal imbalance. Majoritarian politics, as it may be residually compelled to introduce reforms, tends predictably to act in furtherance of the short-term interests of members of dominant coali-tions, taking actions that are necessarily discriminatory in effect. Why should a legislative majority promote the general interest?

In practice, ordinary politics, faced with fiscal crisis in the social-security structure, will introduce means-testing. Persons who meet the age requirement, and whose claims against the system remain valid on either the social- or private-insurance understanding, but who are ob-served to receive relatively high (above median) income from nonsystem sources, become sitting ducks for legislative majorities. In the United States, means-testing was indirectly introduced through differential treat-ment of Social Security income among separate income classes. Moreover, in the 1990s, there has been active discussion of income-wealth criteria for benefit eligibility.

Means-testing may act to eliminate such persons from the beneficiary roles, or it may substantially reduce the value of their claims, and, in the process, convert the general structure of income support for the aged into an overtly discriminatory redistributive scheme, with consequent conflicts of interest between and among identified groups of political constituents. Almost by necessity, the system of retirement income support that, because of its generality features, might have remained effectively "constitutionalized" becomes directly politicized; social security is put back "on the table" of ordinary politics. The general welfare must almost surely lose out as a result.

VI. FISCAL TRANSFERS TO MEMBERS OF TARGETED GROUPS

Much of the analysis of fiscal transfers to the aged, discussed above, can be extended to apply to transfers to persons who qualify as members of specifically targeted recipient groups. Such programs may retain elements of generality if the criteria for eligibility, analogous to age, are objectively identifiable and are not readily amenable to behavioral manipulation. Transfers to the disabled fall under this category, and these transfers are incorporated within the inclusive Social Security system in the United States. As with the old-age system, the transfers to the disabled have been financed by a flat-rate tax on payrolls, and payments to beneficiaries have been income related, as in a private-insurance scheme. Problems arise that are not present in the old-age system, however, from the difficulty of defining criteria for eligibility that are immune from behavioral adjustments by prospective beneficiaries. Experience suggests that this moral hazard operates to undermine the generality of the whole structure and to enhance the potential for distributional conflict which must, in turn, generate pressures for more direct politicization. If the ranks of beneficiaries are extended well beyond the public conception of the "deserving disabled," political entrepreneurs will enter with proposals for reforms, which, in some cases, may overshoot the limits that might be preferred on any social- or private-insurance principles.

I need not discuss in detail programs of direct income support for members of groups that are financed directly from general tax revenues and that contain no insurance elements, either social or private. These welfare programs may be designed so as to satisfy minimal norms for generality if eligibility remains immune from personal behavioral manipulation, and, further, if criteria for eligibility do not seem to emerge directly from the emergent coalitions of majoritarian politics. An example might be disaster relief. A program for transfers to victims of natural disasters financed from general tax revenues might qualify under the generality norm if all potential disasters could be clearly defined in advance, thereby removing the definition of *ex post* beneficiaries from the political decision process. By contrast, tax-financed disaster relief that is implemented piecemeal by legislative majorities or by executive action, motivated in part in response to constituency pressures, would fail the test.

VII. In-Kind Transfers

The modern welfare state is not, of course, limited to the processing of monetary transfers from taxpayers to recipients. Increasingly, welfare-state activities include in-kind transfers that are made to persons directly or indirectly. Medical services come immediately to mind. Governments everywhere either provide medical services directly or subsidize the purchase-provision of these services to all or to designated groups of persons in the polity, with the required outlay financed from taxes, which may or may not be tied to potential benefit eligibility.

Again the question arises as to the possible consistency between the operation of all such in-kind transfer programs and majoritarian politics. Are tax-financed in-kind programs organized so as to meet the generality norm, or do such programs tend to reflect the differentiation in treatment among groups that emerges as a natural consequence of majority rule? If the programs are financed from general taxes, and if criteria for benefit eligibility can be determined objectively and can be extended generally, over the whole membership of the polity, these programs may, effectively, be constitutionalized and essentially divorced from ordinary politics. Difficulties arise, as in other targeted welfare programs, when behavioral adjustments on the part of potential beneficiaries both modify eligibility status and determine rates of utilization under open-ended structures (e.g., medical-care access). And there is still an additional source of difficulty with in-kind programs, one that does not arise with monetary transfers. If specifically designated services are either directly provided or subsidized, an interest in producer groups is established. Such producer interests may exert efforts to secure program expansions beyond preferred levels motivated by prospects of higher rents. (For example, agricultural interests have been among the strongest proponents of the food-stamp program in the United States.)

As is the case with the more general programs of retirement or disabled income support, any means-testing, on either the taxing or benefit side of the account, can only offer a source for conflict on distributional grounds, thereby creating pressures for politicization, with predicted consequences.

VIII. General Welfare in the Modern Welfare State

My purpose in this essay has not been to discuss the many programs that constitute the complex operations of the modern welfare state that we observe. However, I have felt it useful to describe briefly several of the important transfer programs, not for the purpose of presenting institutional detail, but in order to assess their possible consistency with democracy as a political structure. As I noted in Section II, if democracy is equated with majority rule, and if general welfare is defined as the welfare of all members of the polity, the structural contradiction is obvious. As stated before, nongeneral decision-making cannot produce general results.

As I discussed in Section III, however, democracy, as it actually operates, is never described as the unconstrained exercise of majority rule. Majorities are constitutionally constrained. The question becomes: Can welfare programs be constitutionalized in such fashion as to insure the promotion of the general welfare, despite the natural proclivities of majoritarian politics?

Somewhat surprisingly perhaps, the major transfer programs of the welfare state that we observe do, in fact, incorporate elements of generality that counter predictions about the workings of majoritarian democracy derived from elementary public-choice theory. As they participate variously in the political process, persons seem to place moral constraints on overt exploitation of fiscal authority to generate discriminatory results. It is as if the major transfer programs emerged, in part, from constitutional rather than ordinary politics. The old-age support system in the United States has been financed by a flat tax on payrolls, and eligibility has been almost exclusively limited by the age criterion. Means-testing, if this is now introduced in response to threatened fiscal crisis, will move the system away from either its social- or private-insurance principles and must reduce political support for the system by allowing hitherto sublimated distributional conflict to come into play. The same effect of means-testing applies to any other program.

My aim here is not to plead for this or that policy reform, either for implementation or for avoidance. My aim is more comprehensive; it is to suggest that the generality norm or principle, which is still respected to a large extent in the application of law, can be productive when applied explicitly to politics. Constitutional constraints can be effective in preventing majorities from enacting legislation that differentially exploits minorities. And transfer programs can be evaluated in terms of whether or not they meet criteria of generality. Even more importantly, proposed changes in existing programs can be put to the test: Do they move the structure toward or away from generality?

In the debates-discussions of the mid-1990s, proposals to shore up either the Social Security or the Medicare system in the United States by means-testing can only make these programs more vulnerable to political exploitation. Similarly, the earned-income tax credit (which isolates low levels of wage income for special treatment) and the proposed differentially reduced rate of tax on capital-gains income both introduce departures from the generality principle. By contrast, proposals for replacing the complex, loophole-ridden, and progressive tax on incomes by a flat-rate tax make the revenue side of the fiscal account more compatible with democracy, provided that all incomes are brought under the uniform rate.

We do not see the generality principle held up or used as a criterion in the discussion of these and other reforms because this discussion takes place as a part of ordinary politics rather than as a part of a constitutional dialogue and debate. It seems largely gratuitous that some changes, once made, become effectively constitutional. The expressed public dissatisfaction with the modern welfare state may, however, be traced, in part, to the failure to keep transfer programs within the limits of generality that are broadly acceptable. Citizens may indeed tolerate coercive taxes at high rates to finance programs that they consider to promote the general welfare. This support may exist even in the face of widespread public recognition that these programs reduce the rate of aggregate economic growth. But citizens may very quickly withdraw their support for the welfare state if they observe shifting political coalitions to be using their authority to exploit particular groups for the differential benefit of others.

Finally, to return to the question posed in the title of this essay: Democracy can promote the general welfare if democracy, like Ulysses, recognizes that it must bind itself against the opportunistic temptations that its defining institution, majority rule, guarantees must emerge. The general welfare state can survive; the discriminatory welfare state cannot.

Economics, Center for Study of Public Choice, George Mason University

FREEDOM AND MORAL DIVERSITY:
THE MORAL FAILURES OF HEALTH CARE
IN THE WELFARE STATE

By H. Tristram Engelhardt, Jr.

I. An Introduction: Beyond Equality

In his 1993 health-care reform proposal, Bill Clinton offered health care as a civil right. If his proposal had been accepted, all Americans would have been guaranteed a basic package of health care. At the same time, they would have been forbidden to provide or purchase better basic health care, as a cost of participating in a national system to which they were compelled to contribute. A welfare entitlement would have been created and an egalitarian ethos enforced.[1] This essay will address why such egalitarian proposals are morally unjustifiable, both in terms of the establishment of a uniform health-care welfare right, and in terms of the egalitarian constraints these proposals impose against the use of private resources in the purchase of better-quality basic health care, not to mention luxury care.

In framing health-care welfare policy, one must address people's fears of being impoverished while at risk of death and suffering when medicine can offer a benefit. Simultaneously, one must confront significantly different understandings of the appropriate use of medicine, the claims of justice, and the meaning of equality. Any approach to providing health care for those who cannot afford it must come to terms with the substantial disagreements that separate individuals and communities regarding provision of health care by the state. In addition, the attempt to frame a uniform policy must confront the nonegalitarian consequences of human freedom. To be free is to make choices that have nonegalitarian results.

I shall argue that our disagreements about equality, fairness, and justice have a depth similar to that of our disagreements about contraception,

---

[1] The White House Domestic Policy Council, *The President's Health Security Plan* (New York: Times Books, 1993), presents a robustly egalitarian blueprint for health-care policy. In its "Ethical Foundations of Health Reform," the Clinton plan rejects a tiered system: "The system should avoid the creation of a tiered system providing care based only on differences of need, not individual or group characteristics" (p. 11). When the plan recommends that a new federal criminal statute be enacted prohibiting "the payment of bribes, gratuities or other inducements to administrators and employees of health plans, health alliances or state health care agencies" (p. 199), the goal is *inter alia* to proscribe payment to physicians for better basic care. The implications and the stated purpose of the plan are egalitarian. I have developed my critique of the Clinton plan in some detail elsewhere; see, for example, H. Tristram Engelhardt, Jr., "Health Care Reform: A Study in Moral Malfeasance," *Journal of Medicine and Philosophy*, vol. 19 (October 1994), pp. 501–16.

abortion, third-party-assisted reproduction, and physician-assisted suicide, in that they are not resolvable in general secular moral terms. The lesson of the postmodern era is that there are as many secular accounts of equality, justice, and fairness as there are religious groups, sects, and cults.[2] There is no principled basis for choosing a particular content-full account as canonical. As a consequence, establishing a particular content-full notion of equality, fairness, and justice in health care is the secular equivalent of establishing, for a secular national health-care system, the Roman Catholic proscriptions regarding contraception: it would be morally arbitrary and without secular moral justification. Consequently, there are robust secular moral limitations on the establishment of particular views of equality, limitations resulting from the centrality of human persons as the source of secular moral authority. There are good grounds for holding that current health-care policies, such as those embodied in Medicare, which forbid recipients from paying more for better basic care from participating physicians while coercing them to contribute to this program, are immoral. I argue in this essay that welfare rights in health care, if they are to be established, should be recognized as the creations of limited governmental insurance policies and not as expressions of foundational rights to health care or claims of equality or fairness.[3]

II. MEDICAL WELFARE: TEMPTATIONS AND DISAGREEMENTS IN THE FACE OF FINITUDE

Health care claims attention because of the dramatic ways in which medicine and the biomedical sciences address our finitude, vulnerability, and mortality. Political support for the governmental provision of health care often involves the view that to deny someone health care is to deny him or her protection against suffering, disease, disability, and death. The suppressed premise is that such a denial would be unfair. This view has difficulties. First, one must show how and why needs generate rights. Second, unlike food, clothing, and shelter, which can be provided at relatively minimal costs while still being sufficient for health and life, health care frequently confronts disabilities, diseases, disorders, and threats of death that cannot be overcome even with maximum medical efforts and the costs they involve. Often, illness can be cured only in part, suffering ameliorated only to some extent, disabilities remedied only to some degree, and death postponed only for a short time. In many cases, no

---

[2] I take it that the postmodern era is characterized by the circumstance, as a matter of sociological fact, (1) that all people do not share the same moral narrative or account, and (2) that this moral diversity is apparent and widely recognized. Moreover, as a matter of our epistemological condition, (3) there is no way to establish in purely secular terms the correct moral narrative or account without begging the question or engaging in an infinite regress, and (4) this is also widely recognized.

[3] See also H. Tristram Engelhardt, Jr., *Bioethics and Secular Humanism: The Search for a Common Morality* (Philadelphia: Trinity Press International, 1991), esp. pp. 130–38.

matter how much one does, more resources could have been invested with some benefit for some recipients or possible recipients of health care. Just as ever more resources could be invested in avoiding accidental injuries and deaths by improving workplace safety, or invested in diminishing highway deaths by licensing only those cars that have front and side air bags as well as the front-end collision protection available in luxury cars, so, too, in medicine more resources could always be invested in preventive and curative endeavors without ever being fully successful against our finite, vulnerable, and mortal condition. Death and suffering are inescapable, so that we must decide what finite effort we should make to postpone death and avoid some suffering. We must ask whether there is secular moral authority coercively to impose one particular approach and whether it may be an egalitarian one.

The human condition itself conspires against discovering a generally convincing understanding of what should count as a basic adequate package of health-care services. First, there is the problem that medical knowledge is limited and probabilistic. Practicing medicine requires accepting that all life is a gamble, that medicine is a part of life, and that therefore health-care professionals must gamble with the suffering, disability, and death of all whom they treat. Moreover, resources that one might use to improve knowledge and technology are themselves limited. On the one hand, there is not enough money to avoid all suffering, disability, and death. On the other hand, there is not enough knowledge to know with certainty when particular interventions will succeed or fail. As a result, given the finitude of resources and the indefinite range of threats to well-being and life, investments in protection against suffering, disability, and death must take into account probabilities of success and failure. Investments must be limited and one must gamble.

To gamble, one must be willing to lose. Suppose that, as a matter of public policy, one has decided that in order to make good use of resources, one will not provide resources to the poor for a particular intervention—even when it might offer some protection against suffering, disability, and death—because the costs, probability of failure, and/or likely poor quality of results outweigh the possible benefits. In such a case, one must be willing to allow people to experience suffering, disability, and death when the resources are not available. One must also confront the circumstance that those with sufficient resources will purchase protection against death and suffering which is not available to all. In short, since ever more resources could always be invested in health care with some positive benefit, one faces two especially troubling policy questions: (1) May a basic, less-than-optimal package of health care be established for the poor? (2) May individuals, communities, and organizations use their own funds and energies to secure for themselves even better basic protection, as well as supplementary protection, against death and suffering? If secular morality (a) cannot reveal a content-full canonical morality that requires an egalitarian health-care policy, but (b) rather reveals that individuals are the source of secular moral authority, then one will need to endorse a national health-care policy that accepts both moral diversity and inequality.

III. Bad Luck, Unfairness, and Inequality

If the authority of persons over themselves is morally legitimate, then individuals will, through their free choices, set limits to the realization of government-endorsed visions of the good and of human flourishing. Among the goods with which freedom will collide are those of equality and long life. To be free in any way that allows one to pursue particular goods or goals despite risks of death or disability is to be free to place oneself at risk of needing additional health care. To be free in any way that allows the acquisition of wealth as well as the giving and receiving of funds, valuables, and labor is to be free in ways that produce inequalities in opportunity and outcome. If the authority of governments is derived from the free consent of citizens, then citizens can freely limit governmental authority by withholding consent. Freedom brings into question the plausibility of a uniform and equal basic health-care entitlement. Insofar as people are free and have their own resources, some will take greater risks than others and some will purchase better protection than many can afford. Beyond that, one faces other persistent inequalities and a significant diversity of views about how one should respond to inequalities.

All will die, though some will die in their youth and others will live long lives. Inequality in health is, for many, especially vexing, since it involves significant differences in suffering and length of life. Still, differences in health status are not, on average, dramatically related to the level of access to high-cost health care. Cross-national comparative data concerning health-care investments and life expectancies suggest that differences in access to high-technology medicine pale in importance when compared to differences attributable to gender, income, and genetic luck. Women outlive men, the rich outlive the poor, and high-status individuals tend to outlive low-status individuals.[4] For example, in the United Kingdom men and women in 1991 had life expectancies at birth of 73.2 and 78.8 years, respectively, while those in the United States had life expectancies of 72.0 and 78.9 years, respectively, though the United King-

---

[4] See, for example, J. K. Iglehart, "Canada's Health Care System Faces Its Problems," *New England Journal of Medicine*, vol. 322 (February 22, 1990), pp. 562–68; M. G. Marmot, George D. Smith, Stephen Stansfeld, et al., "Health Inequalities among British Civil Servants: The Whitehall II Study," *Lancet*, vol. 337 (June 8, 1991), pp. 1387–93; G. J. Schieber, J. P. Poullier, and L. M. Greenwald, "Health Spending, Delivery, and Outcomes in OECD Countries," *Health Affairs*, vol. 12 (Summer 1993), pp. 120–29; and Schieber, Poullier, and Greenwald, "Health System Performance in OECD Countries, 1980–1992," *Health Affairs*, vol. 13 (Fall 1994), pp. 101–12.

dom invested $1,151 per person for health care, 7.1 percent of its gross domestic product, in comparison with the United States, which invested $3,094 per person, 13.6 percent of its gross domestic product. At age 80, the life expectancy was 6.3 years for men and 8.3 years for women in the United Kingdom, versus 7.2 years for men and 9.1 years for women in the United States. Though the differences in resource investment for health care likely express themselves in these differences in life expectancies at age 80, in absolute terms the differences due to gender still outweighed the differences between the two systems.[5]

Given these data, a national health-care policy which focused on equality in mortality outcomes would most plausibly direct energies toward developing new ways to address the health needs of men and toward preventing pediatric deaths. Indeed, for egalitarians concerned with equality in life expectancies, a cross-national examination of life-expectancy outcomes by gender would seem to mandate a major commitment to the increased study of diseases of men, an increase in the representation of men in research protocols, and the development of better treatments for life-threatening conditions facing men. Such egalitarians would also favor the prevention of pediatric deaths over improvements in geriatric medicine, because of the robust inequalities in life presented, say, in the comparison between having a life span of twelve years versus one of seventy-two years. If one invokes an expository device such as John Rawls's original position,[6] one can easily imagine a characterization of the contractors such that they would regard those dying young as the least well-off, and would therefore direct energies against pediatric life-threatening conditions before directing resources to geriatric care, other than perhaps comfort care.[7] A somewhat similar case can be made for directing medical research toward diseases afflicting the poor and persons of low status. In short, a dedicated pursuit of equality in mortality expectations should give priority to medical research and treatment development for men, children, the poor, and persons of low status.

---

[5] Schieber, Poullier, and Greenwald, "Health System Performance." It is clear that much more would need to be said about differences among countries with regard to achieving morbidity relief. See, for example, Henry J. Aaron and William B. Schwartz, *The Painful Prescription* (Washington, DC: Brookings Institution, 1984).

[6] John Rawls invokes a hypothetical contracting position as an expository device to lay out what he takes to be the defining features of a just and voluntary society. The success of this account in producing the conclusions he wants depends on his prior characterization of the contractors' thin theory of the good, their level of aversion to risk, their absence of envy, etc. See John Rawls, *A Theory of Justice* (Cambridge, MA: Harvard University Press, 1971).

[7] If one of the worst possible outcomes is to die young, and if establishing just health-care policy on the basis of Rawls's original position leads one to adopt the maximin rule—which "tells us to rank alternatives by their worst possible outcomes: we are to adopt the alternative the worst outcome of which is superior to the worst outcomes of the others" (p. 152f.)—then it would seem that contractors in the original position would want first and foremost to protect themselves against pediatric deaths. They would want this because children who die young would count as the worst-off class, and because such deaths would most undermine fair equality of opportunity.

Not all will agree with this approach, either in detail or in its foundations. Since we do not share one concrete morality, the very energies which direct our concerns toward medical issues separate us into disagreeing communities of moral commitment.[8] Disputes regarding bioethics and health-care policy cut to the moral quick regarding equality, not only because individuals and communities differ with respect to the weight assigned to equality interests, but also because of the moral ambiguity of the term itself. If one is to develop an egalitarian policy, one must establish the importance and compelling moral authority of a particular form or understanding of equality. The difficulty is that our understandings of the importance of equality differ substantially.

To appreciate the force of these differences, one might imagine three worlds. The first world has ten people in it, each with six units of goodness or utility. In a second world there are nine people with six units of goodness or utility and one person with ten units. If one is on principle an egalitarian of outcomes, one will regard the second world as worse than the first, even though no one is worse off and the total amount of utility or goodness is greater. If one is morally concerned to rectify the inequalities of the second world, one will incline to what can be characterized as an egalitarianism of envy. That is, one will want all persons to be made equal, even when some have more without dispossessing those who have less. This attitude toward equality can be understood as a form of envy in the sense of an endorsed discontent with the good fortune of others, holding unequalizing good fortune to be unfair, even if it is not at the expense of others. Inequality in and of itself is regarded as a circumstance to be rectified in preference to and in priority over other goods or right-making conditions.[9] Finally, one can consider a third world with nine people with six units of goodness or utility and one person with only one unit. If one wishes to improve the lot of the tenth person as cheaply and efficiently as possible, not because the person's share is unequal, but because that person lacks important goods and satisfactions, one can be characterized as endorsing an egalitarianism of altruism. One is not, in principle, concerned that some have more. Instead, one has sympathy for those who, in having less, lack a good.[10]

---

[8] The claim here is not that disruptive disputes divide polities with regard to health-care allocations and/or delivery. Rather, the claim is that there are real and substantive moral disagreements, even when they may not preclude the imposition of a particular health-care policy. The debates regarding abortion, physician-assisted suicide, and egalitarian health-care policy present these differences even when they do not rule out the possibility of governance.

[9] For a study of the meaning of equality, see Larry S. Temkin, *Inequality* (New York: Oxford University Press, 1993), esp. pp. 157–90, 292–307.

[10] One might interpret the so-called Oregon proposal as driven by an egalitarianism of altruism. Oregon proposed limiting the range of health-care resources available to Medicaid recipients so that all the poor could be covered. The proposal was that all the poor should be insured, although (1) Medicaid recipients would not receive the same level of health care as previously, and (2) the affluent would be able to purchase better basic care, as well as

How one regards the inequalities presented in the descriptions of these three worlds is important for assessing how one regards inequalities in health care and elsewhere. This is especially significant for health-care policy, given that major differences in per-capita investments in health care across nations do not lead to dramatic differences in mortality expectations, once one has achieved a rather modest level of investment (e.g., Greece does very well with $452 of health care per person).[11] One must look to other considerations for the special place of equality in debates regarding health-care policy. Perhaps the special place given to equality in health care depends on (1) the ways in which medicine is felt to bear on our finitude, in particular, on the postponement of death and the blunting of suffering, as well as (2) the difficulties of steadfastly refusing to commit communal funds to rescue persons with expensive health needs, even when (a) some individuals with disposable resources may decide to have themselves treated when they have such needs, and (b) individuals without the funds demand such treatment.[12] If one is to set limits on public health-care expenditures when it has been decided that the costs of such interventions on average outweigh the benefits, while recognizing the authority of persons to make choices about themselves and to use their resources as they wish, one must commit oneself to opposing high-cost last-minute state attempts at medical rescue for the poor and one must accept inequalities in access to health care.

Even if one were resolved to set egalitarian limits on health-care expenditures, one would still be confronted with a diversity of equalities. One would need a basis in principle for choosing among: an equality of opportunity in using one's own resources to pursue one's own health-care goals; an equality of opportunity supported by governmental funds in the acquisition of health care; an equality of opportunity supported by governmental funds and by proscriptions against unbalancing this equality by private purchases.[13] If one pursued an equality of outcome rather

---

luxury care (i.e., there would be a tiered provision of health care with a limited package for the poor and with the affluent left free to purchase whatever they wished and could afford). For discussions regarding the plan, see Martin A. Strosberg, Joshua M. Wiener, and Robert Baker, eds., *Rationing America's Medical Care: The Oregon Plan and Beyond* (Washington, DC: Brookings Institution, 1992).

[11] Schieber, Poullier, and Greenwald, "Health System Performance."

[12] Although a judgment may be made to provide only a certain amount of resources to avoid particular risks of disability and death, when confronted with a particular person actually facing that disability or risk of death, groups will often provide much higher levels of resources. Even if a particular treatment is not considered to be obligatory (given its high cost and low yield), when a particular patient could possibly benefit from the treatment, there may be the inclination to rescue the patient, thus distorting policy developed for the prudent use of communal resources. For a treatment of the difficulties faced in health-care policy when confronted by particular individuals in need of medical rescue, see E. Haavi Morreim, "Of Rescue and Responsibility: Learning to Live with Limits," *Journal of Medicine and Philosophy*, vol. 19 (1994), pp. 455–70.

[13] Norman Daniels provides a justification of an egalitarian approach to health care that, in the service of equality of opportunity, advances arguments for proscribing the purchase

than an equality of opportunity, one would need to choose among: an equality of outcome supported by research and treatment directed toward avoiding the premature death of men, children, etc.; an equality of outcome directed toward equalizing the likelihood of suffering, including the use of nonvoluntary euthanasia; an equality of outcome directed toward equalizing wealth, etc. One would also need a basis for choosing among conflicting views of governmental authority that could be invoked in the coercive realization of a particular ethos of health-care delivery. Does the government have the moral authority only to ensure that the provision of health care will be honest and nonfraudulent? Does the government also have the moral authority to ensure that everyone receives the health care that the government deems to be appropriate? Does the government have the secular moral authority to forbid the rich from leaving the country in order to purchase better health care abroad?

At stake also are conflicting views of what it is for the state to own the resources which politicians might wish to redistribute for egalitarian purposes, and what it is for individuals and groups to have holdings independently of the state. For example, does one own resources because one has produced them or has been given those resources by those who have produced them? Or does one only own resources if such entitlements conform to a governmentally endorsed understanding of a desirable or right distribution of resources? For that matter, why are communal claims to possess resources advantaged over those made by individuals? In addition, one must decide what counts as just, fair, right, and good. For example, do needs generate rights, so that if resources are not available to meet health-care needs, such a state of affairs is unfair?[14] Or are some outcomes simply unfortunate without being unfair? For instance, if certain screening programs can decrease the risk of developing cancer, does such protection against possible death count as a need that generates a right to a service for which others have a moral obligation to pay? Or is the nonprovision of such a service unfortunate, but not unfair? Or, if one's admission to a critical-care unit will convey a small chance of survival at a very high cost, does one have a need for health care that generates a right to the resources of others in order to purchase such critical care? Or

---

of better basic diagnostic and therapeutic interventions. See Norman Daniels, *Just Health Care* (New York: Cambridge University Press, 1985). Daniels was among the advisory members of the White House Task Force on National Health Reform, which developed President Clinton's 1993 health-care reform proposal. See also Dan Brock and Norman Daniels, "Ethical Foundations of the Clinton Administration's Proposed Health Care System," *Journal of the American Medical Association*, vol. 271 (April 20, 1994), pp. 1189–96.

[14] For a discussion of different approaches to how health-care needs may generate rights, see Thomas J. Bole III and William B. Bondeson, eds., *Rights to Health Care* (Dordrecht: Kluwer Academic Publishers, 1991). See also E. Haavi Morreim, *Balancing Act* (Washington, DC: Georgetown University Press, 1995); and H. Tristram Engelhardt, Jr., and Michael A. Rie, "Intensive Care Units, Scarce Resources, and Conflicting Principles of Justice," *Journal of the American Medical Association*, vol. 255, no. 9 (March 7, 1986), pp. 1159–64.

is the nonavailability of such resources, save for the rich, simply unfortunate, not unfair?

There are, in addition, substantive disagreements regarding how to understand the relationship among individuals, communities, societies, and states. These disagreements are functions of different accounts of how one should characterize the communal, societal, and/or political space within which individuals find different kinds of morally authoritative structures.[15] For example, should welfare, in the sense of group-provided insurance against losses in the natural and social lotteries,[16] be provided at the level of the state for all citizens, or instead at the level of particular communities and associations? One might envisage such provision occurring not just through companies, but also through religious and ideological groups. A number of these could transcend national boundaries, such as, perhaps, a worldwide Vaticare health-care welfare system for Roman Catholics, with the payment for care denominated in Vatican lira. Past history indicates that such approaches can succeed quite well even when they are unassociated with a particular religious or moral vision.[17] In our contemporary postmodern world of deep disagreements regarding appropriate moral understandings of health care, such associations offer the opportunity of maintaining moral and religious integrity within structures committed to a particular vision of health care. Under such an arrangement, one will need to tolerate others' doing evil within their own associations; yet when associations (rather than governments) are the social structures which embody content-full moralities, one can distance oneself as a citizen from such undertakings and avoid immediate collaboration with what one recognizes as wrong.

IV. HEALTH-CARE WELFARE PROVISION:
WHY IT IS SO INTRUSIVE AND PROBLEMATIC

The provision of health care as a basic uniform civil right is more intrusive than any other element of the welfare state: health care dramatically touches all the important passages of life, from reproduction and birth to suffering and death. The commitment to a particular package of services brings with it a particular interpretation of the significance of reproduction, birth, health, suffering, death, and equality (e.g., it involves

---

[15] H. Tristram Engelhardt, Jr., "*Sittlichkeit* and Post-Modernity: An Hegelian Reconsideration of the State," in *Hegel Reconsidered: Beyond Metaphysics and the Authoritarian State*, ed. H. Tristram Engelhardt, Jr., and Terry Pinkard (Dordrecht: Kluwer Academic Publishers, 1994), pp. 211–24.

[16] The term "natural and social lotteries" identifies the natural and social forces that advantage and disadvantage individuals irrespective of their deserts: some live long and healthy lives, while others contract serious diseases and die young (examples of the natural lottery); some inherit fortunes, while others are born destitute (examples of the social lottery).

[17] See, for example, David T. Beito, " 'This Enormous Army': The Mutual Aid Tradition of American Fraternal Societies before the Twentieth Century," elsewhere in this volume.

specific positions regarding artificial insemination by donors, prenatal diagnosis with the possibility of selective abortion, physician-assisted suicide, voluntary active euthanasia, and unequal access to better basic health care). A uniform welfare right to health care involves endorsing and establishing one among a number of competing concrete moralities of life, death, and equality. Because of this tie to morally controversial interventions, the establishment of uniform, universal health-care welfare rights directly or indirectly involves citizens, patients, physicians, nurses, and others in receiving or providing health care in a health-care system which they may find morally opprobrious.

Since all elements of personal behavior have some impact on the likelihood of disease, disability, and death, the establishment of a uniform, encompassing health-care welfare system involves the risk of medically politicizing all elements of personal conduct. For example, how should one regard a person who smokes heavily? Does a smoker irresponsibly expose the nation's health-care system to unnecessary costs? Or is such an individual a super-patriot, supporting the long-term fiscal solvency of the government? That is, should one consider such an individual a cost-saver, taking into account not only the costs of health care for smoking-related illnesses, but also the Social Security obligations (which would increase if the person were to live a more wholesome, longer life), possible long-term Medicare costs (which would be incurred if the individual adopted wholesome, nonsmoking behaviors, and thus lived to be eligible), and possible long-term Medicaid costs (which would rise if the individual adopted wholesome, nonsmoking behaviors, lived longer, and developed Alzheimer's, etc.)? Should one also consider the affluence and therefore increased life expectancies that may result from wealth generated from the tobacco industry?[18] Who burdens whom, and under what circumstances, depends on who pays as well as on the freedom of individuals to agree to engage in certain behaviors and to accept the consequences involved.

An encompassing health-care welfare entitlement does not merely tend to impose a particular vision of morality, human flourishing, and responsible risk-taking; it also tends to constrain the free choice of those with disposable resources. The notion of a guaranteed basic benefit package can take on a coercive character, so that individuals are not allowed to purchase better basic care but may only purchase additional care which is not provided through the guaranteed benefit package. For example, after being compelled by state force to contribute to a Medicare system, so-called beneficiaries may not offer more money for a covered service in order to gain access to a premier physician. Current Medicare law forbids Medicare patients from rewarding their physicians and health-care pro-

---

[18] Virginia Baxter Wright, "Will Quitting Smoking Help Medicare Solve Its Financial Problems?" *Inquiry*, vol. 23 (Spring 1986), pp. 76–82.

viders for better basic service. Nor may they legally offer to pay more for a longer, more careful provision of the basic services covered under Medicare. Once covered by Medicare for physician services, for example, they may not volunteer to pay five times the reimbursement schedule (i.e., have Medicare pay its fee and they pay four times that in addition) for a house call by a distinguished internist. In short, their resources are devalued by a system to which they are compelled to contribute and which will then not allow them to benefit from their required contributions if they wish to purchase better basic care. Substantive, coercively imposed health-care policies come into tension with the free and peaceable choices of individuals (e.g., the patient who might wish to purchase better basic care from a willing physician, while still receiving Medicare benefits which that patient has been compelled to fund).

Health-care welfare rights are, for all these reasons, problematic. The framing of health-care policy requires (1) gambling with human life, (2) accepting unavoidable inequalities in morbidity and mortality, (3) recognizing multiple and competing notions of equality in health care, and (4) acknowledging the intrusiveness of health-care rights if they bring with them particular moral visions of reproduction, suffering, and death. It also requires (5) appreciating the dangers of imposing a particular medicalized view of lifestyles in the service of health policy, and (6) noting the temptation to restrict free choices in order to achieve what is taken to be, on some particular understanding, a suitable level of efficiency or equity, while (7) confronting the diversity of our moral visions.

V. Why the Moral Disputes Will Not Go Away, Why We Are Not One Moral Community When It Comes to Matters of Health-Care Welfare Provision, and Why a Particular Substantive Moral Vision of Fairness May Not Be Imposed on All

It is not merely a matter of fact or of sociological circumstance that we possess diverse understandings of the significance of reproduction, birth, disability, suffering, and death, as well as diverse understandings of how one ought to gamble in the face of finitude or how one ought to take account of our inequalities and disparate misfortunes with respect to death and suffering. The crucial point is that we do not possess the basis for resolving such controversies in terms of a content-full morality. The goal of demonstrating that we are one secular moral community—such that we ought to agree as a matter of justice, fairness, or moral probity regarding an all-encompassing health-care welfare system—is elusive. Rather than uniting citizens in a single moral community, the attempt to develop a uniform, encompassing health-care welfare right, as a matter of principle, and not only as a matter of fact, reveals our moral differences concerning the meaning and importance of equality, as well as our differences concerning the proper understanding of reproduction, suffering, and death.[19]

The difficulty in resolving our moral controversies is foundational: one must already possess particular background moral premises, together with rules of moral evidence and inference, in order to resolve a moral controversy by sound rational argument. One needs a perspective from which one can make a morally authoritative choice among competing visions of the right and the good. An appeal to moral intuitions will not suffice. One's own moral intuitions will conflict with other moral intuitions. An appeal to ever-higher levels of moral intuition will not be decisive either, for further disagreements and appeals can in principle be extended indefinitely. Nor will an appeal to a consensus be any more successful. It will simply raise a number of questions: How does any particular consensus confer moral authority? How extensive must a consensus be to confer such authority? And from whom does such authority derive? (The appeal to consensus appears to invoke a secular version of a claim for the divine authority of majorities: *vox populi, vox Dei*.)[20] In short, how much of a majority authorizes what use of force and why? In order to establish policy, one must know which substantive account of the right and/or the good is authoritative. However, the higher-level perspective from which one would make such a choice must itself be informed by an understanding of the right and/or the good.

Imagine that one agrees that a society—through public policy in general, and in health-care policy in particular—should attempt to maximize liberty, equality, prosperity, and security. To calculate and compare the consequences of alternative approaches, one must already know how to compare liberty, equality, prosperity, and security. The comparative consequences of competing approaches cannot be assessed simply by an appeal to consequences. One must already have an independent morality allowing one to compare the different kinds of outcomes at stake, namely, liberty consequences, equality consequences, prosperity consequences, and security consequences. Nor will attempting to maximize the preferences of citizens determine which health policy has the best consequences. One must first know how to compare impassioned versus rational preferences. One must know how, if at all, one is to revise or correct preferences. In addition, one will need to know God's discount rate for preference satisfaction over time; that is, one must have an absolute standard or must know whether each person's own standard should

---

[19] Because of disagreements regarding the proper moral response to inequality, people in good conscience buy into private health-care provision or go to other countries to secure treatment, as occurs with Canadians, egalitarians to the contrary notwithstanding.

[20] For a study of the ambiguities involved in appeals to societal consensus for the authorization of health-care policy, see H. Tristram Engelhardt, Jr., "Consensus: How Much Can We Hope For?" in Kurt Bayertz, ed., *The Concept of Moral Consensus* (Dordrecht: Kluwer Academic Publishers, 1994), pp. 19–40.

be used, whatever it might be, in the moment the person attempts the discounting. Nor will it do to appeal to a disinterested observer, a hypothetical chooser, or a set of hypothetical contractors. If such are truly disinterested, they will have no moral sense and will be unable to make a principled choice. To make a principled choice, they must already be informed by a particular moral sense or thin theory of the good. But of course, the choice of the correct moral sense or thin theory of the good is what is at stake. The same difficulty can be recapitulated for any account of moral rationality or of the decision-theoretic resolution of disputes. In order morally to assess behavior or policy, one must appeal to a standard. To use a standard, however, one must know which standard is morally canonical. The result is that a canonical content-full moral vision can be established as binding by sound rational argument only by begging the question. To choose with moral authority, one must already have authoritative normative guidance. The question is: "Which (and whose) guidance?"

Postmodernity as an epistemological predicament, not merely as a sociological fact, is the recognition that, outside of a revelation of a canonical standard, one cannot authoritatively choose among content-full understandings of moral probity, justice, or fairness without begging the question or engaging in an infinite regress.[21] In order to show how a conclusion is warranted, one must always ask whose moral rationality, which sense of justice, is being invoked.[22] At the same time, one must recognize that there are numerous competing moral accounts or narratives. As we have seen, there are numerous and competing understandings of the importance and significance of equality. In such a circumstance, if all do not listen to God, so as to find revealed to them the canonical content-full notion of moral probity, fairness, justice, and equality, and if all attempts by sound rational argument to establish the canonical content-full account of moral probity, justice, and fairness beg the question, then one can arrive at moral authority when individuals meet as moral strangers, not by drawing authority either from God or from reason, but only from the permission of those who participate.[23] Moral authority will not be the authority of God or reason, but of consent, agreement, or permission. General secular moral authority is thus best construed as authorization.[24] The practice of deriving moral authority from permission makes

---

[21] Though there is no canonical content-full secular moral standard, it does not follow that such a standard is not available through revelation; see H. Tristram Engelhardt, Jr., "Moral Content, Tradition, and Grace: Rethinking the Possibility of a Christian Bioethics," *Christian Bioethics: Non-Ecumenical Studies in Medical Morality*, vol. 1 (1995), pp. 29–47.

[22] Alasdair MacIntyre, *Whose Justice? Which Rationality?* (Notre Dame, IN: University of Notre Dame Press, 1988).

[23] I have explored these issues at length in *The Foundations of Bioethics*, 2d ed (New York: Oxford University Press, 1996), esp. pp. 67–72.

[24] Moral constraints do exist within secular morality; they are derived from the right-making character of appeals to permission as the only source of authority in secular public

possible a sparse practice of secular morality that does not presume any particular content-full view of the right or the good.[25]

In such circumstances, permission or the authority it provides becomes the source of moral authority without any endorsement of permission as either good or bad. The securing of permission provides authority even when it does not provide motivation (permission does secure secular moral authority for the appropriate, albeit limited, use of state coercion, which can motivate compliance with the practice of deriving authority from permission). The point is that it is possible to secure a justification for state coercion and to determine which instances of coercion carry secular moral authority. The question is not "What will motivate moral action?" (though this issue is important), or "What level of moral disagreement makes governance difficult or impossible?" (or, for that matter, "What strategies by governments support public peace or effective governance?"). The question is, rather, "Under what circumstances can those ruling claim secular moral authority, so that those who disobey laws are not only at risk of being punished, but also at risk of being blameworthy?" Acting with permission offers a sparse, right-making condition for the collaboration of individuals who do not share a common understanding of what God demands or what moral rationality requires, but who claim an authority for their common endeavors.

Secular morality is procedural, and its legitimacy is limited by the consent of those who participate in common endeavors. Consequently, the paradigm moral activities of secular morality are the free market, contract formation, and the establishment of limited democracies.

In particular, democracies will have only that secular moral authority which can be derived either from the actual consent of all their members or from the practice of never using persons without their permission. The result will be that one will at most be able to justify the material equivalent of Robert Nozick's ultraminimal state.[26] The point is that, in the absence of a canonical, content-full secular morality, (1) health-care policy must derive its authority from the consent of the governed, (2) not from a prior understanding of justice, fairness, or equality, and (3) may not be all-encompassing, because the scope of its authority is limited by the limits of the consent of those involved. One will need to create policy instead of attempting to discover guidance in secular morality. One must

---

policy. Even if all do not listen to God, and if reason cannot disclose a canonical content-full moral vision, one can still derive authority from common agreement, that is, from permission. See Engelhardt, *The Foundations of Bioethics*, pp. 135–88.

[25] Though the appeal to permission has content-full implications, it does not presuppose any particular content-full account of the good or the right. It does not involve a choice among different rankings of goods, preferences, or right-making conditions. In this sense, the appeal to permission does not involve even a thin account of the good or of the right (of the sort which Rawls, for example, offers in his thin theory of the good, which does involve a lexical ordering of goods; see Rawls, *A Theory of Justice*, pp. 39ff.).

[26] Robert Nozick, *Anarchy, State, and Utopia* (New York: Basic Books, 1974), pp. 26–30.

proceed not by an appeal to a canonical, content-full understanding of the right or the good, but by an appeal to the permission of those involved. There will be no way to discover the correct balance among the various undertakings to which a community could direct its resources (e.g., how one should use common funds when faced with the claims of partisans of whooping cranes versus those of aged humans). As a consequence, limited democracies will be obliged to leave space so that individuals and communities can peaceably pursue their own visions of human flourishing and of appropriate health care. Still, if the state has legitimately acquired common resources, it is at liberty to create limited policy answers. One can explore many of the secular moral limits in health-care policy, without attending to the general secular moral limits on state authority, by assuming that the state possesses legitimately acquired funds.[27]

VI. Taking Moral Diversity and Limited Democracy Seriously

The concern to establish health-care welfare provision is encumbered by a cluster of moral difficulties tied to the inability to establish, by sound rational argument, a canonical morality regarding equality in access, not to mention regarding such important issues as third-party-assisted reproduction, abortion, physician-assisted suicide, and euthanasia. Though there is, on the part of many, a strong desire to establish an encompassing and equal right to health care, there are even stronger grounds for recognizing the morally problematic character of this desire. The substantial and significant differences in moral vision concerning matters of equality—and concerning the appropriate ways to regard reproduction, birth, suffering, and death—make any uniform, governmentally imposed right to health care highly morally problematic. Such an imposition would involve the secular equivalent of establishing a particular religious morality. If we do not share a common understanding of equality, fairness, and justice, and if there is in principle no way through sound rational argument to determine which understanding of justice, fairness, and equality should guide governmental undertakings, and if, in addition, health care is particularly intrusive and morally troubling when it brings with it a content-full moral understanding of reproduction, birth, suffering, and death, then the provision of any general protection against morbidity and mortality is best offered as a limited insurance against losses in the natural and social lotteries.

---

[27] I do not here explore the considerable difficulties faced in providing a general secular moral justification for taxation. Instead, attention is directed to how one ought to proceed in using common resources, presuming that they can be acquired legitimately. For my treatment of issues bearing on the legitimacy of taxation, see *The Foundations of Bioethics*, pp. 154–80.

These considerations argue against any particular universally mandated set of health-care services and in favor of the equivalent of a voucher for the poor, which would allow the purchase of health care from various morally different health-care delivery networks. The limits of secular moral authority require acquiescing in the creation of health-care networks and associations providing morally different forms of basic health care. The only restrictions that may be imposed with secular moral authority will involve the guarantee that participants in the various health-care networks join freely in the particular medical moralities they choose.

In order to establish a limited welfare right to health care without going aground on diverse visions of moral probity and justice, secular health-care provision for the indigent may not be justified in terms of a particular account of equality, fairness, or justice, nor may it establish a particular medical morality regarding reproduction, suffering, and death. The use of vouchers could avoid much of this difficulty if such vouchers could be applied to different alternative, basic menus of service. Different communities or associations with different moral visions could then establish morally competing health-care systems into which individuals could enter for basic services using such vouchers. Better yet would be a policy that avoided even the necessity of establishing basic menus of service and instead allowed the use of health-care purchase accounts to which funds could be provided for the poor to use in purchasing basic medical services.[28]

Under such circumstances, the government would provide basic health-care protection against morbidity and mortality for the indigent without imposing a content-full morality. Medical needs could be both defined and addressed in a range of significantly different terms. In a truly free and limited democracy, competing health-care systems could come into existence to take advantage of the availability of the health-care vouchers (as well as the availability of payments from private insurers and direct payments from patients). For the sake of illustration, one could imagine two systems, one supported by Roman Catholics and another by New Age agnostics. The first would not offer artificial insemination by donors, prenatal diagnosis and abortion, or physician-assisted suicide and eutha-

---

[28] Here focus is given only to the proposal of providing the indigent with a sum of money that can be expended only for health care. At stake is the freedom from the need to establish any particular medical morality in order to provide a voucher or a health-care purchase account (the provision of funds to the indigent for the purchase of health care). Either option—a voucher system or a purchase-account system—would allow recipients to choose among a number of competing morally and medically diverse health-care systems. A health-care purchase account has the further secular moral advantage of providing the indigent with cash, so that they may more freely choose among the different health-care service options available. In this essay no attempt is made to explore the various proposals that have been advanced regarding medical savings accounts. For a recent review of the debates in this matter, see Emmett Keeler, Jesse Malkin, Dana Goldman, and Joan Buchanan, "Can Medical Savings Accounts for the Nonelderly Reduce Health Care Costs?" *Journal of the American Medical Association*, vol. 275, no. 21 (June 5, 1996), pp. 1666–71.

nasia. It would provide limitations on health-care expenditures in terms of religious understandings of the appropriate line between proportionate and disproportionate care, that is, between ordinary and extraordinary care. This line would vary with the social status of the individual (i.e., it would be *proportionem status*).[29] In addition, religiously attentive hospice and comfort care would be offered to all.

In contrast, the system appealing to agnostic New-Agers would offer artificial insemination for unmarried women, prenatal diagnosis and selective abortion, and specially discounted treatment with an agreement to be euthanatized under certain conditions when health care is unlikely to provide a significant extension of life with an acceptable quality. Hospice care would be tied to effective and painless euthanasia.[30] A voucher system or health-care purchase account that took moral diversity seriously would allow individuals to avoid interventions they recognized as morally inappropriate and to purchase in their stead those they saw as acceptable (or to select care so as to achieve a savings of funds). The result would be a policy that provided basic protection against health-care needs without establishing one view of equality and medical moral probity as dominant over the others.[31]

The data indicate that such a basic welfare package would afford significant mortality protection.[32] If individuals were left free to choose particular packages of basic health care (offered within particular medical moralities and constrained only by the free consent of the participants), then help could be provided for the poor while avoiding the significant moral costs of generally imposing one of the many secular medical moralities at the expense of the others. Such an approach to health-care policy would require accepting our finitude, including the limits of governmental moral authority, while acknowledging our moral diversity.

Medicine and Philosophy, Baylor College of Medicine and Rice University

---

[29] The Roman Catholic account of the line between obligatory and non-obligatory care, between ordinary and extraordinary care, includes an acknowledgment of the appropriateness of inequalities in levels of care due to social status, usually correlated with wealth. See, for example, Daniel A. Cronin, "The Moral Law in Regard to the Ordinary and Extraordinary Means of Conserving Life," in *Conserving Human Life*, ed. Russell E. Smith (Braintree, MA: Pope John XXIII Center, 1989), pp. 1–145.

[30] H. Tristram Engelhardt, Jr., "Vecchiaia, eutanasia, e diversità morale: La creazione di opzioni morali nell' assistenza sanitaria," *Bioetica*, 1995, pp. 74–84.

[31] These considerations require the repeal of statutory constraints on the purchase of better basic care of the sort that currently exist with respect to Medicare.

[32] Significant mortality protection appears achievable at a rather minimal level of investment in health care; see Schieber, Poullier, and Greenwald, "Health System Performance."

CITIZENSHIP AND SOCIAL POLICY: T. H. MARSHALL AND POVERTY*

By Lawrence M. Mead

I. Introduction

T. H. Marshall, a British sociologist, gave a series of lectures in 1949 under the title "Citizenship and Social Class."[1] To many American intellectuals, his analysis still offers a persuasive account of the origins of the welfare state in the West. But Marshall spoke in the early postwar era, when the case for expanded social benefits seemed unassailable. Today's politics are more conservative. In every Western country the welfare state is under review. Yet Marshall's conception can still help define the issues in social policy and the way forward.

In Section II, I summarize Marshall's argument for social provision as a dimension of citizenship. I then describe, in Sections III and IV, the two main challenges that have arisen to the welfare state—criticism of its costs and the contention that "welfare" promotes entrenched poverty in the inner city. This second charge, I argue, is the more serious, because it attacks the heart of Marshall's civic case for social provision. After elaborating on the problem of entrenched poverty in Section V, I go on, in Sections VI through IX, to consider several approaches to assuaging poverty, two that are consistent with Marshall's vision and two that are not. I argue that a policy of enforcing work and other civilities is the truest to Marshall's idea and also the most effective. I conclude, in Section X, with some reflections on the implications of the social problem for politics. I believe that dysfunctional poverty threatens the traditional politics of justice, and that only if it is overcome can a debate about justice resume.

II. Marshall's Argument

By "welfare state" we mean the set of income transfers (public assistance, pensions), in-kind benefits (food, housing, health care), and other services that, in affluent societies, protect citizens from the vicissitudes of capitalism. Some of these benefits are designed to replace earnings when

* I gratefully acknowledge helpful comments on the first draft of this essay from Steven Teles, and from Ellen Frankel Paul, David Schmidtz, Daniel Shapiro, and the other contributors to this volume.

[1] T. H. Marshall, "Citizenship and Social Class," in T. H. Marshall, *Class, Citizenship, and Social Development: Essays by T. H. Marshall*, with an introduction by Seymour Martin Lipset (Garden City, NY: Doubleday, 1964), ch. 4.

workers are unemployed, disabled, or retired and presume an earnings history, while others are means-tested, designed to ensure that everyone in the society has enough income and other essentials, such as health care, to live a civilized life.

Marshall argues, first, that the welfare state is an expression of citizenship. Citizenship means the collection of public claims and duties bestowed on people by the political order. It is not changeless. The claims people make on the state have grown over time. In Britain in the seventeenth century, citizenship connoted the civil rights of equality before the law, free labor, and press freedoms. The nineteenth century expanded the suffrage and other political rights until, by 1918, all adults could vote. The twentieth century added social rights such as public education and minimum-income guarantees. In Britain in the late 1940s, at the time Marshall spoke, the Labor Party added guaranteed health care and children's allowances. The welfare state, then, is the operational expression of social citizenship. It provides the material minimums that people now expect as members of the society.

Second, Marshall argues that citizenship is egalitarian as class is not. Something about citizenship commands that public rights and duties be essentially the same for all full members of the political order. Hence, social provision tends to be egalitarian. While some benefits may vary with income, the principle of a "floor" beneath which no one sinks is the same for all. But the very people who are equal as citizens occupy very different economic positions, and thus differ vastly in their income, wealth, and other advantages. Thus, tension develops between citizenship and class. In part, equal citizenship compensates for social inequality and makes egalitarian social reform less imperative. But the political order also pursues "class-abatement." It seeks over time to shift more dimensions of life from class to citizenship, from inequality to equality, or at least to ameliorate inequality. That pressure explains why the content of citizenship has grown over time.[2]

Marshall's conception powerfully expresses the sense many intellectuals have that, at least in rich countries, the welfare state is inevitable. Partly, that sense reflects the argument of Marxists that capitalism inevitably undermines itself, leading to collectivism. A market economy must concede a welfare state in order to shield the populace from economic insecurities and stave off revolution. Even within the non-Marxist social democratic tradition, however, social provision is seen as the inevitable expression of democracy. The welfare state recreates through government the protections against the marketplace that existed in precapitalist society.[3] The politics behind social provision is complex. In some instances, social programs were inaugurated by the anticapitalist left, in other cases

[2] *Ibid.*, pp. 86, 116–17.
[3] Karl Polanyi, *The Great Transformation* (Boston: Beacon Press, 1957).

(notably in Britain and Germany) by aristocrats concerned to forestall industrial poverty or the radicalization of workers. Modern statistical analyses suggest that the welfare state arose to meet prosaic needs to support growing elderly populations and protect societies from international economic pressures.[4]

The Marshallian account is, perhaps, especially applicable to the United States. Citizens of European countries can base their sense of belonging on shared history or ethnicity. Citizens of the United States, with its brief existence and polyglot population, derive their sense of belonging much more from political membership. "Americans" are those who adhere to the individualist creed of the Founders and participate in a democratic political order.[5] There is evidence that, just as Marshall suggests, equal citizenship in America "comforts" inequality. Americans are sufficiently satisfied with equal citizenship that social and economic inequality is seldom resented. Most people think equality *is* equal citizenship; they do not demand equal income or wealth. Status differences are usually ignored in politics provided they do not obtrude on how people are treated by government.[6] What matters, for example, is not that everybody be able to afford the same kind of automobile but that the rich get no precedence in renewing their driver's licenses. Equal citizenship means that they have to queue up at the local Department of Motor Vehicles office like everyone else.

Occasionally, however, the sense that economic disparities violate essential rights and opportunities does arise. That feeling was a powerful impetus to the expansion of government in the United States during the Progressive, New Deal, and Great Society eras. The manifesto of Progressivism was Herbert Croly's *The Promise of American Life*, first published in 1909. Croly's main point was similar to Marshall's: some public intervention in the economy is necessary to vindicate democratic citizenship.[7] Many American academics agree. Equal citizenship in the U.S., Judith Shklar writes, requires equal social "standing," even for out-groups such as racial minorities, and that might require greater social protections than we have.[8] The American welfare state is still incomplete by Western standards, many feel. It does not provide some of the benefits, such as guar-

    [4] Wilensky, Harold, *The Welfare State and Equality: Structural and Ideological Roots of Public Expenditures* (Berkeley: University of California Press, 1975); David R. Cameron, "The Expansion of the Public Economy: A Comparative Analysis," *American Political Science Review*, vol. 72, no. 4 (December 1978), pp. 1243–61.

    [5] Samuel P. Huntington, *American Politics: The Promise of Disharmony* (Cambridge, MA: Harvard University Press, 1981), ch. 2.

    [6] Lee Rainwater, *What Money Buys: Inequality and the Social Meanings of Income* (New York: Basic Books, 1974), pp. 163–73.

    [7] Herbert Croly, *The Promise of American Life*, ed. Arthur M. Schlesinger, Jr. (Cambridge, MA: Harvard University Press, 1965).

    [8] Judith N. Shklar, *American Citizenship: The Quest for Inclusion* (Cambridge, MA: Harvard University Press, 1991).

anteed jobs or child care, often found in Europe.[9] Whether they know it or not, those who assert this argue Marshall's case, that American citizenship should entail greater social rights.

III. Economic Costs

Despite the popularity of social benefits, however, the welfare state is currently in retreat throughout the West. One reason is its cost. Governments find that they cannot afford all the social benefits that politicians have promised, particularly pensions and health care for the elderly. Either they cannot balance their budgets, or the burdens on the economy appear to be excessive. American conservatives charge that exploding social spending is a reason for economic problems in the United States, such as low investment and declining competitiveness. So eligibility for social benefits, and the benefits provided, have been somewhat trimmed in most Western countries since the 1970s. Social spending continues to grow, but mainly because populations are aging, and hence are more in need of health and pension benefits, and because of the skyrocketing cost of health care. In the United States, even the cuts Ronald Reagan inflicted on social programs only momentarily reduced the upward curve of social spending.[10]

As this modest outcome suggests, the economic criticism of the welfare state has not been persuasive enough to date to shake support for social spending in any fundamental way. Skeptics respond that, while social benefits do strain budgets, whether they harm the economy is doubtful. Any link between a nation's social spending and its economic prowess is unclear. Some countries, notably Germany, are socially generous as well as competitive. There is no clear economic limit to the welfare state, only political limits to society's willingness to tax itself.[11]

Even if the cuts were severe, if they were made on economic grounds they would leave the heart of the Marshallian conception unshaken. Even if social provision must be curbed due to scarcity, it still embodies the values of citizenship. It remains a realm of equality relative to the strat-

[9] Margaret Weir, Ann Shola Orloff, and Theda Skocpol, eds., *The Politics of Social Policy in the United States* (Princeton: Princeton University Press, 1988); Sheila B. Kamerman and Alfred J. Kahn, "What Europe Does for Single-Parent Families," *The Public Interest*, no. 93 (Fall 1988), pp. 70–86.

[10] Reagan's cuts came mostly in 1981, after which congressional resistance stiffened. Through 1985, he trimmed social spending less than 10 percent below what otherwise would have occurred. See D. Lee Bawden and John L. Palmer, "Social Policy: Challenging the Welfare State," in *The Reagan Record: An Assessment of America's Changing Domestic Priorities*, ed. John L. Palmer and Isabel V. Sawhill (Cambridge, MA: Ballinger, 1984), pp. 184–86.

[11] Theodore R. Marmor, Jerry L. Mashaw, and Philip L. Harvey, *America's Misunderstood Welfare State: Persistent Myths, Enduring Realities* (New York: Basic Books, 1990), chs. 1, 3; Gary Burtless, "Public Spending on the Poor: Historical Trends and Economic Limits," in *Confronting Poverty: Prescriptions for Change*, ed. Sheldon H. Danziger, Gary D. Sandefur, and Daniel H. Weinberg (New York: Russell Sage Foundation; and Cambridge, MA: Harvard University Press, 1994), pp. 76–83.

ifications of class. It vindicates democratic values. Perhaps citizens decide via politics to rely more on themselves, less on government, but that still is a collective decision that defines terms for belonging for the society. Benefits can always be expanded again if economic conditions improve.

IV. THE COSTS OF POVERTY

Far more threatening to Marshall's vision, I believe, is the current social problem. I refer to the entrenched poverty that, since the 1960s, has plagued most American cities. More recently, similar problems have appeared in Europe. "Poverty" here connotes not only people living below a recognized social minimum but the dysfunctional lifestyle often associated with low income—crime, drug addiction, unwed pregnancy, child abuse, and school failure. Such problems are closely linked to welfare, meaning not the welfare state in general but public assistance and other means-tested benefits. It is families living on aid who most often display a dysfunctional lifestyle.[12]

The challenge poverty poses is very different from the economic problems of the welfare state. The main cost of social provision comes from large benefit programs aimed at the general population, especially unemployment and pension benefits and health care. Such benefits are typically not means-tested or are only partially so. That means that a large proportion of the population receives them, making their cost formidable. The programs thus impose economic strains, but few would call them responsible for the social problems of the inner city. With welfare and other antipoverty programs, the situation reverses. These benefits are means-tested and serve only the neediest, so their monetary cost is minor compared to the middle-class entitlements. The criticism, rather, is that these programs impose social costs by tempting the poor to live improvidently.

Table 1 shows federal spending on major American social programs in 1995.[13] Vastly the most expensive program is Social Security, a huge federal pension system which supports over 40 million retired and disabled people, only a small minority of them poor or on welfare. The next cost-

[12] To avoid definitional disputes, I understand that poverty and welfare dependency are not the same, and that both labels designate larger groups than the "underclass," or the most disordered poor. The "social problem" I refer to here is that of the *long-term* poor, meaning individuals not elderly or disabled, and their families, who are poor by the federal government's definition for more than two years at a stretch. Within this group, I focus particularly on people on welfare for spells of more than two years. The underclass is another subset of the long-term poor. The long-term poor are a small group, perhaps 5 percent of the population in the United States, but they are still strategic to American urban problems. See Lawrence M. Mead, *The New Politics of Poverty: The Nonworking Poor in America* (New York: Basic Books, 1992), pp. 14–15.

[13] The figures in Table 1 are drawn from Office of Management and Budget, *Budget of the United States Government, Fiscal Year 1997* (Washington, DC: U.S. Government Printing Office, 1996), Budget Supplement, pp. 141, 168, and Appendix, pp. 240, 494, 677, 940. Note that figures in Table 1 come from different budget tables and are not precisely comparable.

TABLE 1. *Federal spending on U.S. social programs, fiscal year 1995*

	Spending (billions of dollars)
Social insurance	
Social Security	$333.3
Medicare	156.9
Unemployment insurance	25.2
Means-tested programs	
Medicaid	89.1
All means-tested guarantees except Medicaid	92.5
Aid to Families with Dependent Children	17.1
Supplemental Security Income	26.5
Food Stamps	25.6
Education, training, employment, social services	54.3

liest program is Medicare, a federal health insurance program for the elderly and disabled.

Social Security, Medicare, and unemployment insurance for the jobless are all financed largely by payroll contributions paid by the beneficiaries and other workers while employed. Together, the three programs dwarf in cost all the noncontributory programs. And of the latter, by far the costliest is Medicaid, a health program for the needy whose major benefits again flow to the elderly, for hospital care and nursing homes. Other than Medicaid, all means-tested benefits where all eligible persons are covered cost Washington less than $100 billion a year.

This total includes all of what most people mean by "welfare," or income grants to the younger and more controversial poor. Aid to Families with Dependent Children (AFDC), the main butt of welfare reform efforts, supports female-headed families. Supplemental Security Income (SSI) supports needy persons who are elderly, blind, or disabled, while Food Stamps provides coupons to buy food to poor people of all descriptions. Federal spending for education, work programs, and other social services, most of them targeted on the poor, is only about $54 billion. State and local funding adds somewhat to these totals.[14] While the cost of means-tested programs is significant, it is fair to say that expense is not the main objection to American "welfare," or equivalent subsidies in

[14] The above figures represent only federal costs. About 43 percent of Medicaid costs and 46 percent of AFDC benefit expenses are paid by states and localities. See U.S. Congress, House of Representatives, Committee on Ways and Means, *Overview of Entitlement Programs: 1994 Green Book* (Washington, DC: U.S. Government Printing Office, July 15, 1994), pp. 382, 797.

Europe. Far more significant are the effects these programs may have on the social functioning of the poor.

Dysfunctional poverty threatens the Marshallian conception in a fundamental way, as economic stringency does not. For the argument that equal citizenship necessitates social provision operates only on behalf of people who are accepted as full citizens. Intellectuals emphasize the claims of citizenship, but Marshall also mentions obligations. Modern states impose duties to obey the law, pay taxes, and serve in the military. Education is both a right and a duty, in that government both provides schools and expects citizens to attend them.[15] The current disordered poor, however, commonly violate these expectations. They have significant difficulty in obeying the law and getting through school. For this reason, they are often seen by the nonpoor as less than full members of the society—as "undeserving." In Marshallian terms, this means that they cannot demand aid as a matter of right. Government may still give assistance to them, but as charity, not as something to which they are entitled.

V. The Work Problem

Most academic discussions of the welfare state make little mention of the dutiful side of citizenship. It is simply assumed that the recipients of social benefits are "deserving." In establishing desert, however, work discipline is fundamental, and here many of today's poor adults have a problem.

A. Work and "deservingness"

What legitimizes the social insurance programs is their strong tie to employment. The beneficiaries of unemployment, pension, and health benefits, or their employers, pay premiums while they are working. They then may claim support from the programs with few questions asked when, due to layoff, age, or infirmity, they cannot work.

Historically, the claim of the working class to social protections rested on the disproportion between what it contributed to the society and what it received. Workers, it was presumed, labored harder than the upper class. In the Marxist version, they were exploited, even expropriated, by capitalism. In the populist version more native to America, capitalism is accepted but bosses and Wall Street are resented. If workers received economic guarantees from the society, that was only recompense for the burdens they bore. That conviction generated most of the moral force behind the labor movement and democratic socialism. Social insurance makes it a basis for social policy.

[15] Marshall, "Citizenship and Social Class," pp. 82, 117.

Nevertheless, the founding theorists of the welfare state worried that the premise of work discipline would be forgotten. Marshall and others were concerned, for one thing, that the enactment of rights for unions, an aspect of the welfare state, would make them unwilling to accept wage bargains consistent with the general interest. The refusal of unions to honor wage restraint, even when socialist parties were in power, is a serious problem for collectivist regimes in Europe.[16] It is one aspect of a general problem of free government: the use of political freedoms by economic interests to organize against a free economy.[17]

There was even a danger that people would be less willing to work or otherwise function at all. Beatrice Webb, a founder of British socialism, worried that society would ensure health care and unemployment benefits to workers "without any corresponding obligation to get well and keep well, or to seek and keep employment."[18] William Beveridge, whose wartime planning shaped much of the British welfare state, warned that "[m]en and women in receipt of unemployment benefit cannot be allowed to hold out indefinitely" for preferred jobs; they should have to accept lesser positions or, at least, enter an employment program.[19] Marshall himself feared that work, which was enforced by self-interest as long as there were no social protections, would be tougher to enforce when it was merely "attached to the status of citizenship."[20]

B. Nonworking poverty

In our own time, that danger has come to pass. The chief problem is not that the presence of unemployment benefits makes many of those who lose jobs slower to find new positions, although that is true. It is rather that many adults today do not work regularly enough even to qualify for unemployment coverage, and the dignity that it implies. In the early 1960s in the United States, nearly 60 percent of the unemployed received unemployment insurance, but by the 1980s only a third did, mainly because fewer jobless had held their jobs long enough to qualify. A similar decline in coverage, for similar reasons, is apparent in Great Britain.[21]

---

[16] Ibid., pp. 112–13; Élie Halévy, The Era of Tyrannies: Essays on Socialism and War, trans. R. K. Webb (Garden City, NY: Anchor Books, 1965), pp. 249–85.

[17] Mancur Olson, The Rise and Decline of Nations: Economic Growth, Stagflation, and Social Rigidities (New Haven, CT: Yale University Press, 1982).

[18] Quoted in Daniel Patrick Moynihan, "Toward a Post-Industrial Social Policy," The Public Interest, no. 96 (Summer 1989), p. 18 n. 1.

[19] Quoted in John Burton, Would Workfare Work? A Feasibility Study of a Workfare System to Replace Long-Term Unemployment in the UK (Buckingham, England: University of Buckingham, Employment Research Center, 1987), pp. 28–29.

[20] Marshall, "Citizenship and Social Class," p. 118.

[21] Lawrence M. Mead, Beyond Entitlement: The Social Obligations of Citizenship (New York: Free Press, 1986), pp. 128–32; and Mead, New Politics of Poverty, pp. 95–96; James Riccio, From Welfare to Work among Lone Parents in Britain: Lessons for America (New York: Manpower Demonstration Research Corporation, June 1996), pp. 60–61.

This is not to say that the work ethic has lost its grip. American adults are in fact employed at the highest levels in history. Men have taken extra jobs and their wives have entered the labor force in an effort to keep family income ahead of inflation. They had to do this because wages adjusted for inflation have not risen much for most Americans since 1973. The economy, fortunately, has created jobs in large numbers, albeit often at disappointing pay. In Europe, trends are similar, although the economy, due to a more regulated labor market, creates fewer, higher-paying jobs. Yet in the midst of the work obsession, long-term joblessness for a minority of adults is a serious problem in the U.S. The same tendency has arisen in Britain, provoking official inquiry.[22]

Unfortunately, the work dearth is worst among the poor, who need social provision the most. In the U.S. in 1959, when concern over poverty was just beginning, over two-thirds of the heads of poor families reported working sometime in the year, and almost one-third worked full-time and full-year. But most of the working poor were lifted out of poverty by the rising earnings of the 1960s and early 1970s. Work levels among the remaining poor fell, until by 1975 only half of the heads of poor families reported any earnings and only 16 percent worked full-year and full-time. Those numbers have changed little since, even as the working proportion among the nonpoor has risen.[23]

Among welfare recipients, almost all of whom are poor, reported work levels run even lower, with only 6 percent of welfare mothers saying that they worked in 1992, even part-time.[24] Researchers say that the actual level is somewhat higher, with half of welfare mothers working at some time while on the rolls, often "off the books"; but work is rare among the long-term dependent, who dominate the rolls at any one time.[25] The dependent mothers contrast sharply with single mothers not on welfare, of whom around 85 percent are employed.[26]

Table 2 contrasts work levels among poor and nonpoor American adults in 1991, with separate figures for family heads and female family heads.[27]

[22] House of Commons, Employment Committee, *The Right to Work/Workfare* (London: Her Majesty's Stationery Office, February 13, 1996).

[23] Mead, *New Politics of Poverty* (*supra* note 12), pp. 5–9. "Poverty" here is defined using the federal government's definition. The 1993 figures were 49 percent of poor family heads working at any time, and 15 percent working full-year and full-time. See U.S. Department of Commerce, Bureau of the Census, *Income, Poverty, and Valuation of Noncash Benefits: 1993*, Series P-60, No. 188 (Washington, DC: U.S. Government Printing Office, February 1995), table 19.

[24] Committee on Ways and Means, *Overview of Entitlement Programs: 1994 Green Book* (*supra* note 14), p. 404.

[25] Kathleen Mullan Harris, "Work and Welfare among Single Mothers in Poverty," *American Journal of Sociology*, vol. 99, no. 2 (September 1993), pp. 329–31.

[26] Robert Moffitt, "Incentive Effects of the U.S. Welfare System: A Review," *Journal of Economic Literature*, vol. 30, no. 1 (March 1992), pp. 11, 13.

[27] The figures in Table 2 are drawn from U.S. Department of Commerce, Bureau of the Census, *Poverty in the United States: 1991*, Series P-60, no. 181 (Washington, DC: U.S. Government Printing Office, August 1992), pp. xiv–xv.

TABLE 2. *Employment status of poor and nonpoor American adults, 1991*

	Poor	Nonpoor
Percentage of individuals 15 and over who		
Worked at any time	39.8	72.0
Full-year and full-time	9.0	45.0
Percentage of family heads who		
Worked at any time	50.4	80.5
Full-year and full-time	15.8	61.1
Percentage of female family heads who		
Worked at any time	42.4	76.1
Full-year and full time	9.5	54.5

In all categories, the difference is enormous, particularly for full-year, full-time work.

The Marshallian rationale for social provision, I submit, cannot survive work contrasts as great as these. For such figures reverse the moral presumption of social democracy. If work effort is the measure of deservingness, the affluent now seem more virtuous than the low-income. According to one government study, in 1986 working hours among families in the top fifth of the American income distribution were almost seven times as great as among families in the bottom fifth.[28] High work levels for the general population sustain the citizenship rationale for the social insurance welfare state, but low work levels for the poor put that case in question for welfare and other antipoverty programs. The wide perception that the current poor no longer satisfy the moral presuppositions of citizenship helped justify cuts in means-tested benefits since 1980, although overall spending on these programs, as on social insurance benefits, has continued to expand.

C. Grappling with poverty

Some contend that Marshall's case remains valid without change. Social benefits are still a component of citizenship that everyone should get, and they are needed to inculcate citizenship.[29] Most intellectuals, however, recognize that the current dysfunction at the bottom of the society

[28] Congressional Budget Office, *Trends in Family Income: 1970–1986* (Washington, DC: U.S. Government Printing Office, February 1988), table A-15.

[29] Ralf Dahrendorf, *The Modern Social Conflict: An Essay on the Politics of Liberty* (New York: Weidenfeld and Nicholson, 1988), chs. 7–8; Desmond S. King and Jeremy Waldron, "Citizenship, Social Citizenship, and the Defence of Welfare Provision," *British Journal of Political Science*, vol. 18, no. 4 (October 1988), pp. 415–43.

		Argument based on	
		Citizenship	Effectiveness
Emphasis on	Rights	Entitlement	Investment
	Obligations	Enforcement	Privatization

FIGURE 1. Approaches to the social problem of poverty.

poses a serious political dilemma. Unless the poor display better citizenship, especially by working, generous antipoverty policies could become indefensible.[30] Liberal politics in general has become tarred with the brush of welfare, and that is one motive for the rethinking of liberalism now going on among political theorists.[31]

Either order and effort must be restored at the bottom of society, so that the citizenship argument for antipoverty benefits again persuades, or some non-Marshallian basis for social policy must be found. Figure 1 arrays four possible approaches to the problem of poverty: entitlement, investment, privatization, and enforcement. The two dimensions of the table concern whether solutions focus on rights or obligations, and whether the argument for them rests mostly on citizenship or on the antipoverty effectiveness of the policies. Each approach claims both rationales to a degree, but a difference in emphasis is clear. In the following four sections, I consider briefly the case to be made for each of these strategies.

VI. ENTITLEMENT

Most social policy experts seek to solve the poverty problem with further benefits. They propose additional dimensions of social citizenship. Poverty exists, they contend, because the welfare state is not yet generous or extensive enough. Provide new entitlements and poverty will decline. The main arguments rest on rights, but some experts also claim that new rights would ameliorate the social problem.

A. Universal programs

One version of this case attacks the distinction between social insurance and public assistance. In the United States, that division is profound. The contributory programs, such as Social Security, are work-connected, and hence respectable, but welfare programs, such as AFDC, are means-

---

[30] Amy Gutmann, ed., *Democracy and the Welfare State* (Princeton: Princeton University Press, 1988), introduction and chs. 1–3.
[31] Nancy L. Rosenblum, "Introduction," in *Liberalism and the Moral Life*, ed. Nancy L. Rosenblum (Cambridge, MA: Harvard University Press, 1989), pp. 1–17.

tested, so that dependence on them carries imputations of failure. Social insurance is also distributed according to impersonal rules. Welfare is more demeaning because eligibility hinges to some extent on judgments about the personal "deservingness" of the claimants.[32] As I note below, welfare has asked fewer questions about desert in recent decades, but it is still not respectable.

Proponents of universality want to overthrow this distinction, or at least blur the line between social insurance and welfare. In European countries, people who run out of unemployment benefits have much easier access to welfare than in the United States. Such continuity means that, in Europe, aid recipients tend to be defined as "unemployed," with the dignity that implies, whereas in the U.S. they are seen as nonworking.

Better still, they argue, replace means-tested benefits with universal programs aiding the entire population. Especially, supplement or replace AFDC, the most controversial aid program, with children's allowances, child tax credits, and better child support for the entire population. Replace Medicaid, the costly and troubled health program for the poor, with national health insurance for all. Replace means-tested employment programs aimed only at the poor with wage subsidies and training vouchers for all low-paid workers, and so on.[33]

Universal programs, the contention is, would be better supported and funded than programs just for the poor, which will always be poor programs. The enormous popularity of Social Security and Medicare attests to this. Just as important, to include the poor under the same benefits as the middle-class would dignify them. It would submerge the indigent in a larger and better-functioning population. Their problems would become less visible. They might even function better because they were treated less suspiciously. From greater respect would flow greater self-respect.[34] Universal programs would thus help realize, as well as reflect, equal citizenship.

One objection, of course, is that universal programs cost vastly more than welfare, because so much of the subsidy goes to affluent people who, economically, do not need it. Policy analysts tend to prefer means-testing because of its greater "target" efficiency. More important, however, there is no evidence that universalizing benefits without work stipulations would, by itself, edify the recipients. The dysfunctions of the poor have deep roots in family and ethnic history. They may be exacerbated by invidious treatment; but they are not caused by it, and to replace welfare with

[32] Lawrence M. Friedman, "Social Welfare Legislation: An Introduction," *Stanford Law Review*, vol. 21, no. 2 (January 1969), pp. 217–47.

[33] National Commission on Children, *Beyond Rhetoric: A New American Agenda for Children and Families* (Washington, DC: U.S. Government Printing Office, 1991).

[34] Theda Skocpol, "Sustainable Social Policy: Fighting Poverty without Poverty Programs," *The American Prospect*, no. 2 (Summer 1990), pp. 58–70.

universal but permissive benefits would not overcome them.[35] In Europe, passive, long-term dependency is growing even though the social insurance/welfare division is far less clear than in America. Universal programs would be more edifying if, like social insurance, they presumed work effort. But then they would fail to reach many of the poor, just because they are nonworking.

The case for universality assumes that changing the image of programs can change the reputation of the poor. Unfortunately, the reputation of the recipients seems rather to shape the image of programs. In the U.S., Social Security is respectable because the beneficiaries are retired working people who have "paid their dues." Welfare is disrespectable because the clients are widely seen as "undeserving," and not because their programs are means-tested. The Earned Income Tax Credit (EITC), a wage subsidy for low-paid workers, is means-tested and thus technically welfare. Yet it is popular in Congress. Family Credit, a similar subsidy, is popular in Britain.[36] In both cases, this is because the subsidies premise support on employment, thus ensuring that aid is "earned."

Combining benefits for the needy and the better off is also difficult to do in practice. In the U.S., the aged, blind, and disabled needy were traditionally covered under welfare programs akin to AFDC—partially financed by Washington but with benefits set locally. In 1972, Congress created the more generous, federalized Supplemental Security Income (SSI) program for these groups, on the view that they were more "deserving" than the female-headed families covered by AFDC.[37] SSI was to be administered by the agency running Social Security, in hopes that it would acquire something of the same respectability. But the lives of the people covered did not thereby become less erratic. Their income continued to fluctuate rapidly, as is typical with welfare populations. Benefits had to follow suit, as in any means-tested program. Unused to tracking income, the Social Security Administration had great difficulty determining and updating SSI eligibility, a blow to its morale.[38]

Further, SSI covered the disabled on the presumption that eligibility based on impairment would raise no questions about "deservingness." In the later 1970s and 1980s, however, the rules and procedures that determined eligibility for disability became more lenient. Many people obtained coverage whose impairments were more judgmental or mental

---

[35] Some would fear, as well, that to create new universal aid programs would expose many of the working poor to the incentives to misbehave that now impinge on the dependent poor. This objection is discussed under the privatization option below.

[36] Riccio, *From Welfare to Work among Lone Parents in Britain*, pp. 16–19.

[37] States may still supplement the SSI benefit, and most do, so that benefits still vary across the country; but the federal benefit establishes a significantly higher "floor" than existed before.

[38] James Q. Wilson, *Bureaucracy: What Government Agencies Do and Why They Do It* (New York: Basic Books, 1989), pp. 100–101.

than physical. Moreover, by 1993, the disabled had grown from a minority of SSI recipients to 74 percent of the total.[39] SSI now arouses many of the same questions about "deservingness" as AFDC. Similar doubts have arisen about Disability Insurance, which covers disabled workers as an aspect of Social Security.

Thus, covering the needy with universal programs does not forestall the controversies that surround welfare. A work connection is the touchstone of respectability in social policy, not universal coverage. Unless the recipients who can work do so regularly, the effect of covering them with a broader program will only be to tar social insurance with the brush of welfare.

B. Welfare rights

Another form of the entitlement argument is that welfare should become a right even without becoming a universal benefit. The best-known version, developed by Frances Fox Piven and Richard Cloward, is that welfare "regulates" the poor, supporting them apart from work when the economy is depressed, as in the 1930s, then cutting back support to force them to accept unattractive jobs when times improve. Alternatively, welfare is seen as a concession that government makes to the poor to stave off unrest.[40]

Whether welfare exerts "social control" in this way is controversial among historians,[41] but what is significant here is the Marshallian structure of the argument. Piven and Cloward say, in essence, that the welfare poor are really working people after all. They may not be working now, but they will when conditions improve. They constitute a "reserve army," in Marxist terms. They should be seen as "unemployed," as in Europe, not as malingerers. Thus, AFDC is equivalent to unemployment benefits, and should be given in the same spirit, with no questions asked about lifestyle. Unfortunately, few adults who receive welfare have a steady enough work history to be construed as employees. Few work consistently even when times are good. The level of dependency has only a weak relationship to the state of the labor market. The most noted expansions of the American welfare rolls—in the late 1960s and late 1980s—occurred during economic booms, when unemployment was low rather than high.

---

[39] Committee on Ways and Means, *Overview of Entitlement Programs: 1994 Green Book* (*supra* note 14), p. 209.

[40] Frances Fox Piven and Richard A. Cloward, *Regulating the Poor: The Functions of Public Welfare*, updated ed. (New York: Vintage, 1993). Piven is a political scientist, Cloward a professor of social work.

[41] Walter I. Trattner, *Social Welfare or Social Control? Some Historical Reflections on Regulating the Poor* (Knoxville, TN: University of Tennessee Press, 1983). See the rebuttal in Piven and Cloward, *Regulating the Poor*, pp. 456–66.

Another version of the argument is that welfare recipients should be construed as "deserving" because of their disadvantages. They might not have a work history, but they have suffered racial discrimination and other injustices, and that is morally equivalent to employment as a claim to aid.[42] The trouble with this is that it differentiates citizenship obligations by class. Less is expected of the poor by virtue of their hardships than of the better off. That violates the Marshallian premise that citizenship is egalitarian. If work is taken to be an obligation of citizenship—and in the U.S. it unquestionably is—one cannot exempt the poor from it if one wants to justify provision for them on the basis of citizenship.[43]

A final version of the welfare-rights argument maintains, in effect, that work should be deleted from among the common obligations of citizens. Charles Reich and other law professors argued in the 1960s that some minimum of income and other benefits should be guaranteed under the U.S. Constitution as indispensable to full citizenship, without any demands on citizens in return.[44] The Supreme Court ruled that welfare is not constitutionally mandated, only permitted.[45] It did, however, accept the more limited argument that welfare was a form of property that agencies could not revoke without granting the recipients due process.[46] And it struck down some other rules that conservative states had used to restrict access to aid, particularly in the South.[47]

The effect of these developments, along with liberalizing trends in national and state policy, was to institute a kind of welfare rights by the late 1960s. Aid was given to the vast majority of recipients on the basis of need alone, with fewer questions asked about lifestyle than had been asked formerly. Among the poor, the stigma against dependency broke down and the AFDC rolls doubled. But the victory of entitlement was never accepted by the bulk of voters or politicians. Liberal plans to expand welfare to new groups on the same basis were defeated in the 1960s and 1970s.[48] Similarly, in Britain, the sharp growth of dependency is

[42] Leslie W. Dunbar, *The Common Interest: How Our Social-Welfare Policies Don't Work and What We Can Do about Them* (New York: Pantheon, 1988), ch. 1.

[43] Mead, *Beyond Entitlement* (*supra* note 21), chs. 10–11.

[44] Charles Reich, "The New Property," *Yale Law Journal*, vol. 73, no. 5 (April 1964), pp. 733–87.

[45] *Rosado v. Wyman*, 397 U.S. 397 (1970); *Dandridge v. Williams*, 397 U.S. 471 (1970); *Jefferson v. Hackney*, 406 U.S. 535 (1972); *Lavine v. Milne*, 424 U.S. 577 (1976).

[46] *Goldberg v. Kelly*, 397 U.S. 254 (1970).

[47] In *King v. Smith*, 392 U.S. 309 (1968), the Court disallowed conditions of aid not clearly warranted by the Social Security Act, such as "man-in-the-house" rules that refused aid to mothers cohabiting with men. In *Shapiro v. Thompson*, 394 U.S. 618 (1969), it disallowed residency requirements that denied new migrants to a state the same eligibility for AFDC as older residents.

[48] The most important of these plans were the Family Assistance Plan, proposed by the Nixon administration, and the Program for Better Jobs and Income, proposed by the Carter administration. See Mead, *Beyond Entitlement*, chs. 3, 5.

deeply unpopular despite welfare policies that to date award aid essentially on the basis of need alone.[49]

To suspend the work obligation overtly, one would have to make a political case that it is no longer possible to expect work of the poor. In the prosperous 1960s, it was plausible to argue that automation was destroying low-skill jobs and that society could afford it if the redundant adults received income without employment.[50] The future, however, turned out quite differently. The economy in recent decades has provided many low-skill jobs, while at the same time stagnant real wages for most workers have forced most families to raise their working hours to keep pace with inflation. It is an economy more favorable to the poor than to the middle class, but it also makes most voters want to enforce work on the poor more, not less, than they did before.

C. Opportunity policies

Given the weak support for universal programs or welfare rights, those who wish expanded assistance for the poor have no choice but to attack the employment problem. Traditionally, social democrats made a case for redistribution, but said little about opportunity. They contended that the wages and other conditions available to workers under capitalism were unjust. They argued for regulations and union rights to raise wages, and they wanted social benefits to support the jobless. But they assumed that workers could generally find jobs. If they could not, the reason was unemployment due to the business cycle, as in the Depression. Government should prevent this through activist fiscal and monetary policies, as Keynes advised. The purpose of detailed interventions in the labor market was much more to raise incomes than to create employment.

Under current conditions, the situation reverses. In the United States today, recessions are shallow by the standards of the 1930s, and job creation is prodigious. Unemployment runs higher in Europe, but is cushioned by more generous jobless benefits. The social problem stems less from starvation wages or mass unemployment than from long-term nonwork and dependency for a part of the labor force, particularly youth and racial minorities. This has caused thoughtful liberals to shift their criticism away from wage exploitation to "barriers" that they say prevent poor adults from working at all.

The debate about poverty and welfare among American experts is dominated by discussion of these impediments.[51] Many difficulties have been thought to explain why poor adults seem not to work for long

---

[49] Riccio, *From Welfare to Work among Lone Parents in Britain*, ch. 1.

[50] John Kenneth Galbraith, *The Affluent Society* (New York: Mentor Books, 1958), ch. 21; David Macarov, *Incentives to Work* (San Francisco: Jossey-Bass, 1970), chs. 11, 13.

[51] The following discussion relies heavily on Mead, *New Politics of Poverty* (*supra* note 12), chs. 4–6.

periods when most other adults are employed. The oldest theory, dating to the 1930s, is that this is due to a lack of aggregate demand to sustain a tight labor market. Other theories hold that racial bias shuts the poor, most of whom are nonwhite, completely out of employment, that a lack of available child care prevents welfare mothers from working, and so on. Conservatives, and some liberals, also contend that welfare itself sets up "disincentives" against marriage and employment. Mothers on the rolls are, in effect, paid not to marry or work, for if they did so they would lose benefits.

The most influential "barriers" theory in recent years has been the complex, structural understanding of the inner city developed by the sociologist William Julius Wilson and his followers. Wilson admits that job creation is adequate in the economy as a whole and that racial bias today is a minor cause of nonwork. Nevertheless, the poor face a "mismatch" between the skills they offer and the available jobs. Employers hire mainly in the suburbs, and they demand increasing skills. Poor adults, however, mostly live in the inner city and have limited education. They cannot reach the jobs, or they cannot qualify for them. The inability to work destroys the status of black men in particular. Unless they have steady work, their partners will not marry them, preferring to raise their children on welfare. Failure feeds a culture of defeat and self-destructive behavior, such as drug addiction, on the part of both men and women. The children born of such parents are not raised well, so they tend to fail in school and succumb to nonwork and welfare in their turn.[52]

Another prominent argument, pressed by the economist David Ellwood and others, is that low wages are the chief problem. Work may be available, but earnings have increased little for average Americans since 1973. They have actually fallen for the low-skilled, especially younger men of high school education or less. Thus, even if the poor find jobs, the positions do not pay enough to support families. So again men tend not to work regularly, while mothers go on welfare.[53]

Liberal experts contend that opportunity policies could break down these barriers. Government should guarantee employment by suppressing racial bias in hiring, providing training to the low-skilled, and, if necessary, creating government jobs for people who cannot find their own. Government should "make work pay" through wage subsidies and guaranteed health care. These steps would allow poor men and their partners to work and marry, live regular lives, and thus unwind the pathologies of the inner city.

The case is partly an instrumental one, that such policies would work. But advocates also want opportunity programs understood as a dimen-

[52] William Julius Wilson, *The Truly Disadvantaged: The Inner City, the Underclass, and Public Policy* (Chicago: University of Chicago Press, 1987).

[53] David T. Ellwood, *Poor Support: Poverty in the American Family* (New York: Basic Books, 1988), chs. 4–5.

sion of the welfare state, to be guaranteed to all. Wilson emphasizes that the benefits should accrue to the entire population in need, not simply to blacks or ghetto dwellers.[54] This is another version of Marshall's case for social citizenship. In response to this kind of reasoning, training and employment programs aimed at low-income individuals have grown in importance in the U.S. and Europe since the 1960s.[55]

The argument for attacking "barriers" is vulnerable, however, because it is so brutally empirical. The traditional leftist criticism of capitalism made a case for redistribution based on moral values. The case for opportunity policies is less redistributive and thus raises fewer issues of principle. It depends crucially, however, on showing that the "barriers" are real. This liberals have not done well enough to sustain their case. An ocean of research has sought evidence that lack of jobs or child care, or welfare disincentives, can explain low work levels or the high incidence of unwed pregnancy among the poor. Limited support has been found. It is true that poor adults typically command worse jobs and child care than other people do, and there still is some bias against minorities in employment. But these conditions mostly explain why the poor work at low wages if they work. They do not explain well why so few work regularly at all.

The force of welfare disincentives, which seems strong in theory, has little actual influence on whether poor adults work or marry.[56] Programs that provided training or jobs on a voluntary basis have also shown only small effects. These programs assume that their clients lack only the skills or the opportunity to work, but experience has shown that what they chiefly lack is personal organization. Training programs are aimed less at imparting skills than at trying to motivate their clients to take and hold available positions. Most of the earnings gains they record come from the clients' working more hours at jobs they can already get, not getting better positions.[57] Other efforts to "make work pay," such as allowing welfare recipients to keep more of their benefits when they take jobs, also fail to show much effect on work levels. British experiments in work incentives suggest much the same conclusion.[58]

---

[54] Wilson, *The Truly Disadvantaged*, ch. 7.

[55] In Europe, the motivation was more to reduce measured unemployment and benefit costs for the jobless than to expand opportunity. See Desmond King, *Actively Seeking Work? The Politics of Unemployment and Welfare Policy in the United States and Great Britain* (Chicago: University of Chicago Press, 1995), chs. 4–5; and Katherine McFate, "Trampolines, Safety Nets, or Free Fall? Labor Market Policies and Social Assistance in the 1980s," in *Poverty, Inequality, and the Future of Social Policy: Western States in the New World Order*, ed. Katherine McFate, Roger Lawson, and William Julius Wilson (New York: Russell Sage, 1995), ch. 21.

[56] See Moffitt, "Incentive Effects of the U.S. Welfare System" (*supra* note 26).

[57] Laurie J. Bassi and Orley Ashenfelter, "The Effect of Direct Job Creation and Training Programs on Low-Skilled Workers," in *Fighting Poverty: What Works and What Doesn't*, ed. Sheldon H. Danziger and Daniel H. Weinberg (Cambridge, MA: Harvard University Press, 1986), ch. 6.

[58] Riccio, *From Welfare to Work among Lone Parents in Britain*, ch. 2.

Nonwork and unwed pregnancy are hard to explain, chiefly because they are dysfunctional. It is difficult to grasp why people would get into these behaviors, which make their lives harder, whatever conditions they faced. Low or stagnant earnings would seem to be a reason to work more, as the nonpoor population has done, not less. Dysfunction cannot be a simple reflex of adversity. More likely it reflects the defeatist subculture of the ghetto—what the poverty theorists of the 1960s called the "culture of poverty."[59] The seriously poor share orthodox values and want to get ahead, but feel unable to do so in practice. Since the 1960s, society has become fairer to the poor and nonwhite, but hopelessness lives on in the defeatism parents communicate to their children.[60]

The chief origin of this feeling appears to lie, not in unusual barriers, but rather in the difficult assimilation of some immigrant groups in Western countries. To newcomers, America offers unprecedented opportunity, but it is also a competitive society that makes great demands for work effort and self-reliance. Some members of every incoming group have prospered, as is still true today, but others have succumbed to disorganization. The more successful groups on average, such as English-speaking whites and Jews, have been those that stressed education and were already urbanized in their countries of origin. The less successful were those coming either from rural settings (the nineteenth-century Irish) or the Third World (most Hispanics). Blacks were victims of slavery, but they were also migrants from the rural South to Northern cities, where their adjustment problems have paralleled those of the Irish. Serious poverty in Europe exhibits similar patterns, in that much of it is concentrated among ethnic minorities with origins in former colonies outside the West.[61]

Since the evidence for special barriers is weak, so is the case for further opportunity programs. Employment and training programs have gained a foothold in the United States and Europe, but they have not become in most places a major dimension of the welfare state. That reflects a lack of convincing results, and is not merely a consequence of the conservative politics of the last twenty years.

VII. INVESTMENT

The other benefit-oriented approach to poverty involves various sorts of investment in the personal lives of the needy. By this is usually meant

[59] Daniel P. Moynihan, ed., *On Understanding Poverty: Perspectives from the Social Sciences* (New York: Basic Books, 1969), chs. 7–9.

[60] Lawrence M. Mead, "Poverty: How Little We Know," *Social Service Review*, vol. 68, no. 3 (September 1994), pp. 322–50.

[61] For a further development of this understanding, see Mead, *New Politics of Poverty*, ch. 7. I rely heavily on Thomas Sowell's *Race and Economics* (New York: David McKay, 1975), and his *Ethnic America: A History* (New York: Basic Books, 1981). An ethnic understanding of poverty is more persuasive than a racial one, because the variation in income or status within American racial groups is enormous, far greater than the difference in the averages between groups.

improved child care, health care, early childhood education (such as Head Start in the U.S.), or better schooling. These measures differ from opportunity programs since the focus is on building up the personal capacities of the needy during childhood and youth, rather than on breaking down impediments facing adults. The proposals would improve the health and child care and education that the poor already receive, partly by expanding the amount received but mainly by improving quality and targeting the new resources on the first years of life. While some argue that such benefits should be universal, the case for them is usually not Marshallian. Rather, the benefits would be targeted on the disadvantaged, and the case for them is instrumental—that they would, over time, reduce the incidence of serious deprivation.

The investment approach rests on the perception, which goes back to Aristotle, that the family is the foundation of the political order. Even a regime that values freedom and equality depends for the socialization of citizens on institutions that are unchosen and hierarchical, including the family and also the church and the neighborhood. In the words of columnist George Will, a liberal polity must discover some "sociology of civic virtue" sufficient to produce good citizens, or it will be "ill founded."[62] Involuntary rule, however, is excusable provided its objects are children during their formative years. Once well-formed, individuals will be able to associate freely as equals in a democracy's public arenas, which include the workplace as well as politics.

The argument for investment is similar to the case traditionally made for education as a precondition for democracy. In the nineteenth century, when the suffrage was expanding to universality in Western countries, enlightened leaders of the old order said, "We must educate our masters," meaning the new electorate dominated by the working class. Governments therefore invested in education, which was previously provided privately, on a scale never before seen. In the twentieth century, public education through elementary and secondary school came to be guaranteed and also compulsory.

The contemporary case for investment is focused more on the family and early childhood and less on regular schooling, because of evidence that the incapacities of many poor people develop in the earliest years.[63] Liberals contend that public programs to build up child and health care, guarantee early childhood education to all, and intervene in families in crisis would improve the later capacity of children to profit from schooling and employment. They would recoup their costs many times over

[62] George F. Will, *Statecraft as Soulcraft: What Government Does* (New York: Simon and Schuster, 1983), pp. 18, 135, and *passim*.

[63] James Q. Wilson and Richard J. Herrnstein, *Crime and Human Nature* (New York: Simon and Schuster, 1985), chs. 1, 3, 6–8, 10.

through reduced welfare and law-enforcement expenses.[64] The case made by some conservatives is that society may have to take over child-rearing from the most troubled families, either placing children in orphanages or foster care, or requiring that single mothers and children live in supervised housing.[65]

It is true that some children and family programs have shown success in evaluations, but their effects are not large enough to make a visible difference in the social problem. Small impacts are also found in the compensatory education and training programs for adults referred to above. Although modest, the effects may be large enough to justify the programs' costs, but that is not a sufficient argument for them. Efficacy is the big problem in antipoverty policy, not expense. The great problem is to find any strategy that has a large enough effect truly to improve inner-city conditions. If one were found, justifying the cost would be secondary.

The main drawback of family programs appears to be their limited authority. While they may be informally directive, they do not overtly require that the beneficiaries do anything to help themselves. Most significantly, they do not require that the parents work, and nonwork among the poor largely explains why fathers abandon families and mothers spend years on welfare. Instead, the programs attempt to help children by getting around the parents. The results make clear that the parents usually cannot be gotten around. Unless parents do more to help themselves, there is little prospect of helping the children.[66]

VIII. PRIVATIZATION

The traditional conservative response to the social problem of poverty was libertarian. It argued on principled grounds that, even if serious poverty exists, government has no business doing anything about it. Either it is wrong to redistribute wealth from the rich to the poor, or to do so involves unacceptable interference with the free economy. Some thinkers still make that case today.[67]

Most conservatives, however, prefer the instrumental argument that the entitlement and investment approaches considered above are futile. An extreme version says that the problems of urban poverty have cultural origins beyond the reach of government, and that therefore a policy of

[64] Marian Wright Edelman, *Families in Peril: An Agenda for Social Change* (Cambridge, MA: Harvard University Press, 1987); Lisbeth B. Schorr, with Daniel Schorr, *Within Our Reach: Breaking the Cycle of Disadvantage* (New York: Doubleday, 1988).

[65] James Q. Wilson, "Welfare Reform and Character Development," *City Journal*, vol. 5, no. 1 (Winter 1995), pp. 61–62; Charles Murray, "What to Do about Welfare," *Commentary*, December 1994, pp. 33–34.

[66] Mead, *New Politics of Poverty*, pp. 162–65.

[67] Robert Nozick, *Anarchy, State, and Utopia* (New York: Basic Books, 1974); George Gilder, *Wealth and Poverty* (New York: Basic Books, 1981), chs. 6, 8–12.

neglect is best.[68] Less fatalistic is the view that benefit-oriented programs are counterproductive. Whereas liberals see barriers in the society that stop the poor from functioning, conservatives blame government for unhinging the moral and personal lives of the poor. They especially indict the welfare system, whose disincentives to marriage and work, they believe, largely explain the dissolution of the family in the inner city.

Several conservatives have made this case,[69] but it is most associated with Charles Murray, whose *Losing Ground* became a manifesto for the Reagan administration's attack on liberal social policy. Murray does not question antipoverty programs on grounds of principle or cost. Rather, he contends that rising social spending since the 1960s halted the nation's progress against poverty. Welfare and other aid programs paid their clients to behave in antisocial ways, and they did so. Policy changed the "rules of the game" for them in destructive ways. To overcome poverty, the rules must be changed back so that self-reliance is again affirmed. To this end, Murray would raise educational standards and abolish racial preferences, but above all he would end all welfare for those who are of working age.[70]

Other conservatives argue that the federal government should devolve antipoverty programs to state and local government or, better still, to nongovernmental bodies such as churches or neighborhood associations.[71] These "mediating structures" are more responsive and efficient than public agencies,[72] and they can exert more influence over inner-city culture. Religious bodies have a power to involve the poor in a true community, both aiding them and challenging them to live better, as no public program can do.[73]

If assistance were privatized there would remain no public *claim* to assistance. One might still justify aid on the basis of charity, as a moral duty that the strong owe to the weak.[74] But not all ethical codes have clear distributional implications. The injunctions of the Old and New Testament are addressed to strong and weak alike. On a moral basis, the rich should help the poor, but the poor equally should help themselves. Only a conception of justice, such as Marshall's, can truly justify the welfare

---

[68] Edward C. Banfield, *The Unheavenly City Revisited: A Revision of the Unheavenly City* (Boston: Little, Brown, 1974), chs. 3, 10.

[69] See, e.g., Gilder, *Wealth and Poverty*, chs. 6, 8–10; and Martin Anderson, *Welfare: The Political Economy of Welfare Reform in the United States* (Stanford, CA: Hoover Institution Press, 1978).

[70] Charles Murray, *Losing Ground: American Social Policy, 1950–1980* (New York: Basic Books, 1984).

[71] Stuart Butler and Anna Kondratas, *Out of the Poverty Trap: A Conservative Strategy for Welfare Reform* (New York: Free Press, 1987), chs. 2–4.

[72] Peter L. Berger and Richard John Neuhaus, *To Empower People: The Role of Mediating Structures in Public Policy* (Washington, DC: American Enterprise Institute, 1977).

[73] Marvin Olasky, *The Tragedy of American Compassion* (Wheaton, IL: Crossway Books, 1992), chs. 1–2, 6, 13.

[74] Robert E. Goodin, "Vulnerabilities and Responsibilities: An Ethical Defense of the Welfare State," *American Political Science Review*, vol. 79, no. 3 (September 1985), pp. 775–87.

state. In the world of antigovernment conservatism, no such argument can be made.

The antigovernment case proved persuasive enough after the Republican takeover of Congress in 1994 to provide the main basis for the new welfare reform enacted in August 1996. Whereas the old law guaranteed funding for all applicants eligible for aid, the Personal Responsibility and Work Opportunity Reconciliation Act of 1996 gives federal funding to states as a block grant, with no guarantee that all eligibles will be funded. It limits families to five years on the rolls, although states may exempt a fifth of their caseloads from this limit. States receive much more control over eligibility for welfare, including a right, if they choose, to deny aid to unwed mothers under eighteen and to children born on the rolls. But at the same time, they have to meet stringent new work requirements. As a condition of federal aid, they are directed to move at least half of the adults on aid into work activities by the year 2002.

The libertarian argument, like the liberal case for entitlement or new services, is hostage to the facts. The evidence connecting welfare to the dysfunctions of the inner city is weak. Levels of unwed pregnancy do not vary appreciably around the United States with the level of welfare benefits. Social problems have continued to worsen in the last generation even as the generosity of welfare has fallen.[75] Few poor men live on aid, yet their problems of nonwork and drug addiction are as serious as single-motherhood among women on welfare.[76] Thus, merely to cut back welfare and other benefits would do little to resuscitate the inner city, quite apart from causing hardship.

It is also unimaginable that private institutions could cope with poverty without public resources. Advocates of privatization portray nonprofit service-providers as standing outside government and prepared to take over its responsibilities. In large cities, however, many such organizations are already contractors to government. Typically, they provide

[75] David T. Ellwood and Lawrence H. Summers, "Poverty in America: Is Welfare the Answer or the Problem?" in Danziger and Weinberg, eds., *Fighting Poverty* (*supra* note 57), ch. 4. The real value of AFDC benefits in the median state fell 47 percent between 1970 and 1994, as states failed to increase benefits enough to compensate for inflation, according to Committee on Ways and Means, *Overview of Entitlement Programs: 1994 Green Book* (*supra* note 14), pp. 370–74. This drop was partially offset by a growth in noncash benefits, chiefly Medicaid and Food Stamps. According to Robert A. Moffitt, "The Distribution of Earnings and the Welfare State," in *A Future of Dirty Jobs? The Changing Structure of U.S. Wages*, ed. Gary Burtless (Washington, DC: Brookings, 1990), pp. 210–11, the sum of AFDC, Medicaid, and Food Stamps grew in value between 1969 and 1977, then fell through 1985.

[76] Some poor single men live unofficially off welfare mothers and their benefits. But since a man's earnings would not reduce the mother's benefits unless he were married to her, welfare disincentives cannot explain why such men do not work more regularly. Some conservatives believe that welfare at least relieves a father of the need to support his children. But poor fathers blame their failure to provide less on welfare than on their own inability to work and earn enough to support families. See Elliot Liebow, *Tally's Corner: A Study of Negro Streetcorner Men* (Boston: Little, Brown, 1967); and Frank E. Furstenberg, Jr., Kay E. Sherwood, and Mercer L. Sullivan, *Caring and Paying: What Fathers and Mothers Say about Child Support* (New York: Manpower Demonstration Research Corporation, July 1992).

child care, training, or other services to welfare clients or other poor people, financed by the many social service programs established in the 1960s.[77] Thus, they are virtually part of government already, and the amount of new energy they could bring to overcoming poverty is limited.

It is still true that much of welfare administration can usefully be sub-contracted to nongovernmental bodies. Some of the most effective wel-fare work programs in the United States are run by nonprofit and even profit-making organizations.[78] Even in these cases, however, the pro-grams depend for their effectiveness, not only on public funding, but on their ability to require that recipients participate and go to work as a condition of eligibility for aid. The authority to demand this, and to deny benefits in cases of noncooperation, must ultimately be wielded by public officials. Administration, therefore, must remain essentially public, at least as long as the funding is.

The antigovernment case is also impolitic. While the American people fear the ghetto and do not believe that new benefits or services could overcome it, they still want to protect needy families with children. They will not, as Murray wants, abandon them to the marketplace. For this reason, actual cuts in social benefits have so far been slight. Legislatures may not raise AFDC benefits in step with inflation, causing them to decline in real value, but they seldom cut them. Far more than wanting to reduce the welfare state, the voters want it to work better.[79]

IX. ENFORCEMENT

The final option for antipoverty policy represents a return to a citizen-ship rationale, but this time with the emphasis on obligations rather than rights. The argument is that, if nonwork and other incivilities have weak-ened the welfare state, then work and other duties should be enforced. If the dependent poor become better citizens, especially by working, then

---

[77] Michael B. Katz, *In the Shadow of the Poorhouse: A Social History of Welfare in America* (New York: Basic Books, 1986), pp. 261–65.

[78] These include America Works, a proprietary job-placement firm operating in New York and other states, and various organizations that run reform programs in several Wisconsin counties. See Jan Rosenberg, "Welfare-to-Work: Just the Facts," *City Journal*, vol. 4, no. 2 (Spring 1994), pp. 10–11; and Lawrence M. Mead, *The New Paternalism in Action: Welfare Reform in Wisconsin* (Milwaukee: Wisconsin Policy Research Institute, January 1995), pp. 17–22.

[79] A large body of survey and poll data exists to this effect. See, for example, James R. Kluegel and Eliot R. Smith, *Beliefs about Inequality: Americans' Views of What Is and What Ought to Be* (New York: Aldine de Gruyter, 1986), pp. 151–77, 301–5; Keith Melville and John Doble, *The Public's Perspective on Social Welfare Reform* (New York: Public Agenda Founda-tion, January 1988); and Fay Lomax Cook and Edith J. Barrett, *Support for the American Welfare State: The Views of Congress and the Public* (New York: Columbia University Press, 1992). For summaries, see Mead, *New Politics of Poverty*, pp. 57–61; and James L. Sundquist, "Has America Lost Its Social Conscience—And How Will It Get It Back?" *Political Science Quarterly*, vol. 101, no. 4 (1986), pp. 513–33.

the Marshallian case for aiding them is restored. To do this is also, instrumentally, the best way to solve the poverty problem.[80]

A. Social contract

A notion of "social contract" or reciprocity has displaced entitlement as the leading rubric for welfare reform among U.S. policymakers. The idea is that the needy should receive aid, but only in return for some contribution to the society and not as an entitlement. The public strongly endorses that notion, and most politicians for the last decade have accepted, at least in principle, that adults receiving welfare should have to work for their aid. In the U.S., federal legislation to require adults receiving welfare to enter work programs goes back to 1967; but the idea became dominant only in the mid-1980s, when it provided the political basis of the Family Support Act (FSA) of 1988. FSA's main purpose was to expand mandatory work programs aimed at adults receiving AFDC.[81]

The new requirements were implemented in succeeding years. They have as yet touched only a minority of adults receiving welfare. However, a few states—most notably Wisconsin—have been able to use work programs to drive their welfare caseloads down.[82] Others have gained special permission from Washington to add other requirements that welfare mothers must meet to get aid—such as getting their children vaccinated and keeping them in school.[83] The welfare reform passed in 1996 will force states to expand work programs further, if they are to meet the new work standards. Enforcement programs are explicitly directive, as investment programs are not. They tell the clients how to live. While welfare still remains simply a benefit for most recipients, the day is foreseeable when it will become a regime, able to exact at least some behavioral changes from the recipient.

Similar trends are visible in other Western countries, although they are less advanced. In Britain, the current Conservative government has taken modest steps to require the long-term jobless to look for work or enter training programs as a condition of support.[84] In Ontario, Canada, a

---

[80] For a discussion parallel to what follows, see Desmond K. King, "Citizenship as Obligation in the United States: Title II of the Family Support Act of 1988," in *The Frontiers of Citizenship*, ed. Ursula Vogel and Michael Moran (London: Macmillan, 1991), ch. 1.

[81] Mead, *New Politics of Poverty*, ch. 9.

[82] Lawrence M. Mead, *The Decline of Welfare in Wisconsin* (Milwaukee: Wisconsin Policy Research Institute, March 1996).

[83] Lawrence M. Mead, "The New Paternalism: How Should Congress Respond?" *Public Welfare*, vol. 50, no. 2 (Spring 1992), pp. 14–17.

[84] Department of Employment, *Training for Employment* (London: Her Majesty's Stationery Office, February 1988); Department of Employment, *Employment for the 1990s* (London: Her Majesty's Stationery Office, December 1988); Riccio, *From Welfare to Work among Lone Parents in Britain*, ch. 3.

conservative government has cut welfare benefits but also plans to enforce work for the remaining adults, if necessary through government jobs. Active discussion of work enforcement is occurring in other European countries.[85]

Critics on the left regard these steps as no more than an attempt to undo welfare rights. Before the American welfare-rights movement of the 1960s, social workers often arrogated to themselves the authority to tell welfare mothers how to live as a condition of aid. The new enforcement, critics say, would merely restore that discretion.[86] It is true that, to the extent that behavioral stipulations are attached to aid, it is no longer an entitlement. However, the procedural protections for benefits established in the 1960s remain in place. The goal is to complement welfare rights with obligations, both of them legally codified. While some discretion in implementing rules is unavoidable, it is far more limited than before the welfare-rights movement. It is now liberal experts rather than conservatives who argue for a return to a discretionary, decentralized system, as a way of preserving some aid to the needy that they do not have to earn.[87]

B. Work requirements

The first argument for enforcement is political. It accords with public opinion. As mentioned above, the voters want to hold adults on welfare accountable for effort without denying aid to needy children. The best way to do that is to enforce good behavior within the welfare system, rather than either giving or denying aid without conditions. This approach is so popular that the political mystery is not why policy is following it but why it did not do so until recently. The answer is that policymaking elites were polarized in the more extreme positions of entitlement versus opposition to welfare as such. Enforcement involves a more subtle effort, neither to expand aid as it is nor to deny it, but to change its nature so that support is coupled to employment.[88]

Liberal social-policy experts tend to see public opinion as a "constraint" on the antipoverty policy most of them favor, one that would spend generously on supporting poor families and investing in their

---

[85] I often receive inquiries from European journalists interested in these issues, as do other American experts on poverty.

[86] Piven and Cloward, *Regulating the Poor* (*supra* note 40), ch. 11; Andrew J. Polsky, *The Rise of the Therapeutic State* (Princeton: Princeton University Press, 1991).

[87] Michael R. Sosin, "Legal Rights and Welfare Change, 1960–1980," in Danziger and Weinberg, eds., *Fighting Poverty*, pp. 282–83; Evelyn Z. Brodkin, *The False Promise of Administrative Reform: Implementing Quality Control in Welfare* (Philadelphia: Temple University Press, 1986), pp. 110–11.

[88] See Mead, *Beyond Entitlement* (*supra* note 21), chs. 8–11; Steven Michael Teles, *Whose Welfare? AFDC and Elite Politics* (Lawrence, KS: University Press of Kansas, 1996), ch. 4.

skills.[89] Popular distrust, however, is aimed more at the undemanding character of antipoverty programs than at the principle of helping the poor, which remains popular. The main objection is to the permissive nature of welfare, not its cost. Most people are prepared to spend generously on a reformed welfare system—provided it truly enforced work.[90]

The second argument for enforcement is instrumental: work requirements look like the best way to deal with the employment problem. Since serious welfare work programs appeared in the 1980s, a number have been rigorously evaluated, chiefly by the Manpower Demonstration Research Corporation (MDRC), a nonprofit research firm in New York. Most of these programs tried to train clients or place them in private jobs. Most of the programs mandated participation, but they were not particularly severe. Little use was made of unpaid government jobs to enforce work, and usually only 10 percent of clients incurred cuts in benefits for failure to cooperate.[91]

MDRC uses experimental evaluations, where the effect of a program is gauged by measuring outcomes for a sample of recipients against the same outcomes for a second sample with equivalent characteristics but outside the program. In finished MDRC studies of AFDC work programs to date, clients of the programs gained 16 percent more in earnings and reduced their welfare income by 6 percent more than did the control group. While those effects are still limited, they are larger than those typically recorded by voluntary education-and-training programs. The main reason probably is that mandatory programs can reach a more disadvantaged clientele and thus have more power to cause change.[92]

Mandatory work requirements show more power to raise work levels among the poor than any benefit or incentive where work is left as a choice. The impacts are also understated, because the evaluations do not capture diversion effects, or the power of demanding work programs to deter some people eligible for aid from applying for it.[93] Localities that enforce work firmly can reduce dependency more than the evaluations would suggest. Strong work enforcement plus a strong economy helped Wisconsin drive down its AFDC rolls by a third between 1987 and 1995.

[89] Sheldon H. Danziger, Gary D. Sandefur, and Daniel H. Weinberg, "Introduction," and Hugh Heclo, "Poverty Politics," both in Danziger, Sandefur, and Weinberg, eds., *Confronting Poverty* (*supra* note 11), pp. 15–16, 396–437.

[90] Seymour Martin Lipset and Earl Raab, "The Message of Proposition 13," *Commentary*, September 1978, pp. 42–46; Steve Farkas and Jean Johnson, *The Values We Live By: What Americans Want from Welfare Reform* (New York: Public Agenda Foundation, 1996).

[91] For a review of the studies, see Judith M. Gueron and Edward Pauly, with Cameran M. Lougy, *From Welfare to Work* (New York: Russell Sage Foundation, 1991).

[92] Lawrence M. Mead, "Are Welfare Employment Programs Effective?" in *Effective Social Programs*, ed. Jonathan Crane (New York: Russell Sage, forthcoming).

[93] Robert A. Moffitt, "The Effect of Employment and Training Programs on Entry and Exit from the Welfare Caseload," *Journal of Policy Analysis and Management*, vol. 15, no. 1 (Winter 1996), pp. 32–50.

Much of the decline appears to be due to diversion. It is unclear who the diverted are or what happens to them, but to date anecdotes do not suggest unusual hardship.[94]

The perception of effectiveness, as well as the social-contract rationale, were the main reasons why the Family Support Act focused on expanding welfare employment programs. Despite the current vogue for privatization in Washington, work requirements remain the dominant approach to welfare reform. Bill Clinton promised to "end welfare as we know it" when he ran for president in 1992, and his own welfare reform plan duly sought to enforce work requirements on recipients after two years on the rolls. The Republican Congress elected in 1994 rejected that plan and proposed cuts in welfare unacceptable to Clinton. But the two sides agreed that work enforcement should be strengthened. Any bill they agreed on, then, was bound to include tougher work requirements. Welfare is moving toward a regime where few adults will get aid without having to do something to help themselves.

The implementation of work enforcement, admittedly, is difficult. It means spending lavishly on child care and other support services for the recipients required to work, although the cost is more than recouped in effective programs due to caseload reductions. Just as important, it requires developing administrative systems able to assign clients to varying activities and then monitor their attendance. The most effective programs motivate staffs to enforce participation closely, and then motivate the clients to search for work, and to keep jobs once found. Only programs that do this truly undo entitlement, raise work levels, and produce change.[95]

To date, only a few welfare work programs perform at this level. To achieve widespread enforcement would mean that the welfare state became a state in reality, not just in name. For then welfare would be able, not only to pay out aid, but to enforce the associated obligations, much as government enforces other civilities such as tax payment or obedience to the laws. The welfare state would become a structure for governance as well as for redistribution.

A more civil welfare state might once again expand. That prospect explains why the enforcement strategy, though originated by conservatives, has proven attractive to some moderates and liberals. It would, they hope, reaffirm federal leadership in social policy in an age suspicious of federal

---

[94] The work programs were oriented mainly to private job placement. Since 1994, Wisconsin has implemented more demanding policies involving time limits and government jobs in some counties, but these are too recent to explain more than a small part of the caseload reduction through 1995. See Mead, *The Decline of Welfare in Wisconsin* (*supra* note 82), pp. 1–25.

[95] Eugene Bardach, *Improving the Productivity of JOBS Programs* (New York: Manpower Demonstration Research Corporation, December 1993); Lawrence M. Mead, *The New Paternalism in Action* (*supra* note 78).

power.[96] While liberal social-policy experts do not endorse enforcement overtly, some accept the idea of time-limiting aid without work, and that, in practice, means enforcing work when the grace period runs out.[97]

X. Poverty and Politics

Work enforcement offers the best hope to solve the current social problem, but we should not imagine that it would restore the welfare state as an expression of citizenship in the sense Marshall meant. It might restore civility enough for more generous antipoverty benefits to be justified, but the very need to improve functioning casts a dark shadow over the future of Western politics.[98]

A. Progressive politics

Marshall took for granted a traditional view of politics: that it is a debate about justice, or the proper treatment of citizens. Every definition of citizenship embodies a decision about distribution, because it specifies the claims that the members of the community will have. In Marshall's scheme, the meaning of justice becomes steadily more ambitious, as the content of citizenship expands to embrace political and then social guarantees. At every stage, however, the question faced by the polity is the same: What shall be the terms of belonging in the society? What as a citizen do I give and receive?

That same conception is used by John Rawls and other recent liberal theorists of justice. Several of them conceive politics as a debate among equal citizens about justice. They accept, as Marshall did, that the nature of the economy is to produce inequality but that citizenship is egalitarian. The question is how far, if at all, government should intervene in the society to even out uneven rewards.[99]

This is what I call the progressive issue. Progressive politics—the traditional politics of class in the West—is a debate between those who want more equality through more government intervention and those who want less using a smaller government. Both stances make an appeal to the interests of ordinary people. Liberals promise more redistribution at the

---

[96] Forrest Chisman and Alan Pifer, *Government for the People: The Federal Social Role: What It Is, What It Should Be* (New York: Norton, 1987), chs. 11–14; Mickey Kaus, *The End of Equality* (New York: Basic Books, 1992), chs. 7–9.

[97] Ellwood, *Poor Support* (*supra* note 53), ch. 5. Ellwood was President Clinton's chief welfare planner.

[98] The following discussion extends the discussion in Mead, *New Politics of Poverty*, chs. 1–2, 10–11.

[99] John Rawls, *A Theory of Justice* (Cambridge, MA: Harvard University Press, 1971); Robert Nozick, *Anarchy, State, and Utopia* (New York: Basic Books, 1974); Bruce A. Ackerman, *Social Justice in the Liberal State* (New Haven, CT: Yale University Press, 1980); Michael Walzer, *Spheres of Justice: A Defense of Pluralism and Equality* (New York: Basic Books, 1983).

hands of government; conservatives promise an economy less burdened by taxes and regulations and hence more able to generate jobs and rising incomes. Depending on social and economic conditions, either conception may have greater appeal.

However the progressive debate is resolved, it embodies two premises. First, the issue is the goals of the society rather than facts about social conditions. Nobody disputes that people are unequal; the question is whether to try to make them more equal through some public policy. Second, leaders and voters can make the competence assumption. That is, they can presume that the people they are trying to help are able to advance their own self-interest, if not society's. The progressive debate is an argument among citizens with different preferences about government but a common respect for each other's capacity to run their own lives.

B. Dependency politics

These are precisely the premises violated by current controversies about poverty, which I call dependency politics. The debate about today's social problem is not, in the main, a debate about justice. Conditions in the society are much more in dispute than its values. The question is not what sort of country to have but why some people commit crime and fail to work within a social order that is unquestioned. The issue is not whether to have capitalism but whether poverty is due to an absence of jobs or to misbehavior. Where progressive politics is ideological, a contest among competing social visions, dependency politics is moralistic, a contest among competing views of the opportunity structure and the competence of the poor.

The effect of the poverty problem, in fact, is to drive issues of values and justice off the agenda and bring questions of social disorder on. This tends to conservatize politics, not because society becomes antigovernment, but because issues of justice cannot be raised. Issues of equity have not gone away. The economy continues to generate inequalities as it has in the past. In the United States, global competitive pressures make business less able to provide the public with benefits such as health care than it once was, and wages and incomes have become more unequal. Many intellectuals would like to see those problems get more attention in politics than they do. An old-left case for public intervention in the economy can still be made.[100]

But sharp changes in policy tend to be suppressed by cross-cutting arguments about the inner city. Rising crime and welfare played a major role in halting the social reforms of the 1960s and electing conservatives to office, first in the White House and then in Congress. Conservatives, however, are not necessarily the gainers. Concern over the poor was one

---

[100] Martin Carnoy, Derek Shearer, and Russell Rumberger, *A New Social Contract: The Economy and Government after Reagan* (New York: Harper and Row, 1983).

of the forces preventing Ronald Reagan and now Newt Gingrich from cutting social spending as much as conservatives want. The poverty problem tends to dampen changes in the scale of government either up or down.

Above all, dependency politics is not self-respecting; that is, the claimants who seek aid arouse questions of personal morals and mastery that are suppressed in the structural politics of class. The disputes in poverty politics may appear to be empirical, about whether jobs exist or work is feasible, but much of the real division is about the personality of the poor. Competence is disputed, not assumed. Those who see "barriers" in the society tend to view the poor as victims of whom nothing can be expected, while those who think opportunity exists have a higher view of the competence of the poor and, thus, of their responsibility for their own predicament.

In antipoverty policy, the trends are toward paternalism, or the efforts described above to link support with behavioral requirements. This assumes that adults as well as children need guidance in order to live constructively. Such policies may help restore good citizenship and thus help legitimize welfare. But the very need for them, and the controversy about them, is foreign to Marshall's universe and the central political traditions of the West.

C. How poverty is new

I do not say that poverty is a new issue. It is an old issue, extending back at least to the Elizabethan Poor Law of 1601, which first made assistance a public responsibility in England. The themes of poverty politics—moral responsibility, "deservingness," social control—are timeless. What is new is the seriousness and prominence of the issue. Liberal intellectuals tend to say that welfare is a red herring, a bogey trotted out by conservatives to suppress discussion of the inequities of capitalism.[101] But the social problem is hardly imaginary. In New York City, a million people out of a population of seven million are living on welfare. The society cannot be unified unless poverty and dependency decline.

Before 1960, welfare in America was an issue principally at the local level. In Britain, it became a leading issue only sporadically, preeminently during the controversy over the New Poor Law of 1834, which abolished mass relief outside workhouses. National politics have usually been dominated by issues of class and, in the United States, race. These were the chief disputes that raised the progressive choice between more and less government. Since 1960, however, the inner city has displaced class as the most divisive issue in America, and race, while still urgent, has become

---

[101] Michael B. Katz, *The Undeserving Poor: From the War on Poverty to the War on Welfare* (New York: Pantheon, 1989).

an issue more linked with poverty than with inequality. In Europe, similarly, immigrant minorities have become more controversial than the proletariat. The greatest disputes concern social problems such as crime or dependency rather than economic inequality.

Nor is the point even that incivility marks the dividing line between the old politics and the new. Violence—protest, even revolution—has sometimes been a dimension of progressive conflict. In America, the 1930s and the 1960s, and labor politics in all eras, sometimes involved marches, demonstrations, and battles with police. Britain, notwithstanding its deep commitment to the rule of law, harbors an ancient tradition of popular unrest aimed at the redress of grievance. In Marshallian terms, an old citizenship must sometimes be violated to establish a new and more extensive one.

What divides dependency from progressive politics, rather, is the self-defeating quality of the new disorders. In reviewing a book on British political violence, *The Economist* recently wrote that

> the most striking contrast between 18th-century England and 20th-century inner-city America (and, come to that, 20th-century inner-city England) concerns the adaptation of means to ends. Violence in the 18th century was almost never savage or anarchic. Looting and arson were rare. . . . The 18th-century mob usually had goals and directed its violence to the achievement of those goals. It was aware that too much force would provoke counterforce and end up being self-defeating.[102]

The riots in American and British inner cities, in contrast, are mostly self-destructive, burning down the rioters' own neighborhoods while obtaining few if any concessions in return.

Piven and Cloward attempt to show that disorder is a political virtue. Popular movements must threaten chaos to maximize their effects. If they organize parties or lobby groups, or assume any responsibility for government or policy, they achieve little change.[103] The case persuades only in the most tactical sense. Disorderly violence may startle the authorities and obtain subsidies in the short run. It cannot, however, achieve greater equality. Citizens who harm themselves cannot earn the respect of others and thus cannot negotiate a new dispensation of justice.

The War on Poverty might have produced much more change than it did. What ended it was not so much the election of Richard Nixon as the urban riots and the welfare explosion of the late 1960s. Both dramatized that the poor were not in control of their own lives. The competence assumption was violated, and the poor could no longer be regarded as

---

[102] "Then and Now," *The Economist*, August 8, 1992, p. 81.

[103] Frances Fox Piven and Richard A. Cloward, *Poor People's Movements: Why They Succeed, How They Fail* (New York: Pantheon, 1977).

regular citizens. They were not entitled, therefore, to demand equalizing reforms.

It is not the danger posed by the inner city but its incoherence that pushes fundamental change off the agenda. The traditional working class had far more capacity than today's poor to threaten the status quo. It had the indispensable resources, political as well as economic, that come from employment. During the industrial era, the working class served its own interests extremely well. Through unions and reform parties, it challenged the rest of society to make a place for it. Workers had to be placated with higher earnings and a welfare state. The civil rights and feminist movements showed equal acumen. These, too, were movements on behalf of functioning citizens, and they obtained their major goals. Today's poor, in contrast, are more threatening to themselves than to the society. The main response to dependency is not concession but repression and paternalism. Strikes and marches move politics to the left; crime and welfare move politics to the right.

D. Poverty and community

The expansion of social provision that Marshall celebrated honored the innermost values of Western politics—the individual and community. The growth of the claims of citizenship over time tended more and more to knit up society into a single polity of equal members. Looking to the past, the political scientist Hugh Heclo writes, "inclusion" is "the defining feature of our Western identity," but today that ideal is in danger.[104] Community among citizens can only be built on a basis where individuals show enough self-command to merit the esteem of others. The danger raised by poverty is not that the poor will make excessive demands. They are too few in number to cost impossible sums or to change the society as the labor and feminist movements did. It is rather that the new social minorities no longer display the *personal* organization that makes a community of equal citizens imaginable.

Throughout the West, division will probably no longer arise in the future chiefly from class but from minorities on the periphery of the society. In Europe, the chief problem is immigrant minorities who seem alien to these largely homogeneous societies. In the United States, the problem is not so much ethnic pluralism, which is long-standing, as the tendency of today's poor to be nonworking. Before 1960, poverty levels were much higher than now, but most poor adults were employed, and this tended over time to integrate them. Today, there is less poverty, but the separation of the poor from the economy makes integration more doubtful. Therefore, social programs must promote work, and even enforce it, assuming the function that the workplace did before. Whether

---

[104] Hugh Heclo, "The Social Question," in McFate, Lawson, and Wilson, eds., *Poverty, Inequality, and the Future of Social Policy* (*supra* note 55), ch. 22.

they can do that will largely determine whether "inclusion" remains an operative ideal.

It is difficult to recall an era in Western history when the restoration of order was so much an imperative in and of itself. Looking back centuries, there have been eras of violence, even civil war, but disorder mostly reflected conflict over political ends. It arose from the great issues of nation-building or religious or class conflict. Today's urban disorder is less threatening, in the sense that it no longer betokens any fundamental division in the society. We have disorder linked to poverty but not linked to any larger political agenda, of either the left or the right. Destitution no longer raises issues of justice. By the same token, however, conventional reformism of either a liberal or conservative kind is no longer a solution. The only answer to poverty is a slow building up of community institutions, including antipoverty programs, to the point where they can again enforce the common obligations of citizenship.

The prospect is for a long struggle to restore the self-reliance assumed in Western politics. Only if order is restored in cities, and especially if work levels rise, could the poor become more self-respecting. Only then could they stake claims on the collectivity as equals, rather than seeking charity as dependents. In restoring some coherence to the lives of the poor, the new paternalist social policies, if well-implemented, could make a critical contribution. But as long as they are needed, a truly Marshallian debate about citizenship and equality will be unimaginable. The virtue of poverty politics—perhaps its only virtue—is that it disputes and thus dramatizes the assumption of personal mastery among citizens that traditional politics never questioned. Only when it is again unquestioned and thus drops from view could a debate about justice resume.

Politics, New York University

IDENTITY POLITICS AND THE WELFARE STATE*

By Alan Wolfe and Jytte Klausen

I. Two Principles of Inclusion

Motivated by a deep sense that injustice and inequality are wrong, liberals and reformers in the Western political tradition have focused their energies on policies and programs which seek inclusion: extending the suffrage to those without property; seeking to treat women the same as men, and blacks the same as whites; trying to ensure that as few as possible are excluded from economic opportunity due to lack of resources. Under current conditions, such demands for inclusion take two primary forms, especially in the United States. One is a commitment to using the state to equalize the life chances of individuals. The other is a call for treating groups which have experienced discrimination with full respect. The former leads to the welfare state, while the latter is produced by, and in turn produces, what is commonly called identity politics, the politics of recognition, or the politics of presence.[1]

The welfare state and identity politics, both designed to remedy inequalities, are attractive to those disposed to use the powers of government to correct for the limits of private action. It is therefore not uncommon to hear advocates for one remedy slide routinely into a defense of the other. Thus, Iris Marion Young writes that "[a] democratic cultural pluralism ... requires a dual system of rights: a general system of rights which are the same for all, and a more specific system of group-conscious policies and rights," the latter of which would only apply to "oppressed or disadvantaged groups...."[2] Such a commitment to both general and particular rights helps explain why advocates of racial equality in the United States argue for expanded welfare benefits irrespective of race *and* for race-specific programs such as affirmative action. Along similar lines, one often hears that sympathy for the elderly requires treating those of advanced age as if they were no different from younger people (for example, with respect to employment discrimination) and treating them as

* The authors want to thank Peter Skerry, the other contributors to this volume, and its editors, for their helpful criticism and suggestions.

[1] See Michael Piore, *Beyond Individualism: How Social Demands of the New Identity Groups Constrain American Political and Economic Life* (Cambridge: Harvard University Press, 1995); Charles Taylor, *Multiculturalism and the Politics of Recognition* (Princeton: Princeton University Press, 1992); and Anne Phillips, *The Politics of Presence* (Oxford: Clarendon Press, 1995). For a recent critique of identity politics, see Todd Gitlin, *The Twilight of Common Dreams: Why America Is Wracked by Culture Wars* (New York: Metropolitan Books, 1995).

[2] Iris Marion Young, *Justice and the Politics of Difference* (Princeton: Princeton University Press, 1990), pp. 174, 187.

231

if they were very different (for example, by preserving fee-for-service medical care for them while younger people are transferred into health maintenance organizations), or that women should be included in institutions once reserved for men while men should be excluded from institutions designed to serve the needs of women.

In this essay, we argue that while both the welfare state and identity politics share a commitment to overcoming injustice, the principles behind the one often contradict those behind the other. This is not to suggest that compromises between these principles are impossible; politics is about compromise, and there surely are ways in which both kinds of inclusion can be pursued simultaneously. If such compromises are to be fashioned, however, one first has to understand why they might be necessary. There are a number of ways in which meeting the claims of group demands for recognition runs counter to the logic of equality as understood by most theorists of the welfare state. It is therefore no coincidence that identity politics, although advanced by many who are personally sympathetic to the welfare state, arises at a time when the welfare state has lost its forward momentum. Indeed, while the welfare state is clearly under attack from the right, committed as it is to lower taxes and less governmental regulation, it is also being undermined in significant ways by the left, committed, as *it* is, to particular identities rather than conceptions of common membership in a national community.

II. Liberalism and Particularism

The tension between liberal principles and claims for group recognition is an old one in the history of liberal political theory. Aware that paying particular attention to groups could undermine the universalism they wished to emphasize, classical-liberal thinkers, with very few exceptions, tried to avoid the subject of ethnicity (or, in eighteenth-century terms, nationality) as much as they could.[3] From a liberal point of view, the defense of ethnicity, nationality, or religious and linguistic difference seemed to flirt with a kind of irrational primitivism which was hostile to humanistic universalism.[4] And from the point of view of any specific nationality or ethnic consciousness, liberal principles, which in theory could not stop at the borders of the nation-state,[5] could hardly be expected to stop at the point where groups sought either special rights as groups or exemptions from obligations deemed to belong to all. At their worst moments, liberals imagined individuals as belonging nowhere; at *their* worst moments, na-

---

[3] Jeff Spinner, *The Boundaries of Citizenship: Race, Ethnicity, and Nationality in the Liberal State* (Baltimore: Johns Hopkins University Press, 1994).

[4] Tzvetan Todorov, *On Human Diversity: Nationalism, Racism, and Exoticism in French Thought*, trans. Catherine Porter (Cambridge: Harvard University Press, 1993).

[5] Stephen Holmes, *Passions and Constraints: On the Theory of Liberal Democracy* (Chicago: University of Chicago Press, 1995), p. 39.

tionalists imagined individuals as so much the products of their culture that their choices were illusory and their liberties contingent.

One school of thought believes that by the end of the nineteenth century, when the ideas behind the modern welfare state received their first formulation, the inherent tension between liberal principles and group rights began to moderate. As Will Kymlicka points out, J. S. Mill, John Dewey, T. H. Green, and L. T. Hobhouse emphasized the importance of communities, including, in Hobhouse's case, nationalities of his era which resemble the ethnic and racial groups asking for recognition in contemporary politics.[6] More recent writers, such as Charles Taylor and Kymlicka himself, have insisted that minority rights, properly understood, do not contradict universalistic liberal principles, including principles designed to ensure satisfactory provision for all.[7] Yael Tamir has argued, along similar lines, that liberal nationalism is not only possible but desirable, in that liberalism can temper the extremes of nationalism while nationalism can give context and shape to liberalism.[8]

Efforts to reconcile liberalism and ethnic nationalism under contemporary conditions are based on the premise that the welfare state, in advancing the idea that the national government could be used as a tool to achieve equality within a particular society, took a giant step away from the global universalism attractive to earlier liberal thinkers such as Kant. Once claims for rights are limited to citizens of a particular country, rather than being applicable to all irrespective of place, it is just another step, and one not nearly so gigantic, to the idea that groups within the nation-state ought to be recognized as having legitimate claims for special rights. Behind this way of thinking is the notion that the nation-state is a group like any other group. If Americans can have special claims against the government in Washington which are not available to Mexicans, why can't Mexican Americans have special claims not available to Anglos? Once we come to accept that nationalism represents the triumph of "imagined communities," or that many national traditions are also rather recent inventions, there seems to be no reason why exceptions to universalism, already introduced to make national citizenship possible, cannot be further extended to make group identity more palpable.[9]

Yet it is also possible that the welfare state's move away from universality toward the particularity of specific national citizenships could intensify, rather than moderate, the tensions between universal rights and

---

[6] Will Kymlicka, *Liberalism, Community, and Culture* (Oxford: Clarendon Press, 1989), pp. 206–19.

[7] Taylor, *Multiculturalism and the Politics of Recognition*; Will Kymlicka, *Multicultural Citizenship: A Liberal Theory of Minority Rights* (Oxford: Clarendon Press, 1995).

[8] Yael Tamir, *Liberal Nationalism* (Princeton: Princeton University Press, 1993).

[9] Benedict Anderson, *Imagined Communities: Reflections on the Origin and Spread of Nationalism*, revised ed. (London and New York: Verso, 1991); Eric Hobsbawm, *Nations and Nationalism since 1780: Programme, Myth, Reality* (Cambridge: Cambridge University Press, 1990).

group claims. Individuals may have a rather limited amount of political loyalty to give; if they reserve some of it for ethnic, linguistic, and racial claims, they will have less of it for the demands of national citizenship. "If we want both to have democracy of a more radical kind and envisage a fairly extensive redistributive role for the state," David Miller has written, "it is essential that people should participate politically, not as advocates for this or that sectional group, but as citizens whose main concerns are fairness between different sections of the community and the pursuit of common ends."[10] From this point of view, the welfare state is a precarious compromise in which the national solidarity required for its success can be weakened by global forces beyond it as well as local solidarities within it. Jealous of its sovereignty, the welfare state has to make an effort to control those centrifugal subnational identities which its own claims to nationhood set in motion.

In practice, the growth of the welfare state has not subsumed pressures for more localized identities but seems instead to have fueled them. Both Taylor and Kymlicka have a particular concern with Canada, a country with one of the most expansive and generous welfare states in the world. Yet not only does Canada also have an unusually intensive form of identity politics, it is also in danger of crumbling as a national society. In 1995, for example, not only did residents of Quebec come close to voting for autonomy from the rest of Canada—hardly a formula for emphasizing their ties to English speakers in the rest of the country—but some of their spokesmen denounced "ethnic" opposition to recognition of French-speaking Canadians, a thinly disguised attack on Jews, Moslems, and recent immigrants. If this example is any indication, then, as another Canadian says of Tamir's thesis, liberal nationalism may be a terrific idea, but if it doesn't exist, making a case for it becomes an exercise in abstraction.[11] Canada, of course, may be a special case; both Taylor and Kymlicka recognize that, as Kymlicka puts it, "the right to self-government is a right against the authority of the federal government, not a right to share in the exercise of that authority."[12] But although writers such as Anne Phillips make a strong distinction between the Canadian case and arguments on behalf of the representation of women or racial and ethnic minorities, some form of self-government (or, in the argument of Iris Marion Young,

[10] David Miller, *Market, State, and Community: Theoretical Foundations of Market Socialism* (Oxford: Clarendon Press, 1989), p. 284. A more extensive discussion of these issues by the same author can be found in *On Nationalism* (Oxford: Clarendon Press, 1995).

[11] Bernard Yack, "Reconciling Liberalism and Nationalism," *Political Theory*, vol. 23 (February 1995), pp. 166–82.

[12] Will Kymlicka, "Group Representation in Canadian Politics," in F. Leslie Seidle, ed., *Equity and Community: The Charter, Interest Advocacy, and Representation* (Brookfield: Ashgate Publishing, 1993), p. 74, cited in Phillips, *The Politics of Presence*, p. 140. See also Charles Taylor, "Shared and Divergent Values," in Ronald L. Watts and Douglas M. Brown, eds., *Options for a New Canada* (Toronto: University of Toronto Press, 1991).

a veto-power over government on behalf of specific interests)[13] does lie behind the latter claims, even if in less extreme forms than the demand for an independent Quebec.

In this sense, the Canadian case raises the left's dilemma in its most acute form. On the one hand, devolution of political power away from central authority not only weakens the capacity of the central government to provide benefits and ensure equality among individuals, it also lessens the sense that all members of the national community share a common fate. On the other hand, efforts to protect universal provisions in health care or old-age provision have to be premised on the notion that one is a member of a national community first and a member of a racial or ethnic group second. As Taylor notes, Canadians outside of Quebec often take pride in welfare-state programs such as the national health system (because they are so different from the United States), while Canadians inside Quebec take pride in being from Quebec.[14]

One way to understand the underlying issues raised by the Canadian case—or any other situation in which claims for universal rights seem to contradict claims for particular recognitions—is to go back to the theorists whose ideas shaped the modern welfare state. The concerns that motivated them were quite similar to the issues of today: What constitutes a community? Are the primary beneficiaries of the welfare state individuals or groups? What does equality mean in a pluralistic political system? The way theorists such as T. H. Marshall, William Beveridge, R. H. Tawney, and Gunnar and Alva Myrdal—founders of the British and Swedish welfare states which flourished after World War II—answered these questions can hardly settle our current disputes, for they were writing at different times and under different conditions. But it should become clear from reviewing their ideas that building a welfare state first required building a state. Creating national citizenship was no easy task, given competing claims of class and social standing. If one believes that sustaining national citizenship under today's conditions has become as difficult as creating it half a century ago, one can understand the ways in which identity politics increasingly works at cross-purposes with national solidarity.

III. The Welfare State and the Great Community

The liberal commitment to inclusion has never been more succinctly expressed than in T. H. Marshall's "Citizenship and Social Class," his 1949 lecture presented to the Alfred Marshall Foundation in Cambridge, England. (Thomas Humphrey Marshall was not directly related to Alfred

---

[13] Young, *Justice and the Politics of Difference*, p. 184.
[14] Taylor, "Shared and Divergent Values," p. 66; see also Phillips, *The Politics of Presence*, pp. 132–33.

Marshall.) In T. H. Marshall's view, each of the last three centuries saw the birth of a new set of rights. Civil rights, defined by him as "the rights necessary for individual freedom," such as freedom of speech, property rights, and the right to practice one's religion, came to fruition in the eighteenth century. They were followed, in the nineteenth, by political rights, "the right to participate in the exercise of political power, as a member of a body invested with political authority or as an elector of the members of such a body." Our century, the century of the welfare state, saw the extension of social rights: "the whole range from the right to a modicum of economic welfare and security to the right to share to the full in the social heritage and to live the life of a civilized being according to the standards prevailing in the society."[15]

Marshall emphasized the cumulative nature of these three sets of rights. Not only did each one make the next one possible, there was also no doubt, in Marshall's opinion, that the triumph of each set of rights advanced civilization. "Equality of status is more important than equality of income," he wrote.[16] Social rights, because they contradict the realities of class, were the most inclusive of all. "Rights," Marshall wrote, "are not a proper matter for bargaining. To have to bargain for a living wage in a society which accepts the living wage as a social right is as absurd as to have to haggle for a vote in a society which accepts the vote as a political right."[17] Once the modern welfare state was created, there was no going back. Marshall, after a brief involvement with the Labour Party, moved away from an active identification with socialism—"the Welfare State is not the dictatorship of the proletariat and is not pledged to liquidate the *bourgeoisie*," he wrote in another essay[18]—yet his ideas are compatible with strong restrictions on the market in order to achieve greater political and social equality.

Because Marshall put social rights on the same plane as economic and civil ones, he remains popular among contemporary social theorists on the left, especially those who understand the logic of the welfare state as involving the "decommodification" of labor—or "class abatement," in Marshall's terminology.[19] His ideas have also proven influential among contemporary feminists trying to forge a link between the welfare state and the special concerns of women as women.[20] Feminists have treated Marshall quite differently from the way they have treated other earlier

[15] T. H. Marshall, *Citizenship and Social Class, and Other Essays* (Cambridge: Cambridge University Press, 1950), pp. 10, 11.

[16] *Ibid.*, p. 56.

[17] *Ibid.*, p. 69.

[18] T. H. Marshall, *Class, Citizenship, and Social Development: Essays by T. H. Marshall*, with an introduction by Seymour Martin Lipset (Garden City: Doubleday, 1964), p. 247.

[19] Gøsta Esping-Andersen, *Politics against Markets: The Social Democratic Road to Power* (Princeton: Princeton University Press, 1985); Walter Korpi, *The Democratic Class Struggle* (London: Routledge and Kegan Paul, 1983).

[20] See Birte Siim, "Towards a Feminist Rethinking of the Welfare State," in Kathleen B. Jones and Anna Jónasdóttir, eds., *The Political Interests of Gender: Developing Theory and*

theorists of the welfare state, such as William Beveridge. Because he assumed that women would remain outside the work force, Beveridge is often viewed as paternalistic and hostile to full equality between men and women.[21] But Marshall's emphasis on "social citizenship" can be interpreted to include such provisions as day care, child allowances, and equal pay for women, all of which would permit women to achieve equality with men. Indeed, "social citizenship" is a concept which receives something close to universal endorsement from advocates of a women-friendly welfare state.[22]

Yet there is reason to question whether Marshall would look favorably on the notion that members of groups have rights as group members, rather than as individuals. Marshall was explicit in emphasizing the importance of a common culture, one that in the final analysis had to trump any particularistic claims. "Citizenship," he wrote, "requires a . . . direct sense of community membership based on loyalty to a civilization which is a common possession."[23] His ideas were quite similar to those of other advocates of the British welfare state, such as R. H. Tawney: "What a community requires, as the word itself suggests, is a common culture, because, without it, it is not a community at all." This was especially the case at the start of the Great Depression—Tawney's *Equality* was first published in 1931—because "it is in such circumstances that the need for co-operation, and for the mutual confidence and tolerance upon which co-operation depends, is particularly pressing."[24]

In his effort to show that group solidarity can be reconciled with liberalism, Will Kymlicka points out how many liberal thinkers assigned a priority to community.[25] Yet it is important to emphasize what kind of community was important to them. The communities of which they spoke were bound neither by blood nor by locality, let alone by gender or race. Welfare-state theorists were instead attracted to what Jean Quandt, following John Dewey, has called visions of a "great community," one that uprooted the individual from the generally irrational ties of family and clan and exposed him to the claims of larger groups of strangers.[26] Kymlicka cites Dewey as one liberal who understood the claims of groups. But

---

Research with a Feminist Face (London: Sage Publications, 1988), pp. 160–86; Ann Shola Orloff, "Gender and the Social Rights of Citizenship," *American Sociological Review*, vol. 58 (June 1993), pp. 303–28; and Helga Maria Hernes, *Welfare State and Woman Power: Essays in State Feminism* (Oslo: Norwegian University Press, 1987).

[21] Carole Pateman, "The Patriarchal Welfare State," in Amy Gutmann, ed., *Democracy and the Welfare State* (Princeton: Princeton University Press, 1988), pp. 231–60.

[22] For an exception, see Jytte Klausen, "Social Rights Advocacy and State Building: T. H. Marshall in the Hands of Social Reformers," *World Politics*, vol. 47 (January 1995), pp. 244–67.

[23] Marshall, *Citizenship and Social Class, and Other Essays*, p. 41.

[24] R. H. Tawney, *Equality* (1931; reprint, New York: Capricorn Books, 1961), p. 31.

[25] Kymlicka, *Liberalism, Community, and Culture*, pp. 135–61.

[26] Jean Quandt, *From the Small Town to the Great Community: The Social Thought of Progressive Intellectuals* (New Brunswick, NJ: Rutgers University Press, 1970).

so broad was Dewey's communitarianism that, for all his extensive commentary, he wrote relatively little about ethnicity, and even less about gender, as if he hoped that the particularistic loyalties associated with more permanent group categories would somehow just disappear.[27]

The theorists of the British welfare state shared this concern with the "great" community. Beveridge, writing during World War II, was quite explicit on this point. Emphasizing the need for unity, he worried about the consequences of divided government—indeed, of any loyalties that might potentially conflict with the need to win the war. "One of the weaknesses of many reformers in the past," he noted in a 1942 address at Oxford, "is that they have not taken account sufficiently of the immense feeling of patriotism in the British people, or that loving pride which we have in our country."[28] Going further, he spoke of a "New Britain," one that, in the aftermath of the war, should imagine itself as a large state, not a small one. For this purpose, a reversal of declining birth rates was essential: "unless there are many families with large numbers of children, the British race will not continue. We haven't now anything like enough children being born to keep our race in being."[29] Beveridge's concern with the British birth rate was central to all his thinking. His famous report *Social Insurance and Allied Services* also pointed out the dangers facing Britain from the prospect of fewer British people.[30]

It is important to recall the link between advocacy of the welfare state on the one hand, and fears for what Beveridge called "the quality of the breed" on the other.[31] Beveridge gave the Galton Lecture in 1943 on the same day as the opening of the Parliamentary debate on his *Social Insurance and Allied Services*. In a memo he prepared for the lecture, he addressed the question of whether the provision of children's allowances—payments to the mother on the birth of each child—would increase dysgenic pressures by encouraging poor women to have more children. It would not, he concluded.[32] Rather, children's allowances would neutralize the economic advantages of small families and in that way increase births among all social classes. Whether Beveridge was right or wrong is not the point. What is relevant is his desire to strengthen the British state by strengthening what he took to be the quality of the raw ingredients upon which states build their power. Half a century has passed since Beveridge addressed the issue of "dysgenic" pressures. Now fears of population

[27] John Dewey, *The Public and Its Problems* (New York: Henry Holt, 1927).

[28] Sir William H. Beveridge, *The Pillars of Security, and Other War-Time Essays and Addresses* (New York: Macmillan, 1943), p. 104.

[29] *Ibid.*, p. 93.

[30] *Social Insurance and Allied Services: Report by Sir William Beveridge* (New York: Macmillan, 1942). On the use of declining birth rates and other eugenic concepts by advocates of the welfare state, see Susan Pedersen, *Family, Dependence, and the Origins of the Welfare State: Britain and France, 1914–1945* (New York: Cambridge University Press, 1993), pp. 316–19.

[31] Beveridge, *The Pillars of Security*, p. 164.

[32] Beveridge, "Children's Allowances and the Race," in his *The Pillars of Security*, pp. 164–75.

decline are far more likely to be heard on the right than on the left; for example, the authors of *The Bell Curve* worry that the rate of population increase among the cognitively deficient will outstrip the rate among the cognitively privileged.[33] Despite the fact that supporters of the welfare state no longer worry, as the British Labour Party did in 1945, about the "dwindling" of the domestic population,[34] it is important to recall the degree to which concerns with the great community made dysgenic themes important to the welfare state's expansion.

Beveridge was not the only theorist of the welfare state who was pre-occupied with eugenics. T. H. Marshall himself gave the Galton Lecture in 1953.[35] His theme was social selection, the way in which social institutions such as schools divide different people into the performance of different tasks. We will return to the content of this lecture later in this essay, as it deals with the ways in which Marshall thought about equality. There is little doubt, however, that Marshall, like Beveridge, understood himself as a state-builder. It was not an abstract commitment to equality that Marshall emphasized in his Galton lecture—indeed, as we shall see, he defended particular kinds of inequality—but rather the ways social selection can be managed to strengthen the overall efficiency of the society.

No theorists of the welfare state wrote more directly about social provision and its relationship to the overall strength of society than Gunnar and Alva Myrdal. "It is difficult to avoid the semblance of patriotic pride when writing of one's own country," Alva Myrdal, sounding very much like Beveridge, wrote in *Nation and Family*, first published in an English version in 1941.[36] One of her purposes was to emphasize the almost complete unanimity in Swedish politics around fears of population decline, ranging from the Conservatives, who wrote in a party manifesto that "the population question is literally a question of the life of the Swedish people," to the Social Democrats, who noted that "no people with unimpaired energy and the will to live can observe such a tendency toward its own decline as is now obvious in this country. . . ."[37] There was only one way to alter these dysgenic pressures, in Myrdal's opinion, and that was for the welfare state to provide assistance to all Swedish families so that economic pressures would not force them to have fewer children.

Of course, eugenic theories are no longer associated with efforts to build and sustain the welfare state. Or are they? While fears of population decline have abated, or at least are not as frequently articulated, it is the

---

[33] Richard J. Herrnstein and Charles Murray, *The Bell Curve: Intelligence and Class Structure in American Life* (New York: Free Press, 1994).

[34] The Labour Party, *Let Us Face the Future: A Declaration of Labour Policy for the Consideration of the Nation* (London: The Labour Party, 1945), p. 10.

[35] Marshall, "Social Selection in the Welfare State," in his *Class, Citizenship, and Social Development*, pp. 236–55.

[36] Alva Myrdal, *Nation and Family: The Swedish Experiment in Democratic Family and Population Policy* (New York: Harper, 1941), p. 15.

[37] *Ibid.*, pp. 158, 161.

immigration rate rather than the birth rate which now determines whether the population of a society will be sufficiently large to qualify it as a "great community." In theory, state-builders ought to be sympathetic to immigration, for people are the essential ingredient of statecraft, and if the number of people in the society cannot be increased one way, it ought to be increased another. The line which Beveridge and Marshall began to draw in favor of more births should lead logically to the conclusion that we also ought to have more immigrants.

This has not taken place, however—at least not in this form. Early advocates of the welfare state were not only state-builders, they were also deeply patriotic. Even more importantly, they did not fully trust the then-established ruling classes to look out for the interests of the nation as a whole; reformers and Social Democrats, in their view, were the true patriots, not representatives of business or quasi-feudal landed aristocrats. A certain distrust of globalism runs throughout many of the most articulate attempts to defend welfare-state principles. Gunnar Myrdal put the matter this way: "Planning is national. It is a manifestation of the nation state, which is everywhere becoming stronger. . . . It cannot be helped that everywhere national integration is now bought at the cost of international disintegration."[38] In contemporary politics, Myrdal's preference for the national state over the international community remains the driving force on the left. Pressures toward globalization come primarily from businesses interested in lowering labor costs rather than advancing the interests of primarily national firms, for example. This has led many of those sympathetic to current welfare-state programs to be skeptical of unrestricted immigration, most conspicuously African Americans[39] and (at least in Europe, where feminists tend to be more critical of the benefits of European Union membership) women.[40] If supporters of the welfare state lean in any direction on the question of immigration, it is in a direction hostile to the notion of open borders.

Although hostility toward immigration would seem to stand at odds with the enthusiasm for eugenics once associated with the welfare state, underlying both positions is a concern with the nature of citizenship. The great community had to be large, advocates of the welfare state believed, but it also had to be common. Imagining the great community as one without borders, held together only by the migration of labor and capital to the places in which they will be employed most efficiently, creates too

[38] Gunnar Myrdal, *Beyond the Welfare State: Economic Planning and Its International Implications* (1960; reprint, New York: Bantam Books, 1967), pp. 130–31.

[39] Stephen Steinberg, *Turning Back: The Retreat from Racial Justice in American Thought and Policy* (Boston: Beacon, 1995), pp. 191–92.

[40] Lise Togeby, "Political Implications of Increasing Numbers of Women in the Labor Force," *Comparative Political Studies*, vol. 27 (July 1994), pp. 211–40; EG, *kvinnorna och välfärden. Betänkende av EG-konsekvensutredningarna: Social välfärd och jämställdhet* (Stockholm: SOU, 1993).

thin a conception of community around which any credible theory of rights and obligations could be organized. Protecting the integrity of the national community can therefore be interpreted as a state-building claim which overrides the need for expanding the number of people subject to the state's authority through immigration. For a welfare state to exist, thick conceptions of citizenship are needed, in which individuals feel a sense of obligation to others whose fates are somewhat like their own.[41]

Because state-building remains an important imperative for the welfare state, a tension between the claims of nationhood and the claims of particular identities persists. Since many public policies—especially including affirmative action—have been tied to the size of ethnic and racial groups, pressures exist to expand, not the overall number of Americans, but the number of Mexican Americans or Asian Americans. Often such pressures come, not from those who belong to ethnic and racial categories, but from those who speak in their name; surveys indicate, for example, that Mexican Americans do not support expansive immigration in significant numbers, even from Mexico, but leaders of Mexican-American organizations do.[42] Then there are conflicts, not between one minority group and the larger culture, but between different minority groups, such as the tension between African Americans, whose support of the welfare state is stronger than any other group but who tend to be hostile to immigration, and the leaders of organizations representing Spanish-speaking Americans, who, in welcoming immigration, tend to weaken the ability of the welfare state to target its benefits. (This tension received its most extensive expression in Miami in 1980 when Fidel Castro opened the port of Mariel, sending a number of prisoners and antisocial Cubans to Florida.)[43] The threat to the welfare state which exists from supranational pressures toward globalization meets threats to the welfare state from subnational group power and recognition.

Symbolic recognition of ethnic and racial identity may well be compatible with a strong state and nation. Although state-builders are often jealous of competing loyalties, the welfare state does not presuppose an ethnically homogeneous population. The great community, by embodying what David Hollinger has called a "post-ethnic" perspective, becomes

[41] Michael Walzer, Thick and Thin: Moral Argument at Home and Abroad (South Bend, IN: University of Notre Dame Press, 1994).

[42] See Rodolfo O. de la Garza et al., Latino Voices: Mexican, Puerto Rican, and Cuban Perspectives on American Politics (Boulder, CO: Westview, 1992), pp. 100–101; and Peter Skerry, Mexican Americans: The Ambivalent Minority (New York: Free Press, 1993). Much the same split between rank-and-file opinion and the opinion of leadership organizations on immigration can be seen among African Americans.

[43] Alejandro Portes and Alex Stepick, City on the Edge: The Transformation of Miami (Berkeley and Los Angeles: University of California Press, 1993), pp. 176–202. Immigration is also a more powerful force than color or racial identity; Portes and Stepick note that "Black Americans are profoundly ambivalent about Haitians in Miami, who, though 'brothers' in color, are regarded as a competitive threat in the labor market and business world" (p. 190).

even greater as it renews itself by incorporating newcomers.[44] Mild forms of identity politics are in that sense perfectly compatible with a strong state, so long as there are well-understood principles of assimilation and accommodation. But this process also requires that a strong state be suspicious of formal, explicit, and binding claims by groups within the society for unrestricted immigration of others of their nationality or ethnicity, since the resulting pressures on social services, especially at a time of fiscal limits, will inevitably weaken existing welfare-state commitments. If claims for recognition on behalf of those groups weaken government, such groups may be accorded symbolic equality without government provisions to back them up—a Pyrrhic victory indeed.

Surely welfare states can, and probably will, work out compromise solutions to preserve the national community in the face of global pressures from outside and group pressures from inside. Such solutions will require constant renegotiations of the meaning of citizenship.[45] It would be extreme to conclude that a newly emerging economic order will make national citizenship essentially irrelevant.[46] And, despite the potential unraveling of Canada, it will likely also prove extreme to imagine that the forces of ethnic and racial identity will become so powerful that they will result in a "disuniting" of the United States.[47] Because of the simultaneous presence of supernational and supranational forces, the great community can never be taken for granted. But governments, the collectors of taxation and the providers of public provision, are unlikely to lose their power to define the nation either. The welfare state will have to find a new path in all this, surely as difficult a task as its original founding and expansion.

IV. The "Intense Individualism" of the Welfare State

How can a great community fashion solidarity? What ties people together when their primary loyalty is to the other members of the nation-state? If we increase the number of Americans, Swedes, or Britons, what will they have in common? As odd as it may sound at a time when individualistic theorists of the market generally find themselves locked in combat with collectivist theorists of the state, many welfare-state theorists were proud of what T. H. Marshall called the "intense individualism"

[44] David Hollinger, *Post-Ethnic America: Beyond Multiculturalism* (New York: Basic Books, 1995).

[45] Jytte Klausen, "Citizenship and Social Justice in Open Societies," in Erik Oddvar Eriksen and Jørn Loftager, eds., *The Rationality of the Welfare State* (Oslo: Scandinavian University Press, 1996), pp. 203–27.

[46] See Kenichi Omae, *The End of the Nation State: The Rise of Regional Economies* (New York: Free Press, 1995).

[47] Arthur Schlesinger, Jr., *The Disuniting of America: Reflections on a Multicultural Society* (New York: Norton, 1992).

of the welfare state.[48] One of the consequences of a strong state, in Marshall's view, is that it would break up local concentrations of power, thereby freeing the individual to exercise choices which might have been limited or restricted if subgroups and particular identities had been given full sway. What Americans, Swedes, or Britons would have in common in a great community would be their identities as individuals.[49]

No identity was more deleterious for individual freedom, in Marshall's view, than class. Marshall believed that class membership not only undermined what Britons had in common, but also stifled individuality. Class, in his view, was so pervasive a difference, it so stamped the individual with particular characteristics, that the welfare state, by breaking up the concentrations of tradition, language, behavior, and comportment associated with social class, would enhance individualism, not undermine it. In Marshall's world, in short, the individual and the state could be understood as linked together against the claims of groups, especially including the claims of class.

Marshall, of course, never dealt with the kinds of groups raising questions of identity in contemporary politics. Confronted with them, one could argue that ethnicity, race, and sexual preference speak to differences completely unlike those of class. Kymlicka, for example, argues that

> Marshall's theory of integration does not necessarily work for culturally distinct immigrants, or for various other groups which have historically been excluded from full participation in the national culture—such as blacks, women, religious minorities, gays, and lesbians. Some members of these groups still feel excluded from the "common culture," despite possessing the common rights of citizenship.[50]

Yet there are problems with the notion of making subjective feelings of exclusion from the common culture the criterion by which group claims ought to take precedence over efforts at integration. Without engaging in exercises in comparative victimization, it is easy to forget how the British working class was once felt to belong to another nation, so different was it—in language, attitude, and education—from the dominant elites.

Marshall's own writing, we believe, provides a better "test" of whether a group claim ought to be given a special hearing or whether its demands

[48] Marshall, *Class, Citizenship, and Social Development*, p. 236.

[49] Despite Marshall's emphasis on individualism, the welfare state, at least in its earlier phases, assumed that the family, and not the persons within it, was the main economic unit. For that reason, it was not until the feminist critique of the welfare state developed in the 1970s and 1980s that a truly individualist result was produced, one which disaggregated the family as a unit, so as to increase the rights of all the individuals, including the women (and children) who composed it.

[50] Kymlicka, *Liberalism, Community, and Culture*, p. 180.

for recognition should be overridden for the sake of the larger community than the test provided by Kymlicka's emphasis on self-perceived exclusion. That test would be as follows: if breaking the grip of group loyalty increases membership in the common culture and at the same time increases individual choice, we are justified in overriding group claims for recognition. One way to consider the claims made on behalf of women, minority groups, and other advocates of identity politics in today's discourse is to see how they fare with respect to Marshall's test.

We will argue that most such claims fail the test. Before looking at the United States, we want to offer an example from Scandinavia, where the welfare state is most fully developed. Unlike in the United States, where the left is generally attracted to claims of cultural or linguistic difference, many defenders of the Scandinavian welfare state view efforts to preserve the linguistic and cultural patterns of minorities as a *threat* to the welfare state. Immigrant men, especially from Turkey and other countries in the Middle East, tend to view the female-friendly aspects of the Scandinavian welfare states with great suspicion: day care, child allowances, and public health services, in their view, represent attempts by the authorities to impose secular and egalitarian values upon their religious, traditional, and usually patriarchal beliefs. By insisting that the language of the welfare state is, and can only be, Swedish, welfare authorities try to reach around immigrant men and establish direct contact with the women for whom the services are designed—or, in some cases, to reach around both parents in an effort to target the children. From the perspective of the state, religion and ethnicity simultaneously prevent full membership in the great community *and* limit the options of the individuals affected. If anything, traditional values among immigrants are *more* of an obstacle to incorporation than class ever was domestically. Hence, there would be an even greater requirement *not* to recognize group claims in the case of ethnicity than there was when Marshall wrote about class.

Recognizing special claims based on race can have similar consequences in the United States, as the example of voting rules indicates. Many writers believe that the underrepresentation of African Americans in legislatures, particularly in Congress, is unfair.[51] The Voting Rights Act of 1965, and its subsequent amendments in 1970, 1975, and 1982, combined with expansive Supreme Court decisions, called attention to the phenomenon of "vote dilution." The idea was that if a significant number of members of minority groups were unable to elect representatives of their own race, it would be permissible to draw districts that would increase the chances of members of minority groups winning, so as to

---

[51] Bernard Grofman and Chandler Davidson, "Postscript: What Is the Best Way to a Color-Blind Society?" in Bernard Grofman and Chandler Davidson, eds., *Controversies in Minority Voting: The Voting Rights Act in Perspective* (Washington: Brookings Institution, 1992), pp. 300–317; Douglas J. Amy, *Real Choices/New Voices: The Case for Proportional Representation Elections in the United States* (New York: Columbia University Press, 1993), p. 115.

avoid the effect of having their votes diluted.[52] In *Shaw v. Hunt* and *Bush v. Vera*, decided together in 1996, the Court, and especially Justice Sandra Day O'Connor, objected to bizarrely drawn districts on the grounds that "they convey the message that political identity is, or should be, predominantly racial."[53] In this and previous voting-rights cases, O'Connor worried that the use of race as the dominant reason for drawing district lines deprived everyone of access to a common culture. In the terms we have been using here, the grounds for O'Connor's opposition to racially drawn districts is that they fail the test of encouraging national membership in the society as a whole.

There is a case to be made, however, that such districts also fail the other half of Marshall's test: enhancing individual choice. How this can happen comes out clearly in Justice John Paul Stevens's dissent in the 1996 voting-rights case. Stevens found racial classification benign: "[R]equiring the State to ignore the association between race and party affiliation would be no more logical and potentially as harmful," he wrote, "as it would be to prohibit the Public Health Service from targeting African-American communities in an effort to increase awareness regarding sickle-cell anemia. . . ."[54] His analogy is quite striking, conveying as it does the sense that one's political beliefs and associations are not chosen by oneself but can be equated to a biological or medical condition outside the choice of the person involved. It was precisely to counter such a way of denying individual choice which led Marshall to worry about group-based claims. And it is surely ironic that the "liberal" wing of the Supreme Court endorses claims that identity is not a matter of individual choice while such claims are treated skeptically by the "conservative" wing.

Using race as a criterion for drawing legislative boundaries conflicts with individualism in yet another way. To fashion such districts, black politicians formed alliances with Republicans, who understood that if black voters were concentrated in particular districts, the remaining districts, deprived of a block which usually votes Democratic, would be more likely to elect Republicans. Under racial redistricting, the number of African Americans in Congress increased, but so did the overall number of conservatives and Republicans. Since it is true that black Americans support welfare-state policies in much greater numbers than any other group in the U.S. population, one effect of taking race into account as a way of electing more black legislators was to deprive a much larger group of black voters of the ability to realize their policy preferences.[55] Marshall almost seemed to be anticipating such situations when he wrote that

---

[52] Abigail Thernstrom, *Whose Votes Count? Affirmative Action and Minority Voting Rights* (Cambridge: Harvard University Press, 1987); Lani Guinier, *The Tyranny of the Majority: Fundamental Fairness in Representative Democracy* (New York: Free Press, 1994).

[53] "High Court Voids Race-Based Redistricting," *New York Times*, June 14, 1996, p. A24.

[54] *Ibid.*

[55] Carol Swain, *Black Faces/Black Interests: The Representation of African-Americans in Congress* (Cambridge: Harvard University Press, 1993). There is also evidence that black voters

if groups are fully consulted [on legislative matters that concern them], they should not claim political power; political influence, yes, by the ordinary means of argument, discussion and propaganda. But not power; otherwise group loyalty and citizenship are bound to clash.[56]

Affirmative action also raises interesting questions with respect to Marshall's test. Both supporters and critics of affirmative action often view it as an attempt to establish the claims of groups over the rights of individuals. Michael Piore, who is generally sympathetic to identity politics, notes that in Europe so-called "corporatist" regimes developed policies by using government to negotiate differences among groups, such as employers associations and labor unions, which were given official recognition by the state. Blacks, Piore then concludes, "are the first of the new noneconomic corporate groups in American society."[57] If this is true, then efforts to base public policy on official recognition of corporate groups would surely come at the expense of the rights of the individuals who belong to those groups, for one of the main purposes of European experiences with corporatism was to limit and regulate individual claims against the state. This is no doubt why many critics of affirmative action also view it as a system of group rights; for them, the restrictions on individual choice and identity embodied in affirmative action constitute the strong normative argument against the policy.[58] For such critics, affirmative action, which relies on the power of the state and not on persuasion and argumentation to enforce its rules, is not only misguided, but also harmful to individual rights.

This argument rests on an empirical claim, which is that affirmative action does in fact establish a regime of group claims. That assumption can be challenged. Peter Skerry has argued that black political traditions, like many ethnic political traditions, have not been comfortable with corporatist politics.[59] Blacks, for one thing, are as committed to individualist values as whites.[60] Even when race is used as a category for as-

---

have become more conservative; see Katherine Tate, *From Protest to Politics: The New Black Voters in American Elections* (Cambridge: Harvard University Press, 1993), pp. 29–38. On the differences between black and white opinion, see Jennifer Hochschild, *Facing Up to the American Dream: Race, Class, and the Soul of the Nation* (Princeton: Princeton University Press, 1995).

[56] Marshall, *Class, Citizenship, and Social Development*, pp. 219–20.

[57] Piore, *Beyond Individualism*, p. 25.

[58] See, for example, Carl Cohen, *Naked Racial Preference* (Lanham, MD: Madison Books, 1995); Paul Craig Roberts and Lawrence M. Stratton, *The New Color Line: How Quotas and Privilege Destroy Democracy* (Washington, DC: Regnery, 1995); and Terry Eastland, *Ending Affirmative Action: The Case for Colorblind Justice* (New York: Basic Books, 1996).

[59] Peter Skerry, "The Affirmative Action Paradox: Group Rights and Individual Benefits," unpublished paper.

[60] Terri Susan Fine, "Race and Political Culture: Blacks, Whites, and Commitment to Individualism," *Southeastern Political Review*, cited in Skerry, "The Affirmative Action Paradox," p. 10.

signing government benefits, Skerry points out, individuals get to choose the racial designation which they believe best applies to themselves. From Skerry's perspective, the conditions for establishing strong ethnic and racial groups in American politics have all but disappeared, given suburbanization, the role of the media, and the decline of political parties as ethnic organizers. Under these conditions, affirmative action, whatever the theory behind it, will turn out in practice to support the claims of individuals within groups rather than the claims of groups as groups.

We hope that Skerry is proven correct, but in the meantime it remains the case that most forms of affirmative action—minority set-asides, college scholarships, diversity targets—do become race-conscious in application, leading to the result that individuals can be deprived of benefits to which they would otherwise be entitled in order to satisfy group-based objectives. Affirmative action will therefore only be able to pass Marshall's test when it moves away from classifying people according to relatively fixed categories such as race in favor of classifying them according to relatively fluid categories such as "the disadvantaged."[61] This may already be taking place. Efforts by universities to give special consideration to applicants who have overcome experiences of poverty and discrimination would surely be justified according to Marshall's test, for the purpose is to enhance the life chances of the individual and to facilitate the best use of talents for the great community as a whole. Of course, when affirmative action is applied in this way, we are no longer talking about affirmative action as the term has been recently used but more about fairly traditional efforts of the welfare state to equalize people's life-chances irrespective of the conditions of their birth.

Even though earlier theorists of the welfare state could not have anticipated identity politics as we know it, their ideas are nonetheless relevant to the problems posed by claims for group recognition. It is difficult to imagine a contemporary welfare state possessing sufficient power to provide for uniform social provision if it has to accommodate itself to the claims of entrenched particular interests. The result is a difficult dilemma for identity groups: they can choose to strengthen the group and in the process to weaken the state (whose purpose, presumably, is to provide enhanced benefits back to the group), or they can choose to strengthen the state, thereby expanding benefits to members of the group, but only by weakening the formal political claims of the group as a group. No one can predict how these choices will play themselves out in the future. But it certainly remains within the realm of possibility that identity politics, which is primarily a matter of symbols, will give way to a more traditional politics of bargaining over the substance of social policy. If that happens, the kind of politics produced will prove more compatible with the welfare state than the flourishing of identity politics which we have recently experienced.

[61] Richard D. Kahlenberg, *The Remedy: Class, Race, and Affirmative Action* (New York: Basic Books, 1996).

V. First-Order and Second-Order Inequalities

The theorists of the welfare state were not only state-builders, they were also strong believers in equality; the only state worth building was one that tried to equalize as much as possible the life-chances of individuals. Yet just as the word "community" had a special meaning for them—referring to the great community of the nation-state, not the specific communities of functional groups—so did the word "equality." Both Marshall and Tawney recognized that there were many kinds of equality (and inequality) and that not all of them ought to be pursued (or overcome) in the same way.

The arguments of both men, indeed, while often taken as defenses of radical notions about equality, can also be read as defenses of particular kinds of inequality. It is this desire not to see all inequalities abolished which Marshall took up as the theme for his Galton lecture. The objective of social policy, he wrote, was not to ensure equality of outcomes but to give everyone an equal chance to share in the common destiny which defined British society. So long as that condition was met, inequality would in all likelihood continue. "The right of the citizen in this process of selection and mobility is the right to equality of opportunity," he wrote. "Its aim is to eliminate hereditary privilege. In essence it is the equal right to display and develop differences, or inequalities; the equal right to be recognized as unequal."[62] For Marshall, this "equal right to be recognized as unequal" is a price worth paying if the welfare state is to further individualism at the same time that it recognizes collective obligations and duties:

> If the Welfare State is to bring its two principles [i.e., individualism and collective obligations] into harmony, it must conceive of the basic equality of all as human beings and fellow-citizens in a way which leaves room for the recognition that all are not equally gifted nor capable of rendering equally valuable services to the community, that equal opportunity means an equal chance to reveal differences, some of which are superiorities, and that these differences need for their development different types of education, some of which may legitimately be regarded as higher than others.[63]

Tawney also made it clear that his objective was not "equality of capacity or attainment," but rather "of circumstances, institutions, and manner of life."[64] For him, as for Marshall, different kinds of inequality should be treated differently:

[62] Marshall, *Citizenship and Social Class*, pp. 65–66.
[63] Marshall, *Class, Citizenship, and Social Development*, p. 243.
[64] Tawney, *Equality*, p. 38.

A society which values equality will attach a high degree of significance to differences of character and intelligence between different
individuals, and a low degree of significance to economic and social
differences between different groups. It will endeavor, in shaping its
policy and organization, to encourage the former and to neutralize
and suppress the latter, and will regard it as vulgar and childish to
emphasize them when, unfortunately, they still exist.[65]

Although they did not use this language, Tawney and Marshall were
attacking what could be called "second-order" inequalities while defending "first-order" ones. By first-order inequalities we mean those differences which exist between people in their natural state: some people are
taller than others, some better looking, some with more brain power.
Second-order inequalities, by contrast, are those which are reproduced by
particular kinds of social and economic organization: some privileges are
due to conditions of birth, unequal access to education, or arbitrary actions by employers, all of which work to deny opportunities to people of
merit who ought to have them. Marshall and Tawney believed that these
secondary categories—once again, both writers had in mind the kinds of
differences in education and life attainment determined by class—are
both pernicious and artificial, which means that they can be abolished (or
their effects minimized) through the welfare state. Public policy should
aim to minimize the effects of secondary inequalities—not to fashion a
society in which equality would reign, but to create a society in which
inequalities could persist because there would be nothing morally wrong
with them. Once economic inequality is no longer the major issue, the
natural differences between people, "differences of character and intelligence" in Tawney's words, will be more likely to emerge.

In asking whether or not the principles of identity politics conflict with
the principles underlying the welfare state, one first has to ask what kinds
of differences identity is meant to circumscribe. But that has proven a
very difficult question to answer. An example of how difficult comes from
the arena of sexual preference. In the early years of what would come to
be called "gay liberation," the 1960s and 1970s, most advocates on behalf
of greater recognition of gay identity, under the influence of Michel Foucault,[66] assumed that "gay" and "straight" referred to arbitrary conven-
tions, that gayness, in short, was a construct imposed on homosexuals by
heterosexuals.[67] Their opponents, conservatives opposed to homosexual
rights, assumed, again as a matter of course, that homosexuality was a

[65] *Ibid.*, p. 50.
[66] Michel Foucault, *The History of Sexuality*, vol. 1, *An Introduction*, trans. Robert Hurley
(New York: Pantheon, 1969).
[67] David Halperin, *Saint Foucault: Towards a Gay Hagiography* (New York: Oxford University Press, 1995).

product of innate biological and neurological instincts.[68] During the 1980s, both sides reversed their positions. Realizing that a theory which held that homosexuality was innate could lead to the conclusion that nothing could be done about it, conservatives began to argue that being gay was a choice, one which, having gone one way, could, with either encouragement or punishment, go the other way. Meanwhile, advocates for gay rights, recognizing much the same conclusion, but also pondering their own biographies, began to argue that they never chose to be gay, that their sexual preferences were shaped by forces beyond their explicit control.[69]

Along similar lines, feminists have spent at least two decades trying to theorize about gender, with inconclusive, if not often contradictory, results. Originally, gender was differentiated from sex—the former held to be constructed and artificial, the latter natural and given. This distinction rapidly disappeared. On the one hand, lesbian and radical feminists began to argue that sex itself was socially constructed.[70] On the other hand, gender was viewed as both arbitrary and destructible, yet also so rooted in institutions and structures as to be all but impermeable—that is, incapable of being changed by reform (rather than fundamental change in society).[71] Unable to resolve these different views of gender, feminists took to asserting the truth of both versions simultaneously, pursuing a politics of difference and a politics of equality at the same time.

That particular kind of difference known as race went through a similar transformation. The original impetus of civil rights legislation in the 1960s was to think of racial differences as "second-order" ones. Crucial to the color-blind principles of the Civil Rights Act of 1964 was the notion that racial distinctions are invidious, fraught with the power to deny individuals opportunities for which they otherwise would be eligible; that they are arbitrary, unfair to those classified under them; and that the purpose of public policy ought to be to hasten their disappearance.[72] As everyone by now knows, this inclination to overcome racial differences was replaced by a contrary impulse to think of racial differences as so strong and significant that opponents of racial discrimination had no choice but to take race into account.[73] When the language of color-blindness shifted to the right and center of the political spectrum, the left began to empha-

[68] For an elucidation of psychological, neurological, hormonal, and biological arguments about homosexuality, see Michael Ruse, *Homosexuality: A Philosophical Inquiry* (New York: Basil Blackwell, 1988).

[69] Simon Levay, *The Sexual Brain* (Cambridge: MIT Press, 1993); Richard Mohr, *Gay Ideas: Outing and Other Controversies* (Boston: Beacon, 1992), pp. 221–42.

[70] Judith Butler, *Bodies That Matter: On the Discursive Limits of "Sex"* (New York: Routledge, 1993).

[71] Judith Lorber, *Paradoxes of Gender* (New Haven: Yale University Press, 1994), pp. 292–93.

[72] Andrew Kull, *The Color-Blind Constitution* (Cambridge: Harvard University Press, 1992).

[73] The story of how this happened is well told in Hugh Davis Graham, *The Civil Rights Era: Origins and Development of National Policy, 1960–1972* (New York: Oxford University Press, 1990).

size the notion that racial differences were "first-order" differences: essentialist characteristics which ought not only to be recognized, but which also could be embodied in law. This shift to a new view of racial difference was a controversial move, and a good deal of the resulting public discussion revolves around whether supporters or opponents of affirmative action can best lay claim to the legacy of Martin Luther King. Our purpose in raising the issue, however, is not to take sides on the question, but to highlight the implications for public policy contained in the shift.

The advantage of understanding inequalities as both arbitrary and deeply implanted in society is that such a view justifies taking governmental action to redress them. For Marshall and Tawney, class differences, the product of a particular kind of industrial society, were strong enough to matter but not so strong that they could never be reformed. Central to the way these two theorists understood first- and second-order inequalities was the necessity to focus on the conditions that produced unjustified inequality, but not to the point of eliminating those conditions which enabled justified inequalities to persist. Government intervention therefore had to be stringent, but it also had to be limited. The best way to achieve such a paradoxical result was through indirect state intervention. The aim of the welfare state was not to peer into people's souls to root out instances of bad thinking or improper elitism, but to control for the effects of inequality by restricting only the impact of second-order differences. The language of the welfare state as Marshall and Tawney understood it was one of politics and economics, not sociology and psychology.

Advocates of identity politics, by contrast, have far more ambivalent feelings about second-order inequalities than did Marshall and Tawney. On the one hand, differences in race, gender, and sexual orientation are on proud display when proclaimed by members of the groups affected: some feminists defend the idea that women have a different way of knowing or a different way of acting morally, for example, while similar claims have been made by Afro-centrists on behalf of black learning styles or cultural values.[74] Celebrating such "second-order" inequalities, however, puts advocates of identity politics in a complicated political position, for if there is nothing wrong with the notion that men and women are fundamentally different—for example, that women or blacks think in nonlinear ways—then there is no reason to justify using government for, say, trying to overcome the underrepresentation of women in mathematics or science. Rather than using government to attack deeply rooted inequalities so that less essential ones can persist, identity politics aims to

---

[74] For examples, see Nel Noddings, *Caring: A Feminine Approach to Ethics and Moral Education* (Berkeley and Los Angeles: University of California Press, 1984); Mary Field Belenky, et al., *Women's Ways of Knowing: The Development of Self, Voice, and Mind* (New York: Basic Books, 1986); and Wellesley College Center for Research on Women, *How Schools Shortchange Girls: The AAUW Report: A Study of Major Findings on Girls in Education* (Washington, DC: Association of American University Women, 1992).

preserve and protect deeply rooted differences so that identity can be affirmed.

Yet this is only part of the story. When claims about difference are made by men about women, whites about blacks, or straights about gays, identity-politics advocates often become uncomfortable. Those who advocate laws to prohibit hate speech, for example, such as feminists against pornography, believe that most claims made about racial and gender difference are suspect when made by those who do not belong to the group in question.[75] In these circumstances, governmental action is required to prevent emphasizing (in a presumably negative way) the very second-order inequalities which (in a presumably positive way) identity politics celebrates. In calling for governmental action, advocates of identity seem to be in a position close to the one Tawney and Marshall took with respect to class: now they are saying that racial and gender differences are so arbitrary and invidious that they ought to be abolished. Yet unlike Marshall and Tawney, who believed that equality of opportunity should not lead to equality of outcomes, advocates of identity politics, when they focus on second-order differences, tend to want, not only to abolish them, but to abolish first-order differences as well. Racism, sexism, and homophobia come to be understood as something inherent in the minds of whites, men, and straights. So pernicious are these ways of thinking that every difference becomes suspect. If, for example, standardized tests result in different scores among members of different racial groups, then the tests are suspect. "Differences of character and intelligence," to use Tawney's words once more, cannot be permitted, for fear that such first-order inequalities will perpetuate second-order ones. In this way, the emphasis in the view of Marshall and Tawney is reversed: to achieve equality of results, we have to tamper with equality of opportunity. Whereas Marshall and Tawney argued that not all inequalities were necessarily bad, advocates of identity politics come to distrust any form of hierarchy and generally denounce all forms of elitism as wrong. The result is a conception of equality far more radical than the one advanced by writers such as Marshall and Tawney—if for no other reason than that it is so hostile to merit.

Of course, no one knows how permanent or transitory the categories of identity will ultimately prove to be. Nonetheless, the history of the category deemed by many to be the most intransigent, race, is instructive. Statistical Directive 15, adopted by the Office of Management and Budget in 1977 to settle questions regarding which groups are eligible for which benefits, reads as if the boundaries between races were clear and uncontested: there are four races in the United States according to this directive (white, black, native American, and Asian and Pacific Islander) and one

[75] Mari J. Matsuda, Charles R. Lawrence III, Richard Delgado, and Kimberlè Williams Crenshaw, *Words That Wound: Critical Race Theory, Assaultive Speech, and the First Amendment* (Boulder: Westview Press, 1993).

ethnic group (Hispanic), which presumably means that most Americans can be classified in one category or another.[76] Yet no sooner are racial categories proclaimed than their limits become obvious: not only does it make little sense to include Cuban Americans and Mexican Americans in the same category, but no one knows how to classify black Puerto Ricans or Indians who migrated from Uganda.

Many writers recognize the arbitrariness of these distinctions but insist that African Americans have a special identity because of the legacy of slavery and the persistence of discrimination by whites. Interestingly enough, the notion that black and white are "real" categories is as important to conservatives as it is to advocates of multiculturalism; without racial categories, it would be impossible to write a book like *The Bell Curve*.[77] Yet even this category is increasingly held to be far more ambiguous than it seems. So rapid has been the cross-over of racial and ethnic barriers in the United States that we have witnessed the emergence of a category, "multiracial," which destroys the integrity of all the other categories; indeed, it is multiracial Americans who most insist that Statistical Directive 15 ought to be revoked.[78] If it ever were revoked, the argument that racial differences are so deeply entrenched that special measures are necessary to overcome their secondary effects would find itself losing credibility.

Although it is impossible to know how these understandings of difference will work themselves out in the future, it is possible in the present for those who seek greater justice and equality to work out in more detail what kind of vision they seek to realize. Will their future society be one in which individual whites and blacks (or men and women) are unequal but the inequality between them is not understood as a by-product of their different identities? Or will it be one which, in seeking to overcome difference, finds it necessary to imagine individuals as equal to each other in as many ways as possible? We believe that the former vision is compatible with the welfare state as it was imagined by its founders and developed by its builders, while the latter will require a politics well beyond anything currently within the purview of welfare states as we have known them.

VI. CONCLUSION

In the political and fiscal environment of the late 1990s, welfare states find themselves lucky to hold on to core programs and policies, so much has the *Zeitgeist* been dominated by tax revolts and movements to limit government. For those who have long been committed to the notion that

[76] For an interesting treatment of the directive, see Hollinger, *Post-Ethnic America*, pp. 33–39.

[77] Herrnstein and Murray, *The Bell Curve* (*supra* note 33).

[78] Lawrence Wright, "One Drop of Blood," *The New Yorker*, vol. 70 (July 25, 1994), pp. 46–50ff.

some government regulation of private economic activity is necessary to smooth out the ups and downs of capitalist growth, this era of cutbacks has been hard to accept. One can, of course, blame right-wing politicians for the demise of the welfare state, but so long as the society is democratic, which most welfare states are, such a course leads directly to blaming what is popular, not a particularly fruitful way of building support for one's agenda.

It would be foolish to argue that the left bears primary responsibility for its own political failure, that the limits being imposed on the welfare state have been caused by the left's flirtation with the politics of identity. We do not believe this to be the case: the dynamics of international capital flows, generational imbalances and conflicts, the decline of labor-intensive industry, changes in family life—all these are far more important in explaining the new, and more difficult, environment of the welfare state than affirmative action or feminism. Nevertheless, we do think it fair to make two concluding claims.

One is that a preoccupation with identity politics has prevented the left from developing an appropriate response to these developments. In part, this is because the path of identity politics leads to a politics which often has more to do with symbol than with substance. In part, it is also because, once ensnared within the particularism of identity politics, it becomes difficult to maintain focus on social disadvantage as the main fulcrum around which politics should be organized; Anne Phillips, who wants to preserve at least some role for a class-based politics in a time of identity and recognition, acknowledges that she does not know how to do so.[79] Ultimately, however, the most compelling reason why identity politics runs counter to the welfare state is that the task of building and sustaining national citizenship requires constant vigilance against supranational pressures from without and subnational pressures from within. Cosmopolitanism and group recognition are both good things; yet both, when taken to extremes, undermine the sovereignty of the nation-state. Advocates of identity politics often write eloquently about how capitalism, especially in its global form, undermines national autonomy. What they often fail to realize is that, by asserting the primacy of subnational groups over the claims of national citizenship, they do the same thing.

This leads directly to our second concluding point. Driving the political sentiment behind the attack on the welfare state is a resurgence of sentiment for libertarian ideas: an agenda of privatization, low taxes, suspicion of government intervention, and distrust of bureaucratic rules is as strong in America now as it has been at any time since the New Deal. But before libertarians take credit for these developments, they ought to recognize how much they have in common with advocates of identity politics. It can hardly be surprising that religious parents who object to a

---

[79] Phillips, *The Politics of Presence*, pp. 170–78.

common curriculum in public schools, which they denounce as secular humanism, find themselves using arguments for particular kinds of education which differ little from arguments for special classes for the handicapped or for bilingualism, both of which are often defended by those who are advocates of identity politics.[80] In a similar way, supporters of gay rights or abortion rights not only distrust government as much as any libertarian, they often turn for support to court cases which are seen as limiting the power of government, such as *Lochner v. New York*, which (in 1905) struck down New York State's effort to regulate how many hours bakers could work.[81] Of course, this is not true in all cases; some advocates of identity politics will try to use government to further their objectives—for example, by requiring diversity in hiring—in ways that libertarians would find offensive. Still, there are many ways to undermine the common culture which makes the welfare state possible, and the left's occasional preference for groups over the state can do just as much harm to the welfare state as the right's preference for individuals over the state.

No wonder, then, that the political environment around the welfare state has been changing so dramatically. Between the attractions of groups and individuals, there may be little room left for the kind of state-building which historically made the welfare state possible. Under these conditions, it will become increasingly impossible to pursue the twin inclusive objectives of respect for groups and equality for individuals simultaneously. If, as a result, the welfare state is further weakened, those who left behind the historic concern with creating a common citizenship will have few besides themselves to blame.

Sociology and Political Science, Boston University
Comparative Politics, Brandeis University

---

[80] Stephen Bates, *Battleground: One Mother's Crusade, the Religious Right, and the Struggle for Control of Our Classrooms* (New York: Poseidon Press, 1993), p. 311.

[81] *Lochner v. New York*, 198 U.S. 45 (1905). For two examples of this strategy, see Lawrence Tribe, *Abortion: The Clash of Absolutes* (New York: Norton, 1990), p. 86; and H. N. Hirsch, *A Theory of Liberty: The Constitution and Minorities* (New York: Routledge, 1992), pp. 72–75.

THE PROBLEM OF FORFEITURE
IN THE WELFARE STATE

By Richard A. Epstein

I. Introduction: The Flip Side of Entitlements

Political theory has a good deal to say both for and against the establishment of the modern welfare state. As one might expect, most of that
discussion is directed toward the expanded set of basic rights that the
state confers on its members. In its most canonical form, the welfare state
represents a switch in vision from the regime of negative rights in the
nineteenth century to the regime of positive rights so much in vogue
today. Negative rights—an inexact and somewhat misleading term—
stress the right of an individual to be free from certain kinds of external
interventions.[1] These rights arrange themselves on two basic lists. The
first list generates a set of civil capacities that all individuals enjoy over
their own labor and property: the right to contract, to make wills, to sue
and be sued, to give evidence, and the like. The second list, from which
the term "negative rights" derives, protects all persons from interference,
either by force or by fraud, in the conduct of their own affairs. The
resulting set of rights is short, snappy, and knowable; it is internally
consistent; and it prepares the stage for productive human behavior (exchange) while limiting destructive forms of behavior (theft). Even though
it is not couched in explicit utilitarian language, it can surely be defended
on general functional grounds.[2]

The modern vision of positive rights does not overtly reject this set of
negative rights; nor does it seek explicitly to cut back on the set of correlative duties that it creates. Instead, it optimistically seeks to supplement those rights with a fresh set of entitlements that runs against the
state, not against other persons as such. Thus, individual citizens no
longer have merely the right to buy food, clothing, shelter, and, increasingly, health care, so long as they can find a willing seller. Now they also
have a claim against the state that requires the direct provision of these
key goods and services—without purchase. The precise level of guaranteed services is sometimes in dispute. The more limited version of the
right conceives of it as a claim to receive some level of minimum security.
The more expansive versions of the right treat it as a claim to enjoy

---

[1] See Isaiah Berlin, *Four Essays on Liberty* (London: Oxford University Press, 1969).
[2] For my earlier efforts in this regard, see Richard A. Epstein, "Two Conceptions of Civil
Rights," *Social Philosophy and Policy*, vol. 8, no. 2 (1991), pp. 38–59.

resources at a level attained by those who are able to purchase goods and services for themselves.

The creation of these additional entitlements is not advertised as being in conflict with the set of negative rights traditionally respected and protected by the state, largely because positive rights are said not to run as between persons, but against the state. But legal abstractions do not build widgets; nor do they make decisions on the deployment of either labor or capital. Every statement about the relationship between the state and the individual is at bottom a statement about the relationship among individuals. The actions of individuals are imputed to states, as they are to corporations, by complex agreements, be they state constitutions or corporate charters; but the actions involved are all initiated by individuals, and work for their benefit or to their detriment. Therefore, when the state gives something to A, it means that individuals in positions of power have first taken that something from B. The interposition of the legal entity only obscures the tracks that make the transfer possible. The detective work to pick up the trail is made ever more arduous by the sheer number of parties included on all sides (albeit in different proportions) of a single complex network of transactions. Figuring out who wins and who loses from a system of state-induced transfers is far harder than figuring out who wins and who loses from a simple conversion of property, as when A takes B's horse and uses it as his own.

This obscurantism flourishes both by inadvertence and by design: by inadvertence because it substitutes short and inaccurate phrases for long and clumsy ones; and by design because it lowers the political price that the advocates of redistribution must bear in order to make the transfers in question. The difficulty in disentangling the connections, and in determining the extent of the gains and losses for the individual players, provides a certain cover from political pressure, as opposition groups find it difficult to isolate the transfer and quantify its extent. How much does the public at large lose from price supports for milk or import quotas on sugar? It becomes all too easy to glorify the benefits that fall on concentrated groups, and harder to measure the diffuse losses that fall on the public at large.

Other devices are available for successful groups to cover their political tracks. Abstractly speaking, members of an interest group would rather receive any fixed set of benefits for free than pay for them. In a political goldfish bowl, however, the ability to tell skeptical third parties that you have paid for your Social Security coverage, your Medicare coverage, your flood insurance, or your water allotments negates the most obvious charge that you are a recipient of a naked giveaway. A regime of transfers functions best when both the extent of the benefits and the extent of the burdens can be hidden. The trick therefore is to structure the benefits package and its costs in ways that conceal the net transfer payment built into the system. From the point of view of political cover, it is better to pay

$100 for a $1,000 benefit, than to receive a $900 benefit for free. Well-run institutions want their budget choices to be transparent so that they can make collective choices with full information. But political systems have the opposite incentives: drive the relevant data underground and obtain respectable political coloration.

The inability to trace the linkages between those who pay and those who collect should not, however, blind us to the tight nature of their connection. Rights and duties form a conservative field, such that conferring additional rights on some individuals necessarily imposes correlative duties on others. The only questions worth asking are who gets what, how much will it cost others, and when will they be called on to pay? The choice of a system of rights therefore depends on some estimation of whether the values that inhere in the rights created exceed the costs contained in their correlative duties. Legally each right is matched against a correlative duty in a one-to-one ratio. But the values attached to these rights and duties can increase enormously with the optimal legal arrangement. A sound social system is one where the value of each right to its holder is greater than the cost imposed on the bearer of the correlative duty. In voluntary exchange that condition is satisfied since each person prefers the rights he receives to those he surrenders. Under social-contract theory, the voluntary exchange drops out. Even so, the methodological ideal is to try to replicate the result of voluntary exchanges, by arranging rights and duties in ways that work to the net advantage of all participants in the overall system. It is that search for joint advantage that accounts in practice for the close affinity between social-contract and utilitarian theories, notwithstanding their apparent methodological differences.

In many cases, of course, we cannot measure directly the values found in rights or imposed by duties, which is one reason why social contracts are so much more difficult to construct than practical ones. Notwithstanding these empirical difficulties, however, there is good reason to believe that any set of coercive redistributive transfers is likely, when both public and private incentives are taken into account, to create debits in excess of the credits on the other side of the ledger. The basic difference is simple enough. A system of forced redistribution tolerates win/lose transactions, while a system of voluntary exchanges yields only win/win transactions. It is conceivable that sometimes the "win minus loss" from one transaction could exceed the "win plus win" in a second. But don't bet on it in the long run. The recipients of the transfers are induced to expend labor to secure payment, even though they produce nothing of value thereby. The same is true of those who resist the transfers in question. The actual outcome is in one sense less important than the process, for no matter who wins, there is less wealth left in the society after the process has run its course than before.

The classical-liberal version of takings law seeks to meet this redistributive challenge by limiting the number of forced transactions by the state;

it does so by allowing only those transfers necessary for the creation of public goods, e.g., roads and forts, thereby precluding outright transfers from one private person to another.[3] Needless to say, the rise of the modern welfare state has been matched by a withering away of this public-use requirement.[4] And for those transactions that pass this first hurdle, the law then requires that the person whose property has been taken receive just compensation for his or her loss, thereby blunting the redistributivist element. The overall purpose of this design seems clear: to make any state-initiated transfers imitate the win/win pattern of voluntary arrangements.

For the purposes of this essay, however, I do not want to debate the merits of various programs of public entitlements; instead, I want to focus on the flip side of the fundamental question: What view of individual recipient responsibility is entailed by the shift in basic political philosophy from a regime of negative rights to one where positive and negative rights are conjoined, as exists today? Briefly stated, this problem of forfeiture has several key components: when individuals have a right from the government or under the private law of tort and contract, some conduct on their own part will be regarded as sufficiently wrongful that they will be required to *forfeit* their rights in whole or in part. (An example of forfeiture that might arise under the law of tort is, say, the speeding motorist who seeks to recover damages from another who has run a red light; in this case, the first motorist might be taken to have forfeited all or part of his right to recover, due to his own misconduct. An example that might arise under the law of contract is the seller who demands payment for goods which were not delivered, or which were delivered in damaged condition.) The nature of the present inquiry is to examine the conditions under which the forfeiture of rights takes place under traditional theories of negative rights, and then to ask what transformation in the logic of forfeiture takes place once a set of negative rights gives way (at least in part) to a system of state-operated entitlements.

In principle, there need be no necessary connection between the creation of basic rights and the conditions of forfeiture, but in practice some connection of that sort has surely emerged. The basic relationship seems to be this: the risk of forfeiture looms larger in a world of negative rights and limited government than it does in the modern world of positive rights—a relationship that holds true over the full range of exchange and charitable transactions. In one sense, this result might appear to be unexpected, for the larger the set of original entitlements, the more pressing the need for some counterweight to the right so created. But so simple an argument overlooks the vast changes in intellectual orientation toward the role of individual responsibility that fuel the rise of the welfare state.

---

[3] For a defense of this position, see Richard A. Epstein, *Takings: Private Property and the Power of Eminent Domain* (Cambridge, MA: Harvard University Press, 1985), pp. 161–81.
[4] See, e.g., *Hawaiian Housing Authority v. Midkiff*, 467 U.S. 229 (1984).

The basic assumption of so many legal and social innovations is that individuals are incapable of protecting themselves by contract from exploitation by the large institutions with which they must routinely deal. Once that level of inequality is posited as the justification for the creation of new rights, the same philosophical mind-set carries over to narrow the types of recipient behavior that will either preclude or limit those claims. These same individuals need protection against their own foolish and perhaps even willful actions, which in an earlier day could have led to the forfeiture of rights. The emergent system of entitlements therefore becomes both rigid and enduring. Yet the effort to protect individuals against the consequences of their own folly, mistakes, or incompetence often builds up system-wide pressures that push the losses and inconvenience onto the competent and wise as well. As before, any effort to alter the relationships between ordinary individuals and institutions, necessarily alters the relationships among ordinary individuals as well.

To see how these developments play out, I shall examine the problem of forfeiture in various legal and social contexts under both the earlier conception of rights and the more modern one. In particular, I shall examine how these arguments play out in the context of contract, tort, and charitable relationships. I shall then conclude with some observations as to the systemic consequences of the pronounced shift in orientation against forfeiture.

II. The Nineteenth Century

A. The common law of forfeiture

1. Contract. The question of forfeiture of rights under contract was one of the recurrent issues during the nineteenth century.[5] Generalizations about the law as it developed in the different American states (not to mention the English cases) over long periods of time are somewhat dangerous, and subject to qualification. With that caveat entered, however, the dominant position routinely invoked some doctrine of forfeiture usually to preclude, but occasionally to reduce, the amount of damages recoverable by a plaintiff. The diversity of views on when and how forfeiture should be imposed might be taken to show compromise on the forfeiture issue. But in this context at least, there is less to the point than meets the eye. The conditions of forfeiture varied from strict to quite strict. A review of a few leading cases makes the point.

One constantly litigated question during the nineteenth century concerned employment contracts entered into between farmers and field hands. The typical agreement stipulated that the field hand was to work on the farm for a year and was to receive room and board while in the

---

[5] For a useful set of materials, see Friedrich Kessler and G. Grant Gilmore, *Contracts: Cases and Materials*, 2d ed. (Boston: Little, Brown, 1970), pp. 871-911.

farmer's employ and a cash payment (often set at $120) payable at the end of the year of service. In the cases at hand, the farmhand quit the employ before the end of the year, and then sued for the proportionate part of the cash payment equal to the months served. Thus, if the farmhand worked for nine months, then his claim would be for $90. The question before the courts was whether he should be entitled to recover that payment.

The temptation to allow this recovery was surely substantial. To see why, suppose that the farmhand worked for 364 days of the year and quit the day before the expiration of the contract. Looked at from that time forward, the denial of any cash compensation for the 364 days worked could easily be treated as saying that the allocated payment for the last day's employment was room and board for a day plus $120, for those are the benefits forgone when the farmhand quits the day before. In addition, the farmhand could argue that the defendant is left *better off* by the plaintiff's breach of this contract than by his performance to the letter of the agreement. After all, most farmers would prefer 364 days' work and $120 in hand to 365 days' work and an empty pocket. And if there were any inconvenience in losing a day's labor, such as might arise if the crops were left at risk before harvesting, a payment of $5 or $10 to fill the gap surely would have attracted an extensive queue of otherwise reluctant substitutes.

Yet the dominant legal view in transactions of this sort was that the plaintiff received no cash compensation given the early departure. The explanation here rested on several grounds, all of which suffer severe erosion after the rise of the welfare state. One argument is that nonpayment was understood to be in conformity with the custom of the realm. In *Stark v. Parker* (1824), just this situation arose when the plaintiff, who was entitled to $120 at the end of the year, quit after nine and one-half months and claimed $95 for his labors. Judge Lincoln noted pointedly:

> [T]he usages of the country and common opinion upon subjects of this description are especially to be regarded, and we are bound judicially to take notice of which no one is in fact ignorant. It may be safe to affirm that in no case has a contract in the terms of the one under consideration, been construed by practical men to give a right to demand the agreed compensation, before the performance of the labor, and that the employer and the employed alike universally so understand it.[6]

Immediately, two common themes of the nineteenth-century worldview surge to the fore. The first concerns the problem of knowledge and its relationship to custom. Here, the court has no doubt that everyone understood exactly what the situation was. The custom was very strong, indeed invariant. That is why the court did not hesitate to say that it could

---

[6] *Stark v. Parker*, 19 Mass. 267, 274 (1824).

take judicial notice of a custom not formally put into evidence. Nor did this case amount to any exception to the general rule, for here employer and employee alike, with no differentiation with respect to status, had equal knowledge of the custom and both had contracted in reliance on it. Any thought that inequality of bargaining position, or imperfect information, could upset the contractual relationships is far removed from the passages just quoted. The modern law of unconscionability would not take so dispassionate a view on this question, with employment contracts, or anywhere else.[7]

The second theme concerns the sanctity of the basic agreement. Judge Lincoln proceeds to note that the plaintiff's demand of proration leads to the creation of a contract very different from the "entire" arrangement (the bonus is paid only if the contract is performed by the farmhand in its entirety) agreed to by the parties. "The plaintiff might as well claim his wages by the month as by the year, by the week as by the month, and by the day or hour as by either."[8] The point here is not without its intellectual force. The plaintiff in effect claims the right to redo the arrangement such that it provides that if he leaves after nine months, he is entitled to $90 in cash. If that division is possible, then the original agreement is recast into a series of options not installed in the original agreement, some of which could prove quite disadvantageous to the farmer. Thus, the proration would work a real injustice if agricultural hiring were all done at the beginning of the growing season: if the departure took place within a week or two of the original hiring, then the pickings are slim, as the good farmhands for the year have already taken jobs elsewhere. Once we start to rewrite a contract, it is far from clear which new divisions are unique or even desirable.

The same concern could be raised by looking at the case as a matter of reciprocity of advantage. Thus, if this farmhand is allowed to depart early and claim the proportionate share of the bonus, then is the same right granted to the employer, who could then cast the farmhand out of a job with impunity, so long as he is prepared to pay the proportionate bonus? Yet that solution could easily result in massive inconvenience if the hiring season is over so that the farmhand cannot find on short notice suitable employment for the remainder of the term. The insistence on a strong sense of legal obligation binding on the employee thus offers the employee a substantial benefit: it builds one more bulwark that prevents the erosion of the farmer's contractual obligations. The greater security—that the employer's return promise to the worker means just what it says, no

---

[7] The most famous case on unconscionability is still *Williams v. Walker-Thomas Furniture Co.*, 350 F.2d 445 (D.C. 1965) (use of standard printed contract for seller's lien on property, held unconscionable). Clauses that eliminated recovery against manufacturers for physical injury arising from the sale of their products have also been held unconscionable. See, e.g., *Henningsen v. Bloomfield Motors, Inc.*, 161 A.2d 69 (N.J. 1960).

[8] *Stark v. Parker*, p. 273.

more and no less—is a powerful inducement for farmhands to enter into these contracts in the first place.

In one sense, however, the decision in *Stark* was not driven by both of these considerations. Behind the decision in favor of the employer was its condemnation of the misbehavior of the employee. Over and over again the court stresses the same theme: "Nothing can be more unreasonable than that a man, who deliberately and wantonly violates an engagement, should be permitted to seek in a court of justice an indemnity from the consequences of his voluntary act; and we are satisfied that the law will not allow it."[9] The court had a real sense of outrage that *any person*, regardless of social status or position, would choose voluntarily to breach an agreement and then to sue on the very contract that has been breached. If anything, the only person who should have an action on the contract would be the farmer whose rights have been violated. If he does not sue, the sole explanation is that the unpaid bonus on the contract operates as security in excess of any damages that could be suffered: so self-help, by keeping all the unpaid wages, removes the need of a lawsuit to control the breach of a farmhand.

The law therefore does not lift a single finger to soften the plight of those who break their promises. Yet by the same token, it is alert to advantage-taking on the other side.

> Any apprehension that this rule may be abused to the purposes of oppression, by holding out an inducement to the employer, by unkind treatment near the close of a term of service, to drive the laborer from his engagement, to the sacrifice of his wages, is wholly groundless. It is only in cases where the desertion is voluntary and without cause on the part of the laborer, or fault or consent on the part of the employer, that the principle applies.[10]

A judge who has never heard of "moral hazard" or "bilateral opportunism" has an instinctive sense for the risks that they create, and provides a defense against employer misconduct by fashioning an exception to the

---

[9] *Ibid.*, p. 273. Similar sentiments are found in passages on pp. 271 and 274. That sentiment was also expressed in other contexts. See, e.g., *Smith v. Brady*, 17 N.Y. 173, 186 (1858), where the same sentiment was echoed in connection with building contracts where the plaintiff builder delivers a building that does not comply in all relevant respects with contract specifications. In this case, the builder sought to recover for the benefit conferred, but was rebuffed with sentiments similar to those expressed above:

> Indeed, in this state the sanctity of contracts in this respect at least, has been steadily maintained, and no encouragement has ever been given to that loose and dangerous doctrine which allows a person to violate his most solemn engagements and then to draw the injured into a controversy concerning the amount and value of the benefits received.

[10] *Stark v. Parker*, p. 275.

defense that the employee quit within term and thus forfeited his wages.[11]
Put together, the whole system has an intellectual simplicity and structural integrity that might lead us to assume that it commanded universal
respect.

Nonetheless, the interpretation of this labor contract illustrates once
again that every legal proposition dissolves into a majority and a minority
rule.[12] *Brittain v. Turner* (1834) was the leading authority for the contrary
legal position.[13] There Judge Parker's opinion did not dwell on custom
and common understanding. Rather, Parker allowed the plaintiff's action
(in this case for $95 for nine and one-half months of service) for two
reasons. First, he thought that it was very odd that the defendant should
be left better off in light of the plaintiff's breach than he would have been
if the contract had been performed to the letter. Hence, there was the
concern about the windfall, and, of course, about the possibility that the
astute defendant might, as Judge Lincoln observed in *Stark*, take steps to
procure the breach. Parker understood, however, that the plaintiff in breach
of contract could not sue on the strength of that contract. Rather, he
believed that an action for unjust enrichment (sometimes called an action
for restitution) should allow the worker to recover his proportionate share
of wages, subject to set-off by the employer for the amount of the loss in
question. He thus writes:

> The rule, by binding the employer to pay the value of the service he
> actually receives, and the laborer to answer in damages where he
> does not complete the entire contract, will leave no temptation to the
> former to drive the laborer from his service, near the close of his
> term, by ill treatment, in order to escape from payment; nor to the
> latter to desert his service before the stipulated time, without a suf-
> ficient reason; and it will in most instances settle the whole contro-
> versy in one action, and prevent a multiplicity of suits.
>
> There may be instances, however, where the damage occasioned is
> much greater than the value of the labor performed, and if the party

---

[11] "Moral hazard" refers to the fact that once insurance is provided against a certain
contingency, the likelihood of its occurrence will increase. Here it means that if the worker
can recover the proportionate share of his wages, then he is more likely to quit. "Opportunism" refers to the willingness of self-interested persons to take advantage of whatever
weaknesses they find in their trading partners. The worker who knows that his labor cannot
be monitored precisely may take the opportunity to slack off in midday. The opportunism
is "bilateral" since these opportunities present themselves to both sides: e.g., an employer
who hires a worker by the job may have the incentive to supply him with inferior tools. It
is much more difficult to adjust contractual rules when both sides have the opportunity to
misbehave. Indeed, it is virtually impossible to eliminate both forms of opportunism simultaneously. The sensible contract therefore tries to minimize the cost of opportunism on both
sides, plus the cost of its prevention.

[12] On *Stark* representing the majority rule, see Note in 26 American Decisions (1881), cited
in Kessler and Gilmore, *Contracts: Cases and Materials*, p. 878.

[13] *Brittain v. Turner*, 6 N.H. 481 (1834). Judge Parker is said to have put the citation of this
opinion on his gravestone, so much weight did he attach to the issue.

[i.e., the employer] elects to permit himself to be charged for the value of the labor, without interposing the damages in defense, he is entitled to do so, and may have an action to recover his damages for nonperformance.[14]

This passage narrows the gap between the majority and the minority rule. The source of the convergence is that both decisions are concerned with the possibility of opportunism on both sides of the deal. Here Judge Parker celebrates his rule for precisely the same reason that Judge Lincoln celebrated the opposite rule: it prevents employer abuse to induce breach before the end of term. The only difference is that Lincoln sought to prevent that abuse by reinstating the laborer's action when the employer misbehaved, while Parker was prepared to allow that action in all cases, knowing that the employer would have little reason to induce the farmhand to quit if he were liable to pay for the labor previously expended, *quantum meruit*, for whatever it was worth.

Yet Judge Parker also realizes that misbehavior is a two-way street, and here he provides the farmer with two weapons to combat abuse from the hired hand. The first allows the farmer to use any loss sustained from the farmhand's breach of contract as a setoff against the damages that would otherwise be employed. Thus, if the farmer had to pay $30 in wages to hire a new laborer for the remaining two and one-half months, incurring $10 in additional costs in searching for a new laborer, then presumably the $95 recovery should be reduced by $15 to $80 to compensate for the $5 wage hike and the $10 search cost. Second, Parker's desire to avoid a multiplicity of actions (by allowing the setoff against wages when the employee sued) showed his desire to improve the operation of the system by reducing administrative costs. For all our criticism of the archaic formalism of the nineteenth century, how many cases make it into court today for $25, even adjusted forty-fold (at a guess) for inflation. The legal system today is simply not efficient enough to process many disputes that are worth $1,000 or less.

Place these two decisions side by side, and their similarities dominate their differences. The difference in behavioral incentives created by the two different sets of rules is at most marginal, and largely turns on which legal regime makes the better guess on the distributional question of whether the employee should receive some of the cash promised at the end of the contract. If Judge Lincoln is correct about the custom and usages of the country, then presumably he has the better of the argument by giving the employer the dominant hand. Nonetheless, by treating worker and employer on conditions of rough parity—including their equal ability to commit abuse—both contractual regimes should be equal to the task of policing these employment contracts. Indeed, the main

---

[14] *Ibid.*, p. 495.

difference between the two rules lies less in their incentive effects, and more in who gets to keep the cash payment when the worker quits within term. The dominant view assigned it to the employer in accordance with contract, and the minority view returned it back to the worker. Even here, however, the worker could negotiate a settlement with the employer which resulted in his keeping some portion of his pay. For the long-term operation of the system, the distribution of the cash payment is less important than the incentive problems that any legal rule must confront. There is nothing in *Brittain* that smacks of the protective rules of labor law that are encountered so frequently in modern times, both at common law and by statute. The use of the forfeiture rule, then, is not only important in itself. It is a powerful marker of the theory of individual responsibility that seemed to underlie both the majority and minority approaches to labor contracts in earlier times.

2. *Tort.* The question of forfeiture also arose in connection with the role of the plaintiff's conduct in tort cases. At a formal level, the problem is similar in many ways to the contractual issue. The usual division of the elements of a lawsuit is between the plaintiff's claim and the defendant's substantive defenses to it. The plaintiff's claim focuses on what the defendant has done to the plaintiff. The question of forfeiture arises as a defense that admits the defendant's wrongdoing and then asks whether the plaintiff should be denied recovery because of his own conduct. The critical question is whether the same standards should be applied to the conduct of both parties, or whether the plaintiff should receive some special dispensation that expands the circumstances under which compensation is awarded, or increases the amount that is paid.

The answer to this question depends on the nature of the relationships between the parties. In cases between persons who have no direct contractual connection with each other, there is a good deal to be said for the evenhanded treatment. Thus, when two drivers collide on a public highway, the parties have not previously entered into a cooperative arrangement that could diminish their equal obligation to obey the rules of the road. Neither has assumed any special obligation for the care of the other person. The usual common-law response in these cases has been to treat the standard of care required of the plaintiff as identical to the basic negligence standard required of the defendant. Even today, in dealing with accidents on the highway, we adopt a general position that holds plaintiffs and defendants to the same standards of the rules of the road, and we require teenage drivers to observe the same standards of care as their seniors.[15]

The highway cases are themselves not a good benchmark to gauge the rise of the welfare state. The accidents in question are often caused by

---

[15] See, e.g., *Daniels v. Evans*, 224 A.2d 63 (N.H. 1966), overruling an earlier twentieth-century case—*Charbonneau v. MacRury*, 153 A. 457 (N.H. 1931)—that did allow some leeway for minors in highway accidents.

individuals acting in their individual capacity. Even when the harms in question are caused or suffered by large trucks or other commercial vehicles, very little of what is done can be attributed to some ostensible abuse of their market power. Most people have a sense that it is to some extent a matter of luck who is hurt in a collision, and the overall tendency, even today, has been to think about improvements in traffic rules, road construction, and vehicular safety, in order to minimize the losses in question. The real question of class conflicts arose in connection with the industrial-accident cases, which once again involved the relationship between employers and employees. At first blush, it might be assumed that the same form of parity that was found in the hired-hand cases should carry over to the newer industrial accidents. The same standards of care applicable to defendant employers should be applied with equal force to individual workers.

Yet this conclusion would be premature. The task in accident avoidance is to try to elicit that form of cooperative behavior between the parties that would maximize the net return from their joint investments in safety.[16] The task is not to minimize the number of accidents; nor to minimize the precautions taken to avoid them. It is to minimize the net costs of accidents and their prevention. In dealing with this question, identical precautions between the parties would make sense, if at all, only to the extent that the parties had identical capacities to avoid accidents. In workplace situations, however, that condition is often not satisfied. Workers, in effect, can only take those individual precautions that relate to their own safety. They cannot institute changes in basic structure or capital equipment to avoid the losses in question. In addition, in contrast with the wage cases discussed above, the employee labors under a powerful incentive to take care that operates independently of the liability rule. Be careless and *your* life and limb could be at risk. Employers, for their part, have greater institutional capacity to avoid harm, and less natural incentive, apart from liability, to do it.

The legal system, even in the nineteenth century, responded to this difference in risk. The basic forfeiture position was still in place, for a plaintiff otherwise entitled to recover could be precluded from doing so by his own negligent conduct. By the same token, however, the level of care required of an individual employee was usually adjusted to take into account the perceived differences in position and incentives. While there has been some effort to assert that the law showed a systematic favoritism

---

[16] For a small sample of the enormous history on industrial-accident law, see, e.g., *Farwell v. Boston and Worcester R.R. Corp.*, 45 Mass. 49 (1842); *Lamson v. American Axe and Tool Co.*, 58 N.E. 585 (Mass. 1900); C. B. Labatt, *Commentaries on the Law of Master and Servant*, 2d ed. (Rochester, NY: Lawyers Co-operative Pub. Co., 1913), sections 1433–1533; T. G. Shearman and A. A. Redfield, *A Treatise on the Law of Negligence*, 5th ed. (New York: Baker, Voorhis, and Company, 1898); and Richard A. Posner, "A Theory of Negligence," *Journal of Legal Studies*, vol. 1 (1972), pp. 67–71.

to the defendant,[17] closer examination of the cases undercuts the case for judicial bias.[18] The employer who was in a position to take systematic precautions could be required to protect an individual plaintiff against momentary confusion or mistake.

Some further evidence of the asymmetrical positions of employers and employees with respect to this risk can be found in the rise of workers' compensation systems in the second half of the nineteenth century. These systems began as voluntary contractual responses to industrial accidents, and not as mandatory state programs.[19] These systems all operated around a basic bargain that altered both sides of the common-law equation of negligence and contributory negligence. The injured worker no longer had to prove the employer's negligence as was the case at common law. Instead, the liability of the employer became strict for all "personal injuries by accident arising out of and in the course of employment," i.e., for all work-related injuries. The employee's quid pro quo was that damages were sharply limited. In most cases, a full recovery under the contractual compensation system did not leave the injured party (if alive) as well off as if the injury had never occurred in the first place. Yet that limitation on recovery had its own social function. The worker who knew about the limited level of recovery would stay away from certain dangerous forms of work if his chances of injury were great, or his own risk of loss unusually large, say because of some preexisting health condition. Those workers who did take the job now had a real incentive to avoid injury, precisely because they knew that even with a full recovery they would not come out whole. Moreover, since the damage awards were set low, it followed that the contributory-negligence defense was no longer necessary to curb misconduct by plaintiffs. The upshot was that recovery of damages was forfeited only in cases involving a worker's reckless behavior or willful misconduct.

Although this system formally weakened the level of defenses, it did not ignore the risk of the worker's misbehavior (moral hazard again) that drives the legal response to forfeiture. The reduced recovery means that an employee loses even when he wins: namely, the recovery does not put him back in the position he would have enjoyed if the injury had never taken place. The willful-misconduct doctrine applied more stringent restrictions to the most outrageous forms of worker misconduct: e.g., deliberate self-injury, or drunken misbehavior. The overall situation thus seems to satisfy the two tests of social efficiency. First, its voluntary nature

---

[17] See Lawrence Friedman, *A History of American Law* (New York: Simon and Schuster, 1973), pp. 411–12, where Friedman calls the doctrine of contributory negligence a "cunning trap."

[18] See Gary Schwartz, "Tort Law and the Economy in Nineteenth-Century America: A Reinterpretation," *Yale Law Journal*, vol. 90 (1981), in which Schwartz rejects the Friedman hypothesis.

[19] For this history, see Richard A. Epstein, "The Historical Origins and Intellectual Structure of the Workers' Compensation Laws," *Georgia Law Review*, vol. 16 (1982).

suggests that it marks a systematic improvement over the common-law regimes that it displaced, at least in the settings where the displacement took effect. And second, its incentive properties suggest that it seeks to devise a set of asymmetrical rules to handle the somewhat different positions of the two sides to the arrangements. The great lesson to be learned here is this: Efforts to impose restrictions on defendants to reduce losses cannot ignore the problem of plaintiff's conduct, a problem that requires some doctrine of forfeiture.

B. Charitable obligations

The forfeiture question also arises in cases of charitable support for persons in need. It takes little imagination to see that this question cannot be addressed by a system of market rules that promote mutual benefit through voluntary exchange. The entire object of a system of charity is to work some form of wealth transfer from those who have wealth to those who do not. That system is driven by the common perception that ordinary people can make interpersonal comparisons of utility in their own lives—that is, can decide if other people have greater need for their wealth than they do—even if they cannot quantify them with the precision demanded by welfare economists, who too often dwell on the logical impossibility of such comparisons.

The operation of a system of charitable transfers overlaps in part with voluntary exchanges, for the extensive network of mutual aid societies during the nineteenth century seemed to be a cross between systems of market insurance and a social support network. Thus, premiums or dues could be charged for membership, although it was far from clear that all individuals put in sums that were calibrated in any close sense to their expected payouts.[20] In part, however, that is precisely the point. The charitable efforts flowed from other forms of human interaction and were not kept isolated or distinct from them. For the purposes of this essay, the critical insight is that the dispensation of charitable assistance, in whatever form it took, did not take place in blithe indifference to matters of system design, including those which deal with recipient conduct. Nonetheless, the rules in question have to be adjusted for the matter at hand in two separate domains. The first determines the extent to which charitable

[20] For a sense of the uneasy mix between mutual support, self-sufficiency, and help to those in need in Great Britain, see Stephen Davies, "Two Conceptions of Welfare: Voluntarism and Incorporationism," elsewhere in this volume; and for the analogous American experience, see David Beito, "'This Enormous Army': The Mutual Aid Tradition of American Fraternal Societies before the Twentieth Century," elsewhere in this volume. Precise numbers are hard to come by, but these movements were neither evanescent nor trivial in their scope. The cash payments were only part of the network of support services they provided. For further evidence of the size of these programs, see Marvin Olasky, The Tragedy of American Compassion (Washington, DC: Regnery Gateway, 1992); Olasky notes, for example, that the New York Children's Aid Society helped 91,000 children between 1854 and 1872 (p. 35).

operations are subject to legal sanctions. The second is a set of social rules, difficult to quantify, but which nonetheless guide the operations of any charitable organization in its day-to-day affairs. The connection between these two sets of sanctions is inverse: the broader the scope of the legal rules, the more limited the scope for the social norms.

The nineteenth-century attitude toward this relationship is captured in two concepts. First, in line with earlier thinkers, charitable conduct was regarded as a species of imperfect obligation; the moral duties to assist the poor were not directed to any particular person, and in consequence the enforcement of these duties was left to an uneasy amalgam of moral and social sanctions, or to individual conscience and to expressions of social disapproval. The legal system was cut out from deciding which individuals should have access to charity and which should not.

That systemic view was captured in two related doctrines. The first was that charities were entitled to exclude anyone they chose from the receipt of their services, no matter how great the need.[21] The position stemmed from the strict common-law view that ordinary persons had the right to exclude others from the use of their property and to withhold services to whomsoever they saw fit: exclusion from property, absolute choice of contracting partners, and choice of donees all went hand in hand.[22] The second half of the doctrine was one of charitable immunity for the ordinary negligence of charitable institutions.[23] That doctrine prevented suit against the providers of medical services, first prohibiting suits brought by indigent patients and then by paying patients as well.[24] The position was sensibly qualified in two different ways. First, it was generally recognized that the immunity in question did not extend to various torts that a charity committed against third persons in the ordinary course of its business. A charity could not hide behind its immunity if waste dis-

---

[21] *McDonald v. Massachusetts General Hospital*, 120 Mass. 432 (1876).

[22] Here it is important not to be too dogmatic about the role of exclusion, either at common law or in theory. The traditional common-law rules negated both the right to exclude and with it the right to set prices as one saw fit in all the common-carrier cases, covering stagecoaches and railroads, and innkeepers. A duty to charge only reasonable rates and to avoid discrimination between parties was the price exacted for the creation of the monopoly position. See, e.g., *Allnutt v. Inglis*, 104 Eng. Rep. 206 (K.B. 1810). The questions of monopoly power are not in issue with cases of charitable care, so that the basic rules on exclusivity applied, as in *McDonald* (*supra* note 21).

[23] See, e.g., *Powers v. Massachusetts Homeopathic Hospital*, 109 F. 294, 304 (1st Cir. 1901):

> If, in their dealings with their property appropriated to charity, they [members of the hospital board] create a nuisance by themselves or by their servants, if they dig pitfalls in their grounds and the like, there are strong reasons for holding them liable to outsiders, like any other individual or corporation. The purity of their aims may not justify their torts; but, if a suffering man avails himself of their charity, he takes the risks of malpractice, if their charitable agents have been carefully selected.

[24] *Schumacher v. Evangelical Deaconess Society of Wisconsin*, 260 N.W. 476 (Wis. 1935) (extending the immunity for a paying patient).

charged from its facilities contaminated the well of a neighbor; nor was it immune from liability if its delivery trucks struck and injured a pedestrian. The only persons who presumptively waived the charity's legal liability were those who received medical care. Yet even here the charity could waive all or some of its legal protection by contract. For example, it could purchase malpractice insurance for the protection of its patients.[25]

At first glance, these doctrines seem distinctly unlovely and wholly inhospitable to persons who are in need of medical care. Poor people are asked to run the risk of total exclusion from needed services and to bear the risk associated with the provision of inferior care. Paradoxically, however, the risk of exclusion and of uncompensated injury in large measure spurred the growth of charitable institutions during the last third of the nineteenth century. The explanation for the apparent contradiction lies in the way that these stony doctrines tied in with the broader set of social and moral sanctions used to encourage charitable care. No one was obligated to set up a charitable institution. It was thought, therefore, that one important function of a sound legal system was not to place undue impediments in the path of charitable initiatives. After the fact, it is easy to focus on individual miscarriages of justice caused by charitable institutions left to their own devices. But it is of even greater importance to ask what legal rules will bring forth the greatest burst of charitable activity in the first place. The freedom of action preserved by the common-law approach offers just that powerful inducement. It is easy to dwell on the few individuals who suffered the sting of exclusion or malpractice. But one should never forget the hundreds and thousands of persons whose access to care was made possible precisely because charitable institutions were untouched by any onerous forms of regulation or liability.

The system of charitable care also needed to develop a set of social sanctions to control the need for its services. No individual or group could enter the charitable business with the expectation that recipient fees would cover the cost of doing business. By the same token, however, it was absolutely critical to develop practices to prevent the people who received care for little or no charge from consuming excessive resources. The question of moral hazard, so evident in the employment context, does not disappear just because we have moved over to the charitable arena. Charitable budgets are often fixed, or at least limited. Resources devoted to indigents who do not need treatment are necessarily diverted from those who do. It becomes critical, then, to develop a nonprice rationing system to secure the maximum benefits from charitable care.

It was for just this reason that the classical system created a strong division between the "deserving" and the "nondeserving" poor, with the latter receiving a lower priority of care than the former. Marvin Olasky

---

[25] See, e.g., *Wendt v. Servite Fathers*, 76 N.E.2d 342 (Ill. App. 1947).

has described this system well.[26] From colonial times through the early twentieth century, a powerful moral ambivalence surrounded the dispensation of charitable care. The religious underpinnings for charitable help posited an unquestionable moral obligation to assist the poor in their time of need, but that obligation was consciously tempered by a genuine distrust of many of the poor and their motives. It was not easy to reconcile the abstract duty with the concrete need. Need in and of itself did not guarantee assistance. It was important to know *why* a person was in need of care, and how that condition related to questions of character and moral worth. To speak of the "idle" or the "slothful poor," to berate the poor who were "dissolute," or "stubborn, disorderly, and disobedient," was perceived as commendable realism, not moral smugness or undue character assassination. The prevailing ethos of the time was on constant guard against the sentimental idealism that could lead charitable efforts astray.

To be sure, the term "moral hazard" had not yet been invented, let alone applied to charitable activities. Nonetheless, the early writers on charity, driven in large measure by their religious conception of human sin (original or otherwise) wrote and acted just as if they had patented the term. If sloth and idleness were the enemy, then work, at the direction of the master of the poorhouse, was the antidote. "It would be an evident Breach of the Law of the Gospel, as well as of Nature, to bestow upon those the Bread of Charity, who might earn and eat their own Bread, if they did not shamefully idle away their Time."[27] One pointed irony in the passage should not go unnoticed. The Law of Nature has often been treated as the source of the obligation to provide charitable care. Ironically, however, appeals to the doctrine could cut in both directions, for it was a *breach* of the Law of Nature to bestow charity on those who did not deserve it. Social institutions, such as the poorhouse, were established to force the idle to make do with bread and water while others received a more substantial meal for their labors.

Next the traditional accounts of charity were careful to specify the kinds of causes that merited full assistance for individual victims and their families. These correlated with the conception of an Act of God or *vis maior* at common law. This category includes the victims of storm, fire, earthquake, or other calamity.[28] At the time, no person could be held legally responsible for the harms thus sustained, so there was an evident gap between victim need and legal responsibility that charitable care could fill. Victims of these events had evident need that charitable help could satisfy. That was also true of individuals who were injured or made

[26] For a detailed statement of the attitudes and practices that existed under this system, see Olasky, *The Tragedy of American Compassion* (*supra* note 20), ch. 1.

[27] Charles Chauncy, writing in 1752 to the Society for Encouraging Industry and Employing the Poor, quoted in Olasky, *The Tragedy of American Compassion*, p. 10.

[28] Olasky, *The Tragedy of American Compassion*, p. 7.

ill through drinking or cavorting. In these cases, however, providing aid held out the risk of underwriting socially destructive forms of conduct. It was no coincidence that the temperance movement operated in earnest during this time, and potential recipients of charity were routinely checked for alcoholism.[29] In all cases, the fundamental operating principle was that knowledge of the origin of the loss offered reliable evidence about the recipient's character. Assistance to the victims of natural disasters did not induce any discernible level of the undesirable kinds of conduct that might lead to illness, injury, or disease. Helping dissolute individuals did. Accordingly, the aid was provided in those cases where it was least likely to alter for the worst the primary conduct of the recipient of charity.

The form in which the aid was supplied was critical as well. Often religious groups provided the direct assistance in religious environments. Charity was never made in the form of a simple cash grant.[30] No one received chits or coupons to be spent as he or she saw fit. These could be bartered away, or if used to purchased useful goods, those goods could be exchanged afterwards for prohibited items, such as alcohol or tobacco. In order to avoid the illicit conversion of charitable assistance, the food and service provided had to be consumed in plain view of the charitable provider. Nor were these gifts in kind provided without conditions: the provision of material support was paired with instruction in one comprehensive package, especially for children. In particular, religious orders made it a point to work with (and thereby monitor and guide the conduct of) the recipient so as to prevent the emergence of any untoward behavior.[31] For the most stubborn recipients, the receipt of aid was often dependent on quite literally moving into a poorhouse, a total-control environment, whose master had the power to dispense favors for those who followed the rules and to impose sanctions on those who did not.[32]

Finally, the consensus view was that charitable work had to be done at a very local and immediate level, one recipient at a time. Olasky quotes a wonderful dialogue from McGuffey's Reader—the standard text used in nineteenth-century elementary education—that stresses the importance of modest ambitions properly executed. In response to Mr. Fantom's (McGuffey's names, like Shakespeare's, often make their own point) protestations that he thinks that charity can relieve the miseries *of the whole world* ("It is provinces, empires, continents, that the benevolence of the philosopher embraces; every one can do a little paltry good to his next neighbor"), Mr. Goodman responds, "Every one *can*, but I do not see that every one *does*. . . . [You] have such a noble zeal for the *millions*, [yet] feel so little compassion for the units."[33] Compassion is thus not regarded as

---

[29] *Ibid.*, p. 13.
[30] *Ibid.*
[31] *Ibid.*, p. 14.
[32] *Ibid.*, p. 11.
[33] *Ibid.*, p. 20.

an uncritical social ideal to which we should all aspire. Rather, it is a decidedly mixed blessing that can too easily lead us astray when we become sentimental about the motives and conduct of the recipients of charity. To counter possible abuse, the aid has to be supplied at the local level, by those who know and understand the recipients, and their propensity to misbehave.

The distinction between the deserving or worthy poor, on the one hand, and the undeserving and unworthy poor, on the other, has an unpleasant ring to the modern ear. It smacks of a distasteful mix of moral certitude, complacency, and superiority. It bespeaks a contempt for those less fortunate than oneself. It is, in a sense, far easier to administer a system of care for the poor and needy without having to make dubious evaluations of the moral worth of those persons who receive it.

The unpleasantness was not lost on private organizations in earlier times who sought to administer their own systems of charity. The anxieties of its day-to-day application had to be more evident to those people who policed the line between the deserving and the underserving poor than it would have been to the people who think the line irrelevant. It was considered just as difficult then as it is now to give aid to the wife and the children while denying it to the husband and father who was known to be a drunkard.[34] Aid was a "tied good"; that is, it was quite impossible to aid the drunkard's wife and children without having some benefit spilling over to the drunkard himself. It therefore took a good deal of ingenuity to structure aid so that as much as possible went to its intended beneficiaries. But whatever the embarrassments in the marginal case, the nineteenth-century view placed the distinction between the deserving and the underserving poor center-stage in the operation of the system because charitable organizations understood that many cases lay at either pole. Charities had to find ways to raise the resources needed to discharge their functions, which they could not do if they spent their resources in ways that aggravated the very practices they were seeking to curtail. The threat of forfeiture of the benefit was the best way to constrain misbehavior and stretch out scarce resources in a nonprice environment. The practice of singling out the deserving poor is an attempt, at the cost of some very delicate judgments at the margin, to counteract self-destructive patterns of human behavior by reducing the level of charitable care. It is far more difficult to administer a system that seeks simultaneously to provide charitable care while curtailing access to the system, than it is to administer a system that seeks simply to aid those in need, without regard to how they came to be in their condition.

At every juncture, then, the nineteenth-century view makes it necessary to walk the fine line between the toughness needed to contain asocial behaviors and the guarded sense of compassion for those who have fallen

[34] *Ibid.*

victim to them. Deciding exactly how this dilemma should be resolved is not an easy business, even for those with the best of intentions. It requires hands-on knowledge and long experience to make judgments of this sort—assuming that anyone can make them. And it requires a cadre of unpaid workers whose dominant motivation is often religious and always charitable.

Courts and legislatures cannot duplicate these successes. They cannot draw on an army of volunteers, often motivated by a sense of religious zeal, to administer the programs that they support. Rather, they must hire staff, and must often contend with a complex matrix of hiring rules and union regulations that impede the effective mobilization of their bureaucratic staffs. Nor is it likely that this complex bureaucratic structure can police the full range of substantive issues that caught the attention of the nineteenth-century charitable workers. On the one hand, remote impersonal directives issuing from some bureaucratic center are likely to ignore important differences in individual cases that can be apparent in the field. On the other hand, a grant of large discretion to individual field-workers opens up the specter of abuse in the administration of the laws. The public welfare system therefore lurches between efforts to obtain predictability and efforts to maintain flexibility, and is as likely to miss on both as it is to hit on both. Thus, for example, the constitutional requirement that all welfare recipients receive a hearing prior to the termination of their benefits[35] gives rise to the sensible objection that the wrong people are allowed to milk the system for too long while needy applicants are denied the necessary aid.[36] The point here is empirical and not logical. It is quite difficult to develop any formal bureaucratic structure that can imitate the best features of the earlier charitable system. It seems even more clear that modern programs of welfare reform are doomed to fail if they do not recognize the full range of problems that nineteenth-century theorists confronted when fashioning their own system of charitable relief.

III. The Twentieth-Century Welfare State

The impact of the rise of the welfare state on all of these areas (contract, tort, and charitable provision) is reflected by a shift in two dimensions: in the scope of the basic case for liability or entitlement, as the case may be; and in the grounds on which individuals forfeit their basic protections. Here it is only necessary to trace briefly the transformations in attitude on the question of forfeiture to show how large the gulf has become between the earlier and the modern law. Once again, it is useful to retrace the order of the previous discussion. I shall begin with the private law of contract

---

[35] See, e.g., *Goldberg v. Kelly*, 397 U.S. 254 (1970).
[36] See Jerry L. Mashaw, *Due Process in the Administrative State* (New Haven, CT: Yale University Press, 1985), pp. 34–35.

and tort, and thereafter move on to a discussion of the modern rules that
set the obligations that institutions have to persons in need of assistance.

A. The common-law areas

1. *Contract.* The shift in the attitude on contracts is once again illustrated by a brief tour of employment law. The older regime stressed the
parity of position between employer and employee and sought to set its
rules to counter the opportunism on both sides of the relationship. The
same dual sense of suspicion applied to the legal regulation of other
relationships, including landlord-tenant, producer-consumer, owner-
builder, and the like. But the modern rules start from the opposite direction and often presuppose that one side in the relationship (guess which?)
is powerful and capable of serious misconduct. In contrast, it is assumed
that the other side in the relationship is subject to exploitation but is, at
the same time, largely incapable of its own brand of serious misconduct.
In addition, it is commonly presupposed that various kinds of social
sanctions will not work to curb these perceived excesses: reputation, for
example, is usually treated as an insufficient or unimportant check on
various breaches of social norms, even though large, established firms
spend enormous sums to maintain and enhance their goodwill.

Taken together, these two assumptions largely dictate the form of the
modern law. Once again, it is instructive to focus on the employment
contract. So long as it is primarily employers, and not employees, who are
capable of abuse, then the law should direct all its firepower against the
party that is most likely to do wrong. Where reputation is thought to no
longer afford an effective sanction against misbehavior, the law has to
redouble its efforts to protect the weaker party against exploitation. Indeed, the very use of the term "exploitation" signals a rejection of the
older principle of contract as a potential source of mutual gain, as exem-
plified in the farmer/laborer cases, and brings to the fore a newer principle that treats contracts as akin to theft: the employer gains from contract
only because the employee loses.

Now, clearly, one cannot have a contract law that bans all employment
contracts, so the newer approach exacts its toll in an indirect fashion. One
common form of contract at common law stated that the arrangement
could be "at will" on both sides. There was nothing that prevented the
parties from making the common arrangement that allowed the employer
to fire, and the worker to quit, for good reason, bad reason, or no reason
at all.[37] These contracts at will rank among the most common forms of
employment contract because of their evident simplicity, but they have
increasingly been rejected by courts that insist as a matter of public policy

---

[37] For a discussion of these issues, see Richard A. Epstein, *Simple Rules for a Complex World*
(Cambridge, MA: Harvard University Press, 1995), pp. 151–93.

that wrongful dismissals be sanctioned with heavy damage actions.[38] The same attitude surely carries over in the creation of statutory regulations governing the employment contract, all of which are driven by the vision of contractual exploitation. The American National Labor Relations Act,[39] for example, works on the assumption that competitive markets yield exploitation; and in response, the act creates a complicated bargaining structure that forces an employer to bargain with a union representative chosen by election. In the transportation industry, the workers do not have to face the threat of lockouts or the hiring of permanent replacements, for they are not required to take the economic risk of going on strike.[40] Rather, they receive the power to hold on to the present employment relationship no matter how inefficient it has become with the passage of time.[41] In addition, the constant theme of exploitation spawns minimum-wage laws that can interfere with the operation of employment markets, especially for young and unskilled workers. It also gives rise to the vast proliferation of antidiscrimination laws, which often work at cross purposes to each other: the strong protection given against age-discrimination works a major redistribution from younger to older workers, which will have the long-term effect of reducing the investments in human capital so critical to the maintenance of a productive society.[42]

The transformation in employment law does not deal only with the basic protections, but also with the role of individual conduct. Once an antidiscrimination law or collective-bargaining statute is put into place, it is no longer possible to adopt a legal regime that allows individuals to be dismissed at will. In each and every contested case, it is necessary to

---

[38] For a summary of some of the litigation in this connection, see Paul Weiler, *Governing the Workplace: The Future of Labor and Employment Law* (Cambridge, MA: Harvard University Press, 1990).

[39] National Labor Relations Act, 29 U.S.C., section 141 et seq. (1988).

[40] See *NLRB v. Mackay Radio and Telegraph Co.*, 304 U.S. 333 (1938), which allows for the hiring of permanent replacements in ordinary strikes.

[41] The basic structure of the somewhat misnamed 1926 Railway Labor Act, 29 U.S.C., section 151 et seq. (1988), which since 1936 has applied to airlines, requires both sides to continue with the status quo unless there is mutual agreement to deviate from it. Since the disruption of transportation facilities has such manifest negative third-party effects, the strike and lockout mechanisms applicable under the National Labor Relations Act do not apply. In consequence, unionized workers have vested rights, which de facto make them partial owners of the firm; this is why the restructurings in the airline industry have ended up with workers holding an explicit ownership position, as the price for freedom from their exaction. For a sympathetic account of the Railway Labor Act, see Katherine van Wezel Stone, "Labor Relations on the Airlines: The Railway Labor Act in the Era of Deregulation," *Stanford Law Review*, vol. 42 (1990).

[42] This is a theme that has now been picked up by writers on the other side of the political spectrum. See, e.g., Lester Thurow, "The Birth of a Revolutionary Class," *New York Times Magazine*, May 19, 1996, p. 46, where Thurow notes that today the elderly have far outstripped their children in both net worth and current income. The shift constitutes a major reversal from the situation as recently as twenty-five years ago. In the 1960s, Thurow reports, the average seventy-year-old spent only 60 percent of the amount spent by the average thirty-year-old. Today the seventy-year-old spends 20 percent more than the thirty-year-old.

decide whether the dismissal was made for the reason prohibited by statute. In principle, the employer need not show that incompetence was the reason: sheer caprice unrelated to race, sex, age, or disability would in principle be allowable. It is, for example, permissible to fire someone from an accounting job because he has had the temerity to apply to law school. In most cases, however, the employer's pious claims of permissible irrational behavior will be met with genuine skepticism. In practice, therefore, the employer will usually claim that worker incompetence was the grounds for dismissal. To that claim, the employee will respond with cries of "pretext." Every dismissal or demotion is a potential target for litigation after the fact before a jury that has multiple explanations to choose from: was there really a planned reduction-in-force, or did the plant manager say that the sixty-two-year-old incumbent was "slowing down"?

In addition, the permissible grounds of dismissal have shrunk even in areas that relate to competence. The Americans with Disabilities Act,[43] which prevents discrimination in employment based on the disability of an actual or prospective worker, does not treat alcoholism as a condition that warrants swift dismissal. Today it (or at least past alcoholism) counts as a disability, which the employer is prohibited from taking into account in dealing with individual workers who have relapsed into their former condition. More than one commentator has lamented the stagnation of wages in the United States (not to mention elsewhere) in the past twenty years, especially in the ranks of the blue-collar workers. Yet all too often, the shift in the law's attitude toward contractual freedom is not treated as an important part of the overall story. The changes in legal environment are undeniable, however, and those changes have generated powerful, if perverse, incentives. The broad expansion of basic employee rights is paralleled by a sharp narrowing of the grounds on which dismissal is permissible. A relationship that was once governed by informal sanctions and sensible contractual rules has been taken over by the state, whose own standardized set of required terms does not match well with the requirements of the workplace. And once more, the constant effort to insure the right outcome when termination is at stake works its way back into the system, as job formation becomes an ever more perilous task. Again, more money is taken from the system to resolve the disputes that now arise. These costs are taxes paid in part by employers and employees alike. The effort to secure protection at the termination of the employment relationships that fail makes it more difficult to maintain the relationships that succeed.

2. *Tort.* A similar revolution has taken place in tort. As noted earlier, the traditional tort law adopted an even-handed standard on the question of whether the plaintiff's conduct resulted in the forfeiture of recovery. The nineteenth-century systems could be criticized on the ground that

---

[43] Americans with Disabilities Act of 1990, 42 U.S.C. 12101 et seq.

they allowed that misconduct to block all recovery, even in cases where the defendant was as much responsible for a loss as the plaintiff. The proper response to that criticism is a system of comparative negligence that divides the losses between the parties,[44] not a disintegration of the appropriate standards of plaintiff conduct. But once again the erosion in standards is unmistakable.

Within the area of employment, the tort system today has relatively little sway, as the workers' compensation statutes usually govern recovery for losses due to industrial accidents. Therefore, to understand the decline of responsibility that each individual has for his or her own safety, it is necessary to look at the law of product liability that governs the relationships between the manufacturers of goods and the consumers who use them in their daily lives.

The traditional view of this subject allowed the consumer to recover only to the extent that he made "normal and proper" use of the goods in question.[45] Yet modern product-liability law allows the injured party to recover as long as the product misuse is regarded as foreseeable, which, to an institutional defendant possessed of wide experience of its customers' foibles, it normally is.[46] More than one plaintiff has recovered from an automobile manufacturer for ramming a speeding car into a telephone pole.[47] The older view understood that these foreseeable events were more easily preventable by the individuals who misbehaved. Once again, judges' instincts to respond to the moral-hazard question led them to require that the injured plaintiff forfeit recovery for the harm in question. Today, however, the trend is to treat these forms of individual misconduct as though they are forms of neutral or natural events (like lightning) against which the manufacturer must guard the consumer. It is no coincidence that the same judicial attitude found in the wrongful-dismissal cases carries over to the personal-injury actions. In both types of cases, ordinary individuals are not held responsible for the consequences of their own actions.

[44] The comparative-negligence rule says that when both plaintiff and defendant are at fault, the loss will be divided between them. There are many different schemes for division, some of which require a case-by-case determination, and others of which posit some automatic division. For an exhaustive compilation of every variation of the comparative-negligence law, see Victor Schwartz, *Comparative Negligence*, 3d ed. (Charlottesville, VA: Michie, 1994).

[45] See *Escola v. Coca-Cola Bottling Co.*, 150 P.2d 436 (Cal. 1944). This case is more well-known for its adoption of strict liability for defective products, but its insistence on high standards for plaintiff's conduct was every bit as important to the original synthesis.

[46] See *Barker v. Lull Engineering*, 573 P.2d 443 (Cal. 1978) (covering use in "an intended or reasonably foreseeable manner").

[47] See, e.g., *Dawson v. Chrysler Corp.*, 630 F.2d 950 (3d Cir. 1980), which allowed the driver of a speeding police car that wrapped itself around a steel pole to recover from the automobile manufacturer; and *LeBouef v. Goodyear Tire & Rubber Company*, 623 F.2d 985 (5th Cir. 1980), which held that speeding at 105 miles per hour while drunk was a reasonably foreseeable use. Today, cases of this sort are harder to win before juries than fifteen years ago, but the basic statement of law has not markedly changed.

B. Charitable organizations

The switch in the law's attitude toward charitable organizations has followed many of the same lines that are found in the contract and tort areas. The developments here can be summarized in two stages. First, the judges by common-law decision systematically undid the earlier forms of charitable immunity in the provision of patient care, a development that was largely completed by 1950. At that time, many hospitals and physicians started to resort to contractual devices to limit their liability for medical malpractice in both paying and charitable cases. These contractual protections were themselves judicially invalidated following the watershed 1963 decision of *Tunkl v. Regents of University of California*,[48] which announced that the party with "superior bargaining strength" could not exempt itself from malpractice liability by contract. *Tunkl* paid little attention to the norms of institutional autonomy, but adopted the same worldview as a well-known pair of contemporary product-liability cases, *Henningsen v. Bloomfield Motors, Inc.* (1960),[49] and *Greenman v. Yuba Power* (1962).[50] Those cases explicitly rejected all contractual defenses in personal-injury cases brought by injured consumers against manufacturers.[51] The shift in judicial approach meant that both the commercial and the charitable areas were henceforth organized under judicial norms that explicitly rejected the principle of private ordering. Much of the medical-malpractice and product-liability crises of the next generation could be traced to the inability of private institutions to vary the standard terms on which they did business from the norms prescribed by state judges. As these judges paid increasingly less attention to the risks of the plaintiff's misconduct, the gap between the ideal legal rules and the actual legal rules got ever wider, precipitating the well-known dislocations in both product-liability and medical-malpractice law.

The second half of the attack on the older legal regime was directed toward the ability of private institutions to control the nature of their charitable business. In the early 1960s, there were a couple of legal decisions that hinted at the obligation of charitable institutions to take in all comers so long as they held themselves out as so doing.[52] Any supposed obligation could be avoided if the charitable institution clarified the terms and conditions on which it was prepared to offer service. But the movement to give all persons a strong right to medical care quickly gained speed and resulted in the 1986 passage in the United States of EMTALA (the Emergency Medical Treatment and Active Labor Act), which in its

---

[48] *Tunkl v. Regents of University of California*, 383 P.2d 441 (Cal. 1963).
[49] *Henningsen v. Bloomfield Motors, Inc.*, 161 A.2d 69 (N.J. 1960).
[50] *Greenman v. Yuba Power*, 377 P.2d 897 (Cal. 1962).
[51] For a similar judicial decision having to do with clauses in leases that exempted landlords from tort liability, see *Henrioulle v. Marin Ventures, Inc.*, 573 P.2d 465 (Cal. 1978).
[52] *Wilmington General Hospital v. Manlove*, 174 A.2d 135, 139 (Del. 1961); *Guerrero v. Copper Queen Hospital*, 537 P.2d 1329 (Ariz. 1975).

simplest form requires hospitals to admit, regardless of ability to pay, all persons who arrive in their emergency rooms when in active labor or in need of emergency medical treatment.[53] The hospital retains no power to decide whom to admit, or under what circumstances. Instead, the patient must be treated at institutional expense until stabilized, so long as hospital facilities are available for the treatment. The sanctions here are stiff, and include, in addition to potential malpractice liability, suspension from Medicare and Medicaid programs that, for urban hospitals, constitute a very substantial portion of their patient revenues. Concomitant with the expanded basic obligation is the rejection of any right of any institution covered by EMTALA to refuse treatment because of patient misconduct. It does not matter whether a patient had been treated on numerous occasions before, or at what expense, or with what success; nor does it matter if the patient had voluntarily consumed drugs or alcohol, had misused or refused to take medications, had disregarded medical instructions on diet, exercise, or self-treatment. The central feature of EMTALA is that the expanded right is treated as categorical and absolute: nonforfeitable in the strongest sense of that term.

The repeated justification for so stringent a duty is that individuals will die if hospitals are allowed to choose not to treat them in conditions of dire need.[54] The implicit assumption is that the only changes in consequence are that persons who may once have been excluded from treatment are now covered by it. But that brief account misses all the other signals that are sent out by a statute that sweeps aside everything before it. One major consequence is that the number of available facilities will diminish, as institutions close down or limit the intake of patients in unprofitable units, and that institutions will be most reluctant to expand those units that are able to turn a profit, or at least operate at an acceptable loss.[55] Under the older common-law system, size was an exogenous variable—the size of the facility did not have to be shrunk to keep people out. Now it has become an endogenous variable. One is forced to cut out care to the deserving poor and the paying rich to fence out the high-risk cases that could spell financial doom. In consequence, the capacity gets constrained, and rationing takes place by queuing, not by rational choice on the part of the hospital institutions. On the other end, the ability of

[53] Emergency Medical Treatment and Active Labor Act, 42 U.S.C., section 1395dd.

[54] See, e.g., House Committee on Government Operations, Subcommittee on Human Resources and Intergovernment Relations, *Equal Access to Health Care: Patient Dumping—Hearing before the Subcommittee on Human Resources and Intergovernment Relations of the House Committee on Government Operations*, 100th Congress, 1st session, 1987, pp. 14–20. The early academic comment was generally supportive of the act; see, e.g., Karen H. Rothenberg, "Who Cares? The Evolution of the Legal Duty to Provide Emergency Care," *Houston Law Review*, vol. 26 (1989), p. 21. See also Andrew J. McClurg, "Your Money or Your Life: Interpreting the Federal Act Against Patient Dumping," *Wake Forest Law Review*, vol. 24 (1989).

[55] See Erik J. Olson, "No Room at the Inn: A Snapshot of an American Emergency Room," *Stanford Law Review*, vol. 46 (1994), p. 449.

individuals to force control of their point of entry into the health-care system is increased. There is nothing that says that needy patients have to go to the hospital nearest to them. They can choose to enter the system at any point where the promised care is greatest. Nor is there any ability to withhold care in cases that are regarded as futile or perverse. The most famous case under EMTALA, *Matter of Baby K* (1994),[56] required the hospital to provide extensive care on four separate occasions when a mother brought her anencephalic infant to it for emergency care. The great tragedy of a statute of this sort is that it transfers control from the hospital, which pays the costs, to the government that mandates care for which it will not pay. The dramatic incidents that propelled the EMTALA statute to its passage are not those which are routinely encountered in practice. The current legal regime is a far cry indeed from the nineteenth-century systems. But the present reign of coercion hardly counts as an improvement.

IV. CONCLUSION

In this essay, I have traced the evolution of the ideal of personal responsibility as it has manifested itself in employment and charitable contexts. The nineteenth-century view assumed that legal rules and social practices had to take into account the risks of misconduct from employees as well as employers, and from the recipients of charity as well as charitable donors; the view assumed a universal capacity for mischief. A second assumption was that the ideal set of legal rules had to respond to all the difficulties that arose over the *life cycle* of any social arrangement. It would not do to have a set of rules that worked well on the termination of an employment contract or on the provision of inferior medical care, if that rule could reduce access to jobs, on the one hand, or to medical treatment, on the other. The ability to protect individuals from unfortunate and unjust outcomes within a given relationship should not obscure the need to encourage the formation of these basically beneficial relationships at some earlier time. To recognize the need for these trade-offs was to guarantee that poor, even distasteful results had to occur in individual cases; but these were the unavoidable price for sound basic institutions. The old maxim "Hard cases make bad law" alerted judges to the institutional dangers of seeking to provide remedies in cases of perceived individual injustice.

A third key assumption of the nineteenth-century model concerns its view of the competence of the individuals whose behavior is regulated. In employment contexts, the basic assumption was that all employees were competent to make sound decisions with respect to all matters concerning the wages, terms, and conditions of employment. There was relatively little effort to structure legal rules to counterbalance any perceived advantage that employers had in the workplace.

[56] *Matter of Baby K*, 16 F.3d 590 (4th Cir. 1994).

The nineteenth-century model's approach toward charitable care showed an evident ambivalence on the competence question. No longer could individual competence be assumed as a matter of course, as it is sometimes said to follow from the uncompromising rational-choice models that are the staple of the Chicago School of economics. Quite the contrary, the attitude was much more guarded. No nineteenth-century figure, for example, took the view that the only source of poverty was the lack of funds. The nineteenth-century prescription for dealing with poverty was not a negative income tax, but an elaborate set of restrictions and practices that in some cases was predicated on a lack of respect for the competence of the recipients, and in other cases on a distrust of their motives. The restrictions on giving that were part and parcel of charitable institutions only made sense in a world in which rational behavior was not posited as a matter of course.

The modern views on competence follow the nineteenth-century views on some points but not on others. As regards employment relationships, the attitudes are surely mixed, for while workers are subject to all sorts of protective legislation on the one hand, they are assumed in some contexts to have high levels of sophistication, as for example when they vote in union elections. Yet all too often on matters of contractual behavior, some form of incompetence or incapacity is assumed, and this assumption opens the way for the kinds of risky and counterproductive behavior that any legal system should seek to avoid. In a word, the errors here run in both directions. To assume competence when none is to be had is to run the risk of exploitation and advantage-taking. But to assume that competence is lacking when in fact it is not invites the opposite error, perhaps of even greater magnitude. "Incompetent" workers are given great opportunities to game the system, at the expense of their employers and their more honorable coworkers. In the employment context and other similar areas, I have little doubt that the efforts to relax the older rules have had largely counterproductive effects. The lowering of standards invites decline in personal standards of conduct and a similar decline in the overall efficiency of the social order.

The analysis of competence in the area of charity and welfare is perhaps more difficult to make. As was the case in the nineteenth century, the question of competence is highly contested today, and so too the question of trust, given the incessant demands from some quarters to do something, anything, about welfare cheats and frauds. But the major difference between the two eras goes to the choice of sanctions that should be imposed on those whose conduct and competence is called into question. To the nineteenth-century way of thinking, forfeiture of rights was appropriate even for persons who had limited capacity. The modern view allows far greater forgiveness and seeks to use carrots, but not sticks, to secure compliance with the applicable social norms. The burning question is: Which approach is correct?

Here is one lonely and uneasy vote cast for some cautious return to the sterner morality of an earlier day. It is surely correct that in some cases the forfeiture will be imposed on individuals who could not have done otherwise, or better. In some cases, however, the sanctions will be imposed on individuals who are capable of altering their conduct for the better. When sanctions are imposed on one person, a clear signal is given that others are able to follow. As with employment, both kinds of error have to be taken into account. Just as it is dangerous to make assumptions of universal competence when the opposite is true, so too it is equally dangerous to make assumptions of universal incompetence, especially about those who are not within the throes of the welfare system to begin with. A more exacting standard may help keep some people from falling into a condition of need, and it may keep those within the system from adopting self-destructive habits and practices.

I have little question that by abandoning forfeiture as a means to enforce social norms we have sacrificed the potential for these gains. Yet it is far from clear that we can return to an earlier era. One advantage of the system of private charity is that it resulted in decentralized approaches to the question, which allowed one group of individuals to experiment with strategies not adopted by another. Today, with heavy federal involvement in the system, the scope of decentralized experiments is correspondingly reduced. The state-run programs today are far fewer in number than privately operated ones; yet they account for the largest fraction of the total services delivered. However, the larger source of doubt stems from the common loss of that confident worldview that made implementation of nineteenth-century practices possible. Religious belief in the United States remains strong in some quarters, and, politically, may be growing in strength. But it is not moved by the same mixture of compassion and toughness found in religious thought a century ago. It is quite hazardous to support any radical dismantling of public welfare in the short run when all the private substitutes for it have been allowed to atrophy (or become dependent on federal funds). It is, in a word, far harder to revive a set of practices that have been once rejected than it would be to continue to follow them over time. Thus, while one could hope that elements of the classical systems of forfeiture would be introduced by degrees into the modern system, it is far from clear that the Zeitgeist will support their introduction, no matter who controls Congress in the next generation. Before any legal changes could be introduced, a change in worldview is necessary. As is so often the case, in a world as complex as ours, large changes in philosophical outlook are likely to lead to relatively small changes in social practice. Small perhaps, but vital nonetheless.

Law, The University of Chicago

INDEX